T4-AQN-112

SHAKESPEARE

PR
2989
H267
2009
WEB

SHAKESPEARE

POETRY, HISTORY, AND CULTURE

Jonathan Hart

SHAKESPEARE
Copyright © Jonathan Hart, 2009.

All rights reserved.

First published in 2009 by PALGRAVE MACMILLAN®
in the United States—a division of St. Martin's Press LLC,
175 Fifth Avenue, New York, NY 10010

Where this book is distributed in the UK, Europe and the rest of
the world, this is by Palgrave Macmillan, a division of Macmillan
Publishers Limited, registered in England, company number 785998,
of Houndmills, Basingstoke, Hampshire RG21 6XS.

Palgrave Macmillan is the global academic imprint of the above
companies and has companies and representatives throughout the world.
Palgrave® and Macmillan® are registered trademarks in the United States,
the United Kingdom, Europe and other countries.

ISBN: 978-0-230-61677-6

Library of Congress Cataloging-in-Publication Data

Hart, Jonathan Locke, 1956-
    Shakespeare : poetry, culture and history / Jonathan Hart.
    p. cm.
    ISBN 978-1-4039-6188-4 (alk. paper)
    1. Shakespeare, William, 1564-1616—Criticism and interpretation. I. Title.

PR2989.H267 2009
822.3'3—dc22   2009015906

A catalogue record of the book is available from the British Library.

Design by Scribe Inc.

First edition: December 2009

10 9 8 7 6 5 4 3 2 1

Printed in the United States of America.

For Anne Barton

CONTENTS

PREFACE AND ACKNOWLEDGMENTS

This is a book for general readers, students, and scholars in the field. As a result, I have written the volume in what I hope is an accessible way without sacrificing attention to detail. Another aspect of this study is that it is the work of someone who has published poetry, criticism, and history over a long period. I see criticism and history as arts as well as matters of science. That is perhaps why I have not rushed to bring this book together in a single argument but have left it, perhaps neglectfully, over decades. I have tried to add some notes to allow the reader to see what was done in the field after the writing that seems most relevant to the topic at hand.

The tension among the poet, the critic, and the historian is probably in keeping with those strands in the work under consideration. Shakespeare, however, is an exceptional case. My debt is to the text, the trace before me, of a remarkable artist, practical and theoretical, of the theatre and poetry. He can be Milton's poet of nature and someone who calls attention to theatricality, as Hamlet and the Chorus in *Henry V* do so well. Shakespeare was a poet and a working actor, playwright, and sharer in a theatre company, so it is important, as John Barton has shown, to think also of the text as a score for living theatre. How, for instance, does an actor convey irony? I thank John Barton and others who write for and direct in the theatre for the productions I have seen or workshops given or books written from this point of view.

Earlier parts of some of the book have appeared in journals and collections in Europe and the United States, but some chapters, like those on representing history, gender, and barbarism, appear here in print for the first time even if they were first created some time ago. Some of these parts I wanted to let sit so I could think about whether my approach made sense. Often, my way in was to the evidence of the text itself, providing some context along the way. Some were in areas of controversy, and I did not want to be so caught up in the moment that I would bring more blindness than insight to the matter at hand. After a long time, I have decided to let this method stand, of working from Shakespeare's text, as fluid as that might be, and looking outward when the work suggests that. As Shakespeare's texts are matters of editorial controversy themselves, with variants in spelling, lines, and scenes in places, I have not attempted to standardize any of these, but have gone with the editions I used at the time. After all, present editorial practices meet the elusive quartos (good and bad) and the First Folio and subsequent editions, so I have embraced the flux—or perhaps gone with the flow, if the other metaphor is unpromising and tantalizing in all the wrong ways. What I hope to do here is to bring together in a locus a unified discussion of language and genre in terms of poetry, culture, and history.

In Shakespeare, the greatest most often lies with his language, and that will be a focus of this work. I will try to bring together a thread, a mediation of looking backwards and forwards, to these interpretations of Shakespeare's nondramatic and dramatic works. I am one reader reading, a member of the audience being overheard. There are many admirable Shakespeare scholars past and present. I owe earlier poets, editors, critics, and historians a debt and could not do my work without them. It would be impossible to acknowledge and note them here and throughout the book.

This book I dedicate to Anne Barton, an extraordinary scholar and critic in Shakespeare and other fields, who has been an inspiration to me for a long time now. She invited me to Oxford many years ago and extended her hospitality and showed her generosity to me at Cambridge over the years. Her work on the idea of the play, on comedy—and in many domains—is a model to me and others. This volume is a small token of my thanks to Anne.

As has long been expressed, the faults in a book are the author's, but much of the pleasure of the writing and the credit for the birth of a book, no matter how slow, goes to many others besides the writer. I could not have written this or any other work without the kindness and support of many. I have been fortunate in my teachers and mentors before and after I arrived at university. Some teachers and mentors deserve particular mention and thanks. For many years, R. B. (Brian) Parker has long provided an example with his creativity and knowledge of Shakespeare and theatre. At Trinity, Jill Levenson gave a framework for Elizabethan and Jacobean drama and Michael Sidnell for modern drama, while David Neelands lent me more general support. I remember among others these excellent teachers and Shakespeare and drama at Toronto—Northrop Frye, David Galloway, and John Margeson—and others, like Ronald Bryden, Robertson Davies, Robert Finch, George Ignatieff, and Douglas LePan who encouraged me there. At Harvard, Joanne Dempsey, Heather Dubrow, Gwynne Evans, Marjorie Garber, Harry Levin, Jan Ziolkowski, and others were generous in encouraging, supporting, and responding to my work and deserve thanks. I remember Joanne, Gwynne, and Harry. Harry and Heather were particularly encouraging of my work on the narrative poems, and Gwynne was of my discussion of the sonnets. At the School of Criticism and Theory at Dartmouth College, my thanks to the director, faculty, and participants, and most especially, I remember Thomas Greene and Edward Said. At Alberta, I was fortunate to have welcoming and supportive colleagues in drama and Shakespeare when I joined the faculty, such as Ron Ayling, Patricia Demers, Nicole Mallet, John Orrell, Robert Wilson, and Linda Woodbridge, and in comparative literature, including E. D. Blodgett, Milan Dimić, Uri Margolin, and Edward Możejko, and computing in the humanities, most especially Terry Butler: I also remember John, Milan, and Terry.

Institutions, scholars, librarians, and other friends have been important to my work generally. Thanks, at various times of my tenure, to the provost and fellows of Trinity College, Toronto; the master and fellows of Massey College, Toronto; the president and fellows of Victoria University in the University of Toronto; the director of the Centre for Reformation and Renaissance Studies (Toronto); the master and fellows of Lady Eaton College, Trent; the co-masters of Kirkland House, Harvard; the provost and dean of arts at Alberta, the president and fellows of Clare Hall, Cambridge; the master and fellows of Wilson College, Princeton; and the master and fellows of Churchill College, Cambridge. Some colleagues have been especially kind in their support, some of whom I have thanked and remembered elsewhere, and I cannot enumerate them and their kindnesses. My thanks to friends and colleagues who have made such a difference to me, most particularly Daniel Aaron, Jeremy Adelman, Alfred and Sally Alcorn, John Baird, Sandra Bermann, Jean Bessière, J. Edward Chamberlin, Ross Chambers, Brian Edwards, Stephen Ferguson, Philip Ford, Robyn Gardner, Teresa Grant, Judith Hanson, Tom Healy, Shelagh Heffernan, Roland Le Huenen, Linda Hutcheon, Barbara Job, Wladmir Krysinski, Eva Kushner, Michèle Lamont, Juliet McMaster, Stephen Mobbs, Dale Miller, J. Hillis Miller, Kenneth Mills, Kenneth Munro, Lenore Muskett, Anthony Pagden, Donald and Cathleen Pfister, Harold Shapiro, Peter Sinclair, Irene Sywenky, Andrew Taylor, Gordon Teskey, Pauline Thomas, and Michael Worton. My thanks also to Cindy Chopoidalo and Jane Wong at Alberta for help with the technical matters of the manuscript. To the librarians at Toronto Reference Library, Toronto, Harvard, Alberta, Princeton, Cambridge, Oxford, the British Library, Bibliothèque Nationale, and elsewhere, my thanks. Thanks to my hosts and associations where I lectured or participated in seminars about Shakespeare, theory, poetics, and the Renaissance: the Shakespeare Association of America, the Renaissance Society of America, the Canadian Society for Renaissance Studies, the Pacific Northwest Renaissance Society, the Marlowe Society of America, the American Historical Association, the Modern Language Association of America, the American Comparative Literature Association, the Canadian Comparative Literature Association, the International Comparative Literature Association, and my hosts at Oxford (Terence Cave and Nigel Smith), Wales (Catherine Belsey, Terence Hawkes, and Christopher Norris), Hull (Tom McAlindon and Roland Wymer), Southampton (Ken Hirschkop), Montpellier III (Jean and Angela Maguin), Birkbeck (Tom Healy), Saarlandes (Klaus Martens), Tartu (Jüri Talvet), the Estonian Institute of Humanities (Ülar Ploom), Utrecht (Hans Bertens), Bielefeld (Barbara Job, Josef Raab, and Sebastian Thies), Navarra (Luis Galván), the University of the Basque Country (María Felisa López Liquete), Zaragosa (Dolores Herrero Granado and Susana Onega Jaén), Sorbonne Nouvelle—Paris III (Philippe Daros and Stéphane Michaud), Ljubljana and Villenica (Vanesa Matajc, Darja Pavlič, and Gašper Troha), Institute for Slovene Literature and Literary Sciences (Marko Juvan and Jola Škulj), Koper (Andrej

Blatnik, Krištof Jacek Kozak, Vesna Mikolič, and Marcello Potocco), Calgary (Ron Bond, James Ellis, Pamela McCallum, and Mary Polito), and Cambridge and Harvard (my many hosts in the two Cambridges). To my hosts for talks in other related fields sponsored by or at Sangmyung University in Seoul and Cheonan, Hong Kong, Nanjing Normal in Nanjing, Melbourne, Deakin, Montréal, Toronto, Princeton, Yale, Brown, and elsewhere, I thank you for your many kindnesses. My gratitude also for fellowships from the Social Science and Humanities Council of Canada, and the Fulbright and the Carmargo foundations, as well as visiting fellowships at Toronto, Harvard, Cambridge, Princeton, and elsewhere. Thanks, also, to the University of Toronto for granting me the honor of being the Northrop Frye Professor for this year. To the editors and publishers of *Cahiers Elisabéthains*, *Studies in English Literature*, Farleigh Dickenson University Press, *Shakespeare Yearbook*, and *Aevum* go my thanks for publishing my work and for permission and the courtesy to reprint earlier versions of material in the chapters (specific debts occur in the notes). My editors at Palgrave Macmillan, most recently, Farideh Koohi-Kamali and Brigitte Shull, deserve praise and thanks. I also wish to thank Jennifer Kepler at Scribe and Matthew Robison at Palgrave. It has been a pleasure to work with Palgrave for so many of my books.

Theatre and the arts have been important to my family over generations, and I give thanks to members of my family for their inspiration and support. I thank my father George and remember my mother, Jean. Many thanks to my brothers, Charles and Alan, and my sisters, Gwendolyn, Deborah, and Jennifer. A particular thanks to my wife, Mary Marshall, and our twins, Julia and James. Although I have set out some of the benefits in being slow to put this book together, my one regret is that I did not finish it earlier for those friends and family I have lost along the way.

INTRODUCTION

SHAKESPEARE IS, AS BEN JONSON HAD IT, OF HIS TIME AND endures time itself. Jonson's poem in the front matter to Shakespeare's First Folio (1623) provides a context, one way of many into his contemporary poet and playwright, who defies and invites comparison. Despite the complexity of the verse, with shifts worthy of a master, Jonson (1573–1637) was not afraid to give his dedicatory and commemorative poem a title that signaled his affection for Shakespeare (1564–1616) in whose remembrance he wrote: "To the memory of my beloued, The AVTHOR Mr. WILLIAM SHAKESPEARE: AND what he hath left vs."[1] Like Christopher Marlowe (1564–93), Jonson was a great innovator of verse and drama, and their presence must have kept Shakespeare on his toes and given him a community of rivals who may or may not have been friends (we are not sure what Shakespeare's relation to Marlowe was in life) but who also made each other better as poets and playwrights.

Just as Jonson backed into his praise of Shakespeare, I am backing into Shakespeare through Jonson's words. He begins the poem:

> To draw no enuy (Shakeſpeare) *in thy name,*
>   *Am I thus ample to thy Booke and Fame*
> *While I confeſſe thy writings to be ſuch,*
> *As neither* Man, *nor* Muſe, *can praiſe too much.*[2]

The raising of the issue of envy is something that Jonson brings up in order to praise Shakespeare the more, but the poem might seem to begin with undertow in a kind of ambivalence. Jonson then goes into an analysis of the nature of praise and his own intentions in the way of eulogy and even raises the issue of a dissembling and ironic praise: "*Or crafty Malice, might pretend this praiſe, / And thinke to ruine, where it ſeem'd to raiſe.*"[3] Jonson is a virtuoso who can explore intricacies in this occasional poem and find a deeper way to move the reader with his praise. He calls Shakespeare "*Soule of the age! / The applauſe! delight! The wonder of our Stage!*"[4] The world and the stage, the actual and dramatic time in which Jonson and he lived are Shakespeare's. Jonson creates the oxymoronic image of Shakespeare as being alive in death, a monument that breathes, a book that the reader gives life to:

> *Thou art a Moniment, without a tombe,*
> *And art aliue ſtill, while thy Booke doth liue,*
>   *And we haue wits to read, and praiſe to giue.*[5]

In praising Shakespeare, Jonson places him above Lily, Kid, and Marlowe (Jonson's spelling) and, even though Shakespeare "*hadʃt ʃmall* Latine, *and leʃʃe* Greeke," Jonson summons the names of Aeschylus, Euripides, and Sophocles to honor Shakespeare. Jonson depicts Shakespeare who could "*ʃhake a Stage,*" but finds in his these typologies with the ancients not enough to praise his dead friend:

> *Leaue thee alone, for the compariʃon*
> *Of all, that inʃolent* Greece, *or haughtie* Rome
> *ʃent forth, or ʃince did from their aʃhes come.*
> *Triumph, my* Britaine, *thou haʃt one so ʃhowe,*
> *To whom all Scene of* Europe *homage owe.*
> *He was not of an age, but for all time!*[6]

Shakespeare is of and beyond his age. For all Jonson's classical learning, he comes to favor his contemporary in the triumph, not of England, but of Britain. A British hegemony or empire would triumph if only with Shakespeare in the republic of letters. Here, for Jonson, is a great, or the great, European writer.

There is a kind of migration of this trope of Shakespeare as a poet of nature: the image moves between texts from just before his death through the First Folio and Second Folio (1632). In about 1615 Francis Beaumont had written a poem to Jonson, "To Mr B:J:," in which he says, "And from all Learninge keepe these lines ad deere / as Shakespeare's best are," which appears in the context of heirs hearing "how farr sometimes a mortall man may goe / by the dimme light of Nature."[7] Shakespeare becomes for posterity a poet of Nature. In his poem that appeared in Shakespeare's Second Folio, John Milton (1608–74) praises Shakespeare's folio in much the same image of a living monument as Heminge, Condell, and Jonson do: "Thou in our wonder and astonishment / Hast built thy selfe a lasting Monument" (lines 7–8) and, in "L'Allegro," Milton contrasts the learned Jonson with his contemporary: "Or sweetest Shakespear fancies childe, Warble his native Wood-notes wilde" (lines 133–34).[8] These Miltonic lines echo some of Jonson's in the First Folio. Jonson himself, in his "Conversations with Drummond" (1619), observed that Shakespeare wanted art and reports in *Timber: Or, Discoveries* that Jonson told the players (it appears that he means Heminge and Condell), who, in the prefatory address to readers in the First Folio, praised Shakespeare for barely blotting a line: "would he had blotted a thousand."[9] Jonson says that he justified his own candor because these players commended his friend for his fault—Jonson is on the defensive, not to seem petty, when he immediately adds, "(for I lov'd the man, and doe honour his memory (on this side Idolatry) as much as any" and when he concludes "But hee redeemed his vices, with his vertues. There was ever more in him to be ʃraysed, then to be pardoned."[10] The Jonsonian ambivalence was apparent over time.

But returning to the poem at hand in the First Folio, here, Jonson is more given to praise despite the undercurrent of qualification. Shakespeare's lack of art is not in question as it was, as we have seen, in Jonson's later comments. Instead, Jonson personifies nature to create hyperbole in his laudation of Shakespeare: "*Nature her ʃelf was proud of his deʃignes, / And ioy'd to weare the dreʃsinge of his lines!*"[11] Aristophanes, Terence, and Plautus no longer please but are antiquated "*As they were not of Natures family.*" Here, at least, Jonson admits Shakespeare's art: "*Yet muʃt I not giue Nature all*:

Thy Art, / My gentle Shakeſpeare, *muſt enioy a part."*[12] Jonson sums up this marriage of art and nature: *"For a good* Poet's *made, as well as borne. / As ſuch wert thou."*[13] Nor can Jonson resist alluding to Shakespeare's name, first shaking a scene and then a lance at various points in the poem. Yet Shakespeare is also *"Sweet Swan of* Auon!" whose sight he would like to see in the waters and whose flights he wishes on the banks of the Thames *"That ſo did take* Eliza, *and our* Iames!"[14] In Jonson's imagined scene this swan of the river that runs through Stratford now swims in the Thames and flies to the banks of the Thames where he lived and played in the company of Elizabeth I and "our" James I. The bonding of "our" is the monarchs of Jonson and Shakespeare, who benefitted from the patronage of James, and of the nation, but they appear in the informal address without their princely titles. There is a public or political side to this private friendship between Jonson and Shakespeare, and the First Folio becomes a living monument to it and a triumph of Britain in the translation of culture, study, and power, if not of empire. But the world is not enough. The mythology of metamorphoses, of translating Shakespeare into a swan, something appropriate for a poet of nature, becomes something of the ultimate transformation. Poets, like their creations, can be translated, so Chaucer might join his Troilus and Creseyde and Shakespeare, in happier circumstances, his star-crossed lovers, Romeo and Juliet. But I stray from Jonson's actual translation. Finally, he translates Shakespeare into the stars in the convention of an apotheosis. Jonson addresses Shakespeare as *"Thou Starre of* Poets," whom he asks to shine forth and *"chide, or cheere the drooping Stage,"* which *"hath mourn'd like night"* since Shakespeare fled this life, except *"for thy Volumes light."*[15] What we now know as the First Folio was to cast aside darkness with its illumination.

This context that involves Heminge, Condell, Jonson, and Beaumont, people who knew Shakespeare, plays with the idea of nature and art, their time, and posterity (all time). These friends and acquaintances, accomplished in theatre and the craft of writing, raised issues that would occur to later generations of actors, stage managers (directors), writers, readers, and critics. In many ways, this is the context of my book and all such books on Shakespeare. Milton, who was in his eighth year when Shakespeare died, picked up on the trope of Shakespeare as the poet of nature. We who follow did not know the man or those who knew him. The personal can become occluded and sublimated. Culture is a conversation of the living with the dead. In some ways the dead go between or mediate between the living. They haunt us as we try to understand our own ghostly presences in the brief time that we are given breath. How do we breathe life into death, share in the living monument of Shakespeare's book that Jonson describes? These poetic and existential metaphors can be too direct in a world of professional coolness and objectivity, but in the long course of responses to Shakespeare, there is room for intersubjectivity and the larger questions that Shakespeare asked through his characters like Hamlet. It is good to take the long view from those first responses to Shakespeare by his contemporaries and through Milton, Johnson, Blake, Coleridge, Shaw, Virginia Woolf, and others into the present to see that there is a good deal of latitude in responding to Shakespeare. In the professional world of scholarship (although less so of teaching) sophistication and the traditions of science and institutional protocols, largely developed in the nineteenth and twentieth centuries, can remove our dialogue with and about Shakespeare from the greater community. The delicate balance is to combine a particular professional interest in

Shakespeare with an appeal to all those interested in Shakespeare, each of whom has a personal conversation with him and his work, so to speak.[16] As Jonson intimates, we need to keep our idolatry in check even as we admire Shakespeare, but, conversely, a critical distance that dwindles into carping is hardly helpful.

In Shakespeare we find a protean figure who embodies both the classical and Romantic elements that are so important for our culture. Shakespeare's poetry, dramatic and nondramatic, displays the drama of meaning through a tension between the classical and the Romantic, as we have come to know them. The classic, as Gilbert Murray noted in the inauguration of the Charles Eliot Norton Chair of Poetry, is an interest "Not in things that attract attention or exercise charm at a particular place or moment, but in those that outlive the changes of taste and fashion."[17] This taste Murray attributed to Norton, which embodied a paradox that his taste was for something that was beyond taste—the classic. Elements of what we came to call Romanticism existed before: the horror of Senecan tragedy, the emotionalism of Protestant piety, the emphasis on the folk and on the wildness of nature, the sublime that Longinus had discussed. In other words, it is not surprising if Shakespeare, who drew on the classics, which contained aspects of Romanticism *avant la lettre*, would express himself in ways that we might now term Romantic. He also found a rich source in the Bible and was surrounded by religious debates between Protestants and Catholics in England and Europe while also calling upon popular culture and the folk tales, art and wisdom.

Shakespeare himself was an inspiration to the Germans as they moved from classical to Romantic models. Goethe, Schiller, Tieck, Solger, Müller, the Schlegels, and others, who influenced Coleridge, Thirlwall, and other English writers, for example, in terms of irony, testify to the double if not multiple movement of influence and intertextuality.[18] In these folk elements, often represented in Shakespeare and the Romantics, there is a kind of local exoticism, as if the Middle Ages were remade in the Renaissance and beyond. The uses of magic, prophets, songs, witches, and other aspects of the national past and culture combine pagan and Christian elements into a new context. Shakespeare is of his time and beyond his time, seeming a classic to the Romantics just as Plutarch, Ovid, Virgil, and others were to him. This early modern or Renaissance writer seems to be helping to bring the modern into being, in a kind of drama of meaning between the many aspects of culture that we deem, in shorthand, to be the classical and the Romantic.

None of this is astonishing, except for the sheer beauty, truth, and power of Shakespeare's language and his dramatic and nondramatic worlds. Although I express this in philosophical diction that appeals to terms common to the classical and Romantic, some of which is not to the taste of the times, I do so as someone who sees the paradox of his art, as Murray did in Norton's taste, that Shakespeare represented his times in a way that went beyond them. As a poet, critic, and historian, I am aware of the various levels of what William Lambarde reported Queen Elizabeth as saying to him during the Essex rebellion of 1601, at a time when Shakespeare's players were asked to play *Richard II* to rouse Londoners to his cause: "I am Richard the Second, know ye not that?"[19] Elizabeth was old and childless, without a direct heir, and on a private and at a public level, she was like Richard in prison. And so are we. Caught in our own times, we attempt to go beyond them. We do this through language, character, and action, alone and in a social setting. Shakespeare was able to express the tensions among poetry, culture, and history so well that even when people think they cannot be astonished, they are. In Walter Kaufman's words, "Shakespeare's poetry is the poetry of abundance."[20] In this overflowing fullness there are many contradictions and disjunctions, and the very dramatic tension of representation and meaning, of being caught in one's language, culture, and time creates the unresolved flow and overflow of interpretation.

Shakespeare's poetry in nondramatic and dramatic genres depends on telling the truth of fiction, the possible world of representation, the word, theme, and action that lie between author, character, and audience. The making of poetry is sometimes our unmaking. It bears a close relation to philosophy and rhetoric because of their goal of finding or representing something true. Whether this truth is actual or fictional is another matter.[21] Persuasion and meditations on time are key parts of Shakespeare's narrative poems and sonnets as well as some of his histories and plays in other genres. The rhetoric of seduction suggests that there are negative and positive roles for persuasion in poetry and that there is an ethics of reading and hearing when the power of language is in danger of overpowering characters and the audience. In writing, Shakespeare gives his actors and characters in poems and plays a relation to readers and audience that provides a range of responses that gives cause for reflection. What do private and public acts as expressed in the language of fiction mean for those in the actual world? Both are real although one is fictional and the other actual. Author, actor, character and audience (including readers) all interpret, and one interpretation begets another, which brings us to an interpretation of interpretation.

People are interpreting beings, and this realm of living interpretation is what I mean by "culture." This is as vexed a term as it is important. Those who study culture, like Clifford Geertz, have noted the indeterminacy of the word, the kind of asymptotic quest in defining it, if in fact we are getting any closer to achieving that.[22] And so it is what we cultivate, spreading between in the furrows of the text and the context, word and world. We try to explain, translate, and understand the textual and contextual in the possible and actual worlds that live together but parallel in a kind of comparison, implicit and explicit. Culture is a mediation, a kind of go-between in the relation between the poetic and the historical. The field of human interpretation is enacted and reenacted, so that a poem or play is revived in the reader and audience, and history needs to be relived in the narrative and analysis of the historian and reader. As Aristotle says in *Poetics*, the historian should follow the structure of what happened whereas the poet can explore what might have happened.[23] Shakespeare's history plays make him part historian, part poet, and his time mixed in the bounds of historiography, biography, moral lessons, chronicles, and other kinds of writing that Herodotus, Plutarch, Edward Hall, and Raphael Holinshed and others represented. The testing of the boundaries of genre is one of Shakespeare's many talents. He represents a number of cultures in English from past and present and, paradoxically, like Richard Hakluyt the Younger's and Samuel Purchas' collections of narratives of explorations and travel, helps to create a national identity of Englishness in his time. That Englishness was also a matter of Britishness, because of the Welsh origins of the Tudors, the Scottish connection of James I, and the Irish obsession of English monarchs. Shakespeare represents the desire for solidity and identity in the flux of time, something that seems a constant in the world of culture.

Poetics, as Plato and Aristotle made apparent, have philosophical and historical dimensions and have been given to controversy. Homer is a threat to the republic that the Platonic Socrates envisages but, for Aristotle, a great example of a poet who could write across the genres and a master of comedy as well. The ideological urge is always at the bounds of the claim that poetry is timeless, eternal, and universal, even in the great theorists of universals, Plato and Aristotle. In his *Apology for Poetry*, Philip Sidney came to satirize the historian's work as laboring amidst mouse-eaten records. The minute particulars of William Blake and the historicism of nineteenth-century German classical and biblical scholars given to archeology, dating, editing, and the study of philology or the historicists of recent decades are not the main aesthetic and ethical concerns of Shakespeare's nondramatic and dramatic poetry, even those that concern themselves primarily with history. Shakespeare's poetics are about the play of language, about the relation between speaker and audience, writer and reader, played out in character and action.

The urge in poetry, even in its specifics, can be toward the general, as Samuel Johnson observed, the kinds of choices and decisions embodied in character and the situations in which they find themselves.[24] Lucrece, Brutus, Richard II, and Henry V all have choices to make amid their private and public actions. The mythical and historical urges—one trying to be timeless, the other of its time—find themselves in tension, a productive drama of meaning. Historical poetry, nondramatic and dramatic, pushes at the contested territory between word and world, present and past, mythology and ideology. Poetry can be a form of atonement in a broken and fallen world, but whether that desired wholeness, the redemption of Eden or even secular and natural loss, is possible at all or even for a moment, is debatable. The mythical and historical urges, the ways people build stories and myths from the past to try to control the present and some projected future, represent something Shakespeare's speakers, narrators, choruses, and characters do in lyric, narrative, and dramatic poetry and prose. The originary moment of the rape and death of Lucrece, the plot against and death of Julius Caesar, the overthrow of Richard II, the invasion of France by Henry V, and Cranmer's prophecy about Elizabeth in *Henry VIII* all become contested moments of beauty, myth, and truth, the form, meanings, and interpretations of words worked out in the wrestle of poetry. The beauty and power of Shakespeare's language create a tension between the real and ideal of the actual and possible worlds. Shakespeare's poetry can represent a vast range of thoughts and emotions in an array of characters who act in manifest and multifold worlds.

Shakespeare's poetry and history, his overtly fictional realms, and his use of material for the actual world of the past, find an almost inextricable relation between "history" as story and story about the past. Time is inescapable. The present mediates between a vanishing past and a future that has yet to arrive. The present itself has a presence that is barely here before it is there, a now that seems fleeting and eternal and is gone but with a trace.[25] Shakespeare's facing of the classical past and English history is bold and innovative. John Heminge and Henry Condell, Shakespeare's friends and fellow sharers in the King's Men, defined, as one of the three genres in the First Folio, histories, along with comedies and tragedies. For Heminge and Condell, histories were about the English past. Shakespeare died without collecting his work into a volume, and this was unusual with vernacular plays, something Ben Jonson did in 1616.

Part of this might have been owing to Shakespeare's modesty or busy life, and part of it might have been that there was no copyright law and so the rights of the author were quite different, and it was his acting company that really kept the plays as their property. Here, Jonson broke the mold just before Shakespeare died.

Today copyright would usually be held by a family after an author's death, but it was not until the first decade of the eighteenth century that there was any such thing and not until the early nineteenth century that individualism helped to strengthen the notion of intellectual property. Shakespeare was a sharer or part owner in the Lord Chamberlain's Men that became the King's Men with the ascension of King James. This is perhaps another reason Ben Jonson had spoken about "our Iames," even if Jonson was not a sharer. Jonson, however, was the king's poet laureate, appointed in 1616, the same year his *Workes* were printed in folio.[26] So "our Iames" also meant that Jonson and Shakespeare shared the king's patronage, although not at the same time, as Shakespeare would die within months, whereas James' patronage intensified and continued for Ben Jonson. His triumph, the annual grant of one hundred marks (about sixty-six pounds) that James gave to Jonson on February 1, 1616, was surrounded by the death of friends and colleagues: Philip Henslowe, who paid Jonson ten pounds a play to be staged at various theatres, died in January 1616; Francis Beaumont in March 1616; and Shakespeare in April 1616.[27] To that point, Shakespeare had been the more fortunate playwright in terms of material reward. The King's Men seem to have owned the rights to the plays they purchased or of their sharer, poet, playwright, and actor, William Shakespeare. After his death, two members of the acting company, perhaps with the help of Jonson, who had his works collected and printed in 1616, brought out a collection of Shakespeare's plays. The family is not mentioned as a prime mover in the project, and there are no traces or responses of members of Shakespeare's extended family in regard to this monumental book in the history of English, British, European, and world culture. But they could not have known, perhaps as much as Jonson did, just how great a literary figure Shakespeare was. Yet they were his family and deserve some notice, if only brief, in one of the contexts for Shakespeare's book and this one of many about him. The family was there for the making of Shakespeare and the making of his work and leisure. No matter how exceptional he was, Shakespeare was of them, and no matter how we cannot see the ties between his life and art, there seems to have been a bond with his family to which he returned in retirement. And Shakespeare did not tell us, not living, as we do, in an intensely biographical and autobiographical age, what he thought the connections were between the great events of his life—births, marriages, deaths—and his poems and plays. Even in our age, constructing and reconstructing the conscious and unconscious relations that artists in their lives produce in their art is not a ready task. Elizabeth I, let alone Shakespeare, was not subject to a biography, nor did she leave behind her memoirs or an autobiography. If they were in equivalent positions today, think of how many such books about both of them would exist.

The private and public worlds, the spheres of Stratford and London, are hard to reconstruct in the life and work of William Shakespeare. The First Folio was printed in 1623, but did Anne Hathaway, Shakespeare's wife, see a copy before she died and was buried in that year on August 8? There is no record of whether his sister Joan (or Ione, 1569–46; the first Joan was born 1558 and seems to have died by 1569),

daughters Judith (Iudith, 1585–1662) or Susanna (1583–1649), or Joan's descendents, William Hart (1600–1639), Thomas Hart (b. 1605) or George Hart (d.1702),
and their descendents to this day ever owned a First Folio, or saw the tributes of
Heminge, Condell, Jonson, and others. How much the world of Stratford and London mixed beyond the worlds of William and his brother, Edmund (1580–1607),
also an actor, is something we do not know and perhaps never will. Whereas Edmund
was buried on December 31, 1607 in St Saviour's Church, Southwark, close to the
Globe Theatre on the south bank of London (he is commemorated there), Shakespeare was buried on April 25, 1616, in Holy Trinity Church in Stratford. Immediate
and wider contexts can vanish into the gaps and taciturn entries of records, whether
the mice have eaten them or not.

Heminge and Condell saw the First Folio as a memorial to Shakespeare, and
Jonson construed it as a memory of Shakespeare, who was his own monument.
Shakespeare was all too human, but paradoxically we remember him for the human
and humane poetry that has made him seem almost immortal, at least in terms of
the classical pagan notion of fame. Death would have haunted Shakespeare all the
days of his life. His sister Margareta had died in April 1563, a year before his birth,
but he would probably have heard about her death; Shakespeare'ssister Anne in
April 1579; his son Hamnet in August 1596; his father, John, in September 1601;
his brother Edmund in December 1607; his mother, Mary Arden, in September
1608; and his brother Gilbert in February 1612, probably just to name a few. On
April 17, 1616, William Hart (Hartt), husband to his sister Joan, died just a few
days before Shakespeare succumbed himself.[28] The natural cycle of time and the
biological order was not something that Shakespeare and his contemporaries could
or would attempt to hide or obscure. Until well into the twentieth century, death in
childbirth, infant mortality, and death by infection and disease occurred at fright-
fully high rates. Life expectancy has only recently increased dramatically, mainly
since 1920. The rates of infant mortality were generally lower in Tudor and Stuart
England than in continental Europe, and even in England, a parish like Hartland,
Devon, would have had a much higher life expectancy (fifty-five from 1558 to
1837, which was the national average in 1920) than low-lying marshy and malarial
areas.[29] Epidemics were a prompt of mortality. Shakespeare the writer left behind
more textual traces than Shakespeare the man. In tradition, Shakespeare was said to
have been born and died on the day of the patron saint of England, Saint George—
April 23. Shakespeare became part of the myth of England and then the English
empire and later the British empire.

England had a classical past, traditions of folklore, and the vernacular and religious
tensions and conflicts. It was John of Gaunt's sceptered isle, but it had also began,
however haltingly, to expand. We look back through the lens of empire, through what
John Seeley wrote about at length—the expansion of England—and the spread of
English.[30] None of this was sure during Shakespeare's life, and when he died in 1616,
Jamestown, the first permanent settlement in English America, was uncertain, and
it is only with a backward glance that we can see that it endured. Although Richard
Hakluyt the Younger had made a case for an English empire in northern America, it
was not, as his promotional literature would have it, the place of significance that it
came to be. It was here and then in India that the fate of English language, culture,

history, and institutions were especially forged. The danger in writing from Britain or North America is that a backward glance has a kind of causality, a teleology that makes the triumph of the Anglo-American world inevitable and inexorable. Nothing could be further from the actualities that Shakespeare and his contemporaries faced before the power of Spain and its empire, particularly from 1580 when Portugal and Spain were joined, though their empires were administered separately.

Although Shakespeare was at home in the actual worlds of theatre, city, country, and court, he also created a possible world of nondramatic and dramatic poetry as great as anyone working in the literatures of Europe. Even though I shall discuss culture and context here, the center of my attention will be the language and genres of the works themselves, what might be called the workings of the text. The structure of the book will move from an examination of the narrative poems and the sonnets through a discussion of barbarism and its contexts, Shakespeare's representation of history and the double image or typology of England and Italy, to an extended view of gender in the second tetralogy (*Richard II*, *Henry IV Part 1 and Part 2*, and *Henry V*) and a close analysis of *Henry V* and *Henry VIII*, followed by a brief conclusion. The rationale for this shape is that Shakespeare's *Venus and Adonis* and *Rape of Lucrece* seem to be the only works Shakespeare may well have seen into print. Here, Shakespeare worked out his poetics and a connection with mythology and the classical pasts of Greece and Rome. These poems are in the mode of *epyllia* or minor epics. In this way, they are as redolent of Homer and Virgil as Shakespeare is, despite the classical reach of the Roman plays or the specific themes of Troy and the quest with echoes of the *Aeneid* in *Troilus and Cressida* and *The Tempest*, respectively. The seduction of language and the language of seduction are concerns of *Venus and Adonis* and *The Rape of Lucrece*. The personal world of the former poem involves the meeting of mortal and goddess. In the latter poem, the private and the public come together in the founding of the Roman Republic. The death of that republic links the two Brutuses of Lucrece and of *Julius Caesar* and *Antony and Cleopatra*. Shakespeare's dramatic and nondramatic sonnets take up on the theme of time, which is central to this book. Temporality is something that lovers and kings cannot escape in the poems and the plays.

The nondramatic poems are suggestive in their treatment of language, theme, and character. In *Venus and Adonis*, Shakespeare uses detailed description to establish the body and world, but in representing nature he strives to outdo it. He explores mimesis through reflective imagery, description (or narration) and direct speech, and self-conscious allusions to the laws of nature and their limits. *The Rape of Lucrece* represents the telling of tales during the siege of Ardea. These stories lead to more reports and stories. Principal among these is Tarquin's account of seduction and Lucrece's tale of rape. Shakespeare uses narrative to explore love, lust, and violence. Rhetoric is central to this poetry because persuasion and communication are keys to the poem. One of the questions becomes how the speaker relates to the audience and the writer to the reader. In my interpretation, I call attention to the overlapping categories—characters as narrators, the principal narrator, and the ways the reader is implicated in the narration. In the sonnets, I argue, a conflict occurs between the ruins of time and the gilded monuments of Shakespeare's powerful rhyme. This tension is displaced in the desire between rhetoric and poetics, lust and love. Shakespeare combines formal elegance and compression of the sonnet to meditate on time and timelessness. The verbal world of the sonnets vaunts and overreaches while recognizing the impossibility of the conceit. Shakespeare provides an exploration of the limits and possibilities of poetry and the sonnet. The compression of the lyric, in the case of the sonnet in a collection of these poems or in a play, is a challenge to the expansiveness of time. In some ways, form becomes a theme itself to be explored.

Freedom and slavery are also great themes in love and war in Shakespeare's works. Men and women live between nature and nurture in the living interpretation of culture. Even love can imprison those who try to evade the vicissitudes of time and fortune. People try to cultivate their gardens, something the gardeners in *Richard II* realize is a hard thing to do in a fallen world given to conflict and politics, something that Candide is still advocating centuries later, despite how much Voltaire thought Shakespeare to be barbarous.[31] Culture, cultivation, civility, and civilization are always threatened by barbarism and monstrosity. In Shakespeare's plays and in the texts of encounter and travel this conflict and tension occurs. Text and context become an intertext.[32] Shakespeare represents the intricacies of barbarism, sometimes in ways that echo the representations of Herodotus.[33]

In a chapter that is somewhat of a fulcrum in the book, I examine how Shakespeare represented time and history in poetry and drama, in sonnets, *epyllia* or brief epics, tragedy, romance, and comedy as well as in the histories. Shakespeare's narrators, choruses and characters meditate on the ruins and redemption of time. They also consider the confusing traffic of the world. Shakespeare's history is protean, I maintain, and I suggest five aspects of his representation of history: the meditation on the past, personal and public; the classical past; the biblical past; the European past; the English past. Shakespeare's history also involves his reception and telling and interpretation are bound together in the word "history."

A particular double vision or typology that is a key instance of history is Shakespeare's representation of England and Italy: how, for example, the translation of culture and empire from Italy to England is enacted in his works. Italy and Rome, the Italian and the Roman, are terms that occur through Shakespeare's texts. This occurrence is not surprising, because Rome and Italy were the center of the Roman Empire, of which Britain was a part. They were also the heart of the Western Christian or Catholic Church, which the Church of England had broken with in the 1530s. They provided the origins of the Renaissance and the commercial revolution, especially in accounting and banking. Roman and Italian views are intrinsic at many levels, from commerce and exploration to painting and poetry. Shakespeare represented various aspects of Rome and Italy in his poems and plays. *The Rape of Lucrece* represented a critical moment in the history of Rome. The sonnets owed something to Petrarch. Shakespeare's comedies were indebted to Terence and Plautus and could have had Italian settings. Even Shakespeare's histories defined the English nation in part against Rome and Italy. Shakespearean tragedies, like *Titus Andronicus, Julius Caesar, Othello, Coriolanus*, and *Antony and Cleopatra*, were Roman and Italian. Other comedies, which we have come to call romances and tragicomedies, have similar concerns. Whereas *Cymbeline* explores ancient Britain and imperial Rome, *The Tempest* is set on an island between Italy and Africa. Although I shall suggest a range of Shakespearean constructions of Italy and Rome, I shall focus on ancient Rome and medieval and Renaissance Italy in relation to ancient Britain and England.

History plays provide a common bond between representations of England, which are not unlike those of Rome and Italy in other genres. Shakespeare's second tetralogy, a great accomplishment in the representation of history, leaves women to the margins.[34] Although Shakespeare wrote this group of history plays in the reign of Elizabeth I, who was the center of court and power in England, he represents the marginalization of women from politics and history. In my discussion of gender in *Richard II, 1* and *2 Henry IV* and *Henry V*, I connect the feminine with the masculine and the effeminate because of the interdependence of these gender demarcations. The second tetralogy is a symbolic representation of history in the 1590s of the period from about 1399 to 1422, so there is a dimension when exploring the nature of gender in this genre that involves the Renaissance looking back on the Middle Ages as we look back on Shakespeare's plays as texts from the Renaissance or early modern period. The role of women becomes one important way to understand the role of language, action, character, and thought in one of the great explorations of history in English drama and literature, if not in the drama and literature of the world. In these plays, women are denied action, except by persuading men to act on their behalf. For example, the Duchess of Gloucester, in the second scene of *Richard II*, can only appeal to Gaunt to avenge the murder of his brother and her husband. A woman does not appear on stage until act 2, scene 3 of *1 Henry IV*. Like the first part, the second part of *Henry IV* minimizes the role of women and represents male characters who worry about their masculinity. Although I argue that *Henry V* is partly about the role of Elizabeth I in her time, I am not saying that this is the primary rhetorical emphasis of the play. The Prologue speaks of Mars, war, and kings, and not of women. The marriages and relations between male and female characters in these four history plays lie between the worlds of public and private, at court, in the garden, and in the face and wake of battle.

In some ways Elizabeth I haunts the two history plays that I have chosen to discuss, *Henry V* and *Henry VIII*, because they test their own boundaries in form and the content of what can be represented. Like Elizabeth I giving her speech at Tilbury before the threat of the Spanish Armada, Henry V rouses his troops to heroism against the French. In *Henry VIII*, Cranmer speaks of the greatness and peace that the infant Elizabeth will bring to England, a speech Shakespeare had to wait to produce under a Stuart rather than the last of the Tudor dynasty. In some ways, these aspects of *Henry V* and *Henry VIII*, one a history that is like a problem play and the other like a romance or tragicomedy, are incidental and at the margins of these two plays, but their presence is telling and of some importance. The history play, I argue, is an unstable genre, partly because history is a continuum of time and therefore hard to capture within the limits of a work of art. Its instability partly occurs because the history play is always tending toward something else or is always incorporating other genres.

A kind of metatheatricality occurs in *Henry V*. The Chorus elaborates self-conscious theatricality in the earlier plays of the tetralogy, examining the connection between theatre and world and history play and history.[35] This technique allows the Chorus to raise in the audience an awareness of the problems of representing history on stage. The very structure of *Henry V* calls attention to the debates and questioning of the ideas in the play but also to the problems of representing history. The choric envelope and the main action, for example, are in friction. Moreover, I contend that Henry's violent images and Burgundy's description of France as a ruined garden show

Henry V pressing at the bounds of the genre of the history play because they complicate the marriage at the end and Henry's heroism. This play is self-critical and self-reflexive.

The role of form and content is a central concern. Genre is harder to deny for long. In *Henry VIII* Shakespeare continues to explore imagination and English history as he did in the choruses to *Henry V* and represents the collision of dramatic and historical expectations. The Prologue to *Henry VIII* creates problems for those who would find truth and reveals the disjunction between tragic sadness and celebratory laughter. A tension occurs between the pattern of comedy and exempla in the falls of Buckingham, Katherine, and Wolsey. The tragic and comic aspects of *Henry VIII* make for a creative friction that stresses the variety and problems of history. Like the narrative poems, the lyric voices of the sonnets, the Choruses in *Henry V* and *Henry VIII* are both historical and antihistorical. The very brilliance of the surface of this play questions patterns in history while asserting them. When Shakespeare's history plays most stretch their very bounds, they show their elasticity and their power most manifests itself. The moment of weakness, when the structure might be too loose or compressed to represent time and history, calls attention to the vulnerability of plays and poems and any representation of history.[36] Like characters and people, the power of time is not easily rendered, and getting the better of time is something that can only be temporary.

Shakespeare's poetry, culture, and history are of his time and beyond it. The power of his text is vulnerable. Context and intertextuality apply pressure at the edges, and the stories and histories in their myths represent in various genres the conflict between private and public, mortal and divine, lover and beloved, barbarism and civilization, England and Italy (Rome), men and women, the English and French, Catholics and Protestants, the English and the English. In this conflict and desire for atonement and unity, and the repair of the ruins of time, boundaries shift and Shakespeare explores the intricacies of poetry and theatre. Beauty and truth are of the moment in a world that would not be alloyed. What follows is a sequence of interpretations of text and context focused first on Shakespeare's work and departing from it, and those responses or readings are points of view in search of a thread out of a labyrinth in a tale of abandonment, loss, and exile. Shakespeare's language is the hero of his works and its very virtuosity is what makes his characters and the stories in which they find and lose themselves so spectacular, subtle, and inspiring while being at once exhaustive and regenerative. In my own way, as one in a line of many interpreters of Shakespeare, I hope to appeal to what John Heminge and Henry Condell called in their Preface to the First Folio "*the great Variety of Readers*," that is, "From the moſt able, to him that can but ſpell," the audience they wished for the first great or first collection of Shakespeare's plays.[37] Although in this address Heminges and Condell joke about wide readership because the purse is as important as capacity to the success of the book, in "The Epistle Dedicatorie" to the brothers, the Earls of Pembroke (the Lord Chamberlain) and of Montgomery, they proclaim a higher motive: "vvithout ambition either of ſelfe-profite or fame: onely to keepe the memory of ſo worthy a Friend, & Fellow aliue, as was our SHAKESPEARE, by humble offer of his playes, to your moſt noble patronage."[38] Now, we turn to Shakespeare's poems, which appeared from the early 1590s to 1609 but were not in this book of the theatre that Heminge and Condell, friends and fellow players, produced, with Jonson's help, in loving memory of Shakespeare.

The two narrative poems of the 1590s were dedicated to the Earl of Southampton, whereas the sonnets seem to have been published without the authority of the author. My book is a book for students, readers, and audiences, from those just coming to Shakespeare to those who have dwelt with him a long time—in some sense, all of us, from those who knew him and read and watched his work while he was alive, like Heminge, Jonson, and Condell, to those of us after his death who interpret his work through reading and attending his plays and writing about it. We need not worship Shakespeare or consider him a monument, because that would take away from his very human accomplishment, but to reduce him is also to detract from the gift he has given us. Each interpretation is going to be partial, my own included, and it is really his text and the ways we perform it in the theatre of posterity, in the drama of coming after, that somehow add up to a richness worthy of his name and memory. In other words, even those of us who have spent some time thinking about Shakespeare over many years learn not just from him but from all the others who have responded to Shakespeare in conversations, letters, editions, essays, theatre notes, and performances. It is my view that the conversation is about not one Shakespeare but many and that we should not artificially separate Shakespeare the poet from Shakespeare the playwright. One of the original titles of this book, *William Shakespeare, Poet and Playwright*, might serve as a ghost title and a reminder of why this book includes close attention to the poems and plays separately and together.

PART I

POETRY

CHAPTER 1

VENUS AND ADONIS

IN HIS VERSE TO SHAKESPEARE IN THE FIRST FOLIO, BEN JONSON raised the question of Shakespeare's learning in classical languages and placed him as a dramatist worthy at least of the greatest Greek writers of tragedy and comedy. Whatever the case may be, and however mixed Jonson's touching and touchy tribute may be to his friend and rival, Shakespeare did show an interest in representing and reinterpreting antiquity. His favorite poet might well have been Ovid, whose tales of metamorphoses are as protean as Shakespeare's reworking of classical myths and tales.

Language and mythology are central to Shakespeare's representation of the classical past. Besides his allusions to Greece and Rome and his plays set in Greece and Rome, his narrative poems are keys to his representation of antiquity. The figures of Venus and Adonis were part of the Renaissance "discovery" of the ruins of the classical world. There is no one Renaissance representation of this mythological story of goddess and mortal hunter. Just as we have interpretative divergence today, they did then. For example, Titian, in his painting *Venus and Adonis* (1553), now in the Metropolitan Museum of Art in New York, shows the vulnerability of the goddess building on Ovid's depiction of Venus' infatuation with Adonis in *Metamorphoses*:

> Shee lovd Adonis more
> Than heaven. To him shee clinged ay, and bare him companye.
> And in the shadowe woont shee was to rest continually,
> And for to set her beawtye out most seemely to the eye
> By trimly decking of her self.
> (X.614–18)[1]

Golding's translation captures her clinging devotion, her dressing up so he will fancy her, and Shakespeare continues this image of the most beautiful and divine embodiment of love reduced to pining in a most human way. Ludovico Dolce, also a translator of Ovid's *Metamorphoses*, shows a great subtlety in his response to viewing Titian's painting of *Venus and Adonis*. He says, "Venus is shown from the back, not for lack of art, but to demonstrate double art. Because in turning her face towards Adonis, trying to hold him back with both arms, and half sitting on a purple cloth, she shows everywhere certain sweet and lively feelings, such as one cannot see except in her."[2] The quality of this response, by a translator of Ovid, shows the integration of the arts, and Titian produced these paintings as part of a display for Philip of Spain. This seemingly timeless mythology in art, then, had a context in which culture was part of a display of historical and political power. The erotic power of Titian—something we also find in Ovid's and Shakespeare's representations of Venus and Adonis, had public implications beyond the seduction within the art and of the viewer. Titian called his paintings for Philip (as a prince and then as Philip II) *poesie*—and in doing so emphasized the relation between painting and poetry as Dolce also did in his *Dialogo della Pittura*. In this view, mythological paintings are like poetry because they deal with fiction as opposed to the reality of history. Painters and poets invent, and these paintings arouse the imagination of the viewer through that of the artist. When Titian's paintings were all together in Philip's *camerino*, the different representations of the body from different points of view, they became in a poetic image of the world, as Paolo Tinagli has suggested, erotic.[3] The role of the erotic and seduction from Ovid onward is a key part of the representation of Venus and Adonis, so that Shakespeare's poem on this pair occurs in a vast context. In a sonnet, Pierre Ronsard, for example, alludes to Venus in ways that raise issues in love and gender.[4] Closer to home, Edmund Spenser places—at the heart of book 3 of *The Faerie Queene*—the garden of Adonis that includes descriptions of the beauty of Venus.[5] The role of Elizabeth I, although not my focus here, cannot be ignored. If Prince Philip (later Philip II)—married to Elizabeth's sister, Mary, in the 1550s—could use Titian's *Venus and Adonis* as part of his collection, which was private and public, then Elizabeth had Spenser, Shakespeare, and others to create representations that were part of her mythology, which served her politically, even if she did not commission them directly, as Philip seems to have done.

In writing letters to Elizabeth, Walter Raleigh compared her to Alexander and Orpheus, Diana and Venus.[6] After the breakdown of the Anjou match, it was apparent that Elizabeth would not wed, and after the deterioration of relations with Spain, Elizabeth came to be identified with classical goddesses by different names like Cynthia, Diana, Astrea, Virgo, and Venus.[7] Elizabeth was virtue and virginity in the face of external threats, such as Spanish invasion. Although Shakespeare's poetry is, like Ovid's, a poetic and mythological world unto itself, it has artistic, cultural, political, and historical contexts beyond the years in which he wrote *Venus and Adonis*. It is also important to remember that this poem was immensely popular and was often reprinted between 1594 and 1602.[8]

Another context is that Shakespeare dedicated *Venus and Adonis* and *The Rape of Lucrece* to the Earl of Southampton. More specifically, the relation of Southampton to Lord Burghley is instructive. Southampton became Burghley's ward after the death of his father, and this affected the young man both positively, because Burghley attended to his education carefully, and negatively, because Burghley had a say in who the young man could marry when he turned twenty-one. For our purposes, what is important is that Southampton had taken to the theatre and arts. Shakespeare's role in encouraging him to marry is key here. Burghley had the power to insist on Southampton's match with Burghley's granddaughter or face a fine of his own devising because Burghley was not simply his Master of the Wards. John Clapham, one of Burghley's secretaries, wrote a Latin poem, *Narcissus*, in 1591, and dedicated it to Southampton, who was approaching his twenty-first birthday (October 6, 1594) and needed time to reflect. Like Shakespeare's vernacular poem, this one has the theme that a youth should avoid narcissism and drowning in self-love in the pool where his reflection lies, but marry and procreate, something a young gentleman in search of heirs needed to do.[9] In his dedication, Clapham expresses his bond with the addressee, the young Southampton: "Nonnihil vereor (illustrissime Domine) ne multis ego cum Narcisso meo, cuius in his versibus errores descripsi, ipse etiam videar vmbram affectare propriam, & cum eodem prorsus insanire" (I dread to some degree [most illustrious Lord] that I with my Narcissus, whose errors I have described in these verses, still appear to many to strive for his own shadow even to utter madness).[10] The notion of error is something the poet admits, but he is really in a sense warning the young man to whom he is addressing the poem to avoid the errors of Narcissus. The last line of the poem testi-fies to this end: "Vltima sors haec est nimium infoelicis amantis" (This is the ultimate lot of the most unfruitful lover).[11] The word "infoelicis" has a richness in Latin that English is hard pressed to approximate because it can mean unhappy, unfortunate, unlucky, unproductive, and unfruitful. I have chosen "unfruitful" because it is in the last line of a poem that is, at least implicitly, urging a young man to marry and be fruitful or reproductive, that is to produce an heir. There was a social and public aspect to these poems. Here, having briefly set out a few threads in the web that sur-rounded Shakespeare's poetry, I would like to focus on how the poet through the language he gives to his narrator and characters creates a bond with the reader.

In *Venus and Adonis* Shakespeare uses detailed description to establish the reality of the body and the world but strives to outdo nature and perhaps himself, as Venus says of Adonis, "Nature that made thee, with herself at strife, / Saith that the world hath ending with thy life" (11–12).[12] Shakespeare famishes his lines "amid their plenty," the poem being as reluctant to represent the rage of lust unabated as Adonis is to be carried away (20–36). *Venus and Adonis* begins with a goddess' attempted rape of a "mortal" boy and becomes, in part, a discussion of the reasons Adonis should suc-cumb and her lamentation after he dies not having heeded her reasons and advances. Rationalized arguments for lust frustrate the action. In a poem that has long been recognized as showing strong Ovidian influence, we find that Shakespeare is also doing something different here. He is exploring mimesis through the use of reflec-tive imagery, the tension between description or narration and direct speech, and the self-conscious allusion to the laws of nature and their contravention.[13] The creative disjunction here, which causes interest and dramatic tension as well as frustration, is the expression of art as representation and as supplement. If *Venus and Adonis* is witty and erotic, its characterization in criticism for so long, it is also an experiment, a young artist's exploration of the bounds of art.[14]

REFLECTIVE OR REPRESENTATIONAL IMAGERY

Reflective imagery occurs throughout the poem.[15] The opening line personifies the bright face of the sun, making nature human. In self-interest, wanting to seduce Adonis, Venus transfers the selfishness to him: "Narcissus so himself himself forsook, / And died to kiss his shadow in the brook" (161–62).[16] She misrepresents herself, deflecting attention to a comparison between Adonis and Narcissus, drawing notice to this reflection of the face in nature, self-absorbed human nature in the brook. Later, she compares Adonis with art and also finds his failings in that comparison, for art is not as alive as the real thing:

> Fie, lifeless picture, cold and senseless stone,
> Well-painted idol, image dull and dead,
> Statue contenting but the eye alone,
> Thing like a man, but of no woman bred!
> (211–14)

The context creates the irony as she chides him on aesthetic grounds while she forgets her own moral ground. Venus' face after feigning death imitates the sky: "And as the bright sun glorifies the sky, / So is her face illumin'd with her eye" (485–86). The narrator also says hyperbolically that the sun seems to borrow its shine from Adonis' face and that Venus' eyes "Shone like the moon in water seen by night" (487–92). Here is reflection at two removes, as if her language represents through refraction and distance. Adonis, who has told a tale, himself rebukes Venus for her representations, contrasting the darkness of the night with her reflections: "For by this black-fac'd night, desire's foul nurse, / Your treatise makes me like you worse and worse" (773–74, see 591). He interprets her advances, saying that she seduces every stranger, using increase as an excuse, making reason "the bawd to lust's abuse," but he breaks off because "the text is old, the orator too green" (787–801). Here, the world is a book that must be read; his metaphors attempt to comprehend the world with word. When he leaves her, her cries echo in caves as if to repeat her words perfectly till word and world are joined (829–40). Here is a shunned goddess who suffers human refusal in an ironic reversal, for despair is the human feeling of rejecting the divine will or of being dejected or rejected by it. In this and other places the representation of nature, which is so close and detailed in this poem, can make us forget that a goddess is seducing a mortal, reversing the rough escapades and rapes that Jove forced on mortal women. Venus takes resort in art, in songs and stories. The stylization, mythologizing, and hyperbole that often accompany the precise observation and recording of nature also remind the reader of the friction between mimetic and supplemental art.

The poet's language involves interpreting, just as the readers and characters must face a kind of hermeneutics. Interpretation of the world is something that the narrator warns is difficult for the poor and for Venus herself when she experiences the foreshadowings of Adonis' death:

> Look how the world's poor people are amazed
> At apparitions, signs and prodigies,
> Whereon with fearful eyes they long have gazed,
> Infusing them with dreadful prophecies:
>   So she at these sad signs draws up her breath,
>   And sighing it again, exclaims on death.
> (925–30)

At length, she apostrophizes death, as if to preserve Adonis' life by personifying the death that would take him, as if to insult vacant death into allowing life its fullness (931–55). She would control nature by preventing Adonis' death, trying to translate her language into power, but, ultimately, she can only transform him into something natural and not make him transcend nature. The narrator describes her in reflective terms, the eye and the tears mutual and inseparable: "Her eye seen in tears, tears in her eye: / Both crystals where they view'd each other's sorrow" (962–63). The point of view is destabilized, the viewer and the viewed both part of nature, tending toward identity. In addition the narrator says Venus' tears are "prison'd in her eye like pearls in glass," which implies opacity as well as reflexivity (979–80). Hoping that Adonis is still alive, Venus now insinuates herself with death, whom she has personified, plying him with praise for his art, telling "him of trophies, statues, tombs, and stories / His victories, his triumphs and his glories" (1013–14).

The goddess, who is and is not above nature, humanizes it, caught between her human and divine roles. The narrator amplifies this personified nature, describing, for example, how nearby flowers, grass, herb, leaf, or weed stole Adonis' blood and seemed to bleed with him and says that Venus notices nature's sympathy (1055–62). Nor, as the narrator observes, is the viewer always reliable, her emotions blocking her understanding of Adonis' death:

> Upon his hurt she looks so steadfastly
> That her sight dazzling makes the wound seem three;
> And then she reprehends her mangling eye,
> That makes more gashes, where no breach should be.
>   His face seems twain, each several limb is doubled,
>   For oft the eye mistakes, the brain being troubled.
> (1063–68)

This mistaken eye and troubled brain have implications for mimesis, especially for the representations of love and other intense emotions, so that in agitation, it is easy to exaggerate and misrepresent the object, though perhaps not the very intensity of the subject's passion. Venus herself calls attention to another misrepresentation of the object: understatement. With some wit, she says that her tongue cannot express her grief for one Adonis when she sees two (1069–74). This topos of inexpressibility halves a doubling nature. To bear Adonis' death, she mythologizes him, saying of her dead lover that "To recreate himself, when he hath sung, / The tiger would be tame and gently hear him" and that "When he beheld his shadow in the brook, / The fishes spread on it their golden gills" (1095–96, 1099–1100). This is playing artistically with the mirror held up to nature, for Venus supplements nature, fills the natural absence of Adonis with poetic presence. But she turns to the boar, to a nature that would not have killed Adonis had it seen his "beauteous livery" and "entertainment" (1105–10). This return to violent nature she cannot sustain, so that she humanizes it and would civilize it with art. The representation of nature is not enough.

Venus' struggle between mythologizing Adonis' death and facing it as a natural fact persists in the imagery and language. Her ambivalence over Adonis' death occurs in her desire to kiss him as the boar had and in her realization that Adonis is dead and never heeded her. Nature and art contend in her. She also "stains her face with his congealed blood" but "whispers in his ear a heavy tale, / As if they heard the woeful words she told" (1117–26). The self-reflexive love she found in him has passed with the dimming of his eyes: "Two glasses where herself herself beheld / A thousand times, and now no more reflect" (1129–30). When Shakespeare has the narrator use the echo "herself, herself" in describing Venus looking into Adonis' eyes, he is echoing Venus' description of Narcissus "himself himself" gazing into the brook and her earlier words to Adonis—"So in thyself thyself are made away"—implying that his selfishness is destroying him (763–68). The reflexive, in Venus' case as well, can become self-reflexive. These two points of view, Adonis' eyes, have altered after so many familiar glances into them when she would confirm her notions of herself. As a result of this death, she curses love hereafter, turning nature inside out and upside down (1135f.). Adonis melted into a vapor and was transformed into a purple and white flower like the blood on his pale cheeks (1165–70). Death is sublimated literally and literarily and the human form made a part of nature, but the flower that she places in her bosom is only a substitute for Adonis, a wish fulfillment of intimacy for love that was never requited (1171–76). Besides personifying the flower, she apostrophizes it, imprisoning it with her love as she would have imprisoned Adonis. Weary of the world, she mounts her silver doves, flying in an unnatural way "through empty skies" to Paphos, where she will immure herself and not be seen, as if she will keep herself from a nature that is too hard to bear and guard her flower. She has transmuted nature but will not represent it. Supplementing the lack in the world will be her course for now. Whether or not Venus will later seek intimacy with strangers, as Adonis had charged, Shakespeare leaves open, but, for the moment, Venus is caught up in Adonis' death and her transformation of love.

DESCRIPTION OR NARRATIVE AND DIRECT SPEECH

In the poem a vital tension exists between natural description and action on the one hand and the long speeches on lust and love on the other. Elaborate description and long speeches frustrate desire and action with a metalanguage of lust. In other words, rather than concentrating on Venus' lust in action, the poet represents her talking dirty, sometimes speaking erotically of lust at two removes by using images and analogies, as opposed to making a direct pass at Adonis. Other times she tries to force him physically to succumb to her lust. Shakespeare makes words and action collide in *Venus and Adonis*. The action of seduction and the hunt vie with Venus' lectures and justifications for sexual advances. Through argumentation, selfish Venus' words recoil upon her as she implies a likeness between Narcissus and Adonis (161–62).[17] In this comparison her echoing of "himself" shows Adonis' self-centeredness, "died" his sexual infatuation with himself as well as his actual death from solipsism, and "shadow" the illusion or reflection that is and is not him. Venus uses one of the arguments that the narrator in the sonnets does to persuade the young man to marry—"Thou wast begot; to get it is duty"—and also argues that he will achieve immortality through children (168–75). This is unusual rhetoric for a seduction. Nature is personified: Titan lusts after Venus even as Adonis dismisses love (181–86). The elaborate argument builds up narrative pressure, relying on the frustration of the seduction and of the reader to get to the end of the story. Natural description reveals a tension between reflecting the world and supplementing it. The description of the rabbit fleeing the hunter seems mimetic, but the depiction of the sun is stylized, personified and mythologized, of the horse sexual, of the flower an example of the transformation of sex and nature. If Venus first says that in Adonis nature outdid nature, she chides him for being a "lifeless picture" (211–14). A few lines later, she likens him to a deer, her arms the deer-park, a pun on "dear" but also a natural image. This image implies that she still wishes to be in control, but Adonis will not be a plaything or "Thing like a man, though of no woman bred!" (229–40, cf. 214). Venus cannot avoid physical nature, is caught in her own law of love, "To love a cheek that smiles at thee in scorn" (251–52). There is a strife between art and nature, a painted horse and Adonis' actual horse, so that art excels nature by going beyond an imitation of it by perfecting it, but the narrator uses this metaphor of painting to tell how a horse in life excels another (289–94). It is as if we have Wilde's dictum that life imitates art in the compass of a poem (so that the context is ultimately artistic), something that at times purports to be the world. Venus' sexual images and her argument of lust conflict and fail over more than seven hundred lines of on-again, off-again attempted seduction, Adonis complains of her treatise and abuse of reason in the name of lust (769–92).

This general movement of Venus' argument needs to be supplemented with specifics and the results of her labors. Shakespeare qualifies the argument with imagery; a pattern of lecture, antilecture, and contention; a myriad of elaborate and "artificial" reasons; and apostrophe. The metaphoric and pictorial nature of imagery creates a friction with the logic and abstraction of argument. Part of Venus' argument is erotic imagery: "Graze on my lips, and of those hills be dry, / Stray lower, where the pleasant fountains lie" (234–35). Adonis reacts with disdain to these verbal approaches and the description of Adonis' courser pursuing a jennet only contrasts the coolness of the youth with the hot pursuit of the horse (259–64). In the midst of this juxtaposition between speech and natural description occurs, as we have seen, self-reflexive allusions to the relation of art and life, the nature of nature and the limits of art (289–300). The emblem of the horses complicates speech and natural description, so that Shakespeare's art is not simply mimetic. The description also emphasizes the tension between Venus and Adonis until, at one point, they exchange harsh words (355–90). The extent of the erotic metaphor of the horse calls attention to the broad emblematic use of language in the poem (390–420). Venus also invokes a mermaid voice, the five senses, and a banquet in describing jealousy, while the narrator uses images of the red morning sky, wolf, berry, and bullet, so that the comparisons and images in the description and speech almost overflow in their succession (426–68). Adonis uses natural images to loose himself from Venus' grasp (523–35). She feeds on him with force, which the narrator describes in terms of a wild bird and a roe, but she cannot hold him longer by her (536–82). Animal images may represent lust as much as pastoral example. Venus is like a bird deceived by painted grapes: in all her artfulness, she accuses art of deluding nature (583–606). Speaking to Adonis about hunting, Venus uses images of hunting, of the boar and other less dangerous pursuits (613–720). When Venus suspects but does not want to admit Adonis' death, she uses images of death that we shall examine when we look more closely at apostrophe (931f.).

A pattern of lecture, antilecture, and contention occurs in the poem. Along with the sheer length of Venus' argument and the disjunction that happens because Venus has many reasons for unreason and strains logic to justify lust, this pattern creates comedy and comes close to absurdity. Shakespeare elaborates a comic tension between eroticism and inference. Seven lines into the poem, after a stanza of description, Venus begins her seductive arguments. She flatters Adonis by praising him, promises him secret knowledge if he succumbs (7–24). Just as the opening stanza describes lust and the next three stanzas begin Venus' argument, much of the first half of the poem represents the interspersing of the description and argument of lust (e.g., 25–175). Venus tells Adonis how she tamed Mars for her purposes, asks him to wink and be bold in love, tells him to love before he rots, and finds numerous pretexts to bolster her argument for what she calls love and he calls lust. She will use any strategy she can devise to justify the seduction. Adonis disdains her rationalizations for lust with a smile (241). After the narrator interrupts the argument with a long description of the horses (259–33) and of Venus and Adonis (325–68)—thereby establishing a comparison of equine and human love—Venus and Adonis contend in short bursts of argument (368–450). Adonis has broken his silence that made Venus' pleas seem all the more garrulous. That Venus could be so multifarious and longwinded in justifying her intended seduction helps create a comic atmosphere in the poem. Her vast amassing of reasons reveals the absurd and pathetic limits of her resourcefulness and lust. Not that Adonis avoids self-absorption, but Venus is, ironically, subject to the accusations of solipsism that she makes against him. Seeing that the argument is not working, Venus plays dead, but that strategy has only partial and temporary success and brings about a long and witty speech on how to win her. Adonis argues against her by throwing back natural images in her face (469–535). Once again, Shakespeare repeats the pattern of lecture and counterlecture, both Venus and Adonis claiming moral reason and both using animal imagery, though to different ends. The two lovers squabble (536–720). Venus takes another tack, praising Adonis extravagantly about his outnaturing of nature, repeating once more that he should be prodigal, but he will not take this moralizing and opposes it with a lecture of his own (721–810). He leaves her once more, while once more she pursues him. Adonis is hunted in speech and action and dies from the boar's tusk, if not from Venus' kisses. Her echoing song shows the redundancy of her efforts to restore her loss (817–52). This is her hunt for the hunter (853–88). Her chase is almost tautological, or at least repetitive and frustrating: "A thousand spleens bear her a thousand ways, / She treads the path that she untreads again" (907–8). She cannot see the world in an orderly fashion, and, lacking Adonis to argue with, she takes on death (925–30).

Venus apostrophizes death, a means by which she hopes to gain control over presence and absence in nature, and the narrator then describes Venus' despair. The apostrophe and the description both call attention to the problems of perceiving reality in the world. She still hopes that Adonis is alive—"It was not she that call'd him all to naught"—and shifts her views of death in an apostrophe that tries to make something of nothing, to fill in the O of address. But Venus comes to see that she is dead, and the narrator describes her in animal imagery: as she is and is not part of nature, for she is a goddess participating in nature, she hopes to transcend it but cannot entirely (1015–68). She expresses the difficulty she has in accepting Adonis' death and does so in terms of multiplication and disorienting images of vanishing (1069–92). Using animal images of lion and tiger, she tries to mythologize him but also returns to the grim violence of the boar and Adonis' death. To complicate her reaction more, she then makes his death erotic (1092–22). On the one hand, she sees the coldness of the corpse, but, on the other, she whispers tales in its ear and apostrophizes it. She attempts to animate the inanimate corpse, presenting it with a new law of love, as if Adonis were alive to hear it (1123–64). The narrator then describes the transformation of the body of the youth into a flower, both alike in color but unalike, for, sprouting from his blood, the flower is not identical to his blood. The description also relates how Venus keeps this flower, and she apostrophizes it as if it were a person able to fulfill her sexually. This is another example of her need for mythology. The last stanza rounds out the poem with description as the first stanza had begun it, immuring direct speech with descriptive detail, giving the poem a frame and mythology of its own. It is as if the description and speeches interrupt one another, frustrating the climax of the poem.

THE LAWS OF NATURE AND THEIR CONTRAVENTION

The narrator and Venus call attention to the laws of nature and their contravention.[18] Venus is of nature but a goddess, one of the paradoxes of classical mythology and similar to Christ's incarnation. This transcendence of nature but participation in it causes difficulties for representation. The goddess of love tells Adonis that Nature, which is personified as female, made him and is at strife with herself, for his death will cause a crisis of identity for the world (11–12). Venus accuses him of being unnatural, and yet he will become unnaturally natural (211–16). The conceit about the world ending with the death of Adonis is not true, as the world does not stop with the death, but his transformation into a flower breaks the laws of nature and changes the world.

Personifying the moon and nature, Venus still views nature as being chaotic and full of strife:

> Now of this dark night I perceive the reason:
> Cynthia for shame obscures her silver shine,
> Till forging nature be condemn'd of treason,
> For stealing moulds from heaven, that were divine;
>   Wherein she fram'd thee, in high heaven's despite,
>   To shame the sun by day and her by night.
> (727–32)

The goddess of love is hyperbolic in her own treason against divinity, making Adonis divine and greater than the sun god and moon goddess. It is as if she would translate him into the stars, create an apotheosis, but, ultimately, he will be transmuted into something more earthly: a flower. Nature, for Venus, is counterfeiting even as Venus forges her own mythology. Her charges against nature is that nature herself, as Venus personifies her, bribed destiny, the whole natural course, to frustrate nature's own work or craft, mingling beauty with infirmities, "And pure perfection and impure defeature," making beauty subject to the tyranny of mischance and misery (733–38). In Adonis, Venus finds a mixture of human and divine, and nature's craft is like representation, for it includes his perfection or ideal or his supplement to the natural world on the one hand and his impure disfigurement on the other. Pure and impure interpenetrate in Adonis, nature's workmanship, Venus' language, Shakespeare's poetics, and our interpretation. This mixture is part of a fall into time, suffering, and death. Venus reiterates that the making of Adonis, who is so fair, means the death of nature who made him thus (739–44). Venus recapitulates the fall into death and all our woe (745–50). The fact of death is something that she cannot escape even in her supplementing of nature, for beauty is "sudden wasted." Venus urges the chaste to break the moral laws on earth and hopes to seduce Adonis even still.

Adonis questions Venus' flights of seductive rhetoric. He thinks that her logic is skewed, that her lust is not for increase, that appearance has overtaken actuality in the world, so that her representations are devious and deviant:

> Call it not love, for love to heaven is fled,
> Since sweating lust on earth usurp'd his name;
> Under whose simple semblance he hath fed
> Upon fresh beauty, blotting it with blame;
>   Which the hot tyrant stains and soon bereaves,
>   As caterpillars do tender leaves.
> (793–98, cf. 787–92)

Eschewing idealism and exposing hypocrisy, Adonis warns of illusion in nature, of blaming the victim's beauty while excusing the seducer's lust, using all the time to defend himself a natural image, caterpillars staining leaves. Seducers like Venus are like the caterpillar, victims like Adonis are the "tender leaves." Even in warning against nature, Adonis uses natural images. He also admits that nature has fallen and that a new law governs it.

The facts of nature—Venus' sighting of the blood-mouthed boar—affect her deeply, so that the more she abhors the worst in nature, the more she confronts it by turning away from it (900–901). In other words, she faces fact through mythology and other indirection. Most noticeably, her moods in her addresses to death indicate her circling about the knowledge of Adonis' death. At one moment, she chides her personification of death, as if to start a family squabble: "Now nature cares not for thy mortal vigour, / Since her best work is ruin'd with thy rigour" (953–54). To cope, Venus asserts nature's dominance over death, but as she denies death, she admits it. Venus makes an absence present, in the face of a present absence, making death real while gazing on Adonis' face. With rationalizations, Venus tries to rationalize nature.

If Venus denies the laws of nature but also asserts nature's power over death, she has an ambivalent view of love. The goddess of love apostrophizes love as if it were external to her, thereby attempting to control it and deny that she has anything to do with it. Preceding Othello, she warns love that now that Adonis' beauty is dead, "black Chaos comes again." Fearful, she personifies an outside love that is fearful. At this moment, she hears the huntsman's horn and begins to delude herself that Adonis is still alive and has defied the laws of nature, overcoming death to resume love (1015–26). The narrator likens Venus to a falcon and a snail, natural images, in order to describe Venus' view of the dead Adonis. Her eyes have fled this horrible sight, journeyed to the darkness of the underworld, and reappeared to look in horror at the gored corpse (1027–56). This turning away from and returning to the facts of nature is an action that Venus repeats over the course of the poem. The narrator describes how her eye multiplies Adonis' wounds, transforming nature because she is troubled, so that a view of the world includes the observer (1063–68). In response to Adonis' death, she turns away again, not concentrating on the relation of death and nature but redefining her own law of love. Although she is ambivalent about Adonis' death, she predicts changes in love that will transform nature (1135–64). For Venus, Adonis has left a gap in nature, and to fill it up, Venus turns now from lust to revenge. She in nature will now forge a new strife in order that love will be at cross purposes. Rather than live in this transmuted nature, Venus will take the flower sprung from Adonis and seal herself off from the world. This oxymoronic or paradoxical quality persists in the imagery, description speeches, and the views of death, love, and nature.

Concluding Remarks and Transitions

This poem explores the nature of representation as well as expressing wit and eroticism. Art imitates life imitating art, for Shakespeare describes the "war" between Venus and Adonis in terms of the stage: "And all this dumb play had his acts made plain / With tears which chorus-like her eyes did rain" (359–60). Besides the close representation of nature, Shakespeare also uses stories and personifications of nature and death that challenge mimesis with symbol and allegory (esp. 716–44, 806, 953–1012).[19] A goddess transforms the dead youth into a flower and so breaks the laws of nature, mends the limited possibility of the world with the supplement of art. At the very end of the poem, Venus will leave the scene of Adonis' death and cut herself off from the world. Much of the interest in Venus and Adonis derives from a dilemma: tensions and disjunctions exist between the close mimetic descriptions of nature and the more allegorical and symbolic questionings of representation. Through reflective imagery, the tension between description and speech, and the self-conscious references to the laws of nature and their breach, Shakespeare gives us a poem where nature is vigorous because it strives with itself and with what is beyond it, just as the poem does.

Shakespeare dedicated his two narrative poems to the Earl of Southampton, who had connection with the Earl of Essex.[20] Although I have examined the comic reversal of a goddess pining after a mortal in terms of structure and the expectations based in nature, I have also suggested that any audience familiar with Ovid's representation of the story would find a new and brilliant elaboration on this rendering of mythology rather than a complete surprise. The aesthetic dimension does not preclude the political one. It is a matter of emphasis. In the figure of Venus, Shakespeare might have thought Southampton would recognize Elizabeth, although, as in all allegories, this is not easy to prove. Certainly, in *The Rape of Lucrece*, the founding of the Roman republic and the expulsion of Tarquin as the last Roman king are themes. But so, too, is the chastity of Lucrece a theme that would be in keeping with the cult of the Virgin Queen or at least an understanding of how that mythology operated in the later years of the reign of Elizabeth. It is also true that Shakespeare would later show the fall of the republic and the rise of the empire in *Julius Caesar* and *Antony and Cleopatra*, so it is hard to find a singular representation of republic and empire, people and ruler, monarch and emperor. The reference to Essex in the chorus to *Henry V* and the playing of *Richard II* during the Essex rebellion also complicate matters.

Poetry is textual but also dwells in the context of culture, history, and politics. The seduction in *Venus and Adonis* and *The Rape of Lucrece* is found in language and has erotic and sexual elements that have aesthetic and ethical implications. The political mythology of these poems is one framework and involves tensions between private and public, and if I choose to stress poetics and aesthetics in these poems more than overt politics and ideological allegory, it does not mean that they are without consequence. Shakespeare's language is dramatic and dialogical, creating tension, dialogue, and conflict as well as meditation, soliloquy, and harmony. Between poetics and rhetoric, he creates a language that bristles and wrestles with the dilemma of truth and beauty, as Keats so memorably set out in his poem on a Grecian urn, that "Sylvan historian," in another representation and "recovery" of the classical past.[21] Well known is the controversy over the final two lines of Keats' poem, "'Beauty is truth, truth beauty,'—that is all / Ye know on earth, and all ye need to know."[22] Although Keats admired Shakespeare and Milton, his looking back to the classical world is not theirs, but his suggestive and unresolved assertion prompts more thought on the relation between the aesthetic and ethical. Can form and content ever be separated? While Shakespeare's narrative poems are not Keats' ode, they are poems of such linguistic power, full of thought, emotion, and music, that many who read or hear them are carried away and left to wonder at and about the power of poetry.

CHAPTER 2

THE RAPE OF LUCRECE

VENUS AND ADONIS WAS A GREAT SUCCESS, AND SHAKESPEARE CAME TO dedicate another narrative poem, *The Rape of Lucrece*, to the young Earl of Southampton. In this dedication, Shakespeare had promised to write a more grave work, a promise he fulfilled in this poem about the rape of a virtuous woman and the founding of the Roman republic with the banishment of the king-rapist—Tarquin. Shakespeare takes up a story that Ovid had told in *Fasti* and Livy had included in his *History of Rome*. The chastity of Lucretia is a foundational myth of the Roman republic that Livy and Ovid both represent. The rape of Lucretia has been as much a tale for the late twentieth century as it was for the ancients like Dionysius of Halicarnassus and Diodorus Siculus and for Shakespeare and his contemporaries.[1] For Ovid, the rape of Lucretia was part of a context in which *Fasti* represented the tensions and anxieties of late Augustan Rome by examining Roman monuments, religion, legend, history, and character. His representation, as Carole Newlands has observed, differed from that of Livy, who had made her rape a prelude to the public theme of liberty by stressing that, like Philomela, she had suffered a personal and private tragedy.[2] In other words, Livy's tale of a woman's sacrifice for her country becomes Ovid's exploration of who gets to speak and who remains silent.[3] Ovid is using time, reflecting on the calendar, to consider history and mythology, the politics of ideological foundations. The tension between private shame and public revenge lie at the heart of this story.

Shakespeare's Lucrece represents a connection between private and public virtue and vice. The themes of personal chastity and state corruption involve Lucrece's suicide as a result of her rape by Tarquin, whose lust leads to a revenge by those men loyal to Lucrece. Tarquin goes into exile and with him the Roman monarchy. In some ways Shakespeare brings in Livy's patriotic theme with Ovid's representation of personal integrity.

Still, both Livy and Ovid, despite the division some critics make between the one representing the personal and the other the political, mix patriotism and integrity. Within Livy, there is a balance between private and public. For example, Livy says that in his speech, Brutus "dwelt upon the brutality and licentiousness of Sextus Tarquin, the infamous outrage on Lucretia and her pitiful death, the bereavement sustained by her father, Tricipitinus, to whom the cause of his daughter's death was more shameful and distressing than the actual death itself."[4] This is the private sin of Tarquin and the outrage on the body of Lucrece. In the next sentence, Brutus turns to the public question of Rome in the wake of this rape: "Then he dwelt on the tyranny of the king, the toils and sufferings of the plebeians kept underground clearing out ditches and sewers—Roman men, conquerors of all the surrounding nations, turned from warriors into artisans and stonemasons!"[5] The public decline of Rome is a theme that Brutus connects with the tyrannical king. Ovid has Brutus take up Lucretia's cause, ripping the knife from "her half-dead body," holding "it high as it dripped her noble blood," and delivering the following "fearless words" from a snarling mouth:

> By this courageous and chaste blood I swear to you.
>   And by your spirit, which shall be my god,
> Tarquinus and his exiled line shall pay for this.
>   I have cloaked my manhood long enough.
> (2:841–44, see 838–40)[6]

It is quite dramatic as Brutus bonds with his countrymen, using Lucretia's blood as a sign of her courage and chastity and a means of invoking the spirit of the men he addresses, swearing that "spirit" to be his "god" and stressing that Tarquin and his heirs shall "pay" for this act and that he, Brutus, had hidden his masculinity for "long enough." This train of thought leads to the narrator's blunt description: "This was monarchy's last day" (2:852). This kind of example might cause some problems for Shakespeare's monarch if Ovid, like Livy, is the source for stories about Lucretia in England during the reign of Elizabeth I.

A tension exists politically because in the Elizabethan context, the queen represented a monarch but was mythologized for her chastity or virginity, often to the point of a cult. Whether Shakespeare partakes in this cult is another matter, and certainly one could debate whether John Fletcher or he later gave Cranmer the paean to her in *Henry VIII* during the reign of James I. Shakespeare himself represented what might be called an "Elizabethan republicanism" that seems to allow for the monarch and not a kind of looking back that mixed the virtues and vices of the republic and empire, the two Brutuses and the assassination of Caesar and the Augustan peace. *Lucrece*, *Julius Caesar*, and *Antony and Cleopatra* all combined monarchy, republic, and empire in all their strength and weaknesses. It may be that Elizabeth as monarch was large enough to subsume the exile of a tyrant, the birth of a republic through the private virtue of chastity, the death of a republic through the assassination of Caesar (a tyrant and martyr who had mythological connections with Britain, which he had invaded), and the birth, through the cold Octavius and the sacrifice of the second Brutus (descendent of the first Brutus who avenged the rape of Lucrece and drove Tarquin out of Rome), of empire. Certainly, Shakespeare's art was capacious enough to do so, as we shall see here and in a discussion in a later chapter about the typology of Shakespeare's England and Italy.[7]

Here, I turn from context to the rhetoric and poetics of the text, how the author gives language to the narrator and characters in order to appeal to the reader. This appeal can be to move the reader to virtue or pleasure or both. In it there is a measure of tension between persuasion and seduction on the one hand and consideration and ethical distance on the other. A dramatic tension occurs between form and content, the aesthetics and ethics of reading. In all this, meaning is made and unmade in the poetic and rhetorical contract between writer and reader through narration and characterization through the poetry itself.

The premise of *The Rape of Lucrece* is the telling of tales during the siege of Ardea, a telling which leads to further reports and stories, principally Tarquin's narrative of seduction and Lucrece's tale of rape. Shakespeare's narrative ethic and how he uses narrative to explore love, lust, and violence will be the main concerns of this chapter.[8] My methodology in this discussion of *Lucrece* will be mainly rhetorical because it will analyze the foundations of rhetoric, persuasion, and communication: how the speaker relates to the audience and the writer to the reader. In discussing Shakespeare's poem, I shall examine these closely related and overlapping categories—characters as narrators, the principal narrator, and the ways the reader is implicated in the narration.[9]

The act of interpretation connects the characters, principal narrator, and reader and does not allow any of them to be innocent bystanders to the story. The three categories of characters as narrators, the principal narrator, and the participation of the reader in narrative overlap so much that it is a temptation to discuss them simultaneously to reenact their complex effects, but for the sake of coherence, I shall examine them separately.[10] The narrator helps shape our response as readers by framing and interpreting the tales Tarquin tells to himself and to Lucrece in order to enact the rape, the narratives Tarquin and Lucrece tell each other, the story Lucrece must tell of the rape, and the responses Lucretius, Collatine, and Brutus have to Lucrece's account of Tarquin. The stories come full circle. Narrative may be as much an interpretation of events or a response to another tale as a tale itself. In fact, the tales are contextual, a part of a series. Shakespeare uses the narrator as a telling transition between the narratives of characters and as a means of distinguishing between story and plot, the events and their representation.

THE CHARACTERS AS NARRATORS

As the narrator most often encloses the characters in his narrative or description, this category will include only the narratives that the characters themselves tell in direct discourse. Even though these characters cannot escape the context that the poet creates for them through the narrator, it is informative to examine their own words. If the poet shapes his characters mainly through the narrator, he also gives them their own stories. Although these tales cannot be separated from their setting and from those who listen to them, an attempt at critical, self-conscious separation will clarify the influence of the narrator on our reception of the characters and their narratives.

Tarquin's stories within his interior monologue demonstrate complex narrative techniques (181–357).[11] In a *similitudo* (omoeosis or similitude between two different things), as if to ground his emblem of lust, he likens how he will rape Lucrece to the striking of a flint to begin a fire. Tarquin then addresses his torch and "unhallowed thoughts," condemns the foul act that he is contemplating, and thinks about the "scandal" that will survive him if he forces Lucrece. These scandalous stories that will constitute the reception of the report of his actions concern Tarquin, so that he links physical force and narrative force. In an *attributio*, which involves the attribution of qualities of persons or things to other persons or things, he translates this reaction to a herald marking his coat of arms with a disgraceful and symbolic stroke until Tarquin's heirs will wish he had not fathered them. Tarquin continues to displace the consequences of his actions into skeletal narratives. The "I" who seeks Lucrece becomes the unnamed "Who" and the beggar who gives up eternity and life for a momentary pleasure. This movement from the specific to the general, from the personal to the impersonal, constitutes more than the poet's desire to teach a lesson through adages or moral exempla, because it represents the gap Tarquin explores between his reason and his lust and emphasizes the failure of the former and the agonizing power of the latter.

Tarquin cannot escape the personal. He thinks that if Collatine dreamed of his intentions, then he would rise and in rage ride there to end the siege of his wife. But in this narrative of imagined acts, Tarquin realizes the lasting shame his act will bear and the rationalizations his invention can concoct. Once again, he shifts from the personal—"My will is strong past reason's weak removing"—to the impersonal—"Who fears a sentence or an old man's saw / Shall by a painted cloth be kept in awe" (243–45). These maxims, sayings, and painted cloths, which occur in the stories Tarquin tells himself, represent implied stories and tales. Tarquin also switches the focus of his story to Lucrece's physical nature. This effictio (description) of her body embodies his lust. He says that she "gaz'd for tidings in my eager eyes" because she feared "hard news" about Collatine (254–55). The vocabulary of narrative can be read on the body, and the power of report effects physical changes. Tarquin describes to himself, as we overhear in the translation of writing, the effects of his good news on Lucrece's face— that Narcissus would not have drowned for self-love had he witnessed her transformation. This rhetorical move involves a kind of conformatio (prosopopoeia—animating or personifying objects), because Tarquin gives speech to a look on Lucrece's face, and an exemplum, because he relates a fabulous event to his subject. In this rhetorical vacillation between desire and conscience Tarquin hides behind the power of lust, generalities, and inexpressibility (occupatio or adynaton; "All orators are dumb when beauty pleadeth" [268]) while excoriating his own motives. He personifies "Affection" and tells a brief story about this captain in another of his young man's "saws" (see 244). Personifications of fear and desire follow, and later he humanizes Lucrece's glove by imagining it to be chaste. No matter how much he tells his narratives of resistance and self-doubt, they represent a testatio (a confirmation of the situation through his own experience) because he proceeds to Lucrece's chamber and plots his willful course of action, making foul thoughts into foul deeds. He has changed his diction: "lust" becomes "love" and "sin" now finds "absolution" (350–57).

The actual rape shows Tarquin trying to narrativize this brutal action and to displace the responsibility and guilt for it on to Lucrece (477–672). He says that the color in her face "Shall plead for me and tell my loving tale" and that "the fault is thine" (477–83). In addition to repeating a kind of conformatio, this strategy represents an insidious use of attributio in which he attributes to her face the rhetoric of his desire. He tells her the story, which the reader has just witnessed, of how he tried to resist with reason his desire but could not because of her beauty. This move takes him beyond purgatio, an excuse for an admitted fault, to a blaming of the victim. He threatens her with the future, or hypothetical, narrative of slaying one of her slaves for raping her when in fact Tarquin raped her, with the obloquy (verbal abuse) of her issue (displacing the imagined scandal his heirs were going to rehearse as a result of the rape [204–10]) over her production of a bastard, and with children's rhyming songs citing "thy trespass" (512–25). Rather than describe an imaginary place (topothesia), Tarquin depicts an imagined scene in order to have his way.

The narratives of reputation obsess Tarquin: the effects of narrative become part of the narrative. With natural images he tries to blame nature and not himself for his infamy. He then cuts Lucrece off after her long plea; he swears by heaven that he will not hear her and threatens her once more with force and with his plot of killing the groom as her lover (667–72). His counternarratives against his desire and contemplation of rape and her stories amid her argument against rape possess no ethical effect. The poet implies the impotence of narrative to dissuade vice or to pervert virtue. The power of the word and the tale knows crucial limits. Shakespeare seems to be saying that human life and action are more than language, that we and our lives are not texts.

Lucrece's plea cannot save her from rape (575–666). In the face of Tarquin's minatory rhetoric, she tries to command and warn him. Like Tarquin, she fabulates and uses the impersonal adage, transforming her palpable king into an anonymous woodsman. She also generalizes their situation to man and woman, the latter trying to move the former with moans, tears, sighs, and groans (580–88). Lucrece creates a character in the Tarquin who faces her and who cannot be anything but a "likeness" to the king and warns, as Tarquin had, about the consequences of foul actions. She reminds him of the indelible and written nature of his actions—"For princes are the glass, the school, the book, / Where subjects' eyes do learn, do read, do look" (615–16)—and amplifies this metaphor. She takes up the character of exiled majesty, Tarquin's better self, and asks the likeness before her to let the real king return. This is a form of praeexpositio: she compares what Tarquin ought to have done (and said) with what he did (and said). If Lucrece tells a story, she represents it in a plea full of warnings and imperatives amid tears, to which she calls attention. But Tarquin will not be moved. He rapes her.

After the rape, Lucrece faces the event indirectly (747–1211). Like Tarquin, she uses attributio (conformatio or personification). She speaks of her eyes reacting to the rape: they would rather stay in darkness "To have their unseen sin remain untold" (753). Here, she does not want the body to disclose the story of what happened. In Lucrece's apostrophe to night, which is conventional and extends at least as far back as Troilus and Criseyde, she calls night a register, notary, and stage, so that the writing and enactment of the story represents her worst horror. Like the victimizer, the victim concentrates on reputation, the past events turned into future story. If Tarquin blamed Lucrece's beauty for the rape, she blames the night yet wants perpetual night to hide her shame. These elaborate tropes deflect but heighten Lucrece's grief, as if she were distracted into a language that cannot express her horror. In this soliloquy Lucrece makes herself a character worthy of pity (792–98). Like Tarquin, she is obsessed with future tales of shame. Once again, she exhorts the night:

> Make me not object to the tell-tale day:
> The light will show character'd in my brow
> The story of sweet chastity's decay,
> The impious breach of holy wedlock vow;
> Yea, the illiterate that know not how
>   To cipher what is writ in learned books,
>   Will quote my loathsome trespass in my looks.
> (806–12)

Shakespeare gives to Lucrece a hermeneutic language of self-conscious narrativity. Once again, she uses attributio, as if to give night the power of speech and narrative. The signs of shame become translated into her face and nature itself. Her face will be as a story book even to those who cannot read. The nurse, orator, and minstrels will tell her story: Lucrece dwells on the audience's response to the first and third of these storytellers (813–19). This concern with the audience spills over into the poet's concern with the reader, the reader's sympathetic involvement with Lucrece, and his or her awareness of the necessary detachment of an audience. Lucrece amplifies this concern with the reports and reading of her story (822, 830, 887). Like Tarquin, she piles up natural images to describe the unnatural rape and its consequences and attempts to make sense of the situation with personifications (848ff., 876ff.). Her apostrophe to the personified opportunity makes an impersonal force and a character about whom she can tell a story in which she blames opportunity for allowing Tarquin to rape her and for keeping Collatine away. She then generalizes about Time rather than face her specific circumstance (925ff.).

Amid Lucrece's fear of the written report of her shame, she notes how time changes words. Time's glory, she says, is "To blot old books and alter their contents" (949). This sense of time is double-edged because Shakespeare's Lucrece is one Lucrece in a long line in literature, so that the story has lasted. But reputation is not as important as she thinks (even as the poet seeks his) because language changes and so alters the story. She exhorts time to curse Tarquin as she sets out in her narrative (967ff.). Shakespeare amplifies the notion of the uselessness and powerlessness of words when he has Lucrece proclaim, "Our idle words, servants to shallow fools, / Unprofitable sounds, weak arbitrators!" and say, "This helpless smoke of words doth me no right" (1016–29). Paradoxically, Lucrece needs the help of words to proclaim their helplessness.

She wishes to silence herself with suicide, but since she cannot find a weapon, she talks again about her own story and the bastard in her womb that she intends to silence so Tarquin cannot mock Collatine (1044–78). Lucrece thinks that the sun and birds mock her: she speaks to the bird as Philomel (the narrator calls Lucrece by this name) and wants it to sing its story of ravishment while she tells her parallel tale of rape (1079–92, 1121–48). The story becomes mythologized and generalized, increasing its narrative scope while making Lucrece seem less solitary. The brief allusion to Philomel implies the larger story from mythology and therefore acts as an aenos (a moral added to a fable). After Lucrece's "dialogue" of body and soul, she vows not to die "till my Collatine / Have heard the cause of my untimely death" so he can avenge it (1177–78). She addresses the absent Collatine as if he were present and advises, "How Tarquin must be us'd, read it in me" (1195). She becomes a text to be read and speaks of her will, disbursing her reputation (1198–1211).

The only male voice to make sense is that of Brutus, the man who was thought a fool, whereas the wise appear foolish. Whether the narrator has to be a male is a matter for debate, although I am not aware that anyone assumes the voice to be feminine. If, as critics have assumed, the narrator is male, then the representation of Lucrece's rape occurs through another masculine filter. The plight of this female character has to be sorted out with the awareness that she inhabits a male world that will represent her. This problem has wider implications for male critics even as they attempt to understand the situation in which a male-controlled world has placed Lucrece. Whether writers, readers, and characters are doomed to separate worlds based on differences of gender, race, politics, and religion, whether they are joined through universals, or whether they can find some common experiences despite their differences, become important questions for the critic. My position acknowledges the differences but seeks common ground where, for example, men can understand how patriarchy and male domination can compromise and victimize women. If the narrator is a woman, then we have to ask whether she can be entirely so because Shakespeare, a male writer, creates her. A female narrator in the poem would supplement Lucrece as a dissenting woman, voicing her dilemma in a world that men dominate. Another implication of a female narrator is how much her voice coincides with Lucrece's and why so many critics, who have traditionally been men, have assumed that the narrator is male (and have considered the possibility of it). (I shall assume the maleness of the narrator, keeping in mind these caveats.)

Most males appear silenced by and ineffectual after the rape. After Lucrece's death, her husband stands in stunned silence until her father speaks. Collatine, whose narrative skill apparently so inflamed Tarquin's lust that he raped Lucrece, now grows speechless. Tarquin, who in his hatred abuses her physically and verbally, and Lucretius, who can only react to the death but cannot prevent it, use, contain, and interpret Lucrece in their narratives. Lucretius' direct addresses and apostrophes cannot revive Lucrece (1751–71). Lucretius and Collatine squabble almost comically in their grief over whose woman Lucrece is (1795–1806). Having protected himself at court by pretending to be a fool, Brutus takes charge and speaks justly to Collatine: "Thy wretched wife mistook the matter so, / To slay herself that should have slain her foe" (1826–27). The others follow Brutus in his revenge. If his interpretation of the narrative, rather than Lucretius' and Colatine's impotent and farcical responses, governs the Roman reaction to Lucrece's death, the narrator's words end the poem. The narrator has the last word even if in his narration the reader learns that Lucrece is borne bleeding through the streets and that the Romans banish Tarquin. This principal narrator remains at the center of a study of narrative in the poem.

THE PRINCIPAL NARRATOR

Because all narrators affect and participate in the representation and reception of a tale, a study of that role is necessary for the understanding of stories. In this narrative poem the narrator takes a particularly active role in the interpretation of the poem and thus warrants close attention. Shakespeare's narrator especially acts as a filter between the characters and the reader. He is complicit in the representation and the reception of the poem—which is not a chronicle that lists one tale after the other as if each were equal but rather a study, through the narrative filter, of the consequences for Tarquin of Collatine's tale. The narrator is the primary means Shakespeare uses in changing the tale from being seriatim to a story that allegorizes and moralizes itself and its representation. Shakespeare uses the narrator to report some of the characters' speeches before beginning their direct discourse, so that they never speak entirely for themselves. He also acts in other ways as a transition between the characters and the reader: he comments on the characters' speeches and describes the characters, thereby influencing the reader's interpretation by his own. Once again, the danger is to subsume in this section the three parts of this analysis of *Lucrece*, but to do so is to gain the apparent simultaneous effect of the poem on the reader while losing definition and an understanding of the relation of parts to whole. This section will therefore discuss the narrator's role but will leave to the next section a detailed discussion of his relation to the reader.

Shakespeare's principal narrator wastes no time interpreting each character. In the opening stanza he focuses on "lust-breathed Tarquin" leaving the siege of a town for the siege of a woman, to chase "Lucrece the chaste" (1–7). The narrator then backs up his narrative, telling of how Collatine had "unwisely" told his story about Lucrece, adding his apostrophic editorial on the fragility of happiness and the vulnerability of honor and beauty (8–28). In his interpretation of Collatine's story the narrator calls attention to the power and limits of language: "Beauty itself doth of itself persuade / The eyes of men without an orator" (20–30). Nonetheless, the narrator speaks of beauty as Collatine does: indeed, it is one of the causes of his story. The narrator plays orator and makes an "apology" just as Collatine had, even though he chides this husband for not being possessive enough of his wife (31–35). He properly blames Collatine because his boast about Lucrece has tempted Tarquin, but the narrator also misuses language and women.

The narrator continues to speculate about Tarquin's motives, calling Lucrece a "thing" and saying that Tarquin wanted the happiness of someone of less status: Collatine (36–42). The narrator demonstrates subtlety here because he realizes that Tarquin's motives are as difficult to surmise as any person's: "But some untimely thought did instigate / His all-too-timeless speed, if none of those" (43–44). Assuming a straightforward and singular relation of cause and effect in interpretation, he implies, is not advisable. The narrator moralizes by apostrophizing the heat of the liver, the lust that burns and has long burned within the cold exterior of the lustful man, and he debates, with the very rhetoric he had criticized in Collatine, whether virtue or beauty underpinned Lucrece's fame, although he once more stresses the shame of bragging even as he extols her (45–56). The attitude of the narrator is complex, perhaps as contradictory as paradoxical, so that our reception of his narrative requires discernment.

Although the narrator reports that Tarquin "stories" Lucrece of her husband's fame, he then uses the topos of inexpressibility to express her "wordless" joy for Collatine's success. This negatio (apophasis—a refusal to speak that tells all) gives the speech to the narrator and to Tarquin but not to the silent woman, Lucrece. By saying what Tarquin's face is not yet, the narrator cannot let it be entirely without storm or free from associations with darkness and prison. He also shows that Tarquin cannot control his intentions and pretense. Like Venus' song, Tarquin's conversation passes the night and translates lust (see *Venus and Adonis* 841).[12] The narrator represents Tarquin as being as restless as thieves, cares, and troubled minds. Will's narrator, though less obviously than in sonnets 135 and 136, may be punning on his name Will and thus be speaking about authorial will, or sexual desire and volition, as much as Tarquin's struggle with his will. The author wills his work into being, and his erotic representations can seduce him while serving as moral examples. As the author's view is more oblique and removed from the reader because he hides behind characters and the narrator and represents through them, the reader must take particular care in interpreting that view. Shakespeare uses five consecutive female rhymes through present participles to represent a kind of onomatopoetic wavering of the will until Tarquin seems ready to choose the death of orgasm even if it means his physical death (106–33). The narration here shows a dramatic tension between the restraint of reason and the coursing lust. As T. W. Baldwin points out, Shakespeare through the narrator represents Tarquin's extended ratiocination, for Tarquin asks himself the reason for every statement and looks for the meaning of every successive affirmation (134–40).[13] Through amplification, the narrator describes a lack through surfeit in Tarquin and perhaps in the narrator and reader: "and all for want of wit, / Make something nothing by augmenting it" (153–54). Just as Venus attributes narcissism to Adonis in *Venus and Adonis* partly through a repetition of "himself himself," so too does the narrator call attention to Tarquin's selfishness by repeating this echo twice:

> And for himself himself he must forsake.
> Then where is truth if there be no self-trust?
> When shall he think to find a stranger just,
>   When he himself himself confounds, betrays
>   To sland'rous tongues and wretched hateful days?
> (157–61; see *VA* 161–62)[14]

The narrator represents the destabilization of Tarquin's self into conflicting selves: he becomes vulnerable to slanderous tongues like the narrator's, although slander implies that he has done nothing wrong—yet. He reiterates the harm to the mind as Tarquin "Is madly toss'd between desire and dread" (171; see 167–68, 125–26). The narrator's artifice persists in the repeated images of light and dark, hot and cold, in his debate with "his inward mind," and in his interpretation of Tarquin's words to Lucrece (185, 246–52). When the narrator intercedes between the interior monologues of Tarquin, he is subject to the context, because Tarquin has just closed his appeal to himself in words that call attention to sententiae and conventional pictures akin to the narrator's, no matter how much he disapproves morally of Tarquin (244–45).

The narrator also represents Lucrece ambivalently, especially in relation to Tarquin and the other males in the poem. He repeats the image of the serpent, this time likening Tarquin's eyes to those of the basilisk. In an elaborate descriptive metaphor of wind, earth, and clouds that makes Tarquin the clouds now and not the sun, the narrator reports that Lucrece's words delay Tarquin's haste just as Orpheus charmed Pluto with his music while he retrieved his wife from the underworld. This verbal delay is akin to the narrator's in the first third of the poem. He reverses the sex roles of man and woman by making Lucrece Orpheus, godlike in the power of his music to move rocks and reroute rivers. Lucrece, the narrator may be implying, resembles Orpheus for suffering so much for love, although she is like Eurydice because she is threatened by rape and death and because she fails to prevent her violation and dies amid plaintive sounds. Like a muse, Orpheus and Lucrece each sing but become subject to Pluto. Pluto will also stand between Lucrece and Collatine. Art will lament Lucrece as it did Orpheus and Venus, but art is, perhaps, part of the treason against itself that Shakespeare represents so self-consciously in *Venus and Adonis* and *The Rape of Lucrece*.

Shakespeare also draws attention to the reception of words: Tarquin's "heart granteth / No penetrable entrance to her plaining"; lust is more durable than marble, and life is harder than art (558–60). With eloquence, the narrator tells us that her pleading rhetoric, no matter how gracious, does not move Tarquin. The narrator thereby implies the possible ineffectiveness of his own expressions or the gap between his rhetorical power and her failing words. Either way, males victimize Lucrece. Just as the narrator seeks out metaphors and images in rapid succession to describe the induction to the attempted seduction and the rape itself, he lists the metaphors that Lucrece uses to try to persuade Tarquin to desist (540–74). Lucrece's speech amplifies these metaphors. The narrator uses images to criticize Tarquin but is in danger of sharing his erotic pleasure embodied in a rhetoric like Lucrece's, but also like Tarquin's. Shakespeare and the reader can succumb to the power of lustful language while feeling repugnance for Tarquin's lust and can experience their own seduction by the power of sex and violence.

The narrator and Brutus leave us wondering about the nature of Lucrece's death. Brutus qualifies the betrayal, as his words sway his audience until they swear an oath against Tarquin. The Romans bear Lucrece's body through Rome as a publication of Tarquin's offense, and, as the narrator observes, the Romans banish him forever. Why Lucrece needs to die to awaken the males to action remains a question as much for Shakespeare's sources as for his poem. Although the narrator reports a kind of poetic justice, he implies that Brutus acts where the comic and ineffective duo of Lucretius and Collatine could not. Here is the man who fulfills Lucrece's desire for revenge and justice, but, as at the end of Hamlet, we experience the loss at the end of the work. Why must the woman be silent? Why must she have died? The men have created a situation and society that make Lucrece feel sullied and unable to redeem her honor and to act on her own behalf. The narrator banishes us into silence, to think, perhaps, at least today, why Lucrece could not do as Brutus does. As in Hamlet, the revenge tragedy has its own logic, but the reader in exile, who is both the seducer and the seduced, half-forgetting Tarquin, who left over eleven hundred lines ago, also senses that Lucrece is a present absence.[15] Her silence is with and without power—like Brutus' words, which have power to revenge but not to restore—and at least as disturbing as they are. Perhaps the story calls for the exile into silence, but the narrator's discourse raises questions about the ravishment of poetry and the complicity of poet and readers.

THE READER AND NARRATIVE

The sense of audience connects the characters, the principal narrator, and the reader. Tarquin's hearing of Collatine's tale, Lucrece's hearing of Tarquin's "seduction," his deafness to Lucrece, the confusion that meets Lucrece's recounting of the rape, all demonstrate the importance of audience. The male reactions to her suicide stand in for her own response to events and her act of revenge, as if her life were a praecisio, a speech cut or left off for their interpretation. The many references to scandal, reputation, words, writing, and books also represent a self-conscious awareness of audience and reader inside and outside Lucrece's story. These very references break down the differences between inside and outside, so that Lucrece's tale constitutes only one part, no matter how important, of *The Rape of Lucrece*. The difficulty in separating the responses of character, audience, and reader to the stories of the characters and principal narrator means that, for the sake of coherence, I must limit the scope of this section to a discussion of the response of the characters and the principal narrator to their own stories and shall draw a few general implications for the reader from these examples. More specifically, in this section I shall analyze self-conscious descriptions of, references to, and narratives about art, writing, and storytelling, which call particular attention to the rhetorical relation between speaker and audience, writer, and reader. I shall focus on the narrator's relation of the rape of Lucrece to writing and on some aspects of the inset of the emblem of Troy. The principal narrator is the main filter through which the reader must assimilate and question this metapoetics, and the rape of Lucrece and its aftermath especially focus attention on the problems of reading and interpretation, probably the most interesting aspect of the poem.

The reader must grasp metalepsis (transumptio—the metaphor of a metaphor) as well as a self-conscious representation of writing that implies an informed response in reading. Lucrece speaks to the image of her complaining, so the narrator implies that she represents herself with metaphors about metaphors in a mixture of word and picture (1268–70). The narrator reports the importance and difficulty of writing in Lucrece's reaction to her rape as she asks her maid to get paper, ink, and pen so that she can write to her husband of these events. It is as if she is trying to control the rape and codify her response with the objectification of script. Thought and grief contend as her will revises what her intellect sets down, but the narrator's choice of metaphors almost trivializes the rape with a self-conscious discussion of style—"This is too curious-good, this blunt and ill"—and he describes "her inventions" as a throng like Prince Henry's description in King John of how Death causes a throng of strange fantasies that confound themselves (*KJ*, V.vii.15–20).[16] The narrator uses the precise legal term "tenure" for Lucrece's statement and expresses himself perhaps "too curious good" in witty phrases like "her certain sorrow writ uncertainly" and "Ere she with blood had stain'd her stain'd excuse" (1296–1316). According to the narrator, Lucrece worries that Collatine will suspect her of sin before she accounts for her compromised account of compromise. Written discourse is a defense against the possible accusations that Collatine and the world might level against her: "To shun this blot, she would not blot the letter / With words, till action might become them better" (1322–23). This chiming pun or witty use of the same word in different parts of speech (a form of traductio and polyptoton) links her sin with her words, her interpretation of that blot, rape, and revision.

Shakespeare, the writer, has the written narrator represent writing as a transgression and impediment to action. The narrator's comments might also apply to writing and dumb-shows: the eyes interpret sad sights for the ears (1324–30). The narrator reports the sealing of Lucrece's letter, on which she has written a groping, hyperbolic, and urgent message: "At Ardea to my lord with more than haste" (1332). He extends Lucrece's oxymoronic and ambivalent dementiens (hyperbole) by recording her request that the groom hasten like "lagging fowls before the northern blast" and by calling attention to the limits of language and action: "Speed more than speed but dull and slow she deems: / Extremity still urgeth such extremes" (1336–37). The narrator, Lucrece, and others who hide their guilt "Imagine every eye beholds their blame, / For Lucrece thought he blush'd to see her shame" (1343–44). Lucrece thinks that the groom can read her inner thoughts, the same groom the narrator describes as being obedient and as talking in deeds, but she also misinterprets him by appearances and reads in him her own despair or rage.

From hyperbole, the narrator turns to understatement and silence as sufficient substitutes for speech: he notes that the groom, "this pattern of the worn-out age," gave honest looks, and not words, as his sign of obedience. This mutual displacement of words and images recurs through much of the narration and emphasizes the conflict and complementarity between the verbal and pictorial for character, poet, narrator, and reader (fictional viewer). Through other recurrences or amplifications (faces like fires blushing), the narrator expresses the lack of communication between Lucrece and the groom. Her expression of woe has become stale and so, the narrator implies, she looks for new expression as he does: the parabola (imago) of Troy enables this new expression.

The reader of this poem must be aware of epic conventions, the most important of which is the inset.[17] Shakespeare's use of this convention deserves extensive analysis. He provides his narrative with the inset of an emblem of Troy that is reminiscent of the technique Virgil uses in the *Aeneid* (1:455–93). The narrator reports that Lucrece imagines a painting of the siege of Troy, "Which the conceited painter drew so proud, / As heaven, it seem'd, to kiss the turrets bow'd"—all because of the rape of Helen, an analog to the rape of Lucrece (1371–72). Not only is this the kind of revenge Lucrece wants but also it self-consciously draws attention to the conceits and aspirations of artists. The aspiring supplement to nature the narrator makes explicit: "A thousand lamentable objects there, / In scorn of nature, art gave lifeless life" (1373–74). Shakespeare seems to imagine Ilion and Helen as much through Marlowe as through Virgil. Paradoxically, according to the narrator, art intensifies life, and his possible hyperbole may conform to Quintilian's view of *dementiens*: "When the magnitude of the facts passes all words . . . our language will be more effective if it goes beyond the truth than if it falls short of it" (VIII.vi.67ff.).[18] "The red blood reek'd to show the painter's strife" does not represent the blood shed in battle between Greeks and Trojans, although the conflict leads to bloody strife in the artist just as the rape of Lucrece creates a tension in Shakespeare to represent it. The poet creates for the narrator the fiction of the ingenious painter (as full of conceits as Shakespeare is) to make a Troy that heaven would bow to, it seems, at four mimetic removes.

The reader recreates the poet's description of the narrator's report of Lucrece's recollection of the painter's work. This layering is like amplification itself, as if the reader is drawn into the praiseworthy and praising, the bounding and abundant speakers as they reinforce one another in their representations. As in his *Venus and Adonis* (11) and *Timon of Athens* (I.i.37–38), Shakespeare here represents the painter's, and by extension the poet's, strife in competing with nature (1373–79). The painter creates "A thousand lamentable objects," the blood reeking to show his conflict. Here, Shakespeare's narrator attempts to get inside the painter's mind through Lucrece's and in doing so represents nature mimicking art, or the painter's nature, a kind of reversed intentional fallacy. The poet is creating this hyperbolic lament through the fiction of word-pictures and praises his own work by praising his created painter's creation. The far-off sad eyes are his as much as the Trojans' (1380–86). Perhaps the reader, like these soldiers and the groom, will be caught up in and be part of this imagined piece. All their laments are allegorical for Shakespeare's Lucrece.

The reader must also contend with the narrator's moralizing. The narrator states explicitly his interpretation of Lucrece's interpretation of the painting. In an act of narratorial appropriation of a character's thoughts (as he does elsewhere with voice), he says that she finds company in the misery of the represented figures until she comes to Hecuba, with whom she identifies and who is full of sorrow as she sees her husband bleeding under Pyrrhus. Hecuba to her, as to the First Player in *Hamlet* (II. ii), is a type of sadness and lament. The narrator interprets the painter's allegory of Hecuba: "In her the painter had anatomiz'd / Time's ruin, beauty's wrack, and grim care's reign" (1450–51). This is an example of the critic translating art by denoting its connotations. Like Hecuba, Lucrece finds herself represented as "imprison'd in a body dead" and "shapes her sorrow to the beldam's woes," but the painter has disfigured Hecuba by making her face unrecognizable and by not giving her "bitter words to ban her cruel foes." The narrator sets up a disjunction between his poet and the painter (also a creation of Shakespeare as the narrator is) because the painter, unlike the poet,

> was no god to lend her those,
> And therefore Lucrece swears he did her wrong,
> To give her so much grief, and not a tongue.
> (1461–63)

Although Shakespeare is subject to the limitations of art, he immediately gives Lucrece a speech in which she speaks for Hecuba, whom the painting has silenced. Hecuba's woes are like Lucrece's, so that she obliquely addresses her rape, making herself both Hecuba and Priam, mourner and mourned, because Collatine's response to the rape is not yet represented. Once again, Shakespeare has Lucrece transgress the divisions of gender.

The poet creates a digression that represents eloquence and speechlessness, sympathy and violence, in short, the power and limits of art. He makes his narrator digress in such a way as to create a climax at its end—the identification of Lucrece and Hecuba. Before amplifying this analog through Lucrece's interpretation (1464ff.), Shakespeare expresses Hecuba's lament through seeming inexpression, Lucrece's through Hecuba's, leaving space for the reader to fill out the narrative, a little like making Achilles' spear gripped by an armed hand imply his image (1424). The inset, a fictional painting that is a descriptive narrative, broadens the historical, ethical, and artistic implications of the rape by exploring the relation between art and life, the nature of eloquence, persuasion, and manipulation (thereby implying a comparison between placating Nestor and pleading Tarquin, invader and rapist), the type of Hecuba, the rape of Troy, and the rape of Lucrece. Narrative multiplication complicates the rape of Lucrece and challenges the reader to view it as more than a horrible and discrete event—something that has social implications and a context. Lust and war share hatred and rationalization as well as the attempt to silence the women.

As usual in this poem, the reader must carefully assess the narrator's readings. If the narrator contextualizes Lucrece's interpretation of Hecuba's lot because he sets up her speech and comments on it, he also uses an elaborate metaphor to describe Lucrece's "painted woes." Shakespeare calls attention to verbal as well as pictorial art: Lucrece tells "sad tales" to "pencill'd pensiveness," lends them words and borrows sorrowful looks from the painting (1492–98). For the narrator, Lucrece seems to become the painting as it becomes her, a kind of mutual representation of nature and art. Another context occurs in a parallel analogue: Hecuba is to Lucrece as Sinon is to Tarquin. The description of Sinon provides an analogous inset for Tarquin because each hides with show "his secret evil." By referring to Sinon's "craft and perjury" that "The well-skill'd workman" made, the narrator emphasizes verbal as well as pictorial artifice. Shakespeare gives to his narrator, who gives to the painter, who gives to Sinon, an "enchanting story" that slew Priam and a hyperbolic simile, "words like wildfire" that burned the much-praised Troy until the heavens became humanized in their sorrow and as disorderly as those at Glendower's birth. Sinon's power of words, which depends on the narrator's and ultimately the poet's, can out-hyperbolize Troy itself, the very mirror for the stars, as if the heavens relied on the earth. Shakespeare inverts the mirror for magistrates with Promethean language. Incidentally, he remakes and recontextualizes Virgil (*Aeneid* 2:13–267).

If Lucrece thinks the fictional painter's picture is false, the reader may question Shakespeare's art and workmanship. But the poet also created the portrait of Tarquin, whose outward show and inward corruption seem to corroborate Sinon's (1499–1530). Perhaps Lucrece lacks the experience to recognize moral complexity and to suspect the deception and Machiavellian acting that conceal power and lust: she should not be blamed or praised for this inexperience. Art is a lie insofar as it is of nature but not identical to it. The painter and Shakespeare use contrast to represent the drama of evil in a complicated manner. By making Lucrece seem innocent, Shakespeare may be showing the limited point of view of the narrator, praising his own understanding over that of his characters (a type of dramatic irony) and victimizing his victim.

A complex representation of exempla and description of the characters', narrator's, and author's points of view demands much of the reader. The inset of Troy represents a particularly difficult challenge. Amid suggestion and obliquity, the narrator makes explicit the relation between Sinon and Tarquin and thereby moralizes the exemplum (1534–37, 1562–68). By tearing the "senseless" and imagined portrait of Sinon, Lucrece emphasizes the power of imagination, a reading that has implications for Shakespeare and for the reader as well as for the narrator and her. Shakespeare's narrator represents Lucrece's struggle with equivocation and oxymoron along with gnomic utterance (sententia) and generality as if to generalize her particular suffering as an exemplum (1569–75). By using the analogy of painting, the narrator reminds readers of their relation to the work: the "painted images" make Lucrece forget her own grief. Art deflects and pacifies until the viewer remembers the gap between nature and representation (1576–82). Once again, the narrator reads a character's eyes and tears as an episode in a story, as if the eyes have life themselves. Lucrece's eyes and face, according to the narrator, silence Collatine for a while (1583–96). But Lucrece is also silenced and must yield to the narrator's view—she sighs and is a "pale swan"—until she can tell her story.

Even after Lucrece tells her tale and Brutus avenges the rape within it and the death that ends it, can she escape being represented through the narrator? Can any of the characters' stories be free of the narrator's filter? If the connection between Tarquin and the narrator, the relation of Lucrece to Philomela, the self-conscious awareness of writing and reading, and the inset of Troy make readers more aware of the problems of representation, of the aesthetics and ethics of reading, can they avoid being implicated in the narrator's complicity in the rape of Lucrece and of Troy? This chapter has attempted to demonstrate the complexity of these questions and has constituted one possible answer to them. Representation can misrepresent the subject.

The complicity of the narrator in Tarquin's failed seduction and then rape of Lucrece and the violence in the sack of Troy can embody the author's seduction of himself and of the reader. Although Tarquin's seduction fails and he is exiled for the rape, the very power of Shakespeare's poetry as well as the intricate analogies and contradictions linking the narrator, Tarquin, the poet, and the reader (among others) that I have elaborated suggests that the rhetoric of narrative can be potentially seductive and dangerous. The pleasure of the text creates a tension with the moral of the story. Even if Shakespeare and the reader agree on the moral that Tarquin's rape of Lucrece is brutal and deserves severe punishment, Shakespeare's ability to explore the yearnings, rationalizations, and pleasures of the body and of power tempt the reader and may express an ambivalence within the writer. It is as if we know what is right but do what is wrong in spite of ourselves. Paradoxically, in the tension between the aesthetic and the moral we find our greatest temptation and hope. Perhaps the tension creates a beginning and an opening through which we can know ourselves and understand the nuances, complexities, and complications of desire and hatred in the face of dark forces that we would prefer to ignore, hide, and suppress. By examining narrative closely from the point of view of the relation of the characters, narrator, and poet to the reader, we should understand *Lucrece* better even as the narrative turns rhetorically to and from the world. How much we can translate the ethic of reading into our experience in the world persists as a troubling but vital question.

This space between writing and reading, character and action through language, is also one Shakespeare explores in the sonnets.[19] The human voice that addresses and the eye and ear that are addressed are parts of a rhetorical contract even in poems whose poetics would veer away into lyric moments that try to evade the persuasion and seduction of rhetoric. The intricacies of thought and feelings in word and deed, the reflections and self-reflection, are all subject to the tension between the moment and the long term in regard to a life, to history, and to eternity. Temporality, a theme of Shakespeare's history plays, not to mention the fools of time represented in the tragedies, is also a concern of the poems and a mainstay of the sonnets. The writer represents and the reader reads in the interpretative middle ground in which the poet, his mistress, and the young man, through language, face ethical dilemmas, seduction, revulsion, and a number of the experiences that Shakespeare stresses in *Venus and Adonis* and *The Rape of Lucrece*. The making of poetry in the cultivation of a public–private "history," whether mythological or historical, motivates Shakespeare in the poems and the plays. To explore the dilemma of time, he uses the form of the sonnet in nondramatic and dramatic situations. And to the sonnets I now turn.

CHAPTER 3

THE SONNETS

THE SONNET WAS, LIKE RICHARD HAKLUYT'S COLLECTIONS, PART OF THE MAKING of English culture based on texts and traditions that came from the Continent and beyond. Petrarch's *Canzoniere* and Joachim Du Bellay's sonnets, especially *Antiquitez de Rome* (1558), provided influences and affinities and both contained meditations on time. With great distinction, Edmund Spenser, who had dedicated work to Philip Sidney, translated this text of Du Bellay. He renders into English the beginning of the second sonnet thus: "Great *Babylon* her haughtie walls will praise, / And sharped steeples high shot vp in ayre" and concludes it as follows: "But I will sing aboue all monuments / Seuen *Romane* Hils, the worlds 7. Wonderments," which is not too far off the theme of Shakespeare's Sonnet 55.[1] In the last lines of the first poem of the revision of *L'oliue*, a book of sonnets, in 1550, Du Bellay writes,

> Orne mon chef, donne moy hardieſſe
> De te chanter, qui espere te render
> Egal vn iour au laurier immortel.
>
> [Adorn my head, give me the boldness
> To sing of you, I who hope to render you
> Equal one day to the immortal laurel.][2]

Mortality and immortality are concerns of the Renaissance sonnet, and in this Shakespeare is no different than his predecessors. It is a matter of how he represents this theme—the ways and means—and not the thematics themselves that distinguish him. Some might argue, as A. Kent Hieatt did in the early 1980s, that Shakespearean exceptionalism is at work despite the intertextuality of the sonnet sequences of the European Renaissance because it concentrates themes of time, change, and continuance and on autobiographical elements more than other sequences do.[3] While there is much truth to this observation, it is important, as in many cases of exceptionalism, to see continuities and affinities. The context for the text at hand—Shakespeare's sonnets—involves an emphasis on time that has personal consequences. England was not divorced from Europe, even if an island, as John of Gaunt so eloquently describes in Shakespeare's *Richard II*. Both Edmund Spenser and William Shakespeare, directly and indirectly, could not avoid the influence of Petrarch or Du Bellay. The English predecessors to those poets born in the 1550s and 1560s had already brought Petrarch and Italian language and culture to England.

This was something that some of Shakespeare's contemporaries understood well. In a discussion of the dactyl in Book 2 of *The Arte of English Poesie* (1589), George Puttenham, for example, could see that the "Earle of Surrey & Sir *Thomas Wyat*" were "the first reformers & polishers of our vulgar Poesie much affecting the stile and measures of the Italian *Petrarcha*."[4] Thomas Wyatt and Henry Howard, Earl of Surrey, "translated" the sonnets of Petrarch into the cultural context of England. Wyatt was bold in his translations of Petrarch into English and changed the course of English poetry as a result.[5] Wyatt and Surrey, who both translated 140 in Petrarch's *Canzoniere*, both suffered in the political struggles of the Reformation and at court in Tudor England. Not until Richard Tottel's *Songs and Sonnets* (1557), fifteen years after the death of Wyatt, did this poet's sonnets appear in print.[6] Surrey, whose portrait was painted by Hans Holbein the Younger, died in 1547. Surrey was the cousin of Anne Boleyn (Bullen), who was apparently close to Wyatt before Henry VIII took an interest in her. Henry imprisoned Wyatt on at least two occasions and had Surrey executed just before the king himself died in 1547. These great innovators in English letters, and especially in the sonnet, were caught in the world of court and politics and could not escape the influence, for good or ill, of the monarch. Surrey, who also first used blank verse in his translation of Virgil's *Aeneid*, dwelt at the center of politics in his own country and time. Love, marriage, treason, and love of country all mixed in the textual and actual worlds of their England. There was a private and public dimension of these men, who were also sonneteers, and Sidney, Spenser, Daniel, Shakespeare, and others in a later generation continued this poetic and cultural work. Sidney—author of a sonnet sequence *Astrophil and Stella* (pub. 1592) as well as the great romance *Arcadia* and perhaps the greatest work of literary criticism in Elizabethan England, *The Apology for Poetry* (pub. 1595)—especially led a life that depended on court, receiving recognition on the Continent but not as much at home until his funeral.[7] Sonnets and sonneteers lived and wrote in a space caught between private and public, love and politics. Milton and Shelley later came to write great political sonnets that show the public face of the form more fully. As can be seen in Du Bellay's work, Shakespeare was not the first to mediate on the ruins of time, and he certainly was not novel in contemplating the gilded monuments. The erasure and endurance of time is the dilemma for any person and is all too keen for anyone in love. Yearning, regret, hope, and despair all mix together in sonnets, and Shakespeare's poems are exemplary and virtuoso performances of feelings in and of time.

Time is a theme in Petrarch's sonnets. This is an intricate topic in and of itself, so I will only mention a few instances to suggest that while Petrarch and Shakespeare do not speak about time in the same context or way, they do share a representation of its endurance and evanescence in the context of desire and love. Shakespeare follows Petrarchan conceits but, as is well known, can be positively anti-Petrarchan about them. Part of being a sonneteer is to be clever and to play with the conventions of the form that his or her predecessors spent so much time creating, sometimes through their own reversals of rules. Wyatt, Surrey, and Shakespeare could not ignore Petrarch, but they could make the sonnet their own and translate it into the English language and context. In sonnet 12 of the *Rime sparse*, Petrarch writes,

et se 'l tempo è contrario ai be' desiri,
non fia ch'almen non giunga al mio dolore
alcun soccorso di tardi sospiri

[and if time is hostile to my sweet desires,
at least it will not prevent my sorrow
from receiving some little help of tardy sighs.]
(12:12–13)[8]

Time here might oppose desire but will allow sighs to help his sorrow even if a little late. Petrarch begins sonnet 31 with the image of a noble soul departing this life, "called before its time to the other / life" (*anzi tempo chiamata a l'altra vita*; 31:2).[9] This religious theme between this life and the next is part of the realm of love. In sonnet 32, Petrarch contemplates the last day and sees that time runs fast and light, so that his hope in time (personified as "him" [*lui*]) is fallacious and silly (*"fallace et scemo"*; 32:4). To continue with personification (after humanizing time as a character), Petrarch addresses his thoughts and sees love as an earthly burden that melts like fresh snow (*"come fresca neve"*; 32:7). In this poem, the speaker sees the fall of hope with the advent of peace and a clear recognition of how people advance themselves for doubtful things (*"le cose dubbiose"*) and sigh in vain (32:13). Petrarch has his own conceit about the power of memory and love (one's heart) before monuments, stating that a solid diamond statue (*"un'imagine salda di diamante"*) could come to disappear rather than he forget her (108:6). Petrarch, like Du Bellay after him, represented the theme of time, something that Spenser picked up in his translation of Du Bellay and that Shakespeare developed, varied and amplified in such a memorable way—in time timeless.

In the Sonnets a conflict occurs between the ruins of time and the gilded monuments of Shakespeare's powerful rhyme that is set out in the desire between rhetoric and poetics, lust and love. How in the formal elegance and compression of the sonnet does Shakespeare represent a longing for eternity or a remembrance of things past or a wish for the extension of the evanescence of physical love into some timeless poetic moment? How much of the self-conscious rhetorical hyperbole of a poetics that would outlast other monuments in exploring love represents a conflict that recognizes the impossibility of such a vaunting verbal world? Paradoxically, this overreaching language, especially in conjunction and friction with the leveling rhetoric of lust and death, displays the only hope for love and poetics in the possible world of Shakespeare's poetry.

This attempt to reach beyond language and the forms of poetry also occurs in the sonnets in Shakespeare's plays. While this chapter will emphasize primarily the great sonnet sequence, it will also examine some of the dramatic contests as a means of suggesting how Shakespeare explores time and death in his sonnets generally and how that exploration calls attention to the limits and possibilities of poetry and the sonnet. The chapter begins with a general discussion of the Sonnets, proceeds to a brief examination of Shakespeare's sonnet in various dramatic contexts, and then analyzes some key poems at the beginning, middle, and end of the sonnets. It is impossible to be exhaustive with the sonnets, and no attempt has been made to be so. While the argument takes into account the vexed question of the order of the sonnets, it does not depend on that order.

The sonnets are neither strictly love's argument nor a drama with fully embodied characters. They cannot be resolved into the key with which Shakespeare unlocked his heart, as Wordsworth thought, or a denial of their autobiographical nature, as Browning contended.[10] Criticism is full of partial insights, like those Wordsworth and Browning offered, but taken together these partialities help to address the complexity of literature itself and some of its most perplexing works, like Shakespeare's sonnets.[11] The part this chapter will play in this critical drama is to seek out the limits of Shakespeare's language, his poetics and rhetoric, in these enigmatic lyrics and to do so most especially as he explores the outer boundary of life itself: death. Shakespeare's keeping time in the face of time the destroyer—whether he addresses the young man or the mistress, whether he proclaims the virtues of regeneration or laments the loss of youth and love, whether he contends with time through the boast of words or the heat of lust—constitutes the heart of this exploration of the sonnets.

Shakespeare uses dialectic, rhetoric, and poetics to face the ghost that haunts life, the dark gap of time and the skull beneath the skin. The confrontation of death, sometimes with despair or with the celebration of life, dwells behind the crumbling edifice of language and culture. In the tensions, inverted relations, and paradoxes of love and death lie that unexplored country Hamlet looked into and whose liminality made him shrink back and face those rather than cross the bourn to the afterlife, another world that could only be imagined. The narrator or speaker in the sonnets must, in the drama of time and in the conflicted space between master and mistress, look into the abyss of his existence and express that gaze in a language that attempts to reach beyond its own boundaries, a gesturing that seeks to make the impossible possible.[12] The strains of language at its end leave the speaker, those he addresses, the poet, and the reader seeking a comic ending, the happy circumstance of love, but in a tragic dilemma, as humans are fools of love because they are fools of time. Whether the expression of faith can resolve this sense of tragedy into something happy and comic is the deadly game, the play of the reclamation of wit, the serious but not always solemn procession or fragmentation called the sonnets.

The hope against mortality and the erasure of human life and value in time begins in the first sonnet, and the structure of comedy, despite the wistfulness of loss and the anger over betrayal, persists to the end of the sequence, where Cupid is literally a *deus ex machina*. Shakespeare associates Cupid with sexual and erotic play and the blindness of the love, lust, and lives of humans as part of his responsibility for their star-crossed love and comedy of errors. The great structure of comedy found in the Bible, *The Divine Comedy*, and Shakespeare's romantic comedy involves a move from order through chaos to a new order.[13] Even in this hope for regeneration in the first sonnets and this paean to love in the last two sonnets, a qualification of the drive toward comedy occurs, for the sequence includes poems that express the tragic aspects of love, time, and death. The sonnets intersperse these darker elements with wit and humor, which so often constitute the substructure and content of comedy. Shakespeare's sonnets, as they were printed, are not a conventional comedy—the narrator and the mistress do not overcome the complications of love and lust to marry—but they do have a general comic structure. Moreover, the ending of the sequence is reminiscent of the problem comedies or problems plays, whose conclusions seem theatrically achieved or forced.[14] Part of the problem is notorious: we cannot be sure that the order of Shakespeare's sonnets, any more than Chaucer's *The Canterbury Tales*, is the author's.[15]

Another strain occurs in the fragmentary nature of a series of lyrics, for they are discontinuous in a way that plays are not. The narrative is not straightforward: the telos vanishes, and the story is not a simple series with named characters who develop in linear fashion. This tension plays out in the language of this great sonnet sequence as the words seek to move beyond the limits of love, lust, and death but reinscribe boundaries. The narrator and various players are the innovative creation of a great poet, so that they are part of an experiment in language that pushes back the bounds of expression but that, no matter how successful, cannot escape death and oblivion. If the poet and his creations have religious faith, it is God or the spirit that redeems the fall of language no matter how smooth and able the pen of the poet is. If time, the great leveler, is the ultimate fact, then no amount of virtuosity can overreach the ruthlessness of nature. The wax tablet becomes the wax wings. Shakespeare and his creations share the fate of Icarus.

SONNETS IN THE PLAYS

This disjunctive strain occurs within the sonnet form, a virtuoso genre (kind) where the poet concentrates the vast themes of love and death into fourteen lines in one variation or another of a complex rhyme scheme. Before addressing the sonnets themselves, I would like to discuss sonnets in a few of Shakespeare's plays because they provide a gloss on the sequence itself, calling attention to their difference in form from the wider dramatic contexts in which they appear and they also treat of some similar themes. The sonnet the Chorus speaks as the Epilogue to *Henry V* ends this play and the second tetralogy, yoking a vast, crucial stretch of English history into a compressed poetic form that was traditionally devoted to love. This war story pushes out the bounds of its form: the love lyric yields to the imperial theme. Similarly, the French princess had to succumb to Henry V for dynastic reasons and to please her father's will even as the courtship had, in Shakespeare's version, contained tender and coy moments. Shakespeare's epilogic sonnet gestures toward modesty: "Thus far, with rough and all-unable pen, / Our bending author hath pursu'd the story" (Epilogue, 1–2).[16] This pursuit involves compression of the world into the confined space and time of a play, which has world and time enough compared to the sonnet that ends it: "In little room confining mighty men, / Mangling by starts the full course of their glory" (3–4). The topos of inexpressibility complements the modesty of the author even if he has had the ambition to write about the epic sweep of English history in a series of plays. Whereas Henry V had little time to achieve what he did in the world, Shakespeare has little space to represent that achievement: "Small time; but in that small most greatly lived / This star of England" (5–6). The end of the sonnet is more narrative, describing how Fortune had made him achieve France, "the world's best garden," which he left to his son, Henry VI, whose managers "lost France, and made his England bleed" (12). All this "oft our stage hath shown," so that Shakespeare alludes to his own *Henry VI* plays, which had been popular and had represented the end of the historical sequence before Shakespeare had written the second tetralogy.

Through allusion to more historical time and to other of Shakespeare's plays, the sonnet expands its content and strains its limits even more. This operation is left to the audience to complete, something in keeping with the Chorus' appeal to their imagination throughout *Henry V*. The audience, which in one form also includes the reader, is implicated in the exploration of boundaries in the world and the dramatic and literary forms that represent it. Like the poet and characters like Henry V, the audience is caught in time in the world and art and needs to meditate on it. Without an audience, history is no longer reenacted and embodied and withers away beyond memory. This topos is a courtesy from a begging epilogue, but there is also some credence in the imagined space between author and audience, world and representation.[17]

A choric use of sonnets also occurs in *Romeo and Juliet*, where the Prologue narrates the argument and sets the scene of the play. Once again, the conflict between love and public violence finds expression in the confines of a sonnet. The "new mutiny" and "civil blood" are the context for the children of the two households or foes, "A pair of star-cross'd lovers" (3–6). The love that should have happy conclusion in marriage ends in death: these lovers "Whose misadventur'd piteous overthrows / Doth with their death bury their parents' strife" (7–8). The play, "the two hours' traffic of our stage," is offered to the audience as something that will "mend" what the sonnet has not described and becomes an amplification of "The fearful passage of their death-mark'd love" (12–14, 9). A narrative device, the sonnet calls attention to its own need for supplement that the audience "with patient ears attend," so that the rough and limited art of the playwright needs more space to try to do the story justice (13). The poet emphasizes the bounds of his art as a poet and tries to justify the striving and mending "toils" of his playwrighting (14). The tragedy of what should be a festive comedy about lovers is something the sonnet amplifies through repetition, telling about "the continuance of their parents' rage, / Which, but their children's end, nought could remove" (10–11). The Prologue forewarns about the tragic turn of the play, for the body of *Romeo and Juliet* begins like a romantic comedy with two lovers being smitten and falling in love at first sight, facing obstacles but moving toward overcoming them in order to be united. Something goes wrong in this play when Romeo steps between Tybalt and Mercutio and the former stabs and kills the latter under Romeo's arm, and the young lover then kills Mercutio's killer who is also Juliet's kinsman (III.i.85–137).

Before these deaths in this love tragedy, Shakespeare also uses a sonnet to introduce act 2, and this poem is a comic mock at the changeability of love. The sonnet emphasizes the obstacles to the match between Romeo and Juliet and how Romeo's love has shifted from Rosaline to Juliet (see I.ii.83). Romeo has been spouting the oxymorons of a Petrarchan sonneteer early in the first act until his attentions turn to Juliet, so that by the time the audience hears this prologic sonnet to begin act 2, it is familiar with the shedding of his first love, to whom he had devoted the contradictory and apostrophic phrases—"O loving hate! . . . O heavy lightness, serious vanity"— that expressed the desire of love to yoke emotional extremities in order to exceed and resolve them in unity and the lovers' union (I.ii.175–82). The death of Romeo's love for Rosaline and the birth of his love for Juliet might invoke a shift from false love to true love and do so in the language of eternity and immutability, but the very shift itself questions a love that defeats time and change. This is precisely the monumental love that occurs at the end of the play, but even that union of lovers in death, as in *Antony and Cleopatra*, comes about because of ill fate and error, the star-crossed missings of tragedy. In this early satiric state of love, where Shakespeare has Romeo groaning and oxymoronic under the burden, Romeo will yield, not to the woman he thought his love, but to a woman whose family is his foe. In the metaphorical death of his old love, he has to find new life in love. He inhabits yet another oxymoronic paradox. The Chorus emphasizes this rebirth and regeneration in his opening lines to act 2, and the progress of love finds its imagery in the "death-bed," something that will become a literal stage image at the very end of the play:

> Now old desire doth in his death-bed lie,
> And young affection gapes to be his heir;
> That fair for which love groan'd for and would die,
> With tender Juliet [match'd] is now not fair.
> (1–4)

Although Rosaline is now not counted fair beside Juliet, Romeo and his new love will be heirs to "old desire" in more ironic ways, something the first sonnet spoken by the Prologue has marked out for the audience. Death sets a limit for the language of love even as that love proclaims itself as life itself or as something beyond death. Romeo must "complain" to "his foe suppos'd" and Juliet "steal love's sweet bait from fearful hooks" (7–8). Their situation curtails their love: he is a "foe" and thus cannot swear the vows to which lovers are accustomed; and in this enmity between their two families, she is not free "To meet her new-beloved any where" (12). This danger is an obstacle that comes from parental blocks as it does for the lovers in *A Midsummer Night's Dream*, *As You Like It*, and other Shakespearean comedies. They will seem to defeat time and death, for the sonnet concludes, "But passion lends them power, time means, to meet, / Temp'ring extremities with extreme sweet" (13–14). They can meet owing to the extreme sweetness of their love, and it may be that their love triumphs over time, but in language on earth their tragedy, especially after the deaths of Mercutio and Tybalt, seems inexorable, a waste of youth. Love might conquer all, as Ovid teaches, but, if so, this happens in a space that language can only reach for and whose putative existence draws attention to the very limits of verbal expression and perhaps any form of representation. The expense of spirit in a waste of words is love poetry in action. The very boasts of the language of love address the void of time, which seems like a means but has the power to take away and erase, a kind of heroic hope against the odds.

There are other places in the plays where Shakespeare might have used sonnets. In *As You Like It*, the poems that Orlando has composed for Rosalind, which she, Touchstone, and Celia read aloud in sequence, are decidedly not sonnets, but poems of various lengths composed of rhyming couplets, subject to much satire and critical comment in the scene itself (III.ii.87–250). Perhaps the parody of love poetry as in the plays within plays in *A Midsummer Night's Dream* and *Hamlet* can be more stylized by using more obvious and rudimentary poetic forms. This comic revelry does not call for experiments that push at the bounds of the sonnet form. The Epilogue to *Henry VIII* is a fourteen-line verse in couplets that can be construed as a sonnet, although not formally a usual Petrarchan or Shakespearean sonnet.[18] Shakespeare's epilogic verse incorporates themes found in other begging epilogues in his plays: the inability but desire to please the audience as well as the division between men and women but the hope they will clap in unison. The Epilogue uses "we" instead of "I," possibly suggesting the collaboration of John Fletcher and Shakespeare (4, 7–8, 11; see "ours" at 13). Such instances demonstrate that Shakespeare did not always use the sonnet for love poetry in the plays—in the minor epics, *Venus and Adonis* and *The Rape of Lucrece*, he also represented love, lust, and repulsion—and that his sonnets always explored in rigorous and innovative fashion the bounds of language, the sonnet, and life itself. That lovers, kings, and queens are fools of language and time, a thematic that is explored in the plays in forms other than the sonnet, except in a few rare instances, becomes a central concern in the sonnets themselves. The sonnet itself, a compressed form of musical and semantic time, becomes, in a complex and disjunctive series, a place where the possibility of an enduring art and love—the art of love and the love of art—is called into question. If Shakespeare's art will fail to endure, then what does that mean for lesser mortals and those characters to whom his narrator promises immortality through the monument of verse?

THEMES IN THE SONNETS

The sonnets themselves, whose order may or may not be the one Shakespeare gave to the poems, begins with reproduction as a means to stave off death: "From fairest creatures we desire increase, / That thereby beauty's rose might never die" (1:1–2).[19] The speaker suggests that the youth avoid wasting himself by being too "niggarding" with his "content" and urges him to make an heir (1:11–12). In Sonnet 2 Shakespeare returns to the theme of the death of the beautiful: this time "forty winters shall besiege thy brow, / And dig deep trenches in thy beauty's field" (2:1–2). Once more, a child is held up as an answer to age and death, "Proving his beauty by succession thine" (2:12). More amplification of this concern of procreation occurs in Sonnet 3, where the speaker grows ever blunter: "Or who is he so fond will be the tomb / Of his self-love to stop posterity?" (3:7–8). This warning against narcissism is a persistent theme of the procreation or regeneration sonnets that start Shakespeare's sequence, and Shakespeare will set up this self-adulatory representation as death itself: "But if thou live rememb'red not to be, / Die single, and thine image dies with thee" (3:13–14). The speaker, who hectors the "beauteous niggard" for abusing "beauty's legacy," the gift that Nature has given him, uses hyperbole to reach at the bounds of language in order to make his point that the young man will squander beauty and youth should he be content in himself and not produce an heir: "Profitless usurer, why dost thou use / So great a sum of sums, yet canst not live?" (4:7–8). Shakespeare's numbers, the rhythm of his verse, call on images of numeration and remuneration, of natural and unnatural increase, to drive the point home: "Thy unused beauty must be tombed with thee, / Which usèd lives th'executor to be" (4:13–14). The inexorability of wintry time finds amplification through an insistent repetition, so that the young man whom the speaker addresses cannot miss the message: "For never-resting time leads summer on / To hideous winter and confounds him there" (5:5–6). Beauty is "o'ersnowed" in one image and "summer's distillation," like a perfume, is one way to "remembrance," so that regeneration is a means to preserve substance even while the winter has wrought age and death (8–9, 12–14).

Sonnet 6 returns to winter defacing the young man's summer, to the theme of the previous sonnet, so well encapsulated in the phrase "Make sweet some vial" (6:3, see 5:9–14). Reiterating the imagery of self-killing and usury, the speaker urges his solution with familiar hyperbole:

> That's for thyself to breed another thee,
> Or ten times happier be it ten for one;
> Ten times thyself were happier than thou art,
> If ten of thine ten times refigured thee.
> (6:7–10)

Shakespeare gives his speaker language to refigure the young man in a mimetic regeneration, but, for now, he does not introduce the notion that Shakespeare's verse will make him immortal. That would contradict the argument that regeneration must happen in the world, that an "heir" will make him perpetually "fair" as opposed to being "self-willed," "To be death's conquest and make worms thine heir" (6:13–14). In Sonnet 7 the speaker likens the friend he is addressing to the personified sun, who rises with "gracious light" and "sacred majesty," climbs up "heavenly hill, / Resembling strong youth in his middle age," while mortals still adore his "beauty" and attend "on his golden pilgrimage" and, past the apogee, "Like feeble age he reeleth from the day" and sinks low so that onlookers turn their eyes away (7:1–12). To clinch and telescope the comparison, the speaker concludes, "So thou, thyself outgoing in thy noon, / Unlooked on diest unless thou get a son" (7:13–14). The addressee, who seemed a youth or a young man, is now almost past it and needs the repute and fame that he would gain from a son.

As if there had not been argument or amplification enough, the speaker now turns in Sonnet 8 to music as a means of persuasion. Harmony is not the "singleness" that the young man has chosen thus far but the way toward which the speaker, and perhaps the poet, is urging him, for if the addressee hears "music sadly," it is because he cannot hear properly the "sweets" and "joy" and "the true concord of well-tunèd sounds" that "sweetly chide" him (8:1–8). The speaker urges the young man to "Mark how one string, sweet husband to another, / Strikes each in each by mutual ordering" and, by analogy, "Resembling sire, and child, and happy mother, / Who all in one, one pleasing note do sing" (8:9–12). This harmony in the family is like the music of the spheres, so the microcosm and macrocosm exist in mutual order. The family finds some of its music in paradox and oxymoron, its "speechless song being many, seeming one, / Sings this to thee, 'Thou single wilt prove none.'" (8:13–14). Thus far in the regeneration sonnets the young man has been told of his limits and, by means of hyperbole, paradox and oxymoron where the poet explores the limits of language through the speaker, how to defeat time through the fame, repute, harmony, and reproduced image of an heir. And Sonnet 9 amplifies this theme of "beauty's waste" through an analogy of the world mourning the young man as a widow would her husband, the tragic loss arising because he died childless (9:11). The gaze of others, as in the reception of the sun in Sonnet 7, is a recurrent theme: the widow here keeping her "husband's shape in mind" by looking into their "children's eyes" (9:8). Should the young man die "issueless," then, the speaker concludes in the final couplet, "No love towards others in that bosom sits / That on himself such murd'rous shame commits" (9:13–14). Narcissus, or even Adonis in Shakespeare's narrative poem about his relation with Venus, is an implied comparison for the young man. Even at the limits of nature and language, Shakespeare gives his speaker a language of family and community—the close relation between speaker and addressee has not yet been established. Before the reader learns about the Platonic and close (perhaps sexual) relation between speaker and young man, he or she finds a social and familial context for love.[20] The defeat of time through regeneration, with all the fame and reputation or simply with the domestic moments of seeing oneself or others seeing oneself in one's son and heir, depends on a web of relations and an audience.[21] Remembrance depends on the son or heir, and sometimes the wife. This kind of memorial can be seen, although in a more violent state, when the Ghost of Hamlet senior asks his son specifically, "remember me," and his heir, echoing his father, takes up the challenge literally with a vengeance and much chides Gertrude for her apparent neglect of mourning and remembrance (*Hamlet*, I.v.91–111). Here, the speaker of this sonnet sounds paternal and avuncular, a Polonius who happens to speak a more subtle poetry, which the poet has given him, but not too unlike the kind of advice the king's counselor gives to his own son, Laertes, before he departs for France (*Hamlet*, I.iii.55–81). Age would school youth as if youth were wasted on the young.

The theme of self-shame, so evident in the final couplet in Sonnet 9, finds further expression in the next sonnet, whose first line speaks of "shame" and then proclaims "For thou art so possessed with murd'rous hate" (10:1, 5). The wit of the speaker attempts to leaven the harsh judgment: "O change thy thought, that I may change my mind!" the second clause linking the speaker with the young man through a chiming of the first clause, a play on a "change" that identifies and distinguishes the two characters (10:9). Through the metaphor of the house in the second quatrain, the speaker urges and cajoles and flatters the young man to put his house in order. In the concluding couplet the speaker—while doling out advice that by this point seems to be commonplace or conventional, for him at least—seems to intimate a love more personal: "Make thee another self for love of me, / That beauty still may live in thine or thee" (10:13–14). This line follows up on the recurrent concern of procreation to make beauty endure for the sake of nature, the world, and the young man but might also suggest, as the appeal is now to procreate for the benefit of the speaker, a bond between the two men that involves an admiration of friendship through physical beauty or something more physical still. Sonnet 11 returns to Nature, who is bounteous with those who reproduce, "so fast thou grow'st / in one of thine," but lets others not so wise "barrenly perish" (11:1–2, 9–10). Nature, like a monarch, places her seal on an important document: "She carved thee for her seal, and meant thereby, / Thou shouldst print more, not let that copy die" (11:13–14). This is an aristocratic image, imprinting one's image in wax, but it also conjures the language of degree and law and, possibly, conjoins and confounds the imprinting of court documents and manuscript culture with the mechanical reproduction of print culture. The sonnets themselves are said to have been passed about in manuscript only to be printed as a book with or without the poet's full or even partial participation. Even the author did not intend this meaning; the ambiguity of the seal as imprint and the copies as printed versions would be available to Shakespeare's audience. To go forth and multiply, as if Shakespeare's sonnets were beginning with Genesis in mind, means endurance, but the quality of the image and of the remembrance itself might not be as straightforward as the speaker says it is in his arguments to persuade the young man to regeneration.

Shakespeare regenerates the theme of regeneration: he repeats images in Sonnet 12—clock, sun, flower, person, and nature all move toward death. The sun sinks in "hideous night," and the speaker identifies harvest and funeral. The theme of the "beauty" of the young man "among the wastes of time" is played out once more in the context of the death of beauty in nature and the world, so that the reader can hardly be surprised in encountering the closing couplet: "And nothing 'gainst Time's scythe can make defence / Save breed to brave him when he takes thee hence" (12:9–10, 13–14). This personified or allegorized figure of Time or Death as harvesting humanity, found in emblem books, recurs in various sonnets in Shakespeare's sequence (60:12, 74:11, 100:13–14).[22] Breeding and providing an heir as a loss of "beauty" and a preparation against the "coming end," which was the thesis of the last four lines of Sonnet 12, is a recurrent concern at the beginning of Sonnet 13 (13:1–6). The young man will find himself, his "sweet form," through his "sweet issue," so that, inadvertently or not, a kind of reproductive narcissism is being urged here as it was in earlier sonnets (13:8). The image of the house in decay, this time in a windy winter storm "And the barren rage of death's eternal cold," recurs, its only hope "husbandry in honour" (13:9–12). The speaker asks who would let this house fall and answers in a half-line of the final couplet, "O none but unthrifts," the medial caesura leading to "dear my love, you know," which has ambivalent syntax, proclaiming how dear his love is to the young man or that this youth is his dear love (13:13). Whatever the reading here, the final line proclaims the familiar theme: "You had a father, let your son say so" (13:14). The line of male descent would then be preserved; but the speaker had also urged carrying on the maternal side by calling the youth his "mother's glass" (3:9). The urge to reproduction is dynastic and, while joining the parents in the son, may also blur gender boundaries because the son looks like the mother as well as the father and may not have achieved manhood. Sonnet 14 uses "astronomy" as the trope by which the speaker amplifies the now-familiar theme. He will not use astronomical prediction to judge but will read the young man's eyes, "constant stars," where "truth and beauty shall together thrive" if the addressee "from thyself to store thou wouldst convert" (14:9–12). This Grecian ideal, to which John Keats would later return, is a form of flattery and hyperbole, but Shakespeare relies on the *volta*, or turn, of the sonnet to turn on and qualify this stretching of the limits, because, in the final couplet, the speaker's praise depends on this reproduction, this storing of the young man's seed, for if that does not occur, then the contrary prognostication will obtain: "Thy end is truth's and beauty's doom and date" (14:13–14). This *volta* before the final couplet is far more abrupt and contradictory than in the Italian or Petrarchan sonnet, where it usually occurs between the eighth and ninth lines and where the momentum for the argument is not quite so one-sided. Shakespeare's language is a vehicle against the ruins of time, but, at this stage, it is the reproduction itself in nature that guarantees endurance.

Sonnets 15 and 16 mark the transition between the begetting of an heir and the lasting nature of the speaker's poetry as a means for the young man to find immortality in the face of Time, the destroyer. That rhyme is a means to stave off time goes back, as G. Blakemore Evans notes, to Horace and Ovid, and Shakespeare is not alone among Renaissance European sonneteers in elaborating on this theme.[23] In Sonnet 15 a tension occurs between breeding and writing as a means of defeating time, something Shakespeare works out through a theatrical metaphor, which, in his plays, grows more specific, from metapoetics to metatheatre. Shakespeare may be playing on the heavens in his theatre as a means of bringing astronomical and theatrical art together as a means of amplifying earlier metaphors of the sun rising and falling and prediction by reading the stars. In this conjunction people grow and decay under the sky and fade from "memory" (15:1–8). The speaker returns to a situation that he has outlined to the young man beforehand, one "Where wasteful Time debateth with Decay / To change your youth to sullied night." (15:11–12). In this "war with Time" the speaker has his "conceit," and can thus state, "for love of you, / As he takes from you, I ingraft you new" (15:9, 13–14). The conceit might be that, like a gardener, the speaker as poet creates an image that creates an heir for the young man and, existentially, perhaps implies a kind of sexual union, in the text at least, that does not require the womb that he invokes in Sonnet 4 (4:5). The expression of endurance and immortality is becoming more intricate with each sonnet as the language is the form and the content striving in a bid to proclaim the young man's immortality. Sonnet 16 involves a retreat from pride in the power of poetry and, in questioning the youth, suggests that procreation is "more blessèd than my barren rhyme" in the war with "this bloody tyrant Time" (16:1–4). Here, the speaker advocates the young man's "living flowers" to "you painted counterfeit," so that nature is urged above art and reiterated in the next quatrain (16:9–12). Shakespeare cannot resist a quibble on lines, which are bloodlines and the lines an artist draws, so that his puns may yield to the young man in his repetition of "yourself" and in the final phrase of the poem, "your own sweet skill," but this admission and yielding occur in the language Shakespeare gives to the poet. There are two characters, speaker and addressee, and the implied lives of Shakespeare and the person who may or may not be a friend or lover of the poet. These linguistic domains involve a simultaneous distancing and intimating, for the language of speaker, character, poet, and friend (perhaps the dedicatee) plays on the reader, once apparently a member of an inner circle where the manuscript was circulated and now a changing him or her, himself or herself, caught in the conflict between life and language on the one hand and time on the other. This is another dimension of loss that even monuments, brass and poetic, that proclaim their permanence, face. We all face, inside and outside the poem, then and now, the dilemmas of time and the changes of language that proclaim the changeless, what Alexander Pope said would be Dryden's fate as much as Chaucer's, so the very conceit of endurance in the fallen world of time has a certain pathos to it.

Shakespeare plays with the limits of verse and language in Sonnet 17: "Who will believe my verse in time to come / If it were filled with your most high deserts?" (17:1–2). The hyperbole the poet had been using to praise the young man will, it turns out, dissuade posterity from believing the portrait. The anonymity of the addressee does not seem to occur to the poet, who may have thought that his private circle of friends would know the identity of the young man or the construction of the character, but, in an age before biography was the rage, this identification was not passed on. The speaker qualifies this first question about exaggeration with an assertion that the verse is like the tomb from which it has been trying to rescue the young man, something "Which hides your life, and shows not half your parts" (17:4). By this means, the speaker shows that his verse is unworthy and that its skill in descriptive hyperbole and hyperbolic description is not up to the task and if it were, "The age to come would say, 'This poet lies; / Such heavenly touches ne'er touched earthly faces'" (17:7–8). His numbers cannot number and posterity will think the poet is given more to words than "truth," given to "rage / And stretchèd metre of an àntique song" (17:10–12). The turn in this poem shows the wit and ambivalence of the poet: he displays his nimble gift for words while resolving that the young man can live in heir and poem: "But were some child of yours alive that time, / You should live twice, in it and in my rhyme" (17:13–14). Perhaps, then, there is no true contradiction between nature's regeneration and art's memorial reconstruction. Whether Shakespeare considered this a resolution that in the war with time people should choose both—and rather than either—or is something that the order of the sonnets cannot answer because they do not have the unequivocal authority of the author. As the sonnets stand, as they have since 1609, the poet turns from regeneration to the theme of the power of rhyme. Language here attempts to burst its own limits in the service of love and in the battle with death and time.

THE ORDER OF TIME

While the order of the sonnets may or may not be Shakespeare's, the procreation or regeneration sonnets do seem to cohere. From Sonnet 18 onwards, the sequence has less apparent unity, and, owing to uncertainty over the structure, an analysis based on strands might provide a reminder of this textual instability as well as enable a more focused discussion of each thematic concern in the friction between time and language. Poetry as immortality is a conceit Shakespeare takes up in Sonnet 18, but this time he does so without an apology for the claims of the poet to make the young man immortal. This well-known sonnet, "Shall I compare thee to a summer's day?" reiterates the passing of summer and the turning of the seasons and the declining of the sun, yet sets those familiar tropes up for a turn, in the Petrarchan manner, after line 8: "But thy eternal summer shall not fade" (18:9). Death will not "brag" because "in eternal lines to time thou grow'st" (18:12). The speaker's verse, which has life in the fiction of Shakespeare's verse alone, is like Horace's and Ovid's but, in a Christian context, also resembles the power of God himself to make a man eternal: in the final couplet, the poem achieves this potency through the power of the readers over the generations: "So long as men can breathe or eyes can see, / So long lives this, and this gives life to thee" (18:13–14). The power of poetry is beyond the grave in another time.

Sonnet 19 addresses "Devouring Time," a proverbial expression in English and perhaps an echo of Ovid and Spenser, a figure that also appeared in Sonnet 5 (19:1).[24] Time is asked to have animals and seasons in its power, for example, to blunt the "lion's paws . . . .And burn the long-lived phoenix in her blood" (19:1, 4). The speaker will allow the immortal bird to be consumed again and to grant "swift-footed Time" to do with "the wide world and all her fading sweets" but not "one most heinous crime," that is to devour the young man: "O carve not with thy hours my love's fair brow, / Nor draw no lines there with thine àntique pen." (19:6–10). In a vocative or apostrophic address the poet asks Time not to be a poet and write in hours in nature in such a way as to create lines in the young man's forehead, so that his vaunted forbidding of time is a pleading, a wish that is followed by another, that Time permit the youth to be "untainted," "beauty's pattern to succeeding men" (19:11–12). Whether this physical beauty is a Platonic ideal or a physical icon of desire is left unsaid. In the turn to the couplet the poet dares "old Time" to "do thy worst" because "despite thy wrong, / My love shall in my verse ever live young" (19:13–14). In the poet's hyperbole and hubris, Time has come to devour itself: this verse does something that the phoenix and Time cannot do—regenerate "My love," the poet's feelings and the object of admiration or desire. That double love in one finds regeneration through the best that language can express when it defies its limits. Sometimes the monument against time occurs in the mind of the speaker, the poet, rather than in his writing. In Sonnet 30 in "the sessions of sweet silent thought," he summons "remembrance of things past," but this thought, expressed in the legal terms "sessions" and "summons," finds itself disturbed by action and the sad loss that comes with "my dear Time's waste" (30:1–4).[25] This waste is also of his friends hidden "in death's dateless night" and "many a vanished sight," so that the speaker tells and pays his "sad account" (30:5–12). In a reversal, a kind of *volta* or turn at the level of the structure of the sonnets, the poet proclaims that the young man in the older speaker's thought will defeat time: "But if the while I think on thee (dear friend) / All losses are restored, and sorrows end" (30:13–14). As Ovid contended, but with perhaps more irony, *amor vincit omnia*—love conquers all—and this friend is male and not female. "Thy bosom" begins Sonnet 31, and indeed that breast subsumes the love of the dead friends' that the speaker's heart has lacked, so the friend is later addressed as

> the grave where buried love doth live
> Hung with the trophies of my lovers gone
> Who all their parts of me to thee did give.
> (31:1, 9–11)

Regeneration comes through the young man and the love between the speaker and him, a love expressed as a debt, "That due of many now is thine alone" (31:12). This expression of love in fiscal terms, which credits the young man with defeating death through the speaker's love interest, could not, as much as the speaker, the poet, elides his writing of this account, exist without the writing in which this love union occurs: "Their images I loved I view in thee, / And thou (all they) hast all the all of me" (31:13–14). The poet needs his love for the young man as a topic to use writing as a weapon in the war against time and death, so his "images," whatever they represent in life, are all that is left. If this love were Platonic it would be only these shadows on the wall of the cave that apparently would remain. This monument shifts as if the poet as speaker and Shakespeare as the poet have to devise new strategies in the action against time: his thoughts shift even as they are images in and against a changing world. He is like Richard II before his death, making comparisons between prison and the world in which his brain proves "the female to his soul," the father, "and these two beget / A generation of stillbreeding thoughts" (*Richard II*, V.v.6–8). In the face of death Richard calls into question the efficacy of thought and the unlikelihood that it will make the thinker happy—"And these same thoughts people this little world, / In humors like the people of this world: For no thought is contented" (*Richard II*, V.v.9–11). But the speaker of Sonnet 31 (and of Sonnet 30), as he considers death, ends by putting his faith—he talks about "dear religious love stolen from mine eye"—in images and thought even as he expresses them through the idea of his love for the young man: this is so because the friend's body or physical presence, whatever the claim, can be represented only in the very thoughts the poet seeks to make material (Sonnet 31:6). Indeed, dear religious love is stolen from the eye—the poet's, the young man's and the reader's.[26] The heroic nature of that love, and its expression in poetry, is the hope against time and death even if that stand may not succeed, and the splendor of that endeavor is the mixture of steadfastness and mobility, an ingenuity of expression in a desire for something that endures the wrack of death and the movement of time.

Nearing the center of the sonnets, as they were printed, are Sonnets 54 and 55, which return to the theme of immortality through poetry. The reciprocal pair of beauty and truth, as well as the images of distilling perfume from flowers that Shakespeare employed in Sonnets 5 and 6, represent preoccupations in Sonnet 54. Shakespeare contrasts the rose, which regenerates, with the canker-rose, which dies unto itself, thereby returning to the thematics of Sonnets 4 through 6 (54:5–12).[27] The final lines of Sonnet 54 proclaim, "And so of you, beauteous and lovely youth, / When that shall vade, by verse distils your truth" (54:13–14). Whether "by" (Evans) or "my" (Capell) precedes "verse," the poetry will distil the "truth" of the young man like perfume from flowers as his beauty fades.[28] Shakespeare's best-known conceit of the power of verse in the sonnets comes in 55: "Not marble nor the gilded monuments / Of princes shall outlive this pow'rful rhyme" (55:1–2). This conceit is bold but becomes more equivocal in the wider context of the sonnets, where, whatever order, an oscillation, if not a vacillation, occurs in vaunting of the power of poetry against time and the potency of the temporal.

This boast about the power of rhyme finds qualification in Sonnets 63 through 65, where a disjunction exists between the sad progress of mortality and poetry's immortal qualities. After reiterating the work of "Time's injurious hand," which includes once more "lines and wrinkles" on the beloved's brow, the speaker, the poet, of Sonnet 63 hopes that his "sweet love's beauty" can never be "cut from memory" by "age's cruel knife," appealing again to the comparison of aging with the passing of the seasons (63:1–12). His answer, as it will be in Sonnet 65, is, "His beauty shall in these black lines be seen, / And they shall live, and he in them still green" (63:13–14). The blackness of ink will restore the "greenness" of spring and youth to the beloved and stop "age's steepy night" from making the beloved's "beauties" from vanishing, "Stealing away the treasure of his spring" (63:5–8). The last couplet answers more generally the first twelve lines, which portray the anxiety of erasure, and more specifically, the death of youth and spring that age and death bring. The poet's hand tries to answer another writer, Time, whose "injurious hand" inscribes its lines in nature and brands the beloved's brow with age and death. Sonnet 64 is another meditation on the ruins of Time, once more personified as devouring and decaying, a force that "will come and take my love away" (64:12). The speaker despairs in poetry that such a thought is death, when he possesses his love, both his feelings and beloved, that which the

meditation "fears to lose" (64:14). In the final line, as in line 8, the poet stresses loss
and the act of losing, the mourning of a putative death and the failure to win the
battle with Time. Further, in Sonnet 65, the speaker asks,

> Since brass, nor stone, nor earth, nor boundless sea,
> But sad mortality o'ersways their power,
> How with this rage shall beauty hold a plea,
> Whose action is no stronger than a flower?
> (65:1–4)

Through amplification, the speaker queries further "how shall summer's honey breath
hold out / Against the wrackful siege of batt'ring days" when rocks and steel gates cannot and Time continues to decay (65:5–6). By analogy, the young man is now "Time's
best jewel" and "beauty" and nothing and no one, no "strong hand," can, as the question seems to say, stop the "swift foot" of Time who will have "his spoil" (65:9–12).
In the final couplet, the speaker, the poet, who has already proclaimed "O fearful
meditation!"—answers this question of who can resist time with a short, direct, and
despairing phrase, which he then modifies with a clause of hope: "O none, unless this
miracle have might, / That in black ink my love may still shine bright" (65:13–14).
The miracle is the claim that verse is immortal, that the poet's love for the beloved or
the beloved himself may endure in the ink of this sonnet, perhaps a kind of apotheosis. The starkness of "O none," a kind of sigh of despair, finds qualification not in a
declarative statement of this "miracle" of "black ink" but in a conditional "unless."
Moreover, the conceit of the power of verse has its own limits and depends on the very
abyss of time it labors against. As destructive of humanity as it is, this time is humanized through personification, as it is throughout many of the sonnets and certainly as
it was in the preceding two sonnets (63 and 64).

Whether thoughts, words and deeds can be made into an association against time,
perhaps as Richard II tries to do in prison, is a question that becomes more problematic when the sonnets are considered as a whole. The tension between the sequential
and the overview is especially apparent in a collection of lyrics: the logic and counter-
logic in the form of each poem contends with the gathering of them in a book,
and the reader also traverses the breaks in the spaces between the poems. While I
understand the reasons many editors have doubted that the order of the sonnets was
Shakespeare's, I also see no conclusive evidence against attributing this order to him.
If he had been unhappy with the order, he might have sought to publish an authorized
version, although it has to be said that while he did publish *Venus and Adonis* and *The
Rape of Lucrece* in good order, he did not do so with many of his plays, which would
have come under another kind of ownership, that of his acting company. While it is
impossible to be certain about the teleology or the generic construction of the sonnets
as a whole, for example, whether Shakespeare himself conceived of them as a comic
movement, there are enough qualifying and contradictory notions of writing and
time that the monument of poetry against sluttish time shows its cracks.

LIFE RIVALING ART

In writing against time, Shakespeare gives his speaker, himself the poet, a language that makes writing itself less monolithic and monumental, for authors are subject to style and rivals, so there is not one way to address the young man and to craft words against change and mortal corruption. Time is not the only rival poet to the speaker. Writing is in danger of warring against itself. The paradox for Shakespeare's speaker is that he must change and be constant, to move with the times in order to be immovable in time. To make his love ever young even as time will age and kill him becomes a contradictory task. Nor are the two men—speaker and young man—alone. A new dramatic conflict—rivalry—seizes the center of Shakespeare's sonnet sequence.

The doubting and asserting of the power of his verse while contending with a rival (rivals) becomes the preoccupation of the speaker in Sonnets 76 to 84. The opposition between writing and time devolves into many more conflicts and complexities. Sonnet 76 begins with the questions, "Why is my verse so barren of new pride? / So far from variation or quick change?" (76:1–2). Instead of fighting change with change, the speaker writes in a verse that change is "ever the same," an ever-fixed mark where "you and love are still my argument" (76:5, 10). The oxymoronic old newness and new oldness of his verse gives a different spin to the revolution of the times: "For as the sun is daily new and old, / So is my love still telling what is told" (76:13–14). This love, like the beloved, is a variation on a theme told in a poem, which renews the conventions of previous love poetry. In Sonnet 77, Shakespeare invokes an old tradition, the *memento mori*, to renovate his love and beloved.[29] Here, the speaker sends the young man the sonnet and a blank notebook to fill up with thoughts that, like other measurers of time like his "glass" and "dial," which appear in the opening two lines and find further amplification beyond, will remind him of "Time's thievish progress to eternity" (77:1–8). The book will contain what his memory cannot, so the addressee becomes a writer, the young man's thoughts "children nursed, delivered from thy brain, / To take a new acquaintance of thy mind" (77:11–12). Here is a new kind of procreation sonnet, where the young man begets words for his children instead of children for his words. In all this, the speaker, the poet, is the metaphorical midwife. He and the young man can together produce children through words only—not in the world.

The rival poet or poets challenge the monopoly on writing and the speaker's friendship with the young man (see Sonnets 78–80, 82–86, 126).[30] They write against the grain of the claim by the speaker, the poet, that his verse alone will immortalize the man he addresses in the sonnets. In Sonnet 78 the young man is the poet's muse, but now "every alien pen hath got my use, / And under thee their poesy disperse" (78:3–4). The phrase, "under thee," suggests a sexual image of the rival poets procreating with the young man as well as the notion that, under the young man's patronage, they disseminate their poetry through manuscript or print culture. Returning to hyperbole, the speaker makes the young man a muse who can teach the dumb to sing, make ignorance sing, and add feathers, grace, and style even to the most learned poet. This inspiration, which the poet invokes, raises him up: "But thou art all my art, and dost advance / As high as learning my rude ignorance" (78:13–14). The young man is a muse who becomes all his art, so that he is the only begetter of the sonnets.

Even if this is exaggeration for its own sake as a form of bonding flattery, it may speak as much to the young man as the author of himself and narcissistic reproducer of his own image that poetry is an act of love, where the object of desire transforms the subject to such an extent that their act and words of love are inseparable, a kind of progeny where the traits of the parents are indistinguishable. Sonnet 79 is a sly yielding to a rival poet with "a worthier pen" because the speaker's muse is sick, "his gracious numbers decayed," but he takes away while giving ground to the rival, for that poet can invent virtue and beauty to praise in the young man by stealing it from his life, where it is greater yet (79:6, 3). The *volta* comes with the speaker's critique of the rival poet who empowers the young man, who, as the implication goes, is the source of beauty and virtue and therefore has the power to reinstate the speaker as his poet to make "thy lovely argument" (79:5): "Then thank him not for that which he doth say, / Since what he owes thee, thou thyself dost pay" (79:13–14). In Sonnet 80 the speaker praises the young man's "worth (wide as the ocean is)" (80:5) and, in an image of boats makes himself a "saucy bark," (7) a kind of bold but modest vessel, then "a worthless boat" (11) while the rival is "of tall building and of goodly pride" (12). Thus, retrospectively, the line "The humble as the proudest sail doth bear" (6), makes sense in terms of the rivalry between the humble speaker and the proud rival for the love of the worthy young man and for the chance to praise him in poetry. Although the speaker claims that the rival's "praise" of the young man's name makes "me tongue-tied speaking of your fame" (3–4), he is willing—in the final couplet—to accept his fate: "Then if he thrive and I be cast away, / The worst was this: my love was my decay" (80:13–14). This yielding is an appeal to the unable tongue of true love before someone who would praise the young man with "all his might" (80:3). This gesture toward sincerity, like that of Kent in *King Lear*, is an idealization or suppressed hyperbole of the speaker's virtue and steadfast love and loyalty. This is a far way from the boasts of Sonnets 15 to 19 and Sonnet 55 about the power of the speaker's poetry to make the young man immortal. The tension between these extremes provides dramatic conflict as well as expressing the oxymoronic claims of language to making the human world endure past a single generation and the inability of language to represent people and the world. Whether this modest boastfulness is witty, contradictory, or paradoxical, or all three, is something with which the reader must grapple.

In Sonnet 81 the immortality of the young man in the speaker's poetry resurfaces and intensifies the oxymoronic claims of writing. Creation as procreation and praise as a monument come back in the middle of the segment on the rival poet(s) when the unworthy and tongue-tied speaker has his love alone. Nor do these claims slip in because the monumental nature of the verse, as opposed to the speaker's death, finds amplification: "Your name from hence immortal life shall have, / Though I (once gone) to all the world must die" (81:5–6). Even in death, the speaker will immortalize the young man, a point he reiterates as he envisions the death of his love: "The earth can yield me but a common grave, / When you intombèd in men's eyes shall lie" (81:7–8). Being buried in the eyes of the readers will be his rebirth: "Your monument shall be my gentle verse, / Which eyes not yet created shall o'er-read" 81:9–10). To the eyes, the speaker adds tongues and breath to "rehearse" the words of praise for the dead beloved (81:11–14). This repetition of a meditation on death and how verse can defeat time and mortality qualifies the yielding of the speaker, the poet, to the rival poets, although the fragmentation, agon, and agony of the writing against time in the name of love can never be quite monumental or simply the dust that awaits each person. At worst, writing extends life when posterity recreates the apparently lifeless signs of ink on page.

The next four sonnets explore the nature of praise in such a way as to modify the theme of poetry as monument, as expressed in Sonnet 81, so that this sonnet finds itself in a context that contradicts it and one that creates dramatic tension. Sonnet 82 allows that other rival poets can praise the young man, as there was no oath between the speaker and the youth, no marriage of true minds, and perhaps, as the addressee passes all praise that the poet can muster, it is just as well that others try to come up to the mark and try to better time in these "time-bettering days" (82:1–8). But then comes the *volta*: the speaker, the poet, has spoken plainly and truly—"Thou, truly fair, wert sympathised / In true plain words by thy true-telling friend"—as opposed to those deploying "the strainèd touches rhetoric can lend" (82:9–12). True plain speech—like Kent's in *King Lear*—characterizes the virtue of the poet, whose praise is short of, or at, the mark of the young man's beauty, truth, and virtue, so that this topos of inexpressibility attempts to escape the very rhetorical nature of its ploy. If there was any doubt in the turn, the final couplet defends the realistic and naturalistic virtue of the author of this sonnet: "And their gross painting might be better used / Where cheeks need blood; in thee it is abused" (82:13–14). The final plea is for the plain to triumph over the gross—quite a turn from the conciliatory and understanding position of the first eight-and-a-half lines.

Sonnet 83 picks up on the theme, expressed in the last couplet of Sonnet 82, that the young man does not need "painting" (83:1–2). Here, the hyperbole is that the excellence of the young man shows that life can outpraise art: "I found (or thought I found) you did exceed / The barren tender of a poet's debt" (83:3–4). The parenthetical qualification raises doubt about the young man's status of being beyond the poet's obligation to his patron or the indebtedness of his love for the youth as well as the vacillation in the poet's mind concerning the power of his poetry and the power of the young man's truth and beauty in love. The speaker, the poet, has "slept in your report," in writing about the young man and in the youth's chronicle of him (83:5). Still, the poet has doubts about the young man's "worth," and the silence is a mutual dumbness, even if the poet protests about "being dumb," "being mute," and that other rival poets, those of the "modern quill," would "bring a tomb" (83:7–12). This epistrophic chiming of lines 10 through 12 contrasts the poet being mute and dumb before the worth of the young man with those who would silence their subject in a tomb, although Shakespeare has raised questions about whether the youth does exceed even the "barren tender of a poet's debt" and about his "worth" and "silence" (83:3–5, 8–9). As if to resolve the rivalry between poets and the ambivalence in the speaker and poet of Sonnet 83 about the young man and his power to love or to express in life more than any poetry, Shakespeare reverts, in the final couplet, to what may be called the antimonumental stance, which contravenes monumental sonnets like 55 and 81: "There lives more life in one of your fair eyes / Than both your poets can in praise devise" (83:13–14). This *volta* expresses the paradox that in this eulogy the eye of the young man has more life than the praise of two poets can enact even as Shakespeare's lines represent that commendation.

Sonnet 84, a poem of "rich praise," argues that the young man need be represented only—"that you alone are you" (84:2) and "That you are you" (84:8)—so that embellishment in poetry is not necessary. No matter what the "store" of praise the poet has or the store of seed the young man has, the youth is himself (84:3). Perhaps, as in the procreation sonnets, begetting a son is the only way to produce a like, but not identical, beauty, worth, and truth as the young man possesses. Once again, any poet who wishes to praise the addressee should count on a representational "copy" of "what in you is writ" and not a "fame" begotten by "wit" and "style" (84:9–12). The subject and object are indistinguishable as writers. In the final couplet a turn occurs that, as in Sonnet 83, calls into doubt the perfection and self-praising and self-sufficient representation that is the youth: "You to your beauteous blessings add a curse, / Being fond on praise, which makes your praises worse" (84:13–14). The young man's blessings are praise and elicit praise, which, being foolish, makes this adulation even worse, so that the young man and the poets appear less than perfect. It is possible to say that the criticism might be a double negative or a backhanded compliment: being so perfect, the youth causes others to praise him in ways that, by comparison, fall short, and so this perfection attracts imperfection and thus is imperfect (perhaps through no fault of its own).[31] In this version, there is less of a turn because there might be a pun on "fond on" as "fawned on," so the youth's beauty has the curse of being fond of a praise that is fawning, which makes his "beauteous blessings" worse through a praise that is foolish and falls short. Either way the praise is less than perfect because the young man and what the poets say about him are entwined in this couplet and elsewhere. If the young man is himself, a trope repeated in the poem, he is also the poetry that represents him: even in the separation of life and art a problem arises as set out in the procreation and monumental sonnets— how can this beautiful young man outlast the ravages of time and death?

More than one rival poet appears in Sonnet 85, which elaborates on the theme of praise, something that reaches beyond neutrality, potentially in the direction of flattery and hyperbole. The poem begins with the "tongue-tied Muse" of the speaker, the poet, a conflation of tropes in Sonnets 80 and 82, in the face of the work of others, whose "praise" for the young man is "richly compiled" and who use a "golden quill / And precious phrase" (85:1–4). Once more, the speaker, the poet, is silenced and thinks "good thoughts, whilst other write good words" (85:5). This plainness and silence in the face of aureate rhetoric, this trueness before polish and refinement, is the poet's virtue, as opposed to his rivals' verbosity: they may be true in praising the youth, but the poet and speaker adds "something more"—the love in his thought (85:9–12). The "Amen" of the prayer is, by translation, true, and gives a religious cast to these words that the silent thought supplements with an even greater truth.[32] Nevertheless, the speaker and poet as character and the poet Shakespeare as creator cannot express truth and silence in this lyric poem in any way but words, so that the thoughts, even if one accepts the Platonic split between words and writing, go before words but can only find an outlet in language. The larger framework of praise and patronage—which might well inform the context of the writing and production of the sonnets, although we do not have a direct and easily identifiable dedication as we do in *Venus and Adonis* and *The Rape of Lucrece*—might further suggest that the use of "rank" is also a metonymic suggestion of the relation between poet and patron socially as well as a bond of love through the poet's thought, which ranks above the words that must express it. Just as Richard II chases his thoughts through elaborate metaphors and words in prison, the speaker, the poet, uses an extended metaphor to couch his thoughts as opposed to words in an elaborate chain of verbal association: "Then others for the breath of words respect, / Me for my dumb thoughts, speaking in effect" (85:13–14). These "dumb thoughts" are not as silent as the verbal conceit of silence would make them.

This civil strife among poets in the middle of the sonnets questions their monumentality. The conflict develops a certain vocabulary: for example, Sonnet 86 returns to the imagery of the rivalry with another poet—spirits and ships—that occurs in Sonnet 80. Writing fractures in the contest over who gets to represent the young man and how. According to the speaker, the poet, of Sonnet 86, the rival goes from "the proud full sail of his great verse" in line 1 to being "Bound for the prize of all-too precious you" in line 2.[33] As in Sonnet 85, the speaker examines his own thoughts as worthy reflections of the youth, but, as in an antiprocreational image contra the tropes he used in the first fifteen sonnets, he asks whether the rival's verse makes the "tomb" of the speaker's thoughts "the womb wherein they grew" (86:1–4). The poet wonders whether it was spirits who taught his rivals' spirit to write supernaturally and so silenced or killed the speaker figuratively, but answers that no, these nightly spirits and ghosts, perhaps emissaries of the devil, could not "astonish" or dumbfound his verse (86:5–12). From here on, death as a trope qualifies the death that seemed so final in the procreational and monumental sonnets, so that the power of poetry, even if it cannot be silenced, is phenomenal in a world that might be, even if only figuratively, noumenal. The final couplet stresses that the young man's "countenance"—face and patronage—"filled up his line," so that the speaker, the poet, lacked "matter"—means or a subject—so his line became "enfeebled" (86:13–14). This is the very feebleness of a great sonnet sequence. Sonnet 86 displays the fissures in writing itself through the rivalry and the desire to represent life beyond death, here in a spirit world, however negatively portrayed, and, in the monumental poems like Sonnet 81, in the wish or assertion that the speaker's poet will outlast silence and death. In the middle of the sonnets as we have them, a dramatic tension occurs between poetry as the hedge against death and time, but, whatever the order, an ambivalence takes place between life and art, and a conflict arises between poets that questions the very nature of writing. The art of writing splits between plain speech and rhetorical ornament, although rhetoric is not enough for poetry, even if poems are partly rhetorical. Representing plainness requires rhetorical strategies. Nor in the war against time and death is victory readily achieved through beauty, truth, thought, or words: the fiction of the young man or the speaker's poetry as outlasting their time till doom is a hope caught in the web of the very language in which it is expressed. Sonnet 81 proclaims the monumental and enduring nature of the speaker's poetry but in a context that modifies any such claim, and in other sonnets throughout and toward the end of the sequence, the disjunctions and fragilities of language and life find further exposure.

TRANSITIONS: YOUTH AS THE MISTRESS OF TIME

Sonnet 126, a coda to the poems that are thought to be addressed to the young man and a transition to the sonnets about the mistress (127–52), represents the ravages that time will have on the young man.[34] Despite procreation, the monument of the sonnets, and his own beauty, worth, and truth, he will grow old and die. The reaction to this plight is mixed: as in the previous 125 sonnets, none of these means has triumphed as a way to defeat time and death. In individual sonnets one of these options might gain the upper hand, but even in single poems there is often a tension between two, or among three, of these alternative ways to defiance against temporality and mortality. This poem mixes praise and warning, for the "lovely boy" holds in his power "Time's fickle glass, his sickle, hour" and has "by waning grown" while his lovers withered, and he has benefitted from a Nature May that Time disgrace" by being plucked back from its ruin (126:1–8), but in the *volta* at line 9 the eulogistic mode shifts to the minatory. Of Nature the speaker proclaims to the youth, "Yet fear her, O thou minion of her pleasure, / She may detain, but not still keep, her treasure!" (126:9–10). The aristocratic youth, a "minion," must beware of a more powerful patron, being now in a position that the speaker, the poet, has found himself in regarding the young man, so that he is warned that her pleasure might be to "detain . . . her treasure," which reinforces the earlier "pluck thee back," but she cannot "keep" him. This imagery of commerce, sex, and patronage stresses the power of Nature and the impotence of the young man to be above Nature and to defeat Time, because if he grows as he wanes, as the first eight lines promised, he ultimately will suffer what his lovers, perhaps like the older speaker and poet, will: age and death. The last couplet in this twelve-line sonnet proclaims that the young man is the "quietus" or final settlement that Nature, a personified she, must make with the youth, which, given the earlier discussion of Time, implies that is how she pays the debt to Time. Although the order of the sonnets is not entirely certain, as the sequence stands, the poems begin with procreation and move through a vacillation between the assertion that the speaker's poetry will be a monument to the young man that will outlast time and the doubt that the power of poetry generally and his poetry specifically will counteract the inevitable movement of Nature and Time, despite the favored condition of the young man, to death: "Her audit (though delayed) answered must be, / And her quietus is to render thee" (126:11–12). The poet surrenders his love to debt and death.

This last poem is also a transition to the sonnets about the mistress or dark lady. Sonnet 127 meditates on Nature and art in regard to beauty, a concern that ran through the sonnets addressed to the young man. In this poem the ideal of beauty is anti-Petrarchan, for this mistress is "black" and Laura is blonde:

> ma poi ch'Amor di me vi fece accorta,
> fuor i biondi capelli allor velati
> et l'amoroso sguardo in sé raccolto.
>
> [but since Love has made you aware of me,
> your blond hair has been veiled
> and your lovely gaze kept to itself.][35]

In Sonnet 7 of Philip Sidney's *Astrophel and Stella* (1591) the speaker praises Stella's blackness, so that Shakespeare's poet is part of a larger literary movement in which love and the lady is transformed.[36] Shakespeare sets up a contrast between the dark lady and the fair youth of the preceding sonnets, so that the speaker has shifted his aesthetic of love within the sequence not only in terms of gender but also in regard to color. Fairness and beauty are also matters of fashion. The mistress' eyes are "raven black" and so seem like "mourners": "Yet so they mourn, becoming of their woe, / That every tongue says beauty should look so" (127:13–14).[37] This paradoxical praise, a technique the speaker had used to flatter the young man, bolsters the beauty of the dark lady, transforming nature through the hyperbolic reaches of poetry.

Some of the other poems to the mistress qualify the idea that love conquers all. Time and death, while not as ubiquitous and explicitly present as in the sonnets to the young man, still haunt the poems to the dark lady. In Sonnets 135 and 136, which tease the reader with more autobiographical dimensions, the speaker identifies himself with the author by punning on his name, "Will," but may also refer to other Wills (including, perhaps, the W in the W. H. of the dedication) and the will of sexual appetite, of determination, and of inheritance. The defeat of Death in Sonnet 146 is part of a general address that may or may not be to the mistress. Sonnet 147 represents reason as "the physician to my love" whose prescriptions the speaker will not keep, so that "Desire is death" (147:5–8). The speaker admits that in love and desire his discourse is as random as a madman's, so that he strays from reason and truth (147:9–12). In Sonnet 147 the *volta* turns on the power of blackness that began with the praise of his mistress' dark beauty in Sonnet 127 and on the fever of his longing expressed in the body of 147 itself: "For I have sworn thee fair, and thought thee bright, / Who art as black as hell, as dark as night" (147:13–14). Poetry does not redeem the world but is a subjective madness that desire has induced while the speaker seeks recognition that he has been mistaken in his longing for his mistress— her darkness once seemed beautiful but now is hell itself. The soul of the speaker, the poet, of Sonnet 151 "doth tell my body that he may / Triumph in love," but by the last line of the poem, the poet puts love in quotation marks and in the context of rising and falling as in intercourse and, perhaps, as in a tragic rise and fall on the wheel of fortune (151:7–8, 14).

In Sonnet 152, the last of the poems that address the dark lady, the speaker shows his disgust for his love and lust for which he has lied, adulterated, and perjured his faith, so that while he has accused her, his breach is ten times worse. His "honest faith" in her is lost—in both senses as he is lost in her in sex and his belief in her is gone (152:8). Although the poet has looked into his heart and taken a responsibility tenfold hers, he now, from line 9, comes to blame her, that he did praise her too much in his oaths, making her kind when cruel, in love when not, true when false, constant when fickle, enlightened when not, that he gave eyes to his blindness and made them take oaths against what they actually saw (152:9–12). This self-delusion in praise is another aspect of the problem of the limitations of language, which the speaker also explored in his addresses to the young man, so that the nature of praise and hyperbole in poetry does not necessarily lead to truth and faithful love or a defeat of time and death. Sonnet 152 ends with the wistful and witty paradox: "For I have sworn thee fair: more perjured eye, / To swear against the truth so foul a lie" (152:13–14). The self-accusation moves to self-righteousness in the blame of the mistress: he has perjured his eyes and himself (through the eye/I pun) and his lies about her fairness have fouled the truth. After this reversal and all these shifts can the reader, in this last great *volta*, come to see that the poet has reached a kind a tragic recognition of his error—or does he or she wonder about the ability of the speaker to bring all things in love around to his own way or to his advantage?

This betrayal in love, as represented in the sonnets, perhaps even presaged in the young man's tolerance for rivals, is a betrayal of fairness, not the ideal love that Petrarch had found in his golden Laura (not to mention in Dante's relation to Beatrice) but an infernal and consuming love of the body, a tale of lust and lies. Whether this confession or retraction at the end of things redeems the failures of the language of praise and the possibilities of poetry to defeat time and death remains an open question. That desire and flattery make illusions of love is what the speaker asserts, but whether the speaker's blind claims make it difficult for poetic language to triumph is left in the reader's eye, which has its own sins, faults, and perjuries with which to contend. Certainly, the young man and the dark lady are each left in the last sonnets in this sequence as it was ordered in 1609 to a defeat in time, Nature, death, and language: their beauty in the speaker's love and words of love were to be such eternal truth. Even if in Nature these addressees were of such great beauty, they are represented as fallible in the words and eyes of this poet, and the eyes and ears of posterity will judge them, whoever they might have been in history and fiction, not without prejudice—that which the speaker makes for them and that which the readers bring with them.

Nor are these two "lovers" without mutual relation, as a triangle exists among the speaker, mistress, and fair youth, something represented in Sonnets 41, 42, 133, 134, and 144. Three is not company here: the speaker states his case forcefully, his revulsion, despair, and disgust depending on his point of view. The readers do not have the other sides of the story but can see that the speaker shifts within poems—the nature of the sonnet—and between them. This split unsettles the very unity of faith and truth in love and, like the rival poets, questions the nature of praise and endurance in the speaker's poetry. The accusations and conflicting multiplicities unsettle the single integrity of truth and faith that the poet seems to yearn for in the whole sequence.

DYING AND UNDYING LOVE

Writing in the sonnets can and cannot defeat Time and Death, the very forces of oblivion that they personify. Love and writing are, nonetheless, ambivalent and sometimes self-contradictory, self-effacing, and self-defeating. A few scattered sonnets other than those discussed in this chapter should suggest this intricacy in the larger sequence of sonnets, suggesting that this ambivalence, contradiction, and effacing happen no matter what the order. The poet writes against the temporal and mortal forces as he addresses his Muse and vacillates between the power of the young man in life and nature and that of poetry (Sonnets 100–103). Looking typologically into "the chronicle of wasted time"—as if all history led by prophecy to the youth whom he addresses—the speaker of Sonnet 106 sees that poets, old and new, do not have the power to praise this young man adequately (106:1). Love, "an ever-fixèd mark," is "not Time's fool," so that, the speaker, concludes, if this view is erroneous, "I never writ, nor no man ever loved" (116:5, 9, 14). In Sonnet 41, however, the poet claimed that his mistress and the youth had been inconstant to him: "Hers, by thy beauty tempting her to thee, / Thine, by thy beauty being false to me" (41:13–14). Beauty and truth in love are not always true ways to stave off the vicissitudes of time and death. Wit and flattery are playful parts of writing and qualify the stern constants of ideal love, for Sonnet 137 begins, "Thou blind fool, Love," and Sonnet 138 starts with the proclamation "When my love swears that she is made of truth, / I do believe her, though I know she lies," and ends with the sexually and linguistically playful "Therefore I lie with her, and she with me, / And in our faults by lies we flattered be" (138:1–2). This world of lovers can be full of error, illusion, and flattery and is self-reflexive enough to know that a constant and sincere love is improbable in such a setting, so that, at least in some of the sonnets, the realization and even the celebration of inconstancy and "lying" is a convention. In Sonnet 148, after declaring "Desire is death" in the previous sonnet (147:8), the speaker asks "O how can love's eye be true, / That is so vexed with watching and with tears?" (148:9–10).

The last two sonnets, 153 and 154, end the sequence as we have it with the witty "love is blind," which qualifies that of "love conquers all." Cupid, the key figure in these last two poems, gives the sonnets a conventional and comic ending even to the sometimes tragic aspects of the whole sequence. This pair of sonnets resembles some written in Latin, Italian, and French that treat of Cupid.[38] In Sonnet 153 the "holy fire of Love" possesses "A dateless lively heat," but no bath could cool the poet's passion because there "Cupid got new fire—my mistress' eyes" (153:5–6, 14). Sonnet 154, a kind of diptych with 153, tells how a virgin nymph stole Cupid's "heart-inflaming brand" and tried to quench its "heat perpetual" in a well to provide a remedy for love-sick men, but the speaker, coming there for a cure, learned that "Love's fire heats water, water cools not love" (154:2, 10, 14). The eternal rule of love is that love is too hot to be cooled and that there is no cure for it. As much as the speaker wants a remedy from the vicissitudes of love, the only constant is that there is no cure. Love is too strong for cold water, but has it the strength to defeat time and death? Love is ever changing, a disease to be borne, and the language of love is ever shifting. The speaker of the sonnets seeks out different ways to make the young man live on past the heat of the moment, but that heat is all that love can offer. As the Greeks knew with their many words for "love," even if English puts such strain on the one poor word we have, there are different kinds of love, and Shakespeare's sonnets do explore aspects of *agape*, *caritas*, and *Eros*. The speaker, the poet, suggests procreation and the power of words to represent the young man until doom while showing the betrayals, opportunism, and limitations of physical attraction. The sequence of poems asserts and subverts the power of the poet and of poetry to make love endure, and while the sonnets, as we have had them from 1609, begin with advice to a young man to marry and produce an heir, it ends with an irrational paean to *Eros* itself and to the desire the poet finds in his mistress' eyes.

Shakespeare's dramatic and nondramatic sonnets stretch the bounds of the verse form itself, the desire for peace and the discovery of conflict working within the confines of fourteen lines and a tight formal rhyme and rhythm. His sonnet sequence represents a private love made public in fame, whether their generation in print was authorized or not, an exploration in the oscillation between permanence and oblivion, true and false love that is not always that different from the more seemingly public space of the theatre, where the sonnets in *Romeo and Juliet* and *Henry V* were performed. In *Romeo and Juliet* other tragic elements of love are explored in the sonnets within the play, but whereas the prologic sonnet sets out the tale of woe of the terrible consequences of the meeting of private love and public hatred, of the oxymoronic enemies as lovers, an oxymoron that has a basis in the two lovers but is ignored in the blindness of the feuding families, it is but one type of poetry that Shakespeare uses to explore the errors of love, hatred, time, and death in the play, and one in a minor key. In *Henry V* Shakespeare compresses history into dramatic time, the vast world into a stage, and uses the compression of the sonnet to underscore that great clash. War has a prominent role in the play until a dynastic match, owing at least as much to Mars as to Venus and Cupid, unites Henry and Katherine, France and England. The sonnet goes more public here and gestures toward the more public sonnets of Milton and Shelley. All the while with virtuosity Shakespeare asserts, sometimes modestly and sometimes not, the power of language to speak about love, time, and death. This unsure sureness rests as much in readers' eyes as in mistress' eyes, not to mention in ears, hearts, and minds, the images and music extending in many directions at once.[39]

The sonnets Shakespeare writes in his poems and plays compress content in form and make in this small space a temporality that is of its time and seeks to be for all time. These sonnets have a literary, historical, and cultural context, a suggestion of which I began this chapter. Although I have concentrated on close attention to Shakespeare's texts, I have tried to give a sense that they embody a fictional world that relates to other possible worlds and to the actual world in which Shakespeare and his contemporaries lived. Language is at the heart of culture: it is the medium of poetry and of literature generally. The beauty and power of Shakespeare's language urges its own truth on even the most skeptical. The virtuosity of Shakespeare makes him exceptional, but he is also of his time and culture. Shakespeare plays on and with time in his work, his text being in contexts and almost seeming to rise above them. His language is a medium of culture and history and represented to his time and ours and those after us, not simply in its aesthetic appeal but the ethics of feeling, thought, and action. If culture is about cultivation, it is a metaphor of farming that lies between the civility of civilization and the city with which it has been associated and the barbarity of those outside the language and culture. Shakespeare's negative capability, to return to Keats' phrase, what I have called multiplicity, allows the reader and audience to inhabit the empire of meaning through language as barbarian and not.[40]

PART II

CULTURE AND HISTORY

CHAPTER 4

BARBARISM AND ITS CONTEXTS

IN THE AESTHETIC OF THE SONNETS, IN WHICH POET, MISTRESS, AND young man live in a drama of love, lust, and time, it is difficult, even at the moments of disgust or the mediations on the slipping away of hours, always to remember the breaking in of the world of culture, politics, and history, the minute particulars of those who made the way for Shakespeare and for England in the expansion of Europe. That is not to say that the sonnets in Shakespeare's plays and in the sonnets are really about love's empire or the clash of worlds, but that after examining the nature of time in these sonnets, I would like to shift to contexts and to another range of allusion in the texts of Shakespeare and his contemporaries. The shock of discovery with the expansion of Europe was one of the many great changes that Europeans and other cultures lived through from the fifteenth century onward. The divisions between we and they, and us and other, were temptations, but there was also a making of new hybrid cultures, and in this transla-tion, amid whatever practical problems and suspicions, considerations of barbarity and monstrosity nibbled at the edge of Shakespeare's works and his culture like the monsters beyond the known or in uncertain places on the maps of the time.

Shakespeare lived at a time when England was defensive and was also trying to expand. After the early Portuguese and Spanish voyages to Asia and the New World, the English and French tried to follow suit. By the time Shakespeare was born in 1564 and had begun writing in earnest in the 1580s and early 1590s, Europeans began to look outward and saw a world beyond their imaginations. Neither Aristotle nor the ancients could account for the New World and the parts of the world beyond the torrid zone that were uncharted and where the chart makers could survive. Like Columbus, Pêro Vaz de Caminha, Francisco de Vitoria, Juan Gines de Sepúlveda, Bartolomé de Las Casas, Jean de Léry, Michel de Montaigne, and others, Shakespeare considered the question of the human, who was a slave and who was free, who was monstrous or barbarous and who was not, or perhaps these elements within us all and the societies we inhabit.[1] These ethical questions and the problem of knowledge also affected writing and poetry in work by poets like Luís Vaz de Camões and Shake-speare.[2] The pressure on text from context is so great that while I am focusing most on Shakespeare's text, I cannot help but bring in related texts that create a context for the Shakespearean works discussed here.[3] Monstrosity and barbarism become test cases just as seduction, rape, and time did in our discussion of the poems in the last section. In this one, the discussion will move from the monstrous and the barbarous to questions of history, relations between England and Italy, and gender.

Barbarism was something that Herodotus considered to be an important part of the struggle and battle with the Hellenes or Greeks that deserved some respect. In *The Histories*, Herodotus begins, "This is the display of the inquiry of Herodotus of Halicarnassus, so that things done by man not be forgotten in time, and that great and marvelous deeds, some displayed by the Hellenes, some by the barbarians, not lose their glory, including among others what was the cause of their waging war on each other."[4] This history is a memorial of great actions in war so that the glory of Hellenes and barbarians will persist. "Barbarian," from our Greek antecedents, is, then, not a wholly pejorative term. Monsters do not play a major role in Herodotus' book: the monster of a boar that the messengers mention to Croesus, which reminds him of a prophecy regarding his son, is perhaps the only one. Whereas Herodotus is given to barbarians and barely mentions monsters, Shakespeare does the opposite. Barbarians and monsters can be threats and marvels and are often related to the security of the city or polity.

Civilization and barbarism have long been paired in classical debates and beyond. In the shadow of the Second World War and the Holocaust, a tension occurred between historical idealism and historical materialism. In literary terms, that is similar to the empathy described in Aristotle's discussion of mimesis in *Poetics* and Bertolt Brecht's alienation or estrangement effect with its Marxian inheritance as a critique of Hegel and the line of philosophy back to Aristotle and Plato. Although Aristotle includes both empathy and distancing in his discussion of representation within the scope of poetics, it is apparent that nostalgia or a longing for the past lives in tension with a critical distance or a critique of historical views of the past.[5] Point of view becomes as important in history and culture as in poetics. In *On the Concept of History*, Walter Benjamin makes this point about vantage in history: "The nature of this sadness stands out more clearly if one asks with whom the adherents of historicism actually empathize. The answer is inevitable: with the victor. And all rulers are the heirs of those who conquered before them. Hence, empathy with the victor invariably benefits the rulers" (Thesis VII).[6] Is Shakespeare in *Henry V*, for example, writing from the point of view of the victor? Are European texts about the New World or other colonies or subjugated areas refractions of victory? Benjamin comes up with the suggestive image of the procession, as if art were as much a spoil as Cleopatra would have been to Octavian. Although he quotes Flaubert in this context (Thesis VII), we can extrapolate Shakespeare to some extent as creating a cultural artifact or a poetics that is part of the victory of European expansion or of the extension of the English language and culture that begot it, not to mention its heirs. Benjamin continues, "According to traditional practice, the spoils are carried along in the procession. They are called cultural treasures, and a historical materialist views them with cautious detachment" (Thesis VII). Shakespeare's works are cultural treasures that some have regarded with detachment. This is a useful kind of doubt or skepticism so that textual interpretation or reading do not become a type of blind faith, atavism, or political or cultural chauvinism. Marx, Brecht, and Benjamin were reacting against the excesses of empathy or nostalgia, and they provide a corrective. I tend to see a dramatic and productive tension between empathy and estrangement, which Aristotle noted in *Poetics*. This is part of what I call the drama of meaning between writer and reader, poet and critic.

Benjamin is perceptive in pointing out the problems of culture. Speaking of the historical materialist, Benjamin says, "For without exception the cultural treasures he surveys have an origin which he cannot contemplate without horror. They owe their existence not only to the efforts of the great minds and talents who have created them, but also to the anonymous toil of their contemporaries" (Thesis VII). These treasures come out of an origin—a kind of nightmare of history, to borrow the fictional Stephen Daedalus' phrase—and are as much a product of those who labor obscurely as those great minds, like Shakespeare, who have created them. The sense of dread and admiration coexist in the response to such treasures as those that Shakespeare has produced. All this, then, leads Benjamin to barbarism: "There is no document of civilization which is not at the same time a document of barbarism. And just as such a document is not free of barbarism, barbarism taints also the manner in which it was transmitted from one owner to another" (Thesis VII). Civilization and barbarism are inseparable. Great cultural treasures about barbarism are in some sense barbaric. Writer and reader, perhaps as much as painter and collector, participate in the transmission of culture, which is both civil and barbaric. For Benjamin, the solution is to adopt historical materialism: "A historical materialist therefore dissociates himself from it as far as possible. He regards it as his task to brush history against the grain" (Thesis VII). Trying to distance himself or herself from this situation of the transmission of barbarism, he or she brushes against the grain of history. This approach is fruitful. As I have said, however, as much as I may have used this method in the past or admire it, I am more interested here in the tension between reading with and reading against texts. To some extent, as there has been in the past so much reading against the grain, I may read more with the text than otherwise.

This interest in barbarism in the nineteenth and twentieth centuries might lead us to expect that a great exemplar of English and European culture like Shakespeare would focus on barbarism. It is somewhat surprising, given the importance of the idea of barbarism in the Renaissance and in our era, that Shakespeare does not really use the words *barbarian*, *barbarous*, and *barbarism* very often. In the play in which one might expect these terms, *The Tempest*, they do not appear, but Caliban, who might be expected to be called a barbarian, is, in the repetitive parlance of Stephano and Trinculo, a "monster" (II.ii, III.ii, IV.i).[7] Monstrosity, which, along with barbarity, infuses the verbal and visual mapping of the New World by Europeans, is not my primary focus here but deserves some mention, as it shares a space of outside threat or internal corruption with the barbarous.

The few examples of monstrosity in *The Tempest* and *Othello*, which are plays about otherness and the exotic, yield their own surprises, so that to equate one group with the monstrous based on its gender, race, or class would be too reductive. Gonzalo wonders to Prospero whether anyone in Naples would believe his report of the people of the island, who are "of monstrous shape" but have manners

> more gentle-kind than of
Our human generation you shall find
Many, nay, almost any.

This is a sentiment that Prospero seconds in an aside:

> Honest lord,
> Thou hast said well; for some of you there present
> Are worse than devils.
> (*Temp.*, III.iii.31–6)[8]

The monstrous is also a function of apparently civilized Europeans who are hellish in their monstrosity. Alonso, stunned at the show of the magic visions on the isle, exclaims, "O, it is monstrous, monstrous!" (III.iii.95). As might be expected, *Othello* also emphasizes "monster" and "monstrous." Like Prospero, Iago identifies the monstrous with hell, but, unlike the magus, he celebrates that conflation. In the last two lines of act 1, he proclaims exultantly, "Hell and night / Must bring this monstrous birth to the world's light." Iago's plan is self-consciously monstrous. Speaking with Montano, the Second Gentleman personifies the sea by describing the "high and monstrous mane" of the "wind-shaked surge" (*Oth.*, II.i.13). Ironically, Othello, who describes the private quarrel that Iago has orchestrated as "monstrous," wonders who began it (II.iii.217). Linguistically, Iago and Othello are linked in their monstrosity, the Moor changing with his ancient's poison, and Othello not fully understanding the irony when he says,

> By heaven, thou echo'st me,
> As if there were some monster in thy thought
> Too hideous to be shown.
> (III.iii.107)

Later, but still in the epicenter of the play, in a scene dripping with irony, Iago warns Othello to beware of jealousy, "the green-eyed monster, which doth mock / The meat it feeds on" (III.iii). In this same scene Iago apostrophizes—"O monstrous world!"— in his dissimulating role where, to Othello, he plays the "honest" man who has been wronged (III.iii.166, 377). After his description of Desdemona's supposed infidelity, Iago soon has Othello cursing: "O monstrous! monstrous!" (III.iii.427). Emilia tells Desdemona that jealousy is monstrous: "'Tis a monster / Begot upon itself, born on itself," and her mistress replies, "Heaven keep that monster in Othello's mind!" (III. iv.161–63). There are also monsters from within, as Othello says, "A horn man's a monster and a beast," and Iago responds, "There's many a beast then in a populous city, / And many a civil monster" (IV.i.62–64). Finally, Montano says of Othello's murder of Desdemona, "O monstrous act!" (V.i.190). In both plays those who proclaim the monstrous can be monstrous themselves in someone else's view.

Shakespeare's uses of "barbarian," "barbarous," and "barbarism" in his plays yield intricate and contradictory contexts. In each of the genres—history, tragedy, and comedy (including romance)—he employs these terms and does so in a variety of ways, and their thematic concerns cut across and disturb generic boundaries. Shakespeare represents the classical past, for example, across genres and in this context uses barbarism in a way the Greeks and Romans would recognize and that pertains closely to the New World contexts discussed here. Barbarians are those who are outside the bounds of civility—the *civis*—who become tributaries or slaves to imperial masters.

At the beginning of *Titus Andronicus*, Marcus Andronicus, a tribune, announces that the people of Rome have elected an emperor, his brother, who is summoned "home / From weary wars against the barbarous Goths" (*TA*, I.i.28).[9] In *Troilus and Cressida*, Thersites, a scurrilous Greek, satirizes Ajax and likens him to "a barbarian slave" (*TC*, II.i.47); later, in a soliloquy, he mocks the Greek leaders individually and collectively— "the Grecians began to proclaim barbarism"—that is, they themselves proclaim anarchy and, perhaps by implication, are barbarous (V.iv.16). Thersites, himself an advertisement for Greek weakness as well as its satirist, is the one who speaks of barbarism in this play. In the midst of Britain's revolt against the Romans, Guiderius, a son of Cymbeline, proclaims to his brother, Arviragus, and to a banished lord, Belarius,

> This way, the Romans
> Must or for Britains slay us or receive us
> For barbarous and unnatural revolts
> During their use, and slay us after.
> (*Cym.*, IV.iv.4–7)

Shakespeare and his audience might be cultural heirs to Roman poetry and drama, but they are modern "Britons," who were heirs to inhabitants of a barbarous isle the Romans subjugated but who had been, and continued to be, in a fight with Rome (this time over religion).

In the English histories, barbarism becomes more general: in *Henry VI Part 2*, the First Gentleman, when seeing the head of Suffolk, declares, "O barbarous and bloody spectacle" and predicts revenge at court (*2HVI*, IV.i.144); Pembroke advises King John to mew up his aspiring kinsman, Arthur, and "choke his days / With barbarous ignorance," the kind of experience Orlando experiences in *As You Like It* (*AYLI*, IV.ii.58–9); York, in his metatheatrical "As in a theatre" speech, in which he likens governance and politics to the stage, tells the Duchess that had God not steeled the hearts of men against the spectacle of the fallen Richard II, "barbarism itself [would] have pitied him" (*RII*, V.ii.36); Henry V speaks of his own wanton past, where he gave himself "to barbarous licence" (*HV*, I.ii.271). In these histories, barbarism here is an act of violence and ignorance and a sin within the English and England itself.

Tragedies and comedies mix these meanings. In a private conversation with Roderigo after the Senate considers Brabantio's case against Othello, Iago describes the marriage between Desdemona and the Moor as "a frail vow betwixt an erring barbarian and [a] super-subtle Venetian" that will be broken by Iago's wit and "all the tribe of hell" (*Oth.*, I.iii.355–57). Being classical in his wrath against Cordelia, King Lear swears that the "barbarous Scythian," who eats his progeny, will in the king's

> bosom
> Be as well neighbor'd, pitied, and relieve'd,
> As thou my sometime daughter.
> (*KL*, I.i.116–19)

This perhaps is a nod to Herodotus, who wrote about the customs of the Scythians, and those who read him. Berowne contrasts "angel knowledge" with "barbarism," which he admits to defending above this opposite, but tells the king that he will stay with him and keep his oath: *Love's Labour's Lost* satirizes this making and breaking of promises (*LLL*, I.i.112–13). In a comic *reductio ad absurdum* Holofernes, who is having a pedantic and rhetorical disagreement with Dull over the kind of deer they witnessed at the hunt, proclaims, "Most barbarous intimation!" (IV.ii.13). In choosing among the caskets, the Prince of Aragon declares to Portia in *The Merchant of Venice*,

> I will not choose what many men desire,
> Because I will not jump with common spirits,
> And rank me with the barbarous multitudes

so that barbarism here becomes a function of taste and class (*MV*, II.ix.31–3). When, in *Twelfth Night*, Sir Toby and Sebastian are about to fight, Olivia, taking the young man for Cesario, chastises her uncle: "Ungracious wretch, / Fit for the mountains and barbarous caves" (*TN*, IV.i.47–8). Here, Shakespeare associates barbarism with wildness and nature. With *Pericles* I return to the romance phase of comedy and to classical antiquity, for the play has as a source a Greek romance of the fifth century AD that may have even earlier antecedents. In a scene about the importance of virtue, in which the pirates sell Marina to Boult, an agent for a brothel, she considers the pirates to be "barbarous" (*Per.*, IV.ii.66). In his mounting jealousy, Leontes calls Hermione a "thing" and not "a creature of thy place": here, as in *Othello*, Shakespeare associates barbarity with "quality," jealousy, sexual misunderstanding of a husband for his wife (*WT*, II.i.82–7). Whereas Shakespeare's uses of the cognates of "barbarism" in the tragedies relate closely to the meanings of the term in New World narratives, the comic instances are more general indicators of bad behavior, although there is some blurring in generic lines between the tragic *Othello* and the tragicomic *The Winter's Tale*.[10] The jealous barbarism that occurs in the tragic phase of the romance ends the tragedy.

This rest of this chapter will examine briefly the classical and early modern views of barbarism and will provide background for Shakespeare's representation of the question of barbarism, especially as it relates to Caliban, who is and is not of the New World. Rather than give a close reading of Shakespeare's "barbarians," the following will outline some contexts from England and Europe that should be suggestive for the interpretation of Shakespeare's work. What follows attempts to set out one possible set of cultural frameworks and not necessarily direct sources for Shakespeare's representations of barbarian and colonizer in the interstices of the plays.

A CLASSICAL BACKGROUND

Consciously and not, Shakespeare would have inherited a classical framework for his representations of politics, exoticism, travel, and other related themes as well as allusions to the barbarism and monstrosity and their cognates. In this period, western Europe, including England, were trying to expand trade and political influence beyond their shores to Africa, Asia, and the New World. What was civilized and what was not, what made one a master or a slave, and what was the nature of the human all came into play in this period of expansion. Reading the classical past was part of the European present as they came to terms with other cultures, and especially those that had not been encountered before in the Americas. Here, the barbarian is the focus of discussion.

In the Greek world barbarism has much to do with language and empire. *Translatio imperii*, or the translation of empire, involved a distinction between those inside the polity and those outside. This kind of thinking suggested an appropriation of the myth of empire. In *Orientalism* (1978) Edward Said examined the Greeks' understanding of barbarians, as Anthony Pagden also did in *The Fall of Natural Man* (1982, rev. 1986), as a means of explaining the European views of another culture.[11] The translation of empire begins for the West in the earliest times and continues today for critics of empire like Said.

One of the main recurrent imperial themes is the ways in which colonizers, whether or not they have themselves been colonized, identify with earlier empires and create a myth of continuity. The colonized justify their transformation into colonizers by appropriating the political and military culture of earlier regimes. This is a vast area that stretches back to the earliest history of the Middle East and Europe and may also apply to other cultures. By appealing to European history, I am focusing on European colonialism, one of the underpinnings of postcolonialism. The connection between postcolonialism and colonial expansion from classical to modern periods is key. In such a brief space, all I can do is to sketch the Western tradition or trope of the translation of empire. Here is an aspect of a colonial background to postcolonial studies. I wish to appeal to the ancient and early modern as a means of seeing where the rupture might happen in the colonial moment that allows ways of thinking toward a postcolonial state even in the midst of empire and therefore represents a prolepsis to postcolonialism. This reaching back may help to ground the postcolonial and make the postcolonial problematic a little clearer.

The Athenians were not interested in empire in the sense that Alexander the Great was and the Romans later were. Greece was a loosely related group of city-states and the Greek world was in many ways a commercial "empire." Anthony Pagden's discussion of barbarism is instructive here. Aristotle discussed the term barbarian as did Aquinas and the neo-Aristotelian commentators. The word is, as Pagden notes, unstable, as it was applied over time to the Berbers, Turks, Sythians, Ethiopians, Irish, and Normans, but these uses had one thing in common—"implication of inferiority."[12] The word *barbarian*, which was coined in the seventh and sixth centuries BC, meant "foreigner," and it was applied to, among others, the Egyptians, whom the Greeks respected. By the fourth century BC, however, it had come to mean, and still means, someone of cultural and mental inferiority. The *barbaros*, for the Hellenistic Greeks, meant a babbler who could not speak Greek, someone devoid of the *logos*, of speech and reason. Barbarians were not of the *polis*, the civil society of the Greek family of humankind, the *oikumene* (also *oikoumene*). As Pagden argues, the Greeks' failure to admit the *barbaroi* or barbarians into the Hellenistic community was "a denial of their humanity."[13] Aristotle thought that the birds watching over the temple at Dimedia were able to differentiate between the Greeks and *barbaroi* because while the one group had access to the mysteries through the *logos*, the other did not.[14] Although Aristotle considered the barbarians to be human, he thought that they behaved like beasts, so that the Achaeans and the Heniochi, tribes of the Black Sea, had gone savage and enjoyed human flesh.[15] Cruelty and ferocity, as Pagden says, are the marks of barbarism, and behavior is the key difference between the civilized and the barbarous. The word *civilized*, which derives from the Latin word "civis," or citizen, shows that the Romans also took up a view of the special nature of their city and its privileges in relation to those outside it. This term should also provide a clue to the importance of civic and civil, like of the city or *polis*, to the Greeks, who dwelt there first and to the shaping of their views of those people who lived beyond them. When the barbarians lived in cities, they did so under tyrannous conditions and devoid of freedom. The idea of the barbarian, as Said and Pagden recognize, is crucial for an understanding of xenophobia, of projections onto others, and of imperialism. It is also important for my problematic of translation. Pagden is explicit about this link: "The definition of the word 'barbarian' in terms that were primarily cultural rather than racial made its translation to the largely non-Greek speaking Christian world a relatively easy business."[16] Here, the narrative of conversion or of spreading Christian civilization began. In order to pursue translation of empire, there had to be a sense of the civilized world and those barbarians beyond. Before taking up the Christian notion of a chosen people of the *logos*, it is also necessary to see the move from Athens to Rome of the imperial theme.

An idea of Greek empire is something that must be established before it can be translated to Rome.[17] *Historia* meant an inquiry into the peoples and geography of the *oikumene*, that is, into time and space in the world known to the Greeks. The *Periegesis* of Hecataeus of Miletus looks at geography and his *Genealogies* at time: extant fragments suggest that together these works are the earliest examples of this type of Greek history. Ethnographic and geographic elements still occur in Herodotus' *Histories*, but they are less prominent than before, and Herodotus stresses the Great Persian war. But the Greek attitudes toward empire and barbarians are ambivalent and refractory. As Ernst Breisach says, "Herodotus viewed the Great Persian Wars as the grand battle between forces of despotism and freedom, between Orient and Occident, and between a despotic monarchy and city-states governed by their citizens," but he "pointedly reminded his readers or listeners of the many admirable customs of the Persians, the fickleness of the masses in a democracy, and the contrast between the serene unity of the Persian Empire and the strident discord among the Greek city-states."[18] Apparently, only Herodotus' glorification of the Greeks in the war allowed the Greeks to overlook his appreciation of Persian "barbarians" and his cosmopolitanism, of which they did not approve. In fact, Herodotus represents the Persian court encouraging Xerxes to wage war against the Greeks so that the sun would never set on the Persian empire.[19] It is easy to forget the empires of the East. The mixture of the celebration and the critique of empire in historical representation begins early. Thucydides meditates on the fall of the Athenian empire. His *Peloponnesian War* focuses Greek historiography on the *polis* and the fate of states, as opposed to ethnography and geography, and he interprets war and empire and how the Athenian quest for power backfired. He analyzes how the Athenian desire for power drove Athens to transform the voluntary alliance of Greek city-states against Persia into an empire and how that drive to power and empire aroused the resentment of some of the subjected and its chief rival, Sparta.

The next stage in Greek historiography was an attempt to move to pan-hellenism after the Macedonian triumph of empire and the destruction of the Greek city-state. Theopompus of Chios attempted a pan-hellenist history in his *Philippica*. On the whole, the Greeks would not accept the Macedonians as part of their culture because they viewed them as barbarians, so this enterprise was problematic and not entirely successful.[20] Alexander the Great admired the epics of Homer and had a copy that Aristotle prepared for him. He conquered Persia and took his army into India. The Greek historians did not know what to make of Alexander. Callisthenes, a relative of Aristotle, gave Alexander a heroic if not Homeric ancestry, tracing him back to Zeus and Achilles. Others traced Alexander to Priam and the Trojan nobility. Alexander was a barbarian who had crushed the rebellion at Thebes, and his empire had come to include so many barbarians that the Greeks in that short a time may have had a difficult time assimilating these changes. The historians may have found it challenging to bring them into the narrative of the *oikumene* and to forge a story beyond the *polis* and the failure of empire.[21] One aspect of Alexander's campaign was that the Greeks were now in contact with diverse cultures, and this exchange effected new geographical and ethnographical writings. The Seleucid monarchy, whose eastern lands bordered on India, had to keep on peaceful terms with the powerful kingdom of Chandragupta in northern India. About 300 BC Megasthenes stayed at this court and, in his *Indica*, described the people and territories near the Gandes and Indus rivers. Unfortunately, this work survives in a few small fragments, and not surprisingly, Megasthenes tried to find traces of Dionysius in that region.[22] In reconstructing history, and the history of empire is no different in this regard, we must remember the lost and mangled documents that make our evidence incomplete. That is why this or any sketch of the translation of empire is incomplete and requires ongoing archival and archeological work. The question of law is also problematic in the matter of who is civilized and who is barbarous, who is human and who is monstrous. The exploration of the New World before and during Shakespeare's life provides a good example of law and what came to be called human rights and the relation between us and the other.

SOME LEGAL CONTEXTS

No matter the extraordinary quality of Shakespeare's talent, he is part of a larger context. Before he was born, let alone began to write, Spain, France, and England showed contradictory and ambivalent attitudes toward Natives and attempted to take legal possession of them as subjects and of their lands. This move has early precedents and provides a background to Caliban's claim of the island against Prospero's, even if Sycorax had found it to be unoccupied, as Bermuda was said to be, a kind of *terra nullius*. European representational, legal, and intellectual possession of the New World have comparative contexts. When Columbus, Cabot, and Cartier planted their symbols in the soil of the Americas, they took possession for their respective kings. Equally, however, there is an intellectual and historical enterprise represented by historiographers like Oviedo, Thevet, and Hakluyt.[23] They literally promote themselves to help record the history of the New World and advocate the economic and religious benefits of empire.

Within the representation of the European discovery of the New World, which was a discovery for them, if not for the Amerindians, there is a legal and political dimension. The first sentence of the *Letter of Columbus* declares that he has taken possession of the peoples by means of a royal proclamation, which receives no opposition.[24]

82

Christopher Columbus then proceeds to name the places he encounters: although the
Natives (whom he has already named "los Indios") call the first island Guanahani, he
will name it San Salvador after Christ, who has given them all this. Hernán Cortés
literally takes possession of Montezuma (Mutezuma, Motecuçoma) and dispossesses
him: he records Montezuma's abdication speech, in which the king asks his attendant
lords to swear allegiance to the Spanish king.[25] In Henry VII's letters patent to John
Cabot, the king gives permission to the captain to set up the royal banner and ensign
in the newly found lands: "And that the aforesayd John and his sonnes, or their heires
and assignes may subdue, occupy and possesse all such townes, cities, castles and isles
of them found, which they can subdue, occupy and possesse, as our vassals, and lieu-
tenants, getting unto us the rule, title, and jurisdiction of the same villages, townes,
castles & firme land so found."[26] The license for possession occurs before the English
and French explorers possess the new lands. Cartier takes possession of New France
but gives alternative explanations to the Amerindians that his cross is not a sign of possession but a beacon or marker.[27] But claims of possession can also lead to ideas that
result in conflict. Edward Haie's account of the voyage of Humphrey Gilbert stakes
the English claim over the French claim in the lands north of the Spanish colonies.[28]
There was a whole legal scaffolding to the narratives of contact and possession and the
histories of those events. The papal bull, *Apostolatus officium* (1403), promulgated by
Benedict XIII in 1403 from Avignon, elevated the Spanish war against the Guanches
on the Canaries to a crusade. Nicholas V repeated the provision of Benedict's bull,
but, paradoxically, the church protected the Natives and obtained a papal ban on
Spanish expansion in the islands, so that, after 1465, Spain took over legal action
concerning the Guanches while conquering them. But in the case of Columbus, the
papal bulls were reactions to his discoveries. Alexander VI, a member of the Spanish
branch of the Borgias, issued four bulls from May 3 to September 26, although two
of them were backdated. The second, *inter caetera*, seems to give possession of the
discovered lands if Christian kings or princes do not occupy them. Whether this bull
gave the Spaniards a right to make war on the Amerindians, as Sepúlveda argued, or
not, as Las Casas argued, it did allow for evangelization, which may have been the
reason Ferdinand and Isabella found it useful. Possession finds many ways to include
conflict.[29] The claim could be made, as Prospero does of the sparsely inhabited island
in *The Tempest*, that a newly discovered land was *terra nullius*, or, in John Winthrop's
words, *vacuum domicilium*. Just as the Portuguese had claimed discovery of populated
areas of the African coast in the fifteenth century, the Spanish, English, and French
used the legal fiction of *terra nullius*, that the nomadic Amerindians ranged but did not
inhabit the land as Europeans did, so that their land could be possessed.[30] This kind of
claim, which involved the rights of discovery being invoked in the instance of unoccupied territory, goes back to Justinian's *Institutes* (II.i.12). The trope of the translation
of empire plays a role in the making and triumph of empires, both in law and myth.

    Another form of possession is the promotion, assimilation, and promulgation of
information about the New World. While there are many forms of this national enterprise, the role of official history is one that this chapter will focus on, especially in
the work of Gonzalo Fernández Oviedo, André Thevet, and Richard Hakluyt the
Younger. They all sought official favor for their respective empires, but the major difference is that for Oviedo the settlement was a fact, whereas for Thevet and Hakluyt,

permanent settlement in the Americas was not yet certain for the French and English. The prefatory matter of Oviedo's *Historia Natural de las Indias* (1526), Thevet's *Les Singularitez de La France Antarctique, Avtrement nommée Amerique* (1558) and Hakluyt's first edition of *The Principall Navigations of the English Nation* (1589) show a seeking of royal favor or national prestige, a desire to be an official voice for the promotion of America and empire. Oviedo, Thevet, and Hakluyt all try to define the national project of colonization and give to it a collection or an attempted assimilation of an archive for public consumption. The work of all three historiographers stresses the scholar coming to terms with new knowledge and representing the truth of that record and the eyewitness report of the experienced voyager who had been there. All three are men of action and scholars, though Hakluyt never makes America part of his extensive travels. Oviedo, Hakluyt, and Thevet hope to spur their patrons and government into more effective policies in navigation and colonization in the New World. By building up pride in the nation, each historiographer wants to see a translation of empire from the Romans to his country, even if metaphorically as an inspiration to further exploration. While being implicitly critical of his nation's lack of policy in the New World—they have not possessed enough or well enough—each historiographer wants a favor from monarch and court, so each has to flatter and to seek patronage. They all desire official or quasi-official roles in molding and recording policy in America. They have great expectations for their respective countries in their navigation on the route to empire.[31] Shakespeare is born into this debate and these intricacies of representation and had to negotiate between actual and possible worlds.

THE TRANSLATION OF EMPIRE AND DISTINGUISHING THE BARBARIAN

Shakespeare, then, is not merely drawing on sources directly but is part of a tradition as well as intellectual, cultural, historical, religious, and material contexts. Notions of barbarism extended from the classical world into the European contact with other cultures. There are many contexts, but here I am interested in the New World, which is part of the allusionary world of Shakespeare's *The Tempest*. There are two sources of European triumphalism, the first, which is classical, is the idea or trope of the translation of empire, and the second, which is Christian, is the typological and teleological idea of the victory of Christ and salvation. The trope of the translation of empire is closely related to the notion of barbarism.

The Spanish debate these ideas in the context of America extensively and set the scene for French and British defenses and attacks on colonization. The European contact with the New World creates a sense of triumph, although this meeting also reveals that this idea of the translation of empire and this assimilation of new peoples into a successor to the Greek and Roman empires would be a difficult and new enterprise. Once again the Spanish were there first. The Amerindians represented new peoples whom the Europeans knew nothing about. Even though the American experience was novel, many of the Europeans tried, for obvious reasons, to fit the Amerindians and their lands into the framework of European experience. The very first sentence Columbus writes to Santangel in the letter describes "la gran vitoria que Nuestro Señor me ha dado en mi viaje" (the great victory with which Our Lord has crowned my voyage).[32] In 1519 Charles of Spain became Emperor Charles V of the Holy Roman Empire. In 1521 Magellan's voyage around the globe uncovered a world of diverse peoples that the classical chronicler, Eusebius (ca. 263–339), and his successors did not know. Still, the idea of a universal Spanish monarchy persisted into the 1700s. The universality of the past was not the universality of the future, and this was a problem that the Spanish and the Europeans generally had a hard time facing. Oviedo wrote his universal history with an understanding of *empire* in its traditional Mediterranean and Western European sense and spoke about Charles as being part of a direct line from Caesar. But Oviedo, colonial administrators, and missionaries came to see that the Amerindians had their own traditions. The debate between Las Casas and Sepúlveda over the treatment of the Amerindians represented two ways to incorporate America into European history. Las Casas saw the contact as fulfilling Christian universal history in the conversion of the Indians, who were human and had souls to be saved. Sepúlveda argued for the growth of the Spanish monarchy and empire and was less interested in the conversion of the Amerindians, whom he considered not completely human.

Two explicit examples show that this idea of the translation of empire seems to have been widespread. In 1524 Hernán Pérez de Oliva, a humanist, asked the city fathers of Córdoba to improve the navigation on the river because the center of empire was moving west to Spain owing to the discovery of America. Edward Haie (ca. 1583) had a different version of the westward movement of empire, as he included a movement from southern Europe to northern Europe and southern parts of America to its northern parts. He also saw this movement in terms of Christ and the apocalypse. The greatness of England is the matter here.

In the early work of Spanish exploration—by Columbus, Cortés, and others—a model of contact, possession, conflict, and triumph coexists in the representations of the New World. The ambivalent representation of the Amerindians as timid and fierce, as inhabitants of a pastoral of the golden age, and as treacherous beasts or cannibals at the point of contact helps to complicate the rhetorics of possession, conflict, and triumph. Hakluyt talks about Columbus in the Epistle Dedicatory to the third volume of the second edition of the *Principall Navigations* (1600) and includes other Spanish and French (not to mention other European) examples to educate the English in navigation and empire. The idea of an English empire in America will depend on Spanish precedent and knowledge of other European experiences and writings about the New World. In the history of Spanish colonization, Sepúlveda and Oviedo argued against the humanity of the American Indian, whereas Las Casas defended them. The Synopsis of *A Short Account of the Destruction of the Indies* (1542, pub. 1552) claims that Las Casas spoke for Natives thus:

> Everything that has happened since the marvellous discovery of the Americas—from the short-lived initial attempts of the Spanish to settle there, right down to the present day—has been so extraordinary that the whole story remains quite incredible to anyone who has not experienced it at first hand. It seems, indeed, to overshadow all the deeds of famous men of the past, no matter how heroic, and to silence talk of other wonders of the world.

Prominent amid the aspects of this story which have caught the imagination are the massacres of innocent peoples, the atrocities committed against them and, among other horrific excesses, the ways in which towns, provinces, and the whole kingdoms have been entirely cleared of their native inhabitants. Brother Bartolomé de Las Casas, or Casuas, came to the Spanish court after he entered the Order, to give our Lord, the Emperor, an eye-witness account of these enormities, not a whisper of which had at that time reached the ears of people here. He also related these same events to several people he met during his visit and they were deeply shocked by what he had to say and listened open-mouthed to his every word; they later begged him and pressed him to set down in writing a short account of some of them, and this he did.[33]

Here, once again, is the contradictory voice of cultural appropriation. The Americas are a marvelous discovery, which is quite different from any Native perspective. This "discovery" of otherness is a matter of heroism and wonder, which evokes the traditions of natural history (Pliny), history (Herodotus), epic (Homer, Virgil), and travel literature (Marco Polo). But beside this is Las Casas' outrage at genocide and his defense of the humanity of the Natives, which defies Sepúlveda's application of Aristotle's theory of natural slavery and which draws on a radical New Testament distrust of class and race that institutional Christianity sometimes perverted. Here is opposition from within the us to stand up for them. Las Casas did not have enough of an effect on Spanish policy to save the Indians, but both sides of the European-American contact were complex. The mediation between us and them is also a possibility; for some, crossing cultures is a sell-out, while for others it is the only hope.[34] Here is the tradition of the other from within.

Montaigne also takes up opposition to European abuses against the peoples the Europeans were subjecting. On his first voyage Columbus had divided the Natives into good and bad, depending on how pliable they seemed and how pro-Spanish they were. He subdivided the bad Natives into Amazons and cannibals. Montaigne's "On Cannibals" (pub. 1580) describes an instance when he asked the Natives, who were in Rouen when Charles IX was visiting, what they found most remarkable:

They mentioned three things, of which I am sorry to say I have forgotten the third. But I still remember the other two. They said that in the first place they found it very strange that so many tall, bearded men, all strong and well armed, who were around the King— they probably meant the Swiss of his guard—should be willing to obey a child, rather than choose one of their own number to command them. Secondly—they have a way in their language of speaking of men as halves of one another—that they had noticed among us some men gorged to the full with things of every sort while their other halves were beggars at their doors, emaciated with hunger and poverty. They found it strange that these poverty-stricken halves should suffer such injustice, and that they did not take the others by the throat or set fire to their houses.[35]

The other becomes a way of criticizing the injustice in European politics and economics. The colonized becomes, as Trin T. Minh-ha and Edward Said suggest, a medium for a discussion between Europeans, but, unlike later anthropologists, who are said to have valued scientific objectivity, Montaigne shows his own awareness of the subjectivity and imperfection of his knowledge and his situation.[36] He admits to forgetting the third remarkable thing the Natives observed in Europe and later complains about how bad his interpreter was. His ethnology turns the lens on Europe, but does he do so through cultural appropriation, or does he avoid ventriloquy to counterbalance European prejudice? Perhaps Montaigne foreshadowed the new movement in ethnology to use its own methods to look at European culture as an other. Jonathan Swift has the King of Brobdingnag complain about European ethnocentrism, something that Las Casas and Montaigne also complain about even though they are, by definition, very European in their cultural training. Earlier in his essay on cannibals, Montaigne alludes to the old debate on barbarism (to which we shall return) and speaks about a new spirit that might escape ethnocentrism, perhaps the ideal of a scientific anthropology, even if the practice must fall short: "I do not believe, from what I have been told of this people, that there is anything barbarous or savage about them, except that we all call barbarous anything that is contrary to our own habits. Indeed we seem to have no other criterion of truth and reason than the type and kind of opinions and customs current in the land where we live."[37] Is this cultural appropriation or the distance of criticism saying that we cannot get outside our cultures and times in matters as important as truth and reason?

The English also tried to describe the Natives in the Americas as strangers and barbarians but not always as ironically as Thomas More had done in *Utopia*. William Hawkins, father of John Hawkins, reports his voyages to Brazil in 1530 and 1532. The elder Hawkins, in a fashion not unlike Columbus, says that he took one of the "savage kings" back to England and left as a pledge Martin Cockeram of Plymouth. The encounter here is reversed and takes place in Europe (if still on European terms) because Hawkins presented the Native king to Henry VIII and the nobility, a sight that caused them to marvel. The Native king stayed nearly a year and died at sea as a result of "a change of aire and alteration of diet."[38] Despite the fears of the English, the Natives of Brazil gave back their pledge and traded goods that filled up Hawkins' ship for the return to England. On his first voyage in 1563, John Hawkins takes up the slave trading that Columbus recommends. There he captures by sword and "by other meanes" three hundred Africans on the coast of Sierra Leona and takes them to Hispaniola to trade with the Spaniards.[39] Conflict occurs in Africa as well as in America. The next two voyages involve battles that include English losses in fights with Africans, and on the second they meet a French ship and are told that the Portuguese have been protecting their trade. The slave trade with the Spanish in the New World, which the Spanish crown often forbade, affected English and French experience, so that they were already part of a European framework when they settled among the Amerindians. Hawkins' third voyage also involves a fight with the Spanish in Mexico.[40] Like Columbus, Martin Frobisher also sought gold and Asia.[41] Christopher Hall's account of the first voyage represents the Inuit in descriptive terms: for example, they are like Tartars in appearance.[42] During the second voyage, the representation turns to conflict between the English and the Inuit, from interest in their language to innuendoes about cannibalism and charges of behaving treacherously and like beasts (171–74).[43] The record of Humphrey Gilbert's voyage of 1583, written by Edward Haie, states that the inhabitants have fled the southern coast of Newfoundland because there are too many Christians (presumably the "Portugals, Biscains and Frenchmen" mentioned later), but the Natives on the north coast are "harmelesse."[44] This harmlessness may be similar to what Columbus also assumed until his first conflicts with the Amerindians. In the letter to Raleigh, written in 1584 by either Captain Arthur Barlowe or Philip Amadas, the Natives are described in a way worthy of Columbus: "we found the people most gentle, loving, and faithfull, voide of all guile and treason, and such as live after the maner of the golden age."[45] Raleigh was about twelve years older than Shakespeare and outlived him by about two years, so these contexts of exploration, of encounters with others, which Shakespeare represented in plays like *Othello* and *The Tempest*, were more immediate. The question of slavery, liberty, barbarity, freedom, and who was a monster or not concerned many of those who governed or wrote in Shakespeare's time and country. He was part of a line in western Europe who considered these questions over centuries if not millennia, but it was the Viking and Columbian contact with the peoples of the western Atlantic that intensified these debates in various and sometimes simultaneous expansions and contractions of Europe.

CONCLUSIONS AND TRANSITIONS

Columbus and Shakespeare consider the nature of others that Europeans encounter in new lands, although the one had that experience personally and immediately in the New World, the other wrote about it based on images and texts and perhaps on Natives on display at court or in various places in London and England. Columbus came to divide the world into good friendly Natives and evil and treacherous Natives, the Arawaks and the Caribs; the author of this letter does the same with the inhabitants of Secotan and Pomovik.[46] Does Shakespeare in *Titus*, *Othello*, *Coriolanus*, and *The Tempest* do anything different? What interests me is not that these plays make some of the same kinds of divisions between civility and barbarity but that the language of contradiction is such in representation that whatever the men, Columbus and Shakespeare, intended, their words embodied the drama of in-between states that could not be civilized or barbarous or would be both. I would suggest that we inhabit a similar division and liminality.

Barbarism and its contexts is partly a matter of representation both in Shakespeare's texts and the background surrounding them. England and Europe and their other in the New World and beyond could not, cannot, be hermetically sealed. Keeping time and story are both parts of poetry, culture, and history. How Shakespeare represented love and hatred in the tensions between mythology and ideology, how he explored the connection between private and public, are signal parts of his nondramatic and dramatic poetry. The question of us and those who are not us, the present story and about stories about the past, resonate and suggest the intricacies of representation. Even though close attention to reading Shakespeare's works as poetry and drama is at the heart of this book, some contextual matters may well reconfigure and cast some light from a different angle on how Shakespeare made his art in the time and place he did, partly building on those who went before him, were about him, and came after him. Even those in his time, near and far, were not always known to him, but they helped create a context for him, however obscure. And so we, too, like those who received Shakespeare in his day and those who will after silence has taken us, enter into the drama of meaning. In these Shakespearean texts and those surrounding them, we represent and are represented in doing so.

CHAPTER 5

SHAKESPEARE'S REPRESENTATION OF HISTORY

CIVILITY, BARBARISM, AND MONSTROSITY ALL OCCUPY THE DEBATE ON TIME PAST. Temporality becomes a continuum in which people in the present reach into the past to project something into a present moving into the future. There is a typology between then and now that attempts to make sense of time or to give it an artistic or political shape. Shakespeare and his contemporaries were well aware of the challenges of time in terms of religion, politics, and art. This poet and playwright used many genres to explore the representation of history and was part of the Renaissance discovery of time.[1]

A thread that runs through my study is what Shakespeare makes in time and of time and how he does so through language. Whether it is the reversal of conventions of love through the reinterpretation of a classical myth, the rhetoric of seduction, temporality in the sonnets, or the insertion of the monstrous between the civil and the barbaric, Shakespeare shapes these themes through words. He represents time and history in poetry and drama, in sonnets, *epyllia* or brief epics, tragedy, romance, and comedy as well as in the history plays themselves. His meditation is not always on the ruins and redemption of time but on the confusing traffic of this world. Shakespeare's history is protean, so that I would like to suggest five principal areas that his representation of history opens up: first, the meditation on the past, personal and public; second, the classical past; third, the biblical past; fourth, the European past; fifth, the English past.

History in Shakespeare's canon is many things at once. Here, I have scope to mention but not elaborate on a few aspects of each of these five areas. In Shakespeare's work I would like to discuss the dynamic relation between the historical and the literary because he could not get history out of his mind and he occupies a central position in the European and English-speaking cultures. Elsewhere, I have argued that Goethe, Tieck, Solger, the Schlegels, Kierkegaard, Hugo, and others on the Continent helped to shape the reception of Shakespeare and to make him into a figure of world literature.[2] This aspect of history, that is, of historical reception, reflects my interest in a comparative Shakespeare or a Shakespeare in a comparative context.[3]

Before outlining these five parts of Shakespeare's representation of history, I would like to give a little historiographical or theoretical background. The term *history* itself involves story and inquiry, so that within the etymology there is a tension between the narrative and analytical aspects of the past. Telling and interpretation are bound together in the word. The Greeks, Romans, and early Christians comprise important parts of the context for the representation of history in early modern England. It is hard to know what Shakespeare read in spite of the fine source studies done by Geoffrey Bullough and others, but it is possible to say that the following ideas, available to him directly or not, appear to have constituted material that he used in his poetry and drama.[4] In *The Rape of Lucrece*, *Julius Caesar*, *Troilus and Cressida*, *Antony and Cleopatra*, and *Coriolanus*, Shakespeare explores the classical idea of the epic challenge or journey, the history as central public myth or *muthos*, that Homer tells in his accounts of Achilles and Odysseus and that Virgil represents in his hero, Aeneas, founding Rome. Aristotle distinguishes history and poetry, for the one tells what happened and the other what might happen. Nonetheless, Aristotle implies a rhetorical common ground for these sister arts because what happened in history is what is possible, which is the domain of poetry.[5] Shakespeare plays with this common imaginative element in history and poetry, especially in the choruses to *Henry V*, which invokes a muse of fire to create the epic history, to cram the vasty fields of France into a wooden O.

Like Herodotus, Thucydides, Livy, Tacitus, and other classical historians, Shakespeare uses invented speeches to imagine what a character might have said if there was no evidence of what he or she actually did say. Thucydides imagines Pericles' oration just as Shakespeare gave unto Richard II in prison and Henry V before his troops speeches that perhaps only a poet or poetic historian could conjure (though Pericles would have had much more training in rhetoric than either English monarch). Cicero insists on style, as well as truth, in history, and Shakespeare provides so much style that he has worried some historians. Shakespeare's characterization of Richard III, following Thomas More's mixture of psychological portrait and Tudor propaganda, is so stylized that his representation has so dominated popular views of Richard that historians like Paul Murray Kendall have set out to redress the balance. Pieter Geyl, the great Dutch historian, praised Shakespeare's history for some of the reasons other historians objected to it: Shakespeare embodies history and makes it live in a dramatic present. For Geyl, unlike Quintilian, a great divide does not separate the fiction of poetry and the truth of history. In Shakespeare as well as in Plutarch a chance remark or gesture can tell us more about a historical figure than public deportment. Plutarch himself tried to downplay biography in history, but his narrative qualified his theory. Biography would not be so easily taken out of history. Shakespeare never tried this separation.[6]

The Augustinian Fall, the gap between the City of God and the earthly city, casts its shadow over many of Shakespeare's English history plays, especially in the second tetralogy, from *Richard II* to *Henry V*. The kings and major actors cannot read the signs of God in fallen political action. Perhaps the much-maligned E. M. W. Tillyard was at least partly right to see a great English epic in the English histories, from the fall and death of Richard II to Henry VII's redemption of England and the union of the Houses of York and Lancaster. After all, A. W. Schlegel held this view and passed it into English Shakespearean criticism through Coleridge. That does not mean that this official history should be believed or that it represents the whole of Shakespeare's historical representation. The biblical typological tradition in which the virtuous are rewarded at the Last Judgment in the final act of a human tragedy turned divine comedy through the mercy and grace of Christ is present in this historical cycle but also occurs in Shakespeare's comedy or problem play *Measure for Measure*. Shakespeare used chronicles, like those of Hall and Holinshed, for his domestic history and often went to Plutarch for the classical parts. Those Renaissance chronicles grew out of a lively chronicle tradition in the Middle Ages.[7] Rather than go on with elements of Shakespeare's theory and practice of history, I would now like to turn to five crucial parts of Shakespeare's representation of history.

PRIVATE AND PUBLIC PASTS

The personal is an inextricable part of Shakespeare's history. It would be easy to say that Shakespeare separates the private from the public, the personal from the historical, to relegate that difference in terms of gender. In discussing the second tetralogy, it is true that women do not play a large public role in the plays, whereas in the first tetralogy, from *1 Henry VI* to *Richard III*, they are central public figures. Part of my argument is that the Shakespearean *œuvre*, like the Bible, is contradictory and intricate. I am not interested in closing one eye for the glory of a thesis or a well-shaped argument. In Sonnets 54 and 55, Shakespeare, following Petrarch and others here, uses love poetry to promise that his male friend will outlast official monuments with the power of the poet's language or record. The future will remember the friend through the style and beauty of Shakespeare's words. History will grow out of the personal through the apparently, by way of a printer's possible piracy, public act of communication and publication.

Love is not without its history. In the brief epic or narrative poem, *The Rape of Lucrece,* Shakespeare, who is just one of the European poets to so, represents Tarquin's rape of Collatine's virtuous wife, a personal horror that constitutes one of the foundational myths of Rome: the expulsion of its last king.[8] The men do not hear her throughout the poem, and she becomes a sign in a corrupt narrative. She would rather commit suicide than live with humiliation, dishonored, a sad and solitary equivalent for a Roman woman to Brutus wanting, in defeat, to die on his sword rather than face revilement.

Anthony and Cleopatra shift between survival and honor in their public private lives. King Lear retreats into a private world at the center of his mythical and historical tragedy, a genre that Polonius was on the verge of identifying while Edgar simulates this retreat in Tom of Bedlam's analogous private madness. Lady Macbeth's private ambition changes the polity until she is driven to a madness: history is an interplay of private and public, whose boundaries blur. In *Troilus and Cressida* the lovers run parallel to the great siege, and in *Coriolanus* the protaganist must face his mother as much as the Roman people. Coriolanus' loyalty to her helps to lead to his death. The personal erupts just when public and official history seems to have it in hand. The lives of the great are public as they are private. King Lear tries to understand his past relation with his daughters and his kingdom just as Gloucester does with his sons and nation. Family and national myths, so much a part of the rhetoric of patriotism and national history, are intertwined.

THE CLASSICAL PAST

This personal aspect of public history helps to make up part of Shakespeare's representation of the classical past. This past can be erotic, as in his reconstitution of Greek myth in *Venus and Adonis*, where Shakespeare shows an early preference for Ovid, the poet Augustus was said to have exiled for his verbal or actual erotic indiscretions. Still, Shakespeare can make Octavius Caesar, later Augustus, triumphant, even if the victory seems Pyrrhic to some, at the end of *Antony and Cleopatra*. Whereas the republic is an implicit theme in *The Rape of Lucrece* and the explicit theme of *Julius Caesar*, love gives politics a run in *Antony and Cleopatra*. The use and abuse of *virtù* among the male characters is a primary concern in these classical plays. The men sacrifice love and friendship and grasp at honor after their state is in ruins.

Nor do the Greeks and Trojans in *Troilus and Cressida* mix love and war any better: Helen, Paris, Achilles, Cressida, and Troilus are all sacrificed in a great battle, one of the defining moments of Greek history and poetic mythology. This Shakespearean *Iliad* has a satirical side and is full of rhetorical debate. Although Aeneas appears in the play, Shakespeare does not rewrite Virgil's epic about a foundational moment in Roman history or what we might now call mythological history. And Renaissance Europe, looking back to the classics, took up the trope of the translation of empire and looked to the Greeks and the Romans as models for their own "empires." As with much else in Shakespeare, his representation of the classical past is contradictory and complex. Thersites joins Pandarus, Timon of Athens, and the sulking Achilles—whether Shakespeare lifted them from Homer and Chaucer—in a satirical and all-too-human dimension of human character that official history traditionally tried to sweep aside, except in propaganda, where it helped to discredit an enemy. The classical myths of love and war become a kind of legendary supplement and alternative to the biblical past. Shakespeare did not, like medieval chroniclers, have to rely mainly on providential history.

The classical past is not simply something to revere but a means of complicating Renaissance notions of history. *Comedy of Errors* revisits Plautus' *Menaechmi* and creates another set of twins to complicate identity and comedy in Ephesus. *A Midsummer Night's Dream* is set in a mythological and fantastical version of Athens and a wood nearby it on the occasion of Theseus' betrothal to Hippolyta, queen of the Amazons, but Shakespeare, as is his wont, Englishes his classical or Continental setting by introducing rude mechanicals with English names, habits, and attitudes. Obviously, Shakespeare feels he is free to use the classical past but sometimes to improve on it. He does not show much of the burden of the past or the anxiety of influence here.[9]

The violence of the mythical *Titus Andronicus* shows the decadence, revenge, and horror of the classical world. Probably during the mid-1590s, Henry Peacham produced sketch of a scene from this play where the major figures have more-or-less Roman costumes while the supporting cast wears distinctly Elizabethan garb. Shakespeare's representation of the past of other places so often has much to do with the present England in which he and his audience lived.

Pericles is a redemptive romantic tale of a fictional classical past, set in the eastern Mediterranean, in a movement akin to the salvational movement of Christian providential history. Shakespeare is overt in Englishing this classical past, for he makes John Gower, one of his sources, the Prologue and Chorus.[10] In *The Two Noble Kinsmen*

Shakespeare borrows from Chaucer in examining chivalry, the relation of Palamon and Arcite, nephews to Creon, king of Thebes, in yet another Athenian setting. Theseus, duke of Athens, and Hippolyta, new his bride, make a second appearance in the Shakespearean canon.

Greece and Rome were one of the foundations of Renaissance political iconography and mythology, but they also provided an allegorical distance, a republicanism, a notion of erotic love, and a typological nostalgia for chivalric honor as prefigured by Roman honor, all as alternatives, challenges, and supplements to the Christian tradition. Julius Caesar killed the republic for a kingdom, undoing what Lucrece's virtue had accomplished with the banishment of Tarquin. Four years after the death of Elizabeth I, Cleopatra would appear on the English stage as anything but the Virgin Queen. This typological and allegorical thinking, while sometimes over-ingenious in particular interpretations, intricated the production and reception of Shakespeare's representation of history.

CHRISTIAN AND BIBLICAL HISTORY

Providential views of history, even when the individual characters' interpretations of Providence contradict one another, run throughout Shakespeare's history plays. In *Richard II*, Mowbray and Bolingbroke claim God in their dispute that breaks open the English civil wars. King John defies the pope as a matter of English nationalism and prefigures of Henry VIII's break with Rome and Elizabeth's excommunication in 1570. There is not one Christian authority here.

In *Henry VIII*, that mixture of history and romance, Providence smiles on the birth of Elizabeth in a kind of retrospective prophecy, a version in 1612 of an event in 1533. England becomes an Israel that its people has abused by turning its back on God. Heminge and Condell, friends, members of the King's Men, and editors of the First Folio in 1623, called histories only those plays about English, not Scottish or British history, because it was the life of the nation. They made this decision even though James occupied the Scottish and English thrones, but it was not until 1707 that the England, Wales, and Scotland became Great Britain.

There is, however, a less official use of the Bible in these histories. In *Henry IV Parts 1 and 2*, the rebels and the taverners refer to God as much as the kings and courtiers do. Falstaff may be blasphemous and irreverent, but he also fears hell. His jokes have serious consequences. When the Chief Justice exclaims, "Well, God send the Prince a better companion!" Sir John replies, "God send the companion a better prince!" (*1HIV*, I.ii.199–200). Falstaff uses Puritan cant. Of Shallow, he says, "Lord, Lord, how this world is given to lying!" and thereby echoes his self-righteous and mock-puritanical words to Hal, to whom he had lied about killing Hotspur, in *Part 1*: "Lord, Lord, how this world is given to lying!" (*2HIV*, III.ii.296–8; *1HIV*, V.iv.144–5). Sir John's words echo those of Christ, who says, "Not euery one that sayeth vnto me, Lorde, Lorde, shall enter into the kingdome of heauen, but he that doeth my Fathers will which is heauen." Jesus then talks about those who in the Day of Judgment will cry "Lord, Lord" and claim to have prophesied and done wonderful works in his name, but swears he will reject them, saying, "I neuer knew you: depart from me, yee that work iniquitie" (Matthew 7:21–3).

Whereas Falstaff is obsessed with damnation and cries "Lord, Lord" for amusement, Henry V will speak words like those of Christ, "I know thee not, old man," to begin the rejection speech in *2 Henry IV*. After the rejection, Falstaff falls ill and dies. The Hostess reports his death, when he cried out the name of God three or four times (*HV*, II.iii.18–23). Henry V uses the name of God to justify his actions, either himself or through his surrogates, but Bates and Williams shake his confidence in his identification with God when the king goes disguised among his soldiers and finds he must debate them over God's judgment of whoever is responsible for those who die in the French war (IV.i). On a public and private scale, Providence is a major force in history in the English history plays. Once again, public and private are inescapably connected.

THE EUROPEAN PAST

Shakespeare's history is not simply about the English past but also the Greek, Roman, Danish, British, Scottish, and French pasts, not to mention more mythical settings in or near Italy in plays like *The Taming of the Shrew*, *The Two Gentlemen of Verona*, *Romeo and Juliet*, *The Merchant of Venice*, *Much Ado about Nothing*, *Othello*, and *The Tempest* as well as the Navarre of *Love's Labour's Lost*, the Illyria of the eastern Adriatic (part of what once was Yugoslavia), the Vienna of *Measure for Measure*, and even a Bohemia with a coast in *The Winter's Tale*. But *The Winter's Tale* is partly set in Sicily, and some of the action of *Cymbeline* takes place in Italy. The many Italian settings in Shakespeare reflect a historical cultural debt that England and other European nations, Protestant or not, had to Italy during the Renaissance. There are allusions to Africa and the New World in *The Tempest*, which is set in the Mediterranean near Italy, and *Othello* is set in Cyprus as well as in Venice. The character Othello is a Moor, but a Moor of Venice. The play with the most traveling Continental setting is *All's Well that Ends Well*, which moves from Rosillion to Paris, Florence, and Marseilles.[11]

There is also a geography to Shakespeare's mythology even when, as in some of the comedies, excepting the representation of rulers and kingship and the tension they experience between private and public selves, the historical concerns seem to come close to evaporating entirely. In representing mediations on the British, Scottish, and European past, which I am calling here the European past for short, Shakespeare concentrates his energies even more into the mythical and personal than he did in the English history plays. *Hamlet* is so well known it has its own journal *Hamlet Studies* and is so complex that Harold Jenkins' fine book-length introduction to the New Arden edition cannot include all the issues that the editor would have liked to discuss.[12]

This play, which has its origins in Norse legends, becomes a meditation on the prince's past, an obsessive self-examination through a contemplation of his dead and ghostly father and on what he considers to be the incestuous betrayal of his mother's wedding to his treacherous uncle. Saxo Germanicus' third book of *Historia Danica* (c. 1200, printed 1514) provides a key source for Shakespeare's play, although Amleth boils the Polonius figure and feeds him to the pigs and is much more brisk in his revenge than Shakespeare's character, for he burns down the palace.[13] In good European fashion the story crossed borders. Belleforest's *Histoire Tragiques* (1576) gave Saxo's story a court setting and the so-called *Ur-Hamlet* probably added the ghost.

This transmutation into Shakespeare's difficult and contradictory text has occupied scholars for generations. *Hamlet* is not simply a mediation on kingship or on the ruler, a central concern in Shakespeare's representation of history, but an exploration of love, death, jealousy, and familial ties, to name a few of the topics it probes with such a depth of poetry. Hamlet questions existence itself in the "To be or not to be" soliloquy, but there is also a public dimension to his conflict with his uncle. In one of his own soliloquies, Claudius addresses the absent England, who is his vassal king:

> And England, if my love thou hold'st at aught—
> As my great power thereof may give thee sense,
> Since yet thy cicatrice looks raw and red
> After the Danish sword, and thy free awe
> Pays homage to us—thou mayst not coldly set
> Our sovereign process, which imports at full,
> By letters congruing to that effect,
> The present death of Hamlet.
> (III.iii.58–65)[14]

Shakespeare seldom misses an opportunity to sneak England into a European context, something not yet mentioned in the debate in the Commons over England's place in Europe. The corruption of the body politic leads to many deaths and the uncertainty of Fortinbras as a successor, he whom Hamlet named but whom he had wondered at for fighting over a "straw" or what Fortinbras' captain calls "a little patch of ground" (IV.iv.18, 26, 55). Is this new king an agent of Providence or a lesser breed that follows after the giants of time, the mythical heroes where legend and history meet?

King Lear represents the division of family and kingdom as if they were symbiotically or at least symbolically enmeshed. The play is about Britain, not England, some tale that is mythologically proleptic of England, as is the conflict between Britain and Rome in *Cymbeline*. The dukes of France and Burgundy, as in the history of medieval and early modern Europe, are rivals, this time for the hand of Cordelia, the British king's daughter. Kingship, the division of the kingdom, and rebellion, as well as the relation of the British Isles to the Continent, are as much concerns of Shakespeare in *King Lear* as in the English history plays.

Macbeth centers the evil of ambition in the usurper and his wife in Scotland, a traditional enemy to England but also the home of the newly crowned James I, who was supposed to be descended from Banquo, whom Shakespeare represents as a good man murdered by the monstrous Macbeth. Scottish history—although the descent from Banquo, which is part of contemporary genealogy, probably mythological—becomes a compliment to James I of England, about three years on the throne, though James VI of Scotland before that. The Scottish past becomes an allegory for the English present: the forces of good, represented by James' family, will triumph. The agrarian risings of 1607 in the Midlands, the year after *Macbeth* and the year of or before *Coriolanus*, a tragedy about the conflict between the plebeians and the patricians in Rome, suggest that James' reign was anything but triumphant and peaceful.[15] Stories from the past from the Continent, Britain, and Scotland provided allegories of the present state of England. No nation is an island, not even an island nation.

THE ENGLISH PAST

More insurgent mobs occur in Shakespeare's work. His representation of English history began early, and while he was producing the *Henry VI* plays, he might have been a script doctor on the unfinished, censored play, *Sir Thomas More*, and might have written the 147 lines representing More's handling of the mob.[16] In the first tetralogy, Shakespeare is wrestling with making chronicles into more than chronicle plays. He is shaping histories, and *Richard III* is his first great shaping. The *Henry VI* plays, as interesting as they are and as good as they are in the theatre, seem to ramble structurally from speech to speech as if rhetoric were contending with action. Shakespeare's first history, *I Henry VI*, begins with the funeral of Henry V and so commences the War of the Roses in *medias res*. The decline of England through their warrior-hero's death will slip to the very depths of Richard III's evil only to be redeemed in the victory of Richmond or Henry VII.

If we follow Shakespeare's career as a writer of histories and not the chronology of the historical tetralogies themselves, then the playwright plunged his audience back into the original fall of Richard II and the beginning of the War of the Roses. Henry V's triumph ends the body of the second tetralogy. The Epilogue the Chorus delivers at the end of *Henry V* reminds the audience of the death of Henry V and the misery under the young Henry,

> Whose state so many had the managing
> That they lost France, and made his England bleed;
> Which oft our stage hath shown.
> (*HV*, EP. 11–13)

This takes the audience back to Henry V's funeral and the beginning of *Henry VI*, which they once saw.

Unlike the second tetralogy, the first, especially in the *Henry VI* plays, represent women as powerful. Queen Margaret, daughter of the duke of Anjou and king of Naples and wife to Henry VI, and Joan de Pucelle or Joan of Arc, even if made to be fiend-like, exercise public power and defy the traditional male authority in war. The rivalry with France and the English claims in that country stemming from the Norman conquest preoccupy England in these plays. Shakespeare's histories are so often about loss, and these are about the decline of English power on the Continent. Only in the 1550s, the decade before Shakespeare was born, had the English lost Calais, their last vestige of their French lands. These eight histories about the providential punishment of the War of the Roses represent civil war and rebellion at home and war in France.

If the audience considers the two tetralogies chronologically, then the pattern ends with Henry VII, the king who commissioned John Cabot to seek out lands in the western Atlantic in 1497. Whereas England had lost an empire in France, it was, very slowly, to acquire one in the New World. *The Tempest* alludes to this New World even if the island of the exile of Prospero and Miranda is said to be in the Old World. Shakespeare knew members of the Virginia company. In Shakespeare's romance Ariel has a stopover in Bermuda and the berry drink Caliban remembers as a gift from Prospero is like the one the Bermuda castaways drank in Sylvester Jourdain's *A Discovery of the Bermudas* (1610). Caliban must obey Prospero, who could control Sycorax's god, Sestebos, whom, as Richard Eden mentions in *History of Travaile* (1577), in his description of Magellan's voyage, the Patagonians summoned for help.[17]

As I have written a good deal on colonialism and postcolonialism, I shall end with only a brief analysis of Prospero's account of his history of the island, one that Caliban hotly contests. In Prospero's narrative he found a tyranny on the island. For a crime, Sycorax was banished from Algiers and, pregnant, was brought to the island, where Ariel was her servant. As Ariel would not enact her terrible commands, she imprisoned him in pain in a cloven pine for a dozen years, during which time she died. Only Caliban had a "human shape" on the island when Prospero found it, and only Prospero's "Art" could free Ariel from his howling captivity (284, 291, see 256–93). Even after Ariel responds, "I thank thee, master," Prospero threatens to do unto him what Sycorax had. After Ariel swears his obedience, Prospero gives up the threats and promises to free Ariel in two days. He also commands Ariel to make himself invisible in his next enactment of Prospero's magic.

Prospero claims the barely inhabited island from the bestial yet human Caliban as if it were *terra nullius* or, in John Winthrop's words, *vacuum domicilium*. Just as the Portuguese had claimed "discovery" of populated areas of the African coast in the fifteenth century, so too had the Spanish, English, and French used the legal fiction of *terra nullius*, that nomadic Amerindians ranged but did not inhabit the land as Europeans did, so that their land could be possessed.[18] If we are sympathetic to Prospero, we can say that he usurped the remnants of a penal colony, founded as the result of some unnamed crime, and became the *de facto* ruler through justice. On the other hand, his magic is a deterrent and becomes the force of law, especially in relation to Caliban, the son of the tyrannous Sycorax of Prospero's official version, but also to Ariel.

By 1610 England had a struggling colony in Jamestown. *The Tempest* contains arguments for and against European imperialism—from Caliban's lament and his learning to curse to Gonzalo's description of his ideal commonwealth—that are much indebted to Montaigne. Long before, the Spanish writers like Oviedo, Sepúlveda, Las Casas, and Acosta had begun such a debate on the nature of the Natives and the legitimacy of Spanish rule. The example of Spain, as I have argued elsewhere, is occluded in France and England, but it does illuminate this colonial and postcolonial debate in *The Tempest*.[19] By this time some of the work of these and other Spanish writers about the New World had been translated into English. Through Eden, Nicholas, Hakluyt, and others, Shakespeare and his contemporaries would have been aware of this debate and were remaking it in the context of English identity and the question of empire.

It turns out then that the relations among ideology and mythology, story and argument, underpin Shakespeare's representation of history. That recreation of history takes on many forms, the shape of arguments and stories sometimes joining, sometimes conflicting. At some points, Shakespeare gives the official version, and at others an unofficial and irreverent alternative. He takes the personal and the social and explores England's relation to the classical and biblical pasts, to Europe and to itself. The very power of his drama, which he achieves through language and a multitude of intricate characters, makes it implausible to hammer out the form and poetry and make the content the form itself. Something is lost in the paraphrase, despite what political critics might say. There is no denying the ideological and political dimensions of Shakespeare's history, but to ignore the mythological and aesthetic aspects is to reduce this historical representation and thereby reduce the important act of critique itself. Shakespeare acted on the advice he had Hamlet give Horatio:

> If thou didst ever hold me in thy heart,
> Absent thee from felicity a while,
> And in this harsh world draw thy breath in pain
> To tell my story.
> (V.ii.346–50)

In reading Shakespeare's history, which was hard to tell, readers, audiences, and critics have to realize how difficult it is *not* to recount.

Ideology is a story we tell ourselves, a kind of undetected rationalization. The ideologies of other people in other times is much easier to detect, though the shape of fiction and the language of poetry makes that detection much more recalcitrant. The putative and possible element of poetry, which Aristotle saw, relates it to history because rhetoric, though to a lesser extent, shares with poetics the "what if" and "what might happen." Dramatic historical poetry can escape neither ideology nor mythology. They are intertwined. It does no good, then, to worship Shakespeare as a timeless poet free from his times and politics, as Bernard Shaw observed, but to reduce him to a political pamphlet is too easy a felicity that in the name of historicism denies history itself.[20]

CHAPTER 6

SHAKESPEARE'S ITALY AND ENGLAND

ONE WAY THAT SHAKESPEARE REPRESENTED TIME AND PLACE WAS TO CREATE a double image, and in this chapter, I would like to focus on the doubling of England and Italy. In his nondramatic and dramatic poetry, Shakespeare represented an Italy of the ancients and what we have come to call the Renaissance, taking up this Victorian word. The term *early modern*, which is also a later invention that Shakespeare would not have recognized, has its own problems in terms of teleology, as if the modern could be graduated, the early looking forward to a modern that would then be left post haste. Here, I would like to look at one aspect of the temporal and spatial, a specific case that Shakespeare represented. Rome and Italy held, for England, an example of a place of politics, empire, poetry, culture, and history, *topoi* of ancient wisdom and of bold change.

There is a typology between past and present, there and here. So much depends on point of view. Shakespeare brought together then and now, Italy and England, in the possible worlds of history and fiction that he represented. Italy had been built by the ancient Roman republic and empire, and Britain had been a part of the Roman sphere, first as a colony or province, and later in terms of the western church under the bishop of Rome, whose influence grew in the wake of the fall of the western Roman empire and who became even more prominent after the fall of the eastern empire, when Constantinople fell in 1453. If Byzantium held a fascination for W. B. Yeats, Rome was a preoccupation for Shakespeare.[1]

Rome meant many things to Shakespeare in his representations of the ancient world, as can be seen when considering *The Rape of Lucrece, Julius Caesar, Antony and Cleopatra*, and *Cymbeline*. This theme brings together Shakespeare's nondramatic and dramatic worlds in a drama of representation. Questions of origins, the republic, the empire, and the relations between Britain and Rome find expression in these works. The Renaissance, which included the rebirth of classical languages and learning, as well as the knowledge of mariners and the finances and expertise of bankers, helped to make Italy a great cultural center for Europe. Painters, poets, historians in the Italian peninsula before Shakespeare and during his life helped to transform the intellectual, cultural, spiritual, and material life of western Europe. The Italians themselves looked back to Rome and Greece just as others looked to early modern or Renaissance Italy as they regarded the actual and cultural ruins of Greece and Rome. The popes issued donations in the fifteenth and sixteenth centuries that affected the Mediterranean and Atlantic worlds, especially in how they attempted to give the Iberian powers a division of the unknown world as western Christendom expanded first more within the former Roman empire and later beyond into the Atlantic and Indian oceans and then globally.[2] The English and French resisted these claims, first with the voyage of John Cabot (Giovanni Caboto) and then of Giovanni da Verrazzano and other Italian mariners working for other nations, such as the Christopher Columbus or Christoffa Corombo (the Genoese form of his name) or Cristóbal Colón, as the Casilians knew him when he sailed on behalf of Ferdinand and Isabella. Another Italian explorer, Amerigo Vespucci, a Florentine, worked for Lorenzo and Giovanni de' Medici, who sent him to work for them in Seville in 1492, the year of Columbus' landfall in the western Atlantic. It is not surprising, given the Italian influence in the expansion of Europe, culturally, intellectually and materially, that in *The Tempest* Shakespeare came to allude to the Virgilian world and to have his shipwreck between Tunis and Italy despite the allusions to Bermuda, the long-time unsettled island that the Spaniards used as a way station for food and supplies. Italy was a double image for Shakespeare that doubled in many ways.

These Italian themes, for Shakespeare, occurred in various genres, exploring the tragic, comic, tragicomic, and historical aspects of the poetic life of possible worlds. Readers and audiences now have their own double image of Shakespeare's England and the relation of their own time and place to those of Shakespeare and the Italy that he represented in his works. There is a historical element to Shakespeare's Italy and England, the typology that occupies the heart of this chapter, even if in the First Folio (1623) John Heminge and Henry Condell classified plays about the English past, not those about the Roman or British past, to be histories. England and Britain, especially under the Elizabeth Tudor, were not the same. The Welsh origin of the Tudors and the Scottish provenance of the Stuarts complicated matters, but when under a Stuart Heminge and Condell came to decide on the kinds of plays, they stuck with comedies, histories, and tragedies alone (given in that order on the title page), and that history was English history. Still, there is some slippage in the plays as in the culture about the relations among Roman Britain, Britain, and England. Elizabeth I and James I were descendents of Henry VII, the figure that Richmond in Shakespeare's *Richard III* represents, uniting the Houses of York and Lancaster at the end of the War of the Roses in 1485, part of what E. M. W. Tillyard so aptly called the Tudor myth, something later historicists came to question. Tillyard, a good Miltonist as well, saw Shakespeare's English histories as an epic of England, a kind of implied counterpart to Milton's religious epic.[3] Henry VII was the same king who sent John Cabot, his Italian mariner, out to the western Atlantic in search of Asia as an answer to Columbus, the Italian who had made such a bold move with his landfall in the western part of the Ocean Sea. It seems, then, that Shakespeare's images of Italy and England are not one thing.

Shakespeare's Italy is, for the purpose of this chapter, a matter of the relations between England and Italy, how the translation of culture and empire from Italy to England is enacted in the poet's works. Italy and Rome, the Italian and the Roman, are terms that pervade Shakespeare's *œuvre*, which is not surprising once it be considered that Rome and Italy were the centers of the Roman empire, of which Britain was a part; of the western Christian or Catholic Church, with which the Church of England had broken in the 1530s; of the Renaissance and the commercial revolution, especially in accounting and banking. Italy had been, and was again, the center of Europe, which England was decidedly not. Other countries, like France, Spain, the German states, and England had political and cultural power, but Italy had the authority of ancient Rome, the papacy, and the rediscovery of classical learning. While Italy had lost some of its power to Spain, its finance and its mariners, like Columbus, Caboto, Vespucci, and Verrazzano, had helped in the expansion of European trade and settlement in the Americas. About a hundred years after Columbus, Shakespeare began to write his poetry and plays, and their Italian dimension helped to suggest the continued influence of Italy in English culture.

Shakespeare's Italy and Rome occur early in his writing and maintain a prominent place until his last works. For example, *The Rape of Lucrece*, a minor epic, represented a critical moment in the history of Rome, while the sonnets reshaped a form that Petrarch had made his own; the comedies, which owed much to Terence and Plautus, often had Italian settings; the histories defined the English nation in part against Rome and Italy; the tragedies, like *Titus Andronicus, Julius Caesar, Othello, Coriolanus,* and *Antony and Cleopatra,* had Roman and Italian dimensions and settings; the romances also play on the Italian theme, as *Cymbeline* revisits the relations between ancient Britain and imperial Rome and *The Tempest* performs a Virgilian motif and explores questions of governance, cultural contact, and expansion on an island between Italy and Africa but refracted through Bermuda and the New World. By definition, Shakespeare's Italy and Rome are themselves, but they are also Shakespeare's England, a putative and fictional place that plays out the aspirations and anxieties of the culture and country in which the playwright lived.

Although this chapter will suggest a range of Shakespearean constructions of Italy and Rome, it will focus on ancient Rome and medieval and Renaissance Italy as they relate directly to ancient Britain and to Shakespeare's representation of England. Other work has focused on various aspects of Shakespeare and Rome or Italy, so that to duplicate these efforts would not help to advance our understanding of the topic.[4] The chapter argues that Shakespeare's play and England were haunted by Italy as a source of the classical and imperial past, the center of Catholicism against which English reformers had rebelled, the question of race in imperial expansion. What distinguishes this chapter is an analysis of the *translatio imperii* or the translation of empire as a central concern. This translation is also a cultural matter, a *translatio studii*, which would include the use of geography and history in the universities, at court, among the explorers, and in plays and poems.[5] How at the brink of empire did England look into the importance of its colonial past in the Roman empire, of its relation to Italian mariners and financiers in its own exploration of the New World, of its own recent break with the Roman church, of its own anxiety over race and new lands, of its coming to terms with the classical past (particularly the Virgilian motif), and of its facing of the incommensurability of this "New World" with the Old World? Part of its view depended on a typology between ancient Rome and Britain, Renaissance Italy and England, Europe and America, and combinations thereof, that contributed to a construction, in Shakespeare's works, a framework of meaning through analogy. The

myth of Brutus, the grandson of Aeneas, as the founder of Britain, a story that seems
to have begun with Geoffrey of Monmouth and later been taken up by chroniclers
like Richard Grafton and poets such as Michael Drayton, reiterated this typology.
The political theatre of Elizabeth brought to life such an analogy between ancient
Rome and Elizabethan England. For example, as Roy Strong observes, in November
1588, to celebrate the defeat of the Spanish Armada, Elizabeth emulated the ancient
Romans by riding a "chariot" in triumph.[6] In the wake of Virgil, Columbus, Polydore
Virgil, and others, through an exploration of Rome and Italy in English, Shakespeare,
paradoxically, helps to create an Englishness, the beginnings of a strong new vernacular
and literature, a prolepsis of a new hegemony. The method of this chapter is to read
Shakespeare in a historical context in order to place his work in a new light. The use
of New World materials, which is keeping with my training in history and literature,
should contribute to that illumination. By the time that Othello and Caliban appear on
the English stage, much else had proceeded them: Columbus on the Natives, Caboto's
or Cabot's commission, and Vespucci and Verrazzano on the New World all affected
the views of Richard Hakluyt, John Hawkins, Walter Raleigh, Thomas Harriot, and
others who would have written on English expansion, aspirations, and trade (including
slavery) in Shakespeare's lifetime. Shakespeare's Italy, then, is also Italy's Shakespeare.[7]

This next part of the chapter will examine Rome and Italy in *Cymbeline* and *The
Tempest*, which are located in part or exclusively beyond Rome and Italy. These texts
have perhaps even more implications for alterity and colonialism than those with
mainly Italian settings.[8] The subsequent section will discuss the role of Rome and Italy
in the English histories, which involves an intensification of the superimposition of,
and typology between, Italy and England. Other Italian allusions and constructions
will occur incidentally to these main concerns.

ROME AND ITALY IN *CYMBELINE* AND *THE TEMPEST*

The use of Rome and Italy extends to conflicts with other nations and to the question of colonialism. The alterity that Romans, Venetians, Milanese and Neopolitans,
and other Italians experience in Shakespeare's texts are part of the otherness from the
Elizabethan and Jacobean audiences in England. The English faced the exoticism of
ancient Rome and contemporary Italy in addition to the more exotic cultures encountered through their representatives like Cleopatra, Othello, and Caliban. In *Cymbeline*
it is Rome itself that becomes doubly different from the English, who are presented
with their British past when Britain was a colony of Rome. Jachimo is a Roman other.
The Tempest, set between Italy and Africa in a typically Virgilian setting, does not have
an English character in it, despite the obvious fact that all the characters speak English
and there is an undertext of some English sources concerning the New World and a
slight allusory mechanism that mentions Bermuda, which, although a place encountered by the Spaniards and others, would become an English colony. Shakespeare's
Italy is exotic, but it is, despite its difference, doubly viewed as Shakespeare's England.

The colonial past of Britain as the future hope and inheritor of Rome is a central
concern of *Cymbeline*, which is set in Britain and Italy. Here the superimposition
and typology between the English and the Italian is most visible. The tragicomedy
and romance conventions of this play represent war and division between Rome and

Britain, often in terms of personal conflict and jealousy, but lead ultimately to a comic ending, a reconciliation (like that in *All's Well That Ends Well*, another Shakespearean play with a comic resolution set in Italy) of a falsely jealous husband and his wrongly accused virtuous wife. The reconciled "marriage" in *Cymbeline* is also the reunion of Rome and Britain. Before we arrive at that end, it is important to speak about the center of the play—III.i—a scene that explains the historic connection between Rome and Britain and that represents the same era as do *Julius Caesar* and *Antony and Cleopatra*. Octavius Caesar is now Augustus Caesar. Caius Lucius attends Cymbeline's court, and their exchange provides a historical explanation that in a different play might have appeared at the beginning:

> CYMBELINE. Now say, what would Augustus Caesar with us?

> LUCIUS. When Julius Caesar (whose remembrance yet
> Lives in men's eyes, and will to ears and tongues
> Be theme and hearing ever) was in this Britain,
> And conquer'd it, Cassibelan, thine uncle
> (Famous in Caesar's praises no whit less
> Than in his feats deserving it), for him
> And his succession granted Rome a tribute,
> Yearly three thousand pounds, which, by thee, lately
> Is left untender'd.
> (*Cym*, III.i.1–9).[9]

This recent division between Britain and Rome, which seemed to have reached an accommodation in the years before, will continue because, under the influence of the queen and her son, Cloten, Cymbeline refuses to continue the tribute, an action that leads to war. This exchange contrasts different readings of the history of the relations of Rome and Britain—the pastoral view of mutually beneficial peace and the tragic aspect of Rome's enslavement of a once-free Britain:

> CYMBELINE. You must know,
> Till the injurious Romans did extort
> This tribute from us, we were free. Caesar's ambition,
> Which swell'd so much that it did almost stretch
> The sides o' th' world, against all color here
> Did put the yoke upon's; which to shake off
> Becomes a warlike people, whom we reckon
> Ourselves to be. We do say then to Caesar,
> Our ancestor was that Mulmutius which
> Ordain'd our laws, whose use the sword of Caesar
> Hath too much mangled, whose repair and franchise
> Shall (by the power we hold) be our good deed,
> Though Rome be therefore angry. Mulmutius made our laws,
> Who was the first of Britain which did put
> His brows within a golden crown, and call'd
> Himself a king.

LUCIUS. I am sorry, Cymbeline,
That I am to pronounce Augustus Caesar
(Caesar, that hath moe kings his servants than
Thyself domestic officers) thine enemy.
Receive it from me, then: war and confusion
In Caesar's name pronounce I 'gainst thee; look
For fury not to be resisted. Thus defied,
I thank thee for myself.

CYMBELINE. Thou art welcome, Caius.
Thy Caesar knighted me; my youth I spent
Much under him; of him I gather'd honor,
Which he to seek of me again, perforce,
Behooves me keep at utterance.
(III.i.46–72)

This double vision of Rome, the benefactor-protector and the intruder-enforcer, dwells in Cymbeline's language, for he admits that he was with Caesar and was knighted by him, while he defies Caesar and Rome. Part of the reason for seeking such freedom for Britain, Cymbeline asserts, is the precedent of the armed rebellions of the Pannonians and Dalmatians for their "liberties" (III.i.72–5). For Britain, Rome has been a source of strength and honor and a force that has erased its own preimperial history. The warlikeness to which Cymbeline refers suggests a question of virility, that Britons are brave men who by definition should govern themselves.

Shakespeare often uses a diptych of public and private realms that mirror each other, so the double is doubled and the multiplicity overlaps so that the public involves the private and the converse. In the private sphere of the play, Jachimo comes to represent, for Imogen and for Britain, the aspects of contemporary Italy that are condemned by characters in Shakespeare in English Renaissance books, whether they are railing at the church, the Machiavel, or intrigue and corruption in politics.[10] While speaking with Pisanio, the servant of her husband, Posthumous, Imogen apostrophizes Jachimo and rails against Italy, which some lines before in this scene she had called "drug-damned" and had accused, as if the country were the false woman Jachimo had "made up" as a seductress of Posthumous, of having "outcraftied" her husband (III.iv.15). Imogen continues to rail: "Some jay of Italy / (Whose mother was her painting) hath betray'd him"; and she moves her speech against the foundations of Rome itself:

True honest men being heard, like false Aeneas,
Were, in his time, thought false; and Sinon's weeping
Did scandal many a holy tear, took pity
From most true wretchedness.
(III.iv.49–51, 58–61)

The false appearances of Italy appear here in Imogen's excoriation of Italian vice. She also reinterprets Aeneas, a mythical founder of Rome and a recurrent figure in Shakespeare's Italy, as being as deceptive as Sinon, the Trojan who betrayed Troy to the Greeks, someone whose figure Lucrece would scratch in the tapestry in Shakespeare's narrative poem. Jachimo wants Imogen to think her husband has betrayed her: she seems to be thinking of how Aeneas abandoned Dido of Carthage, the subject of Marlowe's eponymous play, to found Rome, which is, in the story Jachimo has helped her to make, the place of the betrayal that Imogen experiences. This stuff of romance has cultural and political implications as it refracts an ambivalence toward Italy present in Shakespeare's England.

This same Jachimo leads an Italian force, including "the confiners / And gentlemen of Italy," to join Lucius in order to put down the British uprising (IV.ii.337–8). This invasion creates some doubt and doubleness in the British characters over their own identities. For example, Posthumous, who wears Roman and British clothes in the play, has a dream of Jupiter, the Greco-Roman god, who prophesies his personal reunion and the regaining of peace and harmony between Britain and Rome. Posthumous asks Lucius, "my lord of Rome," "Call forth your soothsayer" to construct an interpretation of Posthumous' dream-vision of Jupiter (V.v.425–26f.). Lucius' Soothsayer, using Latin as an aid to interpretation (playing on *mollis aer* and *mulier*), provides a reading of happiness for Posthumous and "peace and plenty" for Britain (V.v.443–52). Even though forgiveness has been granted to Jachimo, who has represented the darker side of Italy, and peace has been proclaimed, there is some doubt about this "construction" (see V.v.432). Britain might be the heir to Rome—each needs the other—but the paradoxical British submission in triumph appears to be expressed in Roman signs religious, political, and, to some extent, linguistic. In response to the Soothsayer, Cymbeline brings Britain back within Roman hermeneutics:

> Well,
> My peace we will begin. And, Caius Lucius,
> Although the victor, we submit to Caesar
> And to the Roman empire, promising
> To pay our wonted tribute.
> (V.v.458–62)

In a kind of interpretative duet, the Soothsayer and Cymbeline reconstruct British and Roman harmony after the chaotic interruption of the ill-meaning queen. Jupiter, who has already performed in a visionary masque for Posthumous, plays a central role for the British king and the Roman reader of signs. The Soothsayer concludes:

> The fingers of the pow'rs above do tune
> The harmony of this peace. The vision
> Which I made known to Lucius, ere the stroke
> Of yet this scarce-cold battle, at this instant
> Is full accomplish'd: for the Roman eagle,
> From south to west on wing soaring aloft,
> Lessen'd herself and in the beams o' th' sun
> So vanish'd; which foreshow'd our princely eagle,
> Th'imperial Caesar, Caesar, should again unite
> His favour with the radiant Cymbeline,
> Which shines here in the west.
> (V.v.466–77)

The signs of Roman heavenly powers, eagle, and Caesar confer, through this Roman reading that Posthumous has requested, their blessing on the containment of the British rebellion and the reestablishment of political peace. To end the play, Cymbeline praises the gods and proclaims, "Let / A Roman and a British ensign wave / Friendly together" (V.v.479–81). He declares that they should march through "Lud's Town" or London, whose name the queen had wrongly attributed to Cymbeline's grandfather, Lud, when in fact London comes from the Latin (III.i.29–33), to ratify the peace "in the temple of great Jupiter" (V.v.481–3). The last couplet of the play, spoken by Cymbeline, depends on the rhyme of "cease" and "peace": there was never an end of war such as this (V.v.484–5). It is as though ancient Rome and Britain embrace in order to translate empire to the new Rome, the new Britain—England—when the wicked queen, a traitor, and the stage Machiavel, Jachimo, perhaps a caricature of Renaissance Italy, provide warnings. If Jachimo represents an English conception of the corruption and deceit of Renaissance Italy, then that "misrepresentation" leaves the way for Renaissance England to carry on the empire of the ancient Romans.

Italy had provided mariners and bankers for the expansion of Spain, England, and France. Genoa and Venice were great rivals within Italy. While Venice had to contend with the Turks, other Italians also looked westward for profit. Concerning the voyages of Columbus and Cabot, Italian ambassadors reported to their families and governments. For example, the dynamic between Italy and England can be glimpsed in a letter of August 23, 1497, that Lorenzo Pasqualigo wrote to his brothers about John Cabot (Giovanni Caboto): "That Venetian of ours who went with a small ship from Bristol to find new islands has come back and says he has discovered the mainland [*terra firma*] 700 leagues away. . . . And these English run after him like mad."[11] Renaissance Italy relied on economic power and did not achieve any extensive expansion overseas as Portugal, Spain, France, England and the Netherlands were to accomplish, with Italian expertise, in the sixteenth and seventeenth centuries.[12] While *The Tempest* is about an island between Italy and Africa and is a play about Italians encountering the strange inhabitants of a Mediterranean island, it also represents English aspirations about empire, about the westering of empire in the tradition Virgil sets out in the *Aeneid*. This Virgilian motif is a vital undercurrent, or subtext, in this play, and is something that critics have noticed for some time.[13] The concerns of this play about authority and dynasty are in keeping with key themes of history and epic. Besides a series of Virgilian echoes, the matter of the "widow Dido" and the "widower Aeneas" of Carthage and Italy, which takes up part of the story in the *Aeneid*, is debated in somewhat comic and pedantic fashion by Gonzalo, Sebastian, Adrian, Antonio, and Alonzo in II.i (see *Temp.*, II.i.68–112, esp. 75, 78).[14] Like Aeneas, Alonso sails from Carthage to Naples. This allusionary Virgilian field suggests a context for the westering of empire, of the translation of empire that underwrites not simply the ostensible Italian and Mediterranean world of Aeneas, Prospero, and Ferdinand but also the imperial hopes of Shakespeare's England, as the audience would know of the shipwreck in Bermuda, a news event of the recent past that was described in the sources that Shakespeare draws on.

This typological scheme of empire keeps the doubleness of Italy and England in Shakespeare's plays. The typology is more complicated, as Carthage and England were also types of each other. In England Dido's first name was sometimes given as Elissa and, in Charles Stephanus' *Dictionarium historicum* (1595), Eliza, so that there is a doubleness or typological identity between Dido and Elizabeth I of England.[15] Just as the Romans had distinguished themselves from the Greeks by constructing a Trojan origin, the English, in this instance, differentiated themselves from the Romans. England was the imperial inheritor of Rome but with a difference. The English were not Renaissance Italians, but they did draw on them for positive and negative models. Renaissance Italy in *The Tempest* was as ambivalent a place as Rome was in *Cymbeline*: Antonio and Prospero, negative and positive examples of Italy, correspond to Jachimo and Augustus Caesar. Jachimo and Antonio are Machiavellian.

English colonialism, however indebted it was to John and Sebastian Cabot (Caboto), became increasingly an enterprise that focused on the rivals of Spain, France, and Holland. The establishment of Virginia and the shipwreck in Bermuda was the backdrop and source for important though few allusions in *The Tempest*, something that Edmund Malone called attention to in 1808. The voyage of William Somers from England to Virginia in the summer of 1609 provided a shipwreck that is typologically connected to the wrecks of Aeneas and Alonso in the context of Rome and of modern Italy. The typology extends to images of the Old World and the New World, a good example of which, as Stephen Orgel has noted, occurs in Thomas Harriot's *A Briefe and True Report of the New Found Land of Virginia* (1590), where he connects the ancient Britons with the Natives of Virginia.[16] Examining the drawings of John White, who drew for Walter Raleigh in 1585 and 1588, and the copper plates Theodor de Bry made of them, which is produced in the Harriot volume alongside the text, an English translation by Richard Hakluyt, it is interesting to see, after the original picture of Adam and Eve in the garden and the maps of Virginia, a typology between Virginian Natives and Picts. The drawings begin with the Indians and move to the Picts: the title page dividing the pictures of these groups explains that these figures of the ancient Britons are there "to showe how that the Inhabitants of the great Bretannie haue bin in times past as sauuage as those of Virginia."[17] Perhaps, then, Caliban is as much about Virginia as about mythological creatures in a Virgilian world. The typology works on multiple levels, and its shifts involve ancient Britain, Rome, Renaissance Italy, and England. Besides the British past, English history, as set out in Shakespeare's histories, has an Italian dimension. This is another layer in an intricate relation between England and Italy in the Shakespearean canon.

ROME AND ITALY IN THE ENGLISH HISTORY PLAYS

The English histories also call on ancient Rome and Italy of the Middle Ages and Renaissance in order to create a typology and comparative framework for Shakespeare's England. The translation of imperial ideals, a colonial relation with ancient Britain, and the clash with the papacy informs, at an allusionary level, one important part of the scaffolding for epic drama of the English nation that Shakespeare represents during the 1590s. This Italian intersection is seen much more readily in the Roman plays but deserves attention in the English history plays.[18] Italy haunts England even as it attempts to tell its own story.

Shakespeare's histories cover the period, on and off, from the first years of the thirteenth century until the birth of Elizabeth I in 1533. The first and second tetralogies range from the 1390s to 1485, although Shakespeare revisits the later historical period in the second group of four histories. Here, I will discuss in the order of composition, as much as possible, the Roman dimension and medieval and early modern Italian elements in Shakespeare's epic drama of England.

The allusions to Rome and a sense of the translation of empire occur in other rival Europeans nations, like France, something that the first tetralogy suggests. Shakespeare's epic representation of the story of England also involves its dynastic struggles in France and the prelude to its break with Rome. This discussion will begin with Thomas More and end with Henry VIII, partly as a means of showing how the break with Rome defined early modern England. The *Thomas More* fragment may have been censored because of this still-contentious episode in the reign of Elizabeth I's father and owing to the tensions between England and Catholic powers and the internal frictions and pressures between Protestants and Catholics. The birth of Elizabeth in *Henry VIII* might have been a retroactive prophecy of hope for Shakespeare and his contemporaries, but she was excommunicated in 1570, and her conflict with Catholic power within and without her kingdom was one of the markers of her reign. Rome was something against which England defined itself even after the break with the Catholic Church.

Shakespeare's first tetralogy contains allusions to Rome, Italy, and Machiavel that, although not frequent, are reminders of the ongoing relation of England to Italy. Shakespeare was writing about England's Catholic past after the rupture of the Reformation. For example, in *1 Henry VI*, the Bastard of Orleans tells Charles of Joan of Arc, who had a vision of driving the English from France: "The spirit of deep prophecy she hath, / Exceeding the nine sibyls of old Rome" (*1HVI*, I.ii.55–6). Along with Warwick, York excoriates Joan (Pucelle), accuses her of being loose sexually and, in this context, when she names one of her lovers as the father of her child, declares: "Alanson, that notorious Machevile?" (V.iv.74).[19] In this play ambivalent references to Italy occurs: Joan is said to be an ancient Roman sibyl, but York thinks of her countryman as Machiavellian. Another Roman allusion suggests a division between church and state, Rome and England. Over the nature of legitimate rule, Gloucester, the Lord Protector, and Warwick clash with the cleric, Winchester, who exclaims, "Rome shall remedy this." Warwick replies with an irreverent pun that challenges the authority of the Roman church "Roam thither then" (III.i.51). In I.iii. Gloucester had threatened Winchester with violence, including the pulling of his beard, the trampling of his cardinal's hat, and the beating of him with a rope, which he rhymes with Winchester's invocation of the pope (I.iii.28–91, esp. 44–53). In *2 Henry VI* the queen tells her lover, Suffolk, her wishes concerning her husband:

> I would the college of the Cardinals
> Would choose him Pope, and carry him to Rome,
> And set the triple crown upon his head;
> That were a state fit for his holiness.
> (*2HVI*, I.iii.61–4)

The unworldly king is worthy of being bishop of Rome but not to rule such a kingdom as England. In *3 Henry VI* Gloucester recalls the matter of Troy, the imperial theme of Greeks and Trojans, the prolepsis of Rome, along with Machiavelli, the intrigue of politics in Renaissance Florence:

> I'll play the orator as well as Nestor,
> Deceive more slily that Ulysses could,
> And, like a Sinon, take another Troy.
> I can add colours to the chameleon,
> Change shapes with Protheus for advantages,
> And set the murderous Machiavel to school.
> Can I do this, and cannot get a crown?
> Tut, were it farther off, I'll pluck it down.
> (*3HVI*, III.ii.188–95)

Here, the Lord Protector would be as deceptive as the Greeks before Troy and teach Machiavelli, so that this translation of empire shows the most powerful person in England outstripping the clever deceit of his antecedents in Greece and Italy. Whereas Sinon was anathema to Lucrece (Imogen also alludes to him), Gloucester embraces him as a model for behavior in the conduct of state (see *Lucrece*, 1520–68).[20]

The division of church and state, Rome and England, that engaged Gloucester in his conflict with Winchester, is also a central concern of *King John*, which represents the strife between the pope and the king of England in the early thirteenth century. This medieval setting foreshadows the later conflict between Henry VIII and Rome. When Pandulph introduces himself as a Milanese cardinal and accuses King John of keeping the legate of Pope Innocent, "Stephen Langton, chosen Archbishop / Of Canterbury, from that holy see" and demands that John reverse that action, the King of England, in the presence of the King of France, openly defies Pandulph:

> What earthly name to interrogatories
> Can taste the free breath of a sacred king?
> Thou canst not, Cardinal, devise a name
> So slight, unworthy, and ridiculous,
> To charge me to an answer, as the Pope.
> Tell him this tale, and from the mouth of England
> Add thus much more, that no Italian priest
> Shall tithe or toll in our dominions;
> But as we under [God] are supreme head,
> So, under Him that great supremacy,
> Where we do reign we will alone uphold,
> Without th' assistance of a mortal hand.
> So tell the Pope, all reverence set apart
> To him and his usurp'd authority.
> (*KJ*, III.i.135–60)

This proleptic clash between England and Rome leads to the isolation of the English monarch and nation from the great continental powers like France. It is as if Henry VIII's Act of Supremacy were being rehearsed here, in a later time representing an earlier period. King Philip of France cannot accept King John's view of the papacy and of Italian influence:

KING PHILIP. Brother of England, you blaspheme in this.

KING JOHN. Though you and all the kings of Christendom
Are led so grossly by this meddling priest,
Dreading the curse that money may buy out,
And by the merit of vild gold, dross, dust,
Purchase corrupted pardon of a man,
Who in that sale sells pardon from himself;
Though you and all the rest so grossly led,
This juggling witchcraft with revenue cherish,
Yet I alone, alone do me oppose
Against the Pope, and count his friends my foes.
(III.i.161–71)

Such defiance prompts the papal legate to excommunicate John, something that
Elizabeth later suffered (about twenty-five years before Shakespeare wrote this play;
III.i.172–9). There is a kind of temporal, and as well as spatial, typology that connects
John, Henry VIII, and Elizabeth I here in relation to the pope and the Church of Rome.

Pandulph's words cause Constance, the widow of Geffrey, John's elder brother, to
curse the legate and the power in Rome that he represents: "O, lawful let it be / That
I have room with Rome to curse a while!" which prompts Pandulph to claim that
he has "law and warrant" to curse John as a heretic. Constance, however, argues that

Law cannot give my child his kingdom here,
For he that holds his kingdom holds the law;
Therefore since law itself is perfect wrong,
How can the law forbid my tongue to curse?
(III.i.180–90)

Different interpretations of "law" occur here. At the English court, John is not alone
in defying the power of the Roman church. Like Caliban, Constance learns how to
curse the colonial power. If Renaissance England takes on the power of ancient Rome
as a means of creating an ambiance or a mythology that might allow its imperial
expansion, it also has to come to terms with its role as colony in the Roman empire
and vassal to the bishop of Rome—the pope. The key question in *King John* is: should
the king of England or the pope in Rome appoint the archbishop of Canterbury to
be the spiritual leader in England? The papal representative also knows how to curse
and to call on other temporal powers, such as France, to fight the pope's war against
the defiant English. Pandulph promises Philip of France the same fate as John: he
must "submit himself to Rome" (III.i.191–8). Shakespeare cannot miss extending the
most dramatic tension here. Philip of France, who has his hand in John's is literally
caught between the pope and the duke of Austria on the one hand and Constance
and Elinor, John's mother. The women are like a chorus, but they cannot save John,
who, like Cymbeline, seems to be caught in a colonialism or vassalage. The scene and
the conflict have many other characters urging Philip one way or another. As part of
the tension of the dialectic, Philip's son, Lewis, would rather him fight England on

his son's wedding day to Blanch, the Spanish niece of King John, than to keep peace within the family (III.i.300–301f.). Rome has that power.

At the beginning of act 5, John's submission to the pope signifies the power of Rome over England. This obeisance occurs in King John's palace in England when Pandulph is there:

> KING JOHN. Thus have I yielded up into your hand
> The circle of my glory. [*Giving the crown.*]
>
> PANDULPH. Take again
> From this my hand, as holding of the Pope,
> Your sovereign greatness and authority.
>
> KING JOHN. Now keep your holy word; go meet the French;
> And from his Holiness use all your power
> To stop their marches 'fore we are inflam'd.
> Our discontented counties do revolt;
> Our people quarrel with obedience,
> Swearing allegiance and the love of soul
> To stranger blood, to foreign royalty.
> This inundation of mistemp'red humor
> Rests by you only to be qualified.
> Then pause not; for the present time's so sick
> That present med'cine must be minist'red
> Or overthrow incurable ensues.
>
> PANDULPH. It was my breath that blew this tempest up,
> Upon your stubborn usage of the Pope;
> But since you are a gentle convertite,
> My tongue shall hush again this storm of war,
> And make fair weather in your blust'ring land.
> On this Ascension-day, remember well,
> Upon your oath of service to the Pope,
> Go I to make the French lay down their arms. *Exit*
> (V.i.1–23)

In this ceremony the authority of the pope legitimizes the hold of John and his heirs on the English crown. John's defiance, like Cymbeline's, leads to containment in the Roman fold. In a translation of empire the pope, as bishop of Rome, takes up where the ancient Roman emperors left off. This defiance of Rome was not in England alone. Lewis of France also defies papal authority when it suits him, for when Pandulph announces,

> King John hath reconcil'd
> Himself to Rome, his spirit is come in,
> That so stood out against the holy Church,
> The great metropolis and see of Rome

Lewis includes in his answer a challenge to Rome:

> And now it is half-conquer'd, must I back
> Because that John hath made his peace with Rome?
> Am I Rome's slave? What penny hath Rome borne?
> What men provided? what munition sent,
> To underprop this action?
> (V.ii.69–72, 95–9)

Shakespeare also mediates England's relation to Rome through other territories like France.

Foreign forces threaten England, which is also divided against itself. John himself, probably against historical record but part of a legend in Shakespeare's era, soon dies as a result of a monk's poison (V.vi.23f.). Whereas Holinshed has John die of an ague after destroying the countryside, John Foxe, in *Acts and Monuments*, a Protestant book, tells the story of a monk, Simon, who poisoned the king.[21] The Bastard ends the play with a call for unity in England and for the loyalty of its nobility. Part of his speech relies on strong myths of unity and independence. The Bastard proclaims that

> This England never did, nor never shall,
> Lie at the proud foot of a conqueror,
> But when it first did help to wound itself

and, in the last two lines of this history play, says: 'Nought shall make us rue, / If England to itself do rest but true' (V.vii.112–14, 117–18). In the first tetralogy, which precedes *King John* in time of composition, and in the second tetralogy, which is begun about the same time, civil war and unrest similar to that which the Bastard describes plague England.

The civil unrest in England is sometimes framed with images of the corruption of Renaissance Italy. Speaking about Richard II and his court, York, his uncle, makes such a comparison when he addresses his brother, John of Gaunt:

> Report of fashions in proud Italy,
> Whose manners still our tardy, apish nation
> Limps after in base imitation.
> Where doth the world thrust forth a vanity—
> So it be new, there's no respect how vile—
> That is not quickly buzz'd into his ears?
> (*RII*, II.i.21–6)

England imitates Italy in a colonial way, a kind of importation from the center of Renaissance culture to a place at the margins of Europe, literally and figuratively. The king has given himself over to Italian fashion, and, in the context of this narrative of the English nation with some of its nativist overtones, this mimicry and importation weakens the traditions and resolve of England.

Richard had exiled Bullingbrook and Mowbray, the latter of whose wanderings ended in Italy. This courtier's death is typological: his death in Italy corresponds to Richard's in England. They would die while Bullingbrook would flourish. In the deposition scene (IV.i), where Richard loses his crown and suspects that he would die, Carlisle announces the death of Mowbray:

> Many a time hath banish'd Norfolk fought
> For Jesu Christ in glorious Christian field,
> Streaming the ensign of the Christian cross
> Against black pagans, Turks, and Saracens,
> And toil'd with works of war, retir'd himself
> To Italy; and there at Venice gave
> His body to that pleasant country's earth,
> And his pure soul unto his captain Christ,
> Under whose colors he had fought so long.
> (IV.i.92–100)

This crusader, who had lamented his loss of England and English with the exile and become involved in his own travel narrative, fought the "enemies" of Europe and died in a pastoral Italy now purified in Christ. Bullingbrook's rivals, Richard and Mowbray, died alienated from England, one from within and the other from without. The new king himself claims that he will go on a pilgrimage as a means of salving his conscience, but, near the opening of *1 Henry IV*, the threat of civil war chases these thoughts of foreign peregrinations. The Bastard's words at the end of *King John* are suggestive for the situation of England after the fall of Richard II.

Other uses of Italy occur in the rest of the second tetralogy. In *2 Henry IV* Rome is an allusion in Falstaff's euphuistic letter that the Prince reads as part of the comic texture of this history: "I will imitate the honorable Romans in brevity" (*2HIV*, II.ii.123). Falstaff tells John of Lancaster, Hal's brother, that he took Sir John Colevile: "He saw me, and yielded; that I may justly say with the hook-nos'd fellow of Rome, 'There, cousin, I came, saw, and overcame'" (*2HIV*, 40–3). Falstaff's invocation of Julius Caesar sets up a comic typology and qualifies the dignity of, and reverence for, Rome.[22] The comic use of Roman allusion, in which the model of military honor and strategy qualify the high seriousness of the translation of empire, continues in *Henry V*. The Hostess remembers the death of Falstaff, when he talked about the Whore of Babylon, a term that Protestants often applied to the Roman Catholic Church, which they thought of as the strumpet of Revelation 17:3–6 (*HV*, II.iii.38–9, see also 989n38–9). Comic and "serious" uses of the classical past modulate in the play. There are also more serious instances of foolishness in the play. For example, the Lord High Constable of France, when speaking to his king, warns that Henry V models himself on Lucius Junius Brutus, the Roman consul who pretended to be a fool in order to avoid the suspicions of his uncle, King Tarquin:

> And you shall find his vanities forespent
> Were but the outside of the Roman Brutus,
> Covering discretion with a coat of folly.
> (*HV*, II.iv.36–8, see 990 37n)

Tarquin haunts Shakespeare's works beyond *Lucrece*, even if sometimes in a minor key. A deadly seriousness also imbues these classical allusions to expansion and empire. In trying to inspire the troops, Henry V calls their fathers "so many Alexanders," great conquerors all (III.i.19). Figures from the Greco-Roman past are invoked to bolster the English present of the play and the glorious past for Shakespeare and his contemporary audience.

A mixture of valor and comedy contribute to the character of Fluellen. A brave Welshman much admired by the king but also an officer caught up in a comic contest and brawl with the aureate hollow man and rhetorical soldier, Pistol, who is full of tags that refer to a heroic past, Fluellen calls upon ancient Rome for his inspiration. Having already praised Captain Jamy—"By Cheshu, he will maintain his argument as well as any military man in the world, in the disciplines of the pristine wars of the Romans" (III.ii.79–82), he looks to Captain Macmorris for a dispute on "the disciplines of the war, the Roman wars," a use of Rome's military past to shed light on their present wars (III.ii.94–101). Nor does Fluellen stop there. He likens the Duke of Exeter to Agamemnon but also says that the ancient at the bridge (which the audience later learns is Pistol) "is as valiant a man as Mark Antony" (III.vi.7, 13–14). Pistol's arrival, not to mention what the audience already knows about him, qualifies this great praise, and the relation between the captain-historian and his Antony turns into a comic brawl because the two men differ over the fate of Bardolph. The Dolphin (Dauphin) of France takes himself seriously when few others, even among the French, do: he compares his horse to Pegasus and claims that the music of his hoof are more beautiful than the pipe of Hermes (III.vii.14–18). Sometimes the use of the classical past is an object of humor and an indication of pomposity. Like Pistol, the Dolphin (Dauphin) is an empty drum. On the other hand, in his debate with Bates and Williams, Henry V uses Greek mythology to help make his point (IV.i.272–7). The English captain, Gower, is happy to show how shifting and mistaken Fluellen's historical geography can be in his role as an agent of the translation of empire, but Fluellen holds on to his comic typology of Alexander the Great and Henry of Monmouth (Henry V): "I warrant you shall find, in the comparisons between Macedon and Monmouth, that the situations, look you, is both alike" (Iv.vii.24–6, see 11–21). In case anyone missed the use of typology (Thomas Aquinas had spoken about types and shadows in one of his hymns), he reiterates, in spite of Gower's skepticism, his belief in such comparisons between Alexander and Henry: "If you mark Alexander's life well, Harry of Monmouth's life is come after it indifferent well, for there is figures in all things" and again: "I speak but in the figures and comparisons of it," and he goes on to make another analogy between the two warriors, the emperors (IV.vii.31–3, 43–4).

Greece and Rome act as a typological scaffolding in this epic story of England's struggle with and in France. Whereas Fluellen compares Henry V to Alexander the Great, the Chorus, ushering in the fifth act, likens him to a triumphant Caesar:

> How London doth pour out her citizens!
> The Mayor and all his brethren in best sort,
> Like to the senators of th' antique Rome,
> With the plebeians swarming at their heels,
> Go forth and fetch their conqu'ring Caesar in;
> As by a lower but loving likelihood,
> Were now the general of our gracious Empress,
> As in good time he may, from Ireland coming,

Bringing rebellion broached on his sword,
How many would the peaceful city quit,
To welcome him!
(Chorus V:24–34)

Roman triumphs in Shakespeare, whether descriptions of the victorious return to Rome of Titus, Caesar, Octavius Caesar, or Coriolanus, can be problematic: Titus alienates his enemies; Caesar stirs up jealousy with his popularity and victories; Octavius would lead Cleopatra in triumph, but she denies him the pleasure; Coriolanus insults the plebeians after saving them through his victory. By association Shakespeare shifts from the ancient Roman Caesar to his queen, Elizabeth I, to whom he gives the title Empress. The allusion to the "General" is problematic, for Essex, the apparent subject of the allusion, a hero who was a commander in Ireland, was to rebel against the queen in 1601.[23] An intricate typology or association of Caesar-Empress-Harry-Essex arises here. Ireland for England, like the Canary Islands for Spain, had served as a harbinger of overseas colonies, especially those in the New World.[24] The typology of English interests in France in the past with its Irish and New World voyages to the Arctic, Newfoundland, and Virginia from the 1570s provides another framework that looks ahead to *The Tempest*.

The religious scope and geographical reach of England had changed from the end of the fifteenth century onwards. The voyages of Columbus and Cabot as well as the advent of Luther's theses, Calvin's *Institutes*, and Henry VIII's divorce changed England. As Shakespeare represents in *King John*, England of the Middle Ages also had its tensions with Rome. In one of his last plays, *Henry VIII* (1613), possibly written in collaboration with John Fletcher, Shakespeare revisited the disjunction between Rome and England. Shakespeare probably needed to wait for Elizabeth I to die before writing about her father and her birth. The play begins with harmony between England and Rome. Wolsey and Henry VIII meet with the papal legate in a much friendlier exchange than the first meeting of Pandulph and King John:

WOLSEY. Rome, the nurse of judgment,
Invited by your noble self, hath sent
One general tongue unto us: this good man,
This just and learned priest, Card'nal Campeius,
Whom once more I present unto your Highness.

KING. And once more in mine arms I bid him welcome,
And thank the holy conclave for their loves;
They have sent me such a man I would have wish'd for.

CAMPEIUS. Your Grace must needs deserve all strangers' loves,
You are so noble. To your Highness' hand
I tender my commission; by whose virtue,
The court of Rome commanding, you, my Lord
Cardinal of York, are join'd with me their servant
In the unpartial judging of this business.

KING. Two equal men. The Queen shall be acquainted
Forthwith for what you come.
(*HVIII*, II.ii.93–108)

Cardinals Wolsey and Campeius will judge Henry's case against his wife, Katherine. Thus far, the king has deferred to the judgment of Rome:

WOLSEY. Whilst our commission from Rome is read,
Let silence be commanded.

KING. What's the need?
It hath already publicly been read,
And on all sides th' authority allow'd;
You may then spare that time.

WOLSEY. Be't so; proceed.
(II.iv.1–5)

In fact, Henry uses the authority of Rome as a means of justifying his actions toward his wife. Katherine reminds them that she is the daughter of Ferdinand, the king of Spain, a reminder of the powerful rival of England during the reign of Elizabeth and, even in James I's reign, the great power. The mentions of Ferdinand, who with Isabella gave Columbus his commission, and of Henry VII, who commissioned Cabot, provide a backdrop of dynastic marriage and imperial designs to the proceedings. Katherine demands Spanish advisors (II.iv.44–57). Wolsey defends the court and, later, his own impartiality when he replies,

How far I have proceeded,
Or how far further shall, is warranted
By a commission from the consistory,
Yea, the whole consistory of Rome.
(II.iv.88–93)

King and queen are split between external authorities: for him, Rome; for her, Spain. Later in the hearing, Campeius says that Katherine intends an appeal to the pope, which leads Henry VIII to say in an aside:

I may perceive
These Cardinals trifle with me; I abhor
This dilatory sloth and tricks of Rome.
My learn'd and well-beloved servant, Cranmer,
Prithee return; with thy approach I know,
My comfort comes along. —Break up the court;
I say, set on.   *Exeunt in manner as they entered.*
(II.iv.237–42)

Henry has another plan to circumvent the show of the authority of Rome.

The representation of the church in *Henry VIII* involves the subtle power and the regrets of Wolsey. Until his downfall and death, Wolsey plots and controls much of the politics of England. For instance, Suffolk thinks that Campeius is under Wolsey's control:

> Cardinal Campeius
> Is stol'n away to Rome; hath ta'en no leave,
> Has left the cause o' th' King unhandled, and
> Is posted, as the agent of our Cardinal,
> To second all his plot

and he replies to Norfolk's query with an analysis of the countervailing role of Cranmer:

> He is return'd in his opinions; which
> Have satisfied the King for his divorce,
> Together with all famous colleges
> Almost in Christendom. Shortly, I believe,
> His second marriage shall be publish'd, and
> Her coronation. Katherine no more
> Shall be call'd Queen, but Princess Dowager.
> (III.ii.56–70)

The king has circumvented the papal representative and comes to rely on Cranmer above Wolsey, who becomes a figure of the religious corruption of the Roman church and particularly its influence in political affairs in England.

Wolsey himself recognizes that he has been found out when the king confronts him with the evidence of the papers that he misdirected to his monarch. Henry's wrath preoccupies Wolsey as he has a moment alone to muse:

> I fear, the story of his anger. 'Tis so;
> This paper has undone me. 'Tis th' account
> Of all that world of wealth I have drawn together
> For mine own ends (indeed to gain the popedom,
> And fee my friends in Rome). O negligence!
> Fit for a fool to fall by! What cross devil
> Made me put this main secret in the packet
> I sent the King? Is there no way to cure this?
> No new device to beat this from his brains?
> I know 'twill stir him strongly; yet I know
> A way, if it take right, in spite of fortune,
> Will bring me off again. What's this? "To th' Pope"?
> The letter, as I live, with all the business
> I writ to's Holiness. Nay then, farewell!
> I have touch'd the highest point of all my greatness,
> And from that full meridian of my glory
> I haste now to my setting. I shall fall
> Like a bright exhalation in the evening,
> And no man see me more.
> (III.ii.209–27)

His personal ambition and double-dealing—the sacrifice of England and his king to pursue the desire to be pope—are central events in the play, and this breakdown of his relation with Henry is a synecdoche for that between Rome and England. Norfolk accuses Wolsey of making the king of England subservient to himself and the pope:

> Then, that in all you writ to Rome, or else
> To foreign princes, "*Ego et Rex meus*"
> Was still inscrib'd; in which you brought the King
> To be your servant.
> (III.ii.313–16)

Amid other accusations, Surrey faces Wolsey with the following charge:

> Then, that you have sent innumerable substance
> (By what means got I leave to your own conscience)
> To furnish Rome, and to prepare the ways
> You have for dignities, to the mere undoing
> Of all the kingdom.
> (III.ii.326–30)

Henry VIII's desire for a divorce also means that Cranmer, not Wolsey, who opposes this option, must gain the king's ear.

Despite the king's desire for a son and heir, he admires his daughter Elizabeth, whose praises Cranmer sings in a duet with the king to end the body of this romance (V.iv). The peace, plenty and blessedness of this "maiden phoenix" will also pass on to another heir, James I (V.iv.40–55). Of James, the prophetic Cranmer predicts,

> Where ever the bright sun of heaven shall shine,
> His honor and the greatness of his name
> Shall be, and make new nations.
> (V.iv.50–2)

While the historical Henry VIII had identified English king with the Roman emperor through a descent through Constantine, the historical James favored masques and other representations that depicted him as the English Caesar.[25] Virginia was named in honor of Elizabeth I, and its first permanent settlement, Jamestown, was called after James I. In the play, Protestant Elizabeth and James will create a new translation of empire even if the Roman inheritance and the troubles with the pope were still ringing in their ears and certainly present in plays such as *King John* and *Henry VIII*. In this English mythology, an ambivalence or double action occurred: Rome was to be imitated and superseded, and classical Rome was to be separated from the Roman church. England was the true inheritor of the Roman empire. England would become—even if it were only in a wish in 1613, for its colonies overseas were tenuous and a great gap existed between the rhetoric of promotion for colonization and their material conditions—a great empire.[26]

CONCLUDING REMARKS AND TRANSITIONS

This chapter can suggest one aspect only of Shakespeare's Italy: the double action of the imitation and the critique of Rome and Italy. The translation of empire involved the desire England had to expand while, after the Reformation, distinguishing itself from Catholic Rome. Ancient Rome, as complex as it is in Shakespeare's poems and plays, became a model for thought about politics and empire. A typology between ancient Rome, ancient Britain, and Renaissance England, as opposed to the corruption of Renaissance Italy and the Roman church, even if it was sometimes complex and triangulated with Ancient Greece and other paradigms, allowed Shakespeare to distinguish medieval and early modern England from Renaissance Italy. Even still, Prospero, a Renaissance prince from Milan, provides, as much as Elizabeth in Cranmer's prophecy or Henry V as Caesar, an example, a mirror for study, in the building of England and those other "English" nations that Cranmer evokes at the end of what is generally considered to be Shakespeare's last play. When Shakespeare died in England, he may have done so without having set foot on Italian soil, but his work was imbued with traces from Roman and Italian texts. One of his frameworks was the Roman and Italian past and the culture of Renaissance Italy. It is not an overstatement to say that Shakespeare's work was itself a translation of study to another culture on the brink of empire. While he was not, like Prospero, born in Italy or, like Mowbray, buried there, the country nourished him through various translations—literary, temporal, and spatial.

For the first thirty-nine years of Shakespeare's life, he lived in the reign of a remarkable queen. Although, for him as much as for her, questions of gender would not be the same as those for people who live in the wake of the suffragette, women's, and feminist movements, there would be some common ground. Love, lust, relations, marriage, and children are constants in the lives of men and women in time. How the institutions and legal, social, and political mores and conventions go is another matter. Texts always have contexts, and Shakespeare's did then and after into the now of new readers and audiences. Lucrece, Calpurnia, Portia, Cleopatra, Fulvia, Imogen, and other female characters are important to Shakespeare's Italian and Roman worlds. The double image of England and Britain and Rome and Italy is one significant aspect of Shakespeare's imaginative creation. Another is his representation of English history. In the next chapter I turn mainly to his great second tetralogy and do so in much more detail than I have in this and previous chapters. The context in which I wrote this analysis was mainly the 1980s and interpretative views that took into account concerns of genre that arose in the wake of the theoretical and social revolution of the 1960s. Part of what I came to explore was—at the height of the Shakespearean history play, when Elizabeth was growing old and there was no heir in sight, at least to the public, and while the privy council considered its options—the absence of women or at least their diffusion or occlusion in the text in terms of political power. In this book, which involves textual explorations over the years and some contexts that might cast some light that rewards close attention to the text from different angles, I have looked for evidence primarily within the poetic, dramatic, and cultural body of Shakespeare's text and its history. The poems may be traces, but the plays are also ghosts of performances never to be seen by those who lived after Shakespeare. Until the advent of radio, film, and television, no recording could give a presence to voice and image, and the vanishing presence of performances serve as a haunting of our interpretations. Readers and audiences always disappear into thin air, a little like the spirits at the end of *The Tempest*.[27]

So I turn from the double image of England and Italy to a reading of gender in the second tetralogy, now a matter of England. This latter interpretation came at a certain time and now appears at another, in pursuit of plays that have come down to uses in imperfect forms, their broken bodies lost in the debates over good and bad quartos, the status of the folios, and the nature of the text and of editing, reading, and critical and theoretical interpretation.[28] All I can do, here and elsewhere, is to present my way as one way into the texts as plays to be read and performed. And what follows is another aspect of one reader reading or one interpreter of culture, history, and poetics trying to find ways of seeing in his own blindness and in the recognition and misrecognition of the world.

CHAPTER 7

SOME QUESTIONS OF GENDER IN THE SECOND TETRALOGY

WHEREAS THE LAST CHAPTER DISCUSSED THE TYPOLOGY OF ENGLAND AND ITALY in past and present, this chapter focuses on England alone. It occurred to me as I studied these four great plays over three decades ago that I could not include all that I wanted to in one study and its variations. When I came back to reshape my discussion of Shakespeare's representation of history in the second tetralogy (*Richard II, Henry IV Parts 1 and 2*, and *Henry V*), I realized that I could not incorporate everything I had explored. Here, I decided to leave my discussion at this charged time, centered most on the 1980s, when feminism had made some exciting changes to the field of Shakespearean studies, including those of the histories. Then, as now, I thought the best way forward was to see what comes from the text itself rather than to make Shakespeare conform to the works of contemporaries, especially those outside literature and particularly drama. Shakespeare helped to transform the chronicle play and helped to create the history play—one of his most original contributions. For better or worse, I decided, and stand my the decision, to take the view that while context is important to Shakespeare's work, it is also crucial to remember the exceptional talent of this great poet, dramatist, and experimenter. Thus, while I place Shakespeare in the context of women critics working in a great age of feminism in Shakespearean studies and found and find that valuable, I also examine what women say and do in his texts and how others react and interact with those words and actions.[1]

Shakespeare's second tetralogy represents the height of the English history play but leaves women to the margins and silences away from the center of power.[2] In the age of Elizabeth I we can observe the marginalization of women from politics and history. In this chapter I have chosen to discuss the feminine in conjunction with the masculine and the effeminate because these gender demarcations are interdependent. The interdependence of genders as well as classes represents a point that Natalie Zemon Davis made some years ago when speaking about historians: "our goal is to discover the range in sex roles and in sexual symbolism in different societies and periods, to find out what meaning they had and how they functioned to maintain the social order or to promote its change."[3] History, in Davis' view, should look at men and women just as it should examine all classes. Some of the female characters in the comedies and Joan of Arc in *Henry VI Part 1* (dress as men and challenge gender codes. Like Jean E. Howard, who looks at cross-dressing in the theatre and society of early modern England, and other materialist or socialist feminists, I recognize the plural nature of women and assume that race, class, and other factors do not allow for a singular and all-inclusive definition of woman.[4] Joan Kelly's famous question—Did women have a Renaissance?—is particularly appropriate in the consideration of the most influential representations of history in Renaissance England if not of Europe in the sixteenth century: Shakespeare's second tetralogy. During the past twenty years, feminist criticism has questioned the marginalization, abuse, and neglect of women in the Roman and English histories and among male critics. But feminist critics, such as Angela Pitt and Marilyn French, have considered Shakespeare's first tetralogy (*Richard III, Henry VI Parts 1, 2, and 3*) much more than his second tetralogy.[5] Linda Woodbridge (L. T. Fitz) questions the sexist attitudes of male reviewers of *Antony and Cleopatra*. Cleopatra, like Elizabeth I, had power over men, which made them idealize and denigrate her. If the male characters cannot face Cleopatra's actual power because she is female, male critics have committed the same error.[6] Woodbridge refers to the work of Lucie Simpson, who thinks that Cleopatra's role in the play is so primary that it should be called *Cleopatra*, and of Rosa Grindon, whose view forms the kernel of Woodbridge's article: "the men critics in their sympathy for Antony, have treated Cleopatra just as Antony's men friends did, and for the same cause."[7] It seems that men have to tell themselves stories about women in authority, and to make them more and less than men, in order to accept such political power. Phyllis Rackin, who focuses on *Henry VI Part 1* and *King John*, describes the role of female characters in Shakespeare's histories as that of antihistorians. Patricia Parker has expanded on Lisa Jardine's comments that the pregnant woman in Renaissance England represented fertility and a threatening sexuality to discuss the copiousness and unruliness of the "body" of female rhetoric. Like Gayle Whittier, Parker discusses Falstaff as a Renaissance "fat lady," looking at Shakespeare's means of associating him with effeminacy and the pregnant earth in *1* and *2 Henry IV* and of actually representing the fat knight as a fat lady in the transvestite scene at IV.iv of *The Merry Wives of Windsor*.[8] In *1 Henry IV*, Hal says to Poins, "I prithee call in Falstaff; I'll play Percy, and that damned brawn shall play Dame Mortimer his wife" (II.iv.106–8). This scene is never played out. Shakespeare does, however, feminize Falstaff in the imagery of the play. Instead, at length, Falstaff and Hal act the patriarchal drama of the king and his son. These critics are among other women who are rewriting the Renaissance by disrupting the male narrative of the Renaissance as the great rebirth of classical learning and European culture. Although I alluded to this silencing and control of women before I was aware of this feminine rewriting of the early modern period, it is this project that led me to amplify my remarks into something at once more systematic and central to my interpretation of the second tetralogy. This project to make history problematic by calling into question male constructions of gender affected the last version of my argument to the extent that it now amplifies the relation between gender and genre—the women in the history play.

Whether one accepts Joan Kelly's assertion, taking up Ruth Kelso's view that the Renaissance was not a revolution for women, that medieval aristocratic women were freer in their sexual and social relations than their counterparts in the Renaissance, one should not ignore the exploration of the hypothesis.[9] Like Ruth Kelso, Kelly herself opposed the view, as set out by writers as disparate as Jacob Burckhardt and Simone de Beauvoir, that men and women were equal in the Renaissance. Although the second tetralogy is a symbolic representation of history in the 1590s of the period from about 1399 to 1422, it seems to support Kelly's view of the Renaissance, although it may not tell us much about the Middle Ages. Even as a fictional reconstruction of the past that bears a complex relation to the world, the tetralogy, like its sources, keeps women on the edges of power and politics. Possibly, Andreas Capellanus' *The Art of Courtly Love* represents an ideal version of the role of aristocratic women in the twelfth century while treating the lower orders with indifference and contempt, so that Kelly's reading of the work may be as optimistic as Michel Foucault's idealization of the episteme in the Renaissance.[10] Whether Kelly, like Foucault and many of us, yearns for a golden world to criticize our fall into exploitation, ideology, or co-optation and to which we can return or on which we can draw to transform our brazen world, she raises a question wholly appropriate for the second tetralogy. I might now translate this question into something more specific and mundane: Why don't the women have power in Shakespeare's best-known English history plays? If women experienced equality with men in the Renaissance, why do Shakespeare's symbolic representations of history deny an equal place to his female characters?

The Renaissance does not seem to grant women an equal status with men. As Kelly points out, Baldassare Castiglione's handbook for the nobility, *The Book of the Courtier*, equates men and women except at an important level: the men are to be trained to take up arms, the women to be charming.[11] Thomas Hoby's translation of this work spread Castiglione's ideas into England. According to Castiglione, a man may handle weapons and ride because they help to constitute the art of war, but a woman is denied both activities precisely because they lack charm. Castiglione defines sex roles. His lady becomes an aesthetic object of his own making. She became social and cultural decoration to her husband, the prince, and gave up her role as educator to a professional cadre of male humanist teachers.[12] Kelly praises Castiglione for rejecting the unfair views of women that Aristotle, Plato, Ovid, and Aquinas held, but says that he helped to establish a connection between love and marriage that included an implicit sexual double standard for men because he includes too many hortatory tales about female chastity in addition to his disapproving comments on male infidelity.[13] Kelly also makes an interesting connection between the loss of power for women and for the aristocracy in sixteenth-century Italy and England, so that as the princes centralized power, so too did men. Noble men gained power as men in the private sphere as they lost power to the prince in the public sphere. They demanded obedience and had obedience demanded of them. In a Neoplatonic flourish, Castiglione represents the idealization of love of woman and prince, a displacement of actual love into a private and imaginative creation of pure beauty. The power of woman and ruler are in the image of God: both demand service. Kelly is right to suspect an emblematic smokescreen here. While, as Kelly suggests, the courtier dominates his beloved and the prince on a symbolic level, he subjects his beloved and takes on "women's ways" in his relation to the prince. Even though Castiglione defends the courtier against charges of effeminacy, the men at court could take on feminine characteristics to manipulate his prince. The male power of the prince controlled the constructed female roles of the men and women of the aristocracy. The ultimate agent of power and "love" was the male in what Kelly implies is a homosocial, if not homoerotic, relation that leaves the women out of the equation. Here, the aristocratic men lose their public power and, as a consolation prize, gain private power over their wives, whose bodies they dress and suppress as their influence is suppressed while being clothed in ceremony and title. The noble woman becomes dependent on her husband and her prince.[14] The Duchess of Gloucester cannot persuade Gaunt to take revenge on Richard, and Queen Isabel cannot sway Richard II. Hotspur will not listen to Kate to tell her anything about his political and military plans, and Mistress Quickly must put up with Falstaff's control and lies. Bolingbroke is wifeless, and Falstaff tells Doll, "You make fat rascals," or accuses her in misogynistic fashion of tempting men to loose living, to make a lean deer bloated (*2HIV*, II.iv.41). *Henry V* begins with a long debate on the Salic law, which disinherits women from the right to the French crown and ends with the promise of marriage between Henry and Katharine, when France, Burgundy, and Henry speak about her as a town ready to be entered by force. This political marriage is set out in male terms, in which the male characters construct Katharine within their language of "love" and politics.

RICHARD II

Richard II begins with the king's address to his uncle and patriarch, "Old John of Gaunt, time-honoured Lancaster," in a play that represents few female characters. No woman speaks in the first scene, and, if the stage directions are reliable, no woman appears until the second scene. In the opening scene Mowbray declares to Bolingbroke (Bullingbrook),

> 'Tis not the trial of a woman's war,
> The bitter clamour of two eager tongues,
> Can arbitrate this cause betwixt us twain.
> (I.i.48–50)

This declaration reveals what Coppélia Kahn calls the "maternal subtext" of Shakespeare's plays, "the imprint of mothering on the male psyche, the psychological presence of the mother whether or not mothers are literally represented as characters."[15] Kahn aptly cites Nancy Chodorow's work on the Elizabethan family, where she argues that the fundamental masculine sense of self takes place through a denial of the male's first link with the feminine. Chodorow asserts that this denial taints the male's attitudes toward women and inhibits his general ability to affiliate[16] Mowbray's appeal to deeds as opposed to words, which is in keeping with the popular saying current in Elizabethan England—"Women are words, men deeds"—that Patricia Parker has discussed.[17] In the world of *Richard II* and of the second tetralogy as a whole, manly action takes precedence over the femininity of words. It is as if the male characters are afraid of appearing effeminate and so, as Chodorow and Kahn point out, must consciously and unconsciously oppose the maternal and the feminine. This male preference for action does not prevent Mowbray from continuing to answer at some length Bolingbroke's long accusation. The male characters do not always follow their own advice regarding words and seem to use this ploy of denouncing speech as feminine as a ritual formula that allows them to continue speaking without fear of being called effeminate. Part of male speech is to differentiate itself from feminine speech even when there is no difference. Amid their mutual recriminations, Bolingbroke and Mowbray will not listen to Richard and Gaunt, who want to resolve the conflict with words of forgiveness rather than with combat (I.i.152–205). Words are serious because they can slander honor and reputation: Mowbray and Bolingbroke want deeds to mend the damage words have done to their honor. A deed—the murder of Gloucester—informs these accusations, which led to further violent action, until, as the audience hears in III.i, Richard chooses words over combat to resolve the issue. His choice does not, however, prevent further bloodshed.

In the world of these plays women are denied action, except by persuading men to act on their behalf. In the second scene the Duchess of Gloucester can only appeal to Gaunt to avenge the murder of his brother and her husband, "Thomas my dear lord, my life, my Gloucester" (I.ii.16). Although this murder is the source of conflict at the opening of the play, it is not until the second scene that the audience can observe the Duchess' grief and impotence.[18] The Duchess alludes to "that womb" that gave birth to Gaunt and her husband, but spends more rhetorical energy appealing to manhood and to male inheritance from the king, their father:

> Thou dost consent
> In some large measure to thy father's death
> In that thou seest thy wretched brother die,
> Who was the model of thy father's life
> (I.ii.25–28)

But Gaunt will not be moved. In his well-known rejoinder, he argues that God will attend to the actions of His substitute the king if that king is behind the murder. The Duchess rightly observes that she then has no recourse. When Gaunt says that her complaint must be to God, "the widow's champion and defence," the Duchess emphasizes Gaunt's age and impotence and puts her hope for revenge in young Herford. She also imagines Mowbray's remorse weighing down his horse so much that it will break its back but realizes that her only companion as she approaches death is grief. The Duchess is subject to men, both in their murder of her husband and as her means of revenge. When her persuasion fails, she can only hope for male action to help her cause. She will retreat to her "empty lodgings and unfurnish'd walls" to die with groans as her words have failed (I.ii.68). The two scenes that surround her speech involve the conflict between Bolingbroke (Herford) and Mowbray. In this history play we have arms and the man: the women can only plead and groan toward exile and death.

Part of Gaunt's advice to his son as he faces exile is to suppose "The flowers fair ladies, and thy steps no more / Than a delightful measure or a dance," so that he can endure the hardship (I.iii.290–91). Bolingbroke's reply is similar to Mowbray's and foreshadows Gaunt's musings about England as a mother or female earth. Richard had implied that male warfare could harm the female earth: "And grating shock of wrathful iron arms, / Might from our quiet confines fright fair peace" (I.iii.136–37). After the sentence of exile, Mowbray worried about losing his mother tongue, which he associates with the person who had taught him: "I am too old to fawn upon a nurse" (I.iii.170). Bolingbroke associates England and the earth with female nurturing: "Then, England's ground, farewell; sweet soil, adieu, / My mother and my nurse that bears me yet!" (I.iii.306–7). He recognizes the womb that Gaunt turned from in his exchange with his sister-in-law but to which, after the exile, he returns. But the male characters use their apprehension about losing power or someone else abusing it in terms of seduction and sexual excess. Richard fears Bolingbroke's "courtship" and "wooing" of the common people (I.iv.24,28). York speaks of the "Lascivious metres" that the courtiers use to flatter Richard (II.i.19). For these men, speech can be a dangerous seduction. To York's fears, Gaunt responds with a personification of England:

> This fortress built by Nature for herself
> Against infection and the hand of war,
> . . .
> This blessed plot, this earth, this realm, this England,
> This nurse, this teeming womb of royal kings.
> (II.i.43–44, 50–51)

The nurse and the womb serve men, give birth to sons, "Renowned for their deeds," especially in crusades in the service of "Mary's son." England is "Dear for her reputation through the world" (II.i.53–60). This is a female land that Richard is ruining: he is not acting like a royal king but is disregarding his noble lords. Gaunt's England becomes a goddess of war with all the marks of male aggression: "That England that was wont to conquer others, / Hath made a shameful conquest of itself" (II.i.65–66). By identifying so closely with England, he has apparently displaced on to his country his own sense of "feminization" as well as his desire to be more chivalrous and warlike. His rhetoric contrasts with his otherworldly speech to the Duchess.

During the queen's first appearance, she speaks one line in a long and controversial scene in which Richard engages in a verbal fight first with Gaunt then with York. After she greets Gaunt, she falls silent (II.i.71). The reader, as opposed to the audience, is only reminded of her continuing presence on stage when, after expropriating Gaunt's land and goods, ignoring York's warnings, speaking to Bushy, proclaiming York Lord Governor in the king's absence, Richard, almost as an afterthought, says, "Come on, our queen, to-morrow must we part; / Be merry, for our time of stay is short" (II.i.222–23). Instead of hearing the queen's views, the audience hears those of Gaunt, York, and Richard and then the rebellious thoughts of Northumberland and the other lords. If York complained that Richard blocked Bolingbroke's marriage, Ross says that Bolingbroke is "gelded of his patrimony" and Northumberland calls Richard a "degenerate king," implying that he does not live up to his progenitor or father (II.i.167–68, 237, 262). According to Richard's critics, he is not the man his father was partly because he has tried to make Bolingbroke less of a man than is his right. In this patriarchy the queen is silenced in public.

In private the queen speaks. Kelly says that the patriarchal system enforces this dubious division between public and private, so that it can relegate women to the private sphere and thereby leave public life open to men. Only when Richard is in

Ireland and the queen speaks with Bushy (in the presence of the strangely silent Bagot) in private does she speak her mind. The queen, who historically was eleven years old, is here a mature woman who misses her husband and, to serve the prophetic and dramatic sense that disaster after disaster is happening to Richard, says that her "inward soul . . . at something grieves, / More than with parting from my lord the king" (II. ii.12–13). When Bushy attempts to interpret the queen's sorrow for her, she answers that this may be so but her "inward soul / Persuades me it is otherwise" (II.ii.28–29). And the queen will not discount imagination, as Bushy does, but takes seriously and understands with wit her "nameless woe" (II.ii.33–40). Like Gaunt, the queen is a prophet who has the benefit of Shakespeare's backward glance. When Greene enters and announces that Bolingbroke has landed at Ravenspurgh, the major port on the Humber, the queen likens her prophecy to a monstrous birth:

> So, Greene, thou art the midwife to my woe,
> And Bolingbroke my sorrow's dismal heir;
> Now hath my soul brought forth her prodigy,
> And I, a gasping new-deliver'd mother,
> Have woe to woe, sorrow to sorrow join'd.
> (II.ii.62–66)

This passage shows that Isabel, not Bushy, is right about the future, that she thinks independently, that she translates Greene into a midwife, that metaphorically she seems to take responsibility for Bolingbroke's monstrous insurrection. These men are attendant to or derive from her soul. For a moment, these men take shape through a feminine rhetoric. The queen will not listen to Bushy's urging of hope, which she personifies as a flatterer and parasite in the service of death (II.ii.67–72). In her despair she sees the political situation as it is. Bushy, on the other hand, mythologizes it. Like the queen, York assesses the situation accurately: "Comfort's in heaven, and we are on the earth" (II.ii.78). The death of his sister, the Duchess of Gloucester, confirms this state of sorrow (II.ii.90f.). The queen leaves with York, who is flustered at the political chaos, but Bushy, Bagot, and Greene, favorites to the king, stay behind to consider the widespread hatred for them and the impossibility of defeating Bolingboke (II. ii.121f.). The queen returns to silence in the public realm in which York must find a way to solve the crisis.

For the male characters, England and its soil is female. When York confronts Bolingbroke, he asks his nephew why his legs

dar'd to march

> So many miles upon her [England's] peaceful bosom,
> Frighting her pale-fac'd villages with war
> And ostentation of despised arms?
> (II.iii.91–94)

As in the opening scenes, where Richard and Gaunt appealed to the concord of words to save the country, here York's words fail in the face of Bolingbroke's rhetoric, behind which he conceals his rebellious actions. All York can do is repeat that were he as strong as he was when he was young, he would raise an army to teach Bolingbroke and his followers how wrong rebellion is. The words of aged men are like those of women—powerless. They embody the despair of Gaunt, York, the Duchess of Gloucester, and the queen. Nostalgic words, curses, and prophecies represent a rhetorical power in which the old men, the women, and, later, Richard himself take refuge. The military power of Bolingbroke lends force to his words.

Through report and prophecy, the text shows how Richard's power is slipping away, whereas Bolingbroke asserts his power in person (II.iii, iv; III.i). Behind this issue of verbal and actual power lies the problem of gender in its sexual, social, and political manifestations. Bolingbroke accuses Bushy and Greene:

> You have in manner, with your sinful hours,
> Made a divorce betwixt his queen and him,
> Broke the possession of a royal bed.
> (III.i.11–13)

In *The Riverside Shakespeare* G. Blakemore Evans does not comment on this passage, but in the Arden edition Peter Ure, nearly twenty years before, includes a long note, which begins, "An accusation unsupported by history and inconsistent with the portrayal of Isabel's relations with Richard in the rest of the play."[19] Ure's assumption that texts and characters must be consistent is no longer as current as it was in the heyday of new criticism. An exception and an anomaly may tell as much about a text as the normative detail that an author constructs with care. In psychoanalytical terms, the traces of the unconscious are as important as the conscious revisions. If Bolingbroke's assertion derives from an earlier draft of the play, it cannot be dismissed as such because it still comprises part of a text that may constitute a series of writings and revisions at different times. In deconstructive terms, the exception is more interesting than the rule because it undoes the order of the text that the author has worked so hard to establish. In terms of sexual politics, it is often all right to concede that Marlowe might have been a homosexual but not that the Bard was. This is a fallacious extrapolation and correspondence, as if because Marlowe has the queen accuse Gaveston of a homosexual relation with Edward that Marlowe himself was necessarily a homosexual (although it is certain that he was either homosexual, heterosexual, or bisexual). Similarly, if Shakespeare makes Richard bisexual or homosexual, it does not necessarily imply that he shared this sexual orientation with his character. This kind of controversy has especially marked criticism of the sonnets, probably because the sonnet is a lyric form that, for many, signals a more private and personal voice that can be readily associated with the author. As Alan Bray and Eve Sedgwick are among the first literary scholars to do extensive work on homosexual and homosocial roles, it is not an exaggeration to say that this subject was taboo in literary criticism for many years.[20] Ure is not making the naive connection between Richard's possible sexual interest in other men and Shakespeare's, but behind his learned note, there may be an uneasiness about sexual regularity as well as textual regularity. Among the six possible readings that critics have made, Ure accepts five, including the possibility that Shakespeare is echoing Marlowe's *Edward II* (I.iv.150f.). But while Ure does not rule out affairs between Richard and his favorites ("Nothing that Bolingbroke says here need imply"), he favors the reading of the favorites as flatterers like those that Machiavelli, Erasmus, and Castiglione vilify. This uneasiness about sexual orientation is a critical extension of the cultural forces that Shakespeare represents in his male characters. They are sometimes afraid of being effeminate or unmanly. Two other possible readings that Ure discusses are that Bolingbroke is being the queen's champion or that he is lying for his political advantage. In both cases the queen is being used to enhance Bolingbroke's political image: he is her protector because her husband could not be or she is a character in his fable that allows him to eliminate his enemies because they were not good to the queen. Bolingbroke would then seem to revere women and the office of queen even if he is engaging in deceit. This proliferation of possible meanings demonstrates the openness of the text to the reader or audience, but although these meanings are conceivable, I am not sure that they are primary. They may, in part, represent an attempt to evade the uncomfortities of the text (to use Kristian Smidt's term) and the complexity of the personal and sexual relations at Richard's court.[21] Nonetheless, these interpretations of Bolingbroke as champion or liar do serve a useful purpose, especially when after lecturing the favorites and summarily condemning them to death, he turns to York, who is now firmly on his side, and, as if in an afterthought, asks that his uncle commend him to the queen. This yoking of the ruthless and the tender keeps one guessing how concerned and how deceitful Bolingbroke is. The queen is no threat to his power and finds her rhetorical topos between the favorites and Glendower who threaten Bolingbroke (III.i.1f., 42–44).

When Richard lands in Wales, he addresses the earth as if it were alive and once more uses the image of men of war wounding the peaceful earth (III.ii.4f.). But Richard shifts this image of mother earth to one of the earth as child:

> As a long-parted mother with her child
> Plays fondly with her tears and smiles in meeting,
> So weeping, smiling, greet I thee, my earth.
> (III.ii.8–10)

Richard now sees himself as a nurturing mother. From the beginning of the play, in his public rhetoric at least, the king, like Gaunt, said that he wanted words of peace and not deeds of war. But this cooperative "feminine" rhetoric gives way to the equally feminine rhetoric of the curse that the Duchess of York used (III.ii.12f.). Scroope echoes Richard.

The rage of Bolingbroke, according to Scroope, is covering Richard's "fearful land" with steel and hearts as hard as steel. He adds that even "White-beards" and "distaff-women" arm themselves against the king: moreover,

> boys, with women's voices,
> Strive to speak big, and clap their female joints
> In stiff unwieldy arms against thy crown.
> (III.ii.113–15, see 106–12, 116–19)

Scroope implies, as others do elsewhere in the play, that boys and old men are weak like women. They are joining females in their rebellion against Richard.

Behind the masculine there are more signs of the feminine. Like the Duchess, Gaunt, Isabel, and York, Richard expresses his lack of earthly power in terms of heavenly revenge. To Northumberland, Richard says:

> But ere the crown he looks for live in peace,
> Ten thousand bloody crowns of mothers' sons
> Shall ill become the flower of England's face,
> Change the complexion of her maid-pale peace
> To scarlet indignation and bedew
> Her pastures' grass with faithful English blood.
> (III.iii.95–100)

England is a woman whose peaceful face the ten thousand sons of mothers will mar until she grows to indignation and, apparently, intensifies the war. This personification makes mother England peaceful by disposition but capable of a fury mortal men cannot stem. Richard had appealed unsuccessfully to God and the sun to play similar personified superhuman roles but now tries another name on which to displace his hopes for power and his anxieties over its loss (III.ii.36f.). He tries to mother the earth, and when that strategy does not work, he decides to have the earth mother him. That mothering involves an idyllic image of peace, a place free from conflict, and of revenge, an instrument to devour his foes. In both instances Richard requires protection from the image of the mother he creates. But nothing protects Richard. He soon calls the earth base and assures the Lord Protector, York, that his uncle's tears signify love but cannot resolve Richard's situation or the tears themselves (III. iii.190–91, 202–3).

The garden scene (III.iv) is important partly because it represents Isabel's reaction to Richard's fall. It is an allegorical scene, located at the home of the Duke of York, who often comments obliquely on Richard's misfortunes and fall. It is also the only scene in the play in which the audience observes female characters alone. This exclusive female presence, putting aside for the moment the boy actors' playing of female roles, lasts for twenty-three lines. The queen rejects her own suggestion and those of one of her ladies to play a game, dance, tell tales, sing, or weep to drive away their cares. The women can only react to the world: even moving from symbolic activities to weeping itself will not prove cathartic. They are kept from direct action. The queen wagers her grief that the gardener and his two helpers, who have arrived on the scene, will talk of state. The women become secret observers of the men, so that this removal serves a symbolic or thematic purpose as much as dramatic irony. Sure enough, like the queen, the gardener and his man allegorize problems of state (III.iv.29). The man asks in a way that makes even more obvious, though perhaps no less effective, the allegory: why should they keep law, form, and proportion when England, "our sea-walled garden," is full of weeds and overrun by caterpillars (III.iv.40–47)? In the personification he feminizes his country. The narratives of the gardener and the man cause the queen to speak. In part, she speaks against her own gender, for she asks the gardener: "What Eve, what serpent, hath suggested thee / To make a second fall of cursed man?" (III.iv.75–76). After ordering the gardener to tell her the news of the deposing of Richard, she listens and laments that she is the last to know, as if the gardener kept the news from her. Her only way to express her frustration is to curse his garden (III.iv.93–101). As a woman, Isabel hears news of the state last, even when it most concerns her husband.

Unlike Elizabeth I, this queen is not a *hortus conclusus*. As Peter Stallybrass reminds us, that state and virgin are gardens enclosed, walled off from enemies, and that, in the Ditchley portrait, where she stands on a map of England, she symbolizes and is symbolized the *hortus conclusus* as she, the "imperial virgin," ushers in a golden age.[22] But no matter how much Elizabeth I tried to exempt herself from her own gender, she could not. If we can believe John Harington's letter, unless it is a written manifestation of a wish to escape and control the authority of his godmother, when Essex returned to court from Ireland without the queen's permission, she swore to Harington, "By God's Son I am no Quen; that man is above me;—Who gave him commande to come here so soon? I did sende hym on other busynesse."[23] As Louis Montrose says, Elizabeth's rule was not an attempt to undermine male hegemony but represented a differentiation between the queen and other women. In 1563, in a written response to parliament, she recommended marriage for "private women" but not for herself, "a prince."[24] Queen Elizabeth would act as the image of the queen for Shakespeare's audience, so that Isabel might be judged according to the reigning sovereign. Owing to Elizabeth's view of herself as a prince, the audience might also judge Richard II and the other kings in the tetralogy according to her. As Francis Bacon notes, a married queen lost credit to her husband, whereas an unmarried queen could not.[25] Allison Heisch and Joan Kelly assert that Elizabeth is a virago, an honorary male, whose propaganda argued that she was an exception to the law of nature. Elizabeth's famous speech at Tilbury is a good example of this viragoistic strategy: "I know I have the body of a weak and feeble woman, but I have the heart and stomach of a king, and a King of England too."[26] If gender is ambivalent for men in the public sphere, so too is it for women. In the private sphere women must be obedient to their husbands.[27] Kelly quotes Alymer and Spenser but does not differentiate the words of a cleric from those of a fictional character.[28] Still, both attitudes are similar.

If Richard sometimes sees himself as female, Isabel defines herself in terms of him. In the deposition scene, Shakespeare gives to Richard, as he addresses his image in the mirror, a speech that seems to echo Faustus' speech to Helen in Marlowe's *Dr Faustus*, so that the king plays male and female in an address to an image in a way that is even more apparent than Faustus' delusory speech (IV.i.281–89). Richard breaks the illusion almost immediately, whereas Faustus continues his delusion until the very end of Marlowe's play. Isabel often thinks of herself in relation to Richard: "Here let us rest, if this rebellious earth / Have any resting for her true king's queen" (V.i.5–6). Both monarchs are affectionate to each other. The queen, however, will not listen when Richard appears pliant and weak. She wants him to be more the king and man who helped to define her role:

> What, is my Richard both in shape and mind
> Transform'd and weaken'd? hath Bolingbroke depos'd
> Thine intellect? hath he been in thy heart?
> The lion dying thrusteth forth his paw
> And wounds the earth, if nothing else, with rage
> To be o'erpow'r'd, and wilt thou, pupil-like,
> Take the correction mildly, kiss the rod,
> And fawn on rage with base humility,
> Which art a lion and the king of beasts?
> (V.i.26–35)

Ever since A. P. Rossiter's opposition to E. M. W. Tillyard's thesis on the Elizabethan world picture, critics have tended increasingly toward finding ambivalences, subversion, and exceptions in the Shakespearean *oeuvre*.[29] Isabel—like Richard, Gaunt, and Carlisle—subscribes to the establishment view that kings are like God, sun, and lion. Whereas critics now criticize the order of the ruling class, the rulers in the plays seldom do, unless they have lost power. Like the Duchess of Gloucester's appeal to Gaunt to behave like a proper warrior and revenge her husband's death, Isabel wants Richard to behave like a manly king. When Macbeth wants to have no more to do with the plans to murder Duncan, Lady Macbeth berates Macbeth for not being a man:

> When you durst do it, then you were a man;
> And to be more than what you were, you would
> Be so much more the man."
> (*Riverside*, I.vii.49–51)

After Lady Macbeth has talked in a way she would like to hear Macbeth adopt—in a manly or brave fashion—he responds,

> Bring forth men-children only!
> For thy undaunted mettle should compose
> Nothing but males.
> (*Riverside*, I.vii.72–74)

Perhaps Lady Macbeth's ruthless masculinity helps to drive her mad. Richard does not respond as well as Macbeth does, possibly because Isabel and he are at the end of their power and life together, whereas Macbeth and Lady Macbeth think that they are embarking together on a long reign. Instead, Richard displays the woe that the Duchess of Gloucester and Isabel have shown and finds self-pity in words rather than courage for actions. The king advises that she tell tales that with a magical power of metaphor will put out fires and, like Richard's earlier tale on his landing, will tell the sad tale of his fall (V.i.35–50). But then Richard does use his last verbal power to vindicate himself before his wife. Like the Duchess of Gloucester, Gaunt, Isabel, and Carlisle, he uses a mixture of prophecy and curse to condemn his enemy, this time, Northumberland (V.i.55f.). Apparently, then, the language of dispossessed and victimized males and females takes on a similar rhetorical cast. Richard upbraids Northumberland for divorcing him from his crown and his wife, but he cannot help his penchant for pathos. This so-called degeneration in Richard actually makes him a more compassionate character than he was when he banished Mowbray and Bolingbroke, wished Gaunt dead and seized Bolingbroke's lands. Northumberland is literally an interloper with his "policy" when he breaks in on the rhyming stichomythic exchange between Richard and Isabel. The language helps constitute the role Northumberland plays in the scene: he must separate king and queen and send them to their respective exiles. Richard and Isabel will not, however, be prevented from showing their paradoxical situation: they are more married than ever as they are forced to separate. The language helps to comprise the bond they feel as they lose it. In a ritual they play verbally on the conceit in Elizabethan sonnets that in kissing they will give up their hearts. In this exchange Richard's last lines end in a rhyme, "part" and "heart" and Isabel begins with the identical rhyme (V.i.95–98). Isabel and Richard share the woe that they have shared so much since Bolingbroke's landing, though they have done so separately. Here, both speak the language of lovers: both say they will restrain their sorrow. Neither characterizes this language as something that can be gendered.

The next scene also represents domestic relations (V.ii). The Duchess of York wants to hear the rest of the narrative of the arrival of Richard and Bolingbroke into London because York's weeping had interrupted it. York observes the seal of a letter hanging from Aumerle's breast, and no matter how much the Duchess tries to defend Aumerle, York pursues what is in the letter, which happens to be a plot to kill Bolingbroke. York refers to his wife as a "fool," "foolish woman," "mad woman," and "fond woman" (V.ii.68, 80, 95, 101). He would expose his son's treason to save his honor; she would hide it to save her only son. The Duchess appeals to childbirth as a way of shaming York:

> Had'st thou groan'd for him
> As I have done, thou wouldst be more pitiful.
> But now I know thy mind: thou dost suspect
> That I have been disloyal to thy bed,
> And that he is a bastard, not thy son.
> Sweet York, sweet husband, be not of that mind;
> He is as like thee as a man may be,
> Not like to me, or any of my kin,
> And yet I love him.
> (V.ii.102–10)

The appeal that Shakespeare gives to the Duchess is almost a parody of the male obsession with cuckoldry that appears in so many Renaissance and Restoration comedies. How much this speech represents a spillover from Shakespeare's comedies or the Duchess' gentle chiding of her husband for not being enough of a man to have sense about the love and value of children is difficult to say. It is as if the Duchess is turning the male anxiety on its ear by forgiving York for having a child that does not look like her and so may not be hers. This assertion represents, for us at least, more of a comic inversion than a biological fact. Even though, as Stephen Greenblatt has shown, the understanding of gender was uncertain in Renaissance medicine, it was obvious that a woman could not have a child who was not her own.[30] Uncertain paternity, as Linda Woodbridge notes, underlies "the Renaissance fanaticism" on cuckoldry.[31] York calls his wife "unruly"—she will not be ruled (V.ii.110). He will not even tolerate her voice in the privacy and home, where women were given more scope. Parker aptly summarizes a tendency in rhetorics in sixteenth-century England: they figure women as "far-fetched," uncontrollable, garrulous, and "moveable" or inconstant (110). The Duchess is immovable in her determination to save her son from York's decision to tell Bolingbroke of his plot (V.ii.111f.)

Before Aumerle, York, and the Duchess arrive at Windsor Castle, Bolingbroke laments his son's three-month absence in a less exalted places—the tavern and lanes—with loose and criminal companions and calls him a "young wanton, and effeminate boy" (V.iii.10). This charge possesses a historical context different from our own and deserves pause. Bray says that when scholars translated Chapter 6 of the first epistle to the Corinthians for the Authorized Version of 1611, they translated two Greek words associated with homosexuality as "effeminate" and as "abusers of themselves with mankind," whereas the translators of the Revised Standard Version of 1952 used the word "homosexual," which entered the language in the 1890s. In the Renaissance, as Bray reminds us, "effeminate" did not have the specific homosexual connotation it later acquired.[32] The *OED* gives several definitions that were current during the Middle Ages and the Renaissance: a person who has become like a woman; "Womanish, unmanly, enervated, feeble; self-indulgent, voluptuous; unbecomingly delicate or over-refined." It cites a few well-known instances. Speaking of things in *The School of Abuse*, Stephen Gosson, who was involved in the attacks against the theatre, writes, "Effeminate gesture to rauish the sence." In what might have been Sidney's reply to Gosson, *The Apology of Poetry*, Philip Sidney speaks about "An Art . . . not of effeminateness, but of . . . stirring of courage." George Puttenham's *The Art of English Poesie* contains this sentence: "The king was supposed to be . . . very amorous and effeminate." Thomas Nashe's *The Unfortunate Traveller* shares a usage with the example from Gosson: "Their handes had no leasure to aske counsell of their effeminate eyes."[33] Gosson's use is an allusion to feminine seduction, Sidney's to the opposition between womanly weakness and manly courage, Puttenham's to voluptuousness, and Nashe's to the division between active manly hands and the passive feminine eyes. In *Richard III* the Duke of Buckingham says, "we know your tenderness of heart / And gentle, kind, effeminate remorse" (III.vii.211). As in all the examples from fiction, the context is important and tells something about the ethos of the speaker and the audience, the narrator and narratee. The Douay Bible of 1609 translates "*effeminati*" of the Vulgate 1 Kings 14 as "effeminates," whereas the Authorized Version only two years later translates it as "Sodomites," a term, as Bray says, that includes but is not synonymous with homosexuals, the plural of a word that makes it into the *OED Supplement* and which cites Havelock Ellis (1897) as the first instance in English.[34] There is, then, no explicit homosexuality in *Richard II*, though Bolingbroke's charges of "effeminacy" against his son might include it and our modern notions of the word might push interpretation in that direction. The notion of being womanlike in a warrior culture remains, for most of the male characters in the second tetralogy, an insult or an indictment. Weakness is the inexcusable political error in these plays, and being effeminate implies in a patriarchal system softness and weakness.

When the Duchess of York arrives on the scene, in the wake of her son and husband, she seems to usher in a comedy. At least, that is Bolingbroke's view. When Bolingbroke asks, "What shrill-voic'd suppliant makes this eager cry?" the Duchess responds by defining herself: "A woman, and thine aunt, great king" (V.iii.73–74). The Duchess must flatter Bolingbroke and must reinforce his implied definition of woman as the one that speaks shrilly and unlike a man. Her response opposes "A woman" and "great king" and tries to reconcile and balance the opposition with the intercession of "and thine aunt." Here is a woman, but one who is related to Bolingbroke, and whose begging speech should therefore be heard. For whatever reason, the arrival of a woman to beg forgiveness for her son makes Bolingbroke think of a comedy, "The Beggar and the King." The scene now continues York's shift to rhyming couplets, a kind of light, artificial, and contrapuntal music to the graveness of Aumerle's conspiracy to assassinate Bolingbroke. When York insults his wife as a "frantic woman," she calls him "sweet York," which shows how much she must ingratiate herself to her husband as well as to the "king." The contest for Boling-broke's will persists. The Duchess contrasts the fullness of the prayers for pardon that Aumerle and she offer Bolingbroke with the empty prayers that York gives, a strategy that convinces the king. Indirectly, the Duchess reminds Bolingbroke that a woman taught him speech: "And if I were thy nurse, thy tongue to teach, / 'Pardon' should be the first word of thy speech." (V.iii.111–12). Here is a woman, who must beg a powerful man to save her son, who must teach this man how to speak of mercy with pity, but all hangs on the supposition: "And if." This is one of the conditions of a grammatical, if not rhetorical, fiction that this woman must use to effect what she wants in the action of the actual world. York tries to interrupt this plea, to keep this female voice from weakening the king's resolve to punish York's son. But his use of French—that the king says pardon me in a language others will not understand—fails because the Duchess comprehends and uses his ploy to contrast her own sincere use of language against his sophistry: "Ah, my sour husband, my hard-hearted lord, / That sets the word itself against the word!" (V.iii.119–20). The Duchess will not stand until Bolingbroke utters the word "pardon" twice, as if she cannot believe him or her ears. Her response to Bolingbroke is that he is "A god on earth" and to her son that he is an Old Adam who needs to be baptized to become a new man. Bolingbroke will execute all the other conspirators, including his brother-in-law, the Earl of Huntingdon. The king praises the Duchess for praying so well on Aumerle's behalf. This woman's words perform deeds—indirectly, through male agency.

No female character appears for the rest of the play. The audience is left with the recesses of male power. Exton will kill the deposed king because it is Bolingbroke's wish (V.iv). In prison, alone, Richard speaks about his brain proving "female" to his soul, the father, and together they will breed thoughts to people the world. The fallen king is both male and female. In this private sphere of punishment, which arises from the political need to be rid of opponents and rivals, Richard can admit his "daintiness of ear" for music and speak of his tears in this sad time (V.v.45–60). He thinks not about his wife but about his horse. The Groom tells him how the horse "betrayed" him by supporting Bolingbroke. Richard is left to his Keeper and the murderers. Violence concludes this play that began with males and ends with them. In jaunty rhymed couplets, Bolingbroke speaks about rebellion and hears about the execution of the rebels. The new king allows Carlisle Richard's wish, to die in religious isolation (V.vi). The playwright emphasizes the contrast between Carlisle and Richard when Exton brings in the coffin of the deposed monarch. Bolingbroke banishes Exton and wants to spill blood in the Holy Land to atone for this murder. Shakespeare has evacu-ated the women from this play. The ruin of male violence remains.

1 HENRY IV

Like *Richard II*, *1 Henry IV* begins with the king's speech. Both opening scenes exclude women and involve talk about physical conflict. After Henry IV's speech about going on a crusade to expiate Richard's murder, Westmoreland gives him news about the civil war in England. Westmoreland focuses on the thousand dead English soldiers,

> Upon whose dead corpse there was such misuse,
> Such beastly shameless transformation,
> By those Welshwomen done, as may not be
> Without much shame retold or spoken of.
> (*1HIV*, I.i.42–46)

Westmoreland's narrative strategy uses occupatio or paralepsis, which allows Henry and the audience to imagine whatever barbarities they wish. The "transformation" to which Westmoreland alludes, "mutilation," also occurs in Holinshed, who reports, "the shamefull villanie used by the Welsh-women towards the dead carcasses, was such, as honest eares would be ashamed to heare, and continent toongs to speake thereof."[35] Henry's only reaction is that his plans for the crusade must be broken off. This reticence may have to do in part with the nature of Westmoreland's occupatio, which appeals to the honest, and by implication, the civilized, to note the enormity of the women's crime by being brief or silent in the face of it. In part, Henry's silence may have to do with his own mutilation of Richard and his inability to get beyond his guilt over it and his desire to atone for his sin with a crusade. This response helps to suspend the issue of the Welsh-women as exotic enemy. Instead, the king talks about a long list of noble men and compares his son unfavorably to Hotspur. This apparently aberrant fact—which equates women with dishonor, cowardice, and monstrosity—is lost in the rolls of military honor and the king's anxieties over the heir's ability to succeed him. Fortune is feminine: her pride is Hotspur and not Hal. In absence of women in this opening scene the allusion to "transformation" implies an endless monstrosity to the Welsh women because of their foreignness and their gender.

Nor does Shakespeare introduce women to the world of the other plot—unless, of course, we consider Falstaff a figurative literary fat lady, as Patricia Parker does.[36] As Parker notes, in the *Henry IV* plays he is called corpulent on many occasions and is associated with harlotry and verbal copia, and in *The Merry Wives of Windsor* he actually appears as the "fat woman of Brainford." But Falstaff's case, as Shakespeare oversees it, is one of male appropriation, ventriloquy, and transvestitism, so that the question of the "effeminate" male arises once more. The prince characterizes Falstaff's world as one that centers on drink and prostitutes and that, in a kind of tropical transference of gender, might transform the "sun himself" into "a fair hot wench on flame-coloured taffeta" (I.ii.9–10). Falstaff would rather serve the female moon than the male sun—"let us be Diana's foresters"—and Hal agrees that they are "the moon's men" because they are thieves whose fortune ebbs and flows with the taking and spending (I.ii.25–38). The prince's speech reminds Falstaff of the hostess: "is not my hostess of the tavern a most sweet wench?"[37] These male characters cannot help but allude to females and the feminine. Manhood is also an important topic for them. When speaking to Hal, Falstaff equates theft to manhood and royal lineage: "There's neither honesty, manhood, nor good fellowship in thee, nor thou cam'st not of the blood royal, if thou darest not stand for ten shillings" (I.ii.135–37).

A woman does not appear on stage until act 2, scene 3. That absence keeps the female voice from representing itself. Instead, men characterize women and demonstrate their anxiety over "effeminacy" among men. As Woodbridge notes, "Male effeminacy is a recurrent theme in the formal satires of the 1590s: the satires of Marston, Hall, and Guilpin are full of commentary on foppishness; and such other specialized

perversions of true manliness as female impersonation, male prostitution, and bug-
gery in academe receive mention as well."³⁸ Like Woodstock in the eponymous play,
Accutus in *Every Woman in Her Humour*, and Hamlet, when he satirizes Osric, Hotspur makes fun of the effete courtier. Speaking of Osric, Hamlet says to Horatio, "A
did comply with his dug before a sucked it" (*Ham*, V.ii.184). G. Blakemore Evans
glosses "did comply" as "bow politely" while Harold Jenkins uses "pay courtesies to."³⁹
Like Hamlet, Hotspur criticizes the circumlocution, delicacy, and indirection of the
courtier's speech and the outlandishness of his dress. Hotspur reports to Henry that
on the battlefield, one of the king's courtiers "With many holiday and lady terms /
. . . question'd me" and spoke about war like a "waiting-gentlewoman" (I.iii.45–46,
54). In Hotspur's satire lies the opposition between Hotspur, the gruff, direct, and
plain-spoken soldier, and the courtier, the haughty, sheltered, and circumlocutory
interloper. Here, Hotspur leans on his sword while the courtier skirts around the dead
with choice and womanly verbiage. He attempts to contrast wordy womanhood with
active manhood, but the courtier is a man, an effeminate man, and Hotspur himself is
so good with words that, like Hamlet, he overshadows the courtier that he satirizes. If
words are effeminate, then the eloquence of Hotspur and Hamlet makes them so. The
opposition, which occurs in Thomas Howell's *Devises* (1581), breaks down.⁴⁰ The
sticking point between Hotspur and Henry is the marriage between Mortimer and
Glendower's daughter. Henry regards this marriage as a sign of Mortimer's betrayal.
Richard, deposed with Hotspur's help, had also named Hotspur's wife's brother, Mortimer, heir. In private Northumberland, Worcester and Hotspur rehearse their part in
Richard's murder and the claim that Mortimer has to the throne. As Worcester says,
Hotspur "apprehends a world of figures here, / And not the form of what he should
attend" (I.iii.207–8). Hotspur resents the king's order not to talk about Mortimer
and defies Henry by rehearsing how he shall speak about nothing but Mortimer.
This is the same Hotspur whom, in the opening scene, Henry had wanted for his
son. Northumberland makes explicit what has already occurred to the audience: that
Hotspur is, in his own terms, womanly in his speech. Northumberland berates his
son: "Art thou to break into this woman's mood, / Tying thine ear to no tongue but
thine own!" (I.iii.234–35). This traditional misogynistic comment—as if women are
solipsistic and can only prattle—is intended to bait his son for being effeminate so
that he will snap out of this condition and prepare himself for the sober business of
rebellion. In 1 Timothy 2:11–12, which has been controversial, St. Paul speaks about
the limited role of women in church, and in *De studiis et litteris* Leonardo Bruni, a
humanist, declares that rhetoric is outside the province of woman.⁴¹ Although these
male characters speak in public, they are afraid to be taken for garrulous, a trait with
which they impeach women.

 Hotspur remains an eloquent critic of eloquence. He criticizes the language of
those who would not be manly soldiers. Later, he reads aloud parts of a letter from
a lord who will not support his rebellion and interrupts the letter with comments
like "you are a shallow cowardly hind" (II.iii.15). This particular allusion yokes shal-
lowness, cowardice, and a female deer and applies them to the lord. More obviously,
Hotspur displays his need to convince himself of how he will teach effeminate men
how womanly they really are: "'Zounds, and I were now by this rascal I could brain
him with his lady's fan" (II.iii.22–23). To shore up his own manhood, Hotspur makes

those who oppose him into fops whom he can bait. He does divide himself and goes to buffets.

Unlike the scene between Brutus and Portia in *Julius Caesar*, the exchange between Hotspur and Lady Percy does, as A. R. Humphreys notes, show comic elements.[42] Kate and Hotspur are affectionately parodic with each other. The comedy is partly founded on Hotspur's exclusion of his wife from his military secrets and on his choice to exercise his male prerogative. The comic spirit is often based on tensions of age, gender, and class. The line between tragedy and comedy is often not clear. Dr. Johnson, as Harry Levin says, pointed out how incomplete and arbitrary the "complementary masks" of tragedy and comedy were in representing human experience and so freed Shakespeare from the objections of neoclassicists.[43] Hotspur informs Kate that he will be leaving her within two hours, which is hardly consultation. Hotspur is a typical noble in the open lineage family system because he is violent and will not trust his wife or anyone else. As Lawrence Stone deduces in his discussion of this kind of family, which lasted more than a thousand years until the late sixteenth century, "The extraordinary amount of casual inter-personal physical and verbal violence, as recorded in legal and other records, shows clearly that at all levels men and women were extremely short-tempered."[44] Stone also reports that William Wentworth, in a letter of advice to his son, the future Earl of Strafford, tells him to assume that wife, children, friends, neighbors, patrons, and servants are untrustworthy and, therefore, to exercise self-control, reserve, secrecy, and even duplicity.[45] Hotspur seems to be short tempered and not to trust even his wife (although he later believes his uncle's treacherous words that lead him away from pardon and into battle). Kate wonders why Hotspur is alone, why for a fortnight she has not been in his bed, and what is the cause of his anxiety and ill temper. Has Hotspur, in Kate's words, "given my treasures and my rights of thee / To thick-ey'd musing, and curst melancholy?" (II.iii.47). Ophelia could have spoken these words to Hamlet. For someone Hotspur has tried to keep from his wars, Kate knows her military terminology and uses it to tell Hotspur about what he mutters in his fitful slumber. She asks to know Hotspur's business, "else he loves me not" (II.iii.65). A servant interrupts, and Hotspur has not been listening. They banter, but Hotspur will not tell her whether her suspicions are correct that her brother, Mortimer, is growing rebellious over his title. Even in sport, Hotspur belittles the domestic world of women as trivial:

> Away, you trifler! Love! I love thee not,
> I care not for thee, Kate; this is no world
> To play with mammets, and to tilt with lips;
> We must have bloody noses and crack'd crowns,
> And pass them current too. God's me! my horse!
> What say'st thou, Kate? What wouldst thou have with me?
> (II.iii.91–96)

Shakespeare begins *Romeo and Juliet* with a sonnet, continues the Petrarchan spirit throughout, and intensifies it after the death of Mercutio, whose bawdy and counter-if not anti-Petrarchism modifies the young love. In *Hamlet* Ophelia's reports of the prince's love for her as well as Hamlet's letter to her mark a Petrarchan aspect to their love, but his love soon dwindles into misogyny then leaves him to guilt and regret over her death. While Kate wants more of a Petrarchan lover and wonders whether Hotspur is jesting, he will not relent. Woodbridge has defined the stage misogynist as "a kind of humours character, whose governing trait is a testy disregard for the female sex" and suggests that "pure" types are Benedick in *Much Ado About Nothing*, Algripe in Fletcher's *The Nightwalker*, Gondarino in Beaumont and Fletcher's *The Woman-Hater*, Accutus in the anonymous *Every Woman in Her Humour*, and Joseph Swetnam in the anonymous *Swetnam the Woman-hater Arraigned by Women*.[46] One of the nondramatic literary antecedents for the stage misogynist is "the returning soldier figure from the debate over the unisex tendencies of peacetime."[47] The humor might modify Hotspur's misogyny, but it is not undercut. It is a simple but too-frequent interpretative slip for critics to equate a character's view with the playwright. Woodbridge rightly cautions against this slippage, but I am less optimistic that the dramatists use context and humor to undercut their misogynist characters. I may be quibbling here, but I prefer the words "modify" and "qualify," both of which imply a doubling or multiplication of effect that lessens the single focus and intensity of the misogyny but that does not allow it to dissipate or disappear entirely. Whether contempt for women can be "genuine," as Woodbridge argues, is debatable, so that while I agree that the stage misogynist may not exemplify this trait, I doubt whether any similar nondramatic type can and whether this dramatic woman-hater can be pure. Woodbridge concludes her discussion of the stage misogynist with the following assertion—"Paradoxically, the stage misogynist is a figure belonging to the defense of women."[48] Whereas this claim is deduced from a large number of examples in Renaissance drama and may shed light on the subject, it rests on a view of dramaturgy and irony that assumes that if something that comes after an event or a speech attempts to negate it, it does. My view of irony—which is not a solid truth but a matter of a different perspective—leads me to favor scenic and ironic juxtaposition as means of qualification, modification, and complication. One perspective does not undercut the previous one but leads to a multiplication of perspectives. Like some of the new historicists, for instance Greenblatt and Mullaney, and some feminists, like Kristeva and Cixous, I tend to be wary of the ability of the powerful to contain subversion.[49] The powerful are often men. Patriarchy, as it is refracted in Renaissance drama, whether or not the playwrights represent it consciously, seems to reproduce itself. Constance Jordan's discussion of the humanist defenses of women qualifies but does not undercut Woodbridge's observations. More specifically, Jordan observes, "Even such an ostensible feminist as Vives could not renounce the main tenets of Aristotle's antifeminism. In fact Vives' *De institutione foeminae christianae* (1523), which argues for the humanist education of women, paradoxically concludes with his condemnation of women in public life."[50] Paradox depends on perspective. As I, and all male writers sympathetic to the unfair stereotyping of women, should be aware, the male defense of women can become patronizing or a means of social control through the very empathy or sense of justice that makes us speak out. But speaking out and speaking for are different discourses. One is an alliance with women where men listen to them and learn from their work on gender. The other is ventriloquy that uses the voices of women to contain them. The past and present are necessarily different historically, but then as now, male writers bear a refractory relation to their texts because their intentions are not directly enacted in the work as writing, like reading, represents an unconscious as well as conscious activity. In the Renaissance women's voices most often spoke through the filters of male writers who worked with the attendant difficulty of alliance and problem of ventriloquy. Shakespeare's women and the views of male characters about women and "effeminate" men are not exempt from this situation.

Hotspur will not allow Kate to question him about his political and military plans. Even in jest, he condescends with his wife:

> I know you wise, but yet no farther wise
> Than Harry Percy's wife; constant you are,
> But yet a woman; and for secrecy
> No lady closer, for well I believe
> Thou wilt not utter what thou dost not know;
> And so far will I trust thee, gentle Kate.
> (II.iii.108–13)

Even though Hotspur tells Kate that she can join him tomorrow, he does not entrust her with his plans. The jest is serious. For Hotspur, women are inconstant, unreliable, and garrulous. His wife is no exception. Kate is contented with these arrangements "of force." Comedy, as Levin says, often represents the unfair male prerogatives in society.[51] When we laugh with and at Hotspur and Kate, in a society where gender roles are rapidly changing, we are uneasy. It is as if we are experiencing a distancing effect from an earlier period, the 1590s and 1950s. Rather than Brecht's alienation effect, which focuses most on class, we participate in gender alienation.[52] Writers consider these social changes as they modify genres, but readers and audiences also alter genres through reception. No matter how much historical imagination and archaeology we use, we engage historical writing as much as the present's critique of the past as the past as a means to criticize the present for present purposes.

The evidence of misogyny or gender stereotyping may be found in the speeches of many of the male characters, so that the context cannot simply undercut Hotspur's misogynist remarks. The prince parodies Hotspur and Kate, making them both trivial in their attitude toward those Hotspur has killed in battle. Their love of war is their war of love. Hal wants to play Percy and have Falstaff play Dame Mortimer (II. iv.96–109). Hal's transvestite Falstaff never plays the part of Kate, and, instead, swears his exaggerated valor "if manhood, good manhood, be not forgot upon the face of the earth" (II.iv.125–26). Instead, he will play Hal's father and then Hal in a playlet in which Hal gets the better of him. In the tavern scene the Hostess plays a serving role: she lets the prince know that one of the king's officers wants to speak with him. She speaks amidst the sexual jibes of Falstaff and Hal. Falstaff parodies Glendower for giving Lucifer horns and thereby making him a cuckold. Hal connects the heat of war with the sexual pliancy of women: "it is like if there come a hot June, and this civil buffeting hold, we shall buy maidenheads as they buy hob-nails, by the hundreds" (II.iv.357–59, see 333). While Falstaff responds favorably to the sexist jest, he raises his concern: "But tell me, Hal, art not thou horrible afeard?" In the play extempore, speaking passionately in King Cambyses' vein, Falstaff makes the Hostess his "sweet Queen" and "tristful Queen" but then quiets her laughter with more tavernly personifications—"pint-pot" and "tickle-brain" or strong liquor (II.iv.385–92). But the principal drama is between king and heir, Falstaff and Hal. Falstaff continues to satirize male anxiety over the faithfulness of their wives. Speaking as Henry, Falstaff says, "That thou art my son I have partly thy mother's word, partly my own opinion, but chiefly a villainous trick of thine eye, and a foolish hanging of thy nether lip, that doth warrant me. If then thou be son to me, here lies the point—why being son to me, art thou so pointed at?" (II.iv.397–400). In fact, elsewhere in the play, we never see or hear about Henry's wife. When the sheriff interrupts the play, the Hostess acts as a watch and messenger. The male roles continue to dominate the play.

The scene shifts from the competition between Falstaff and Hal to that between Hotspur and Glendower, both of whom the prince and the fat knight parodied in the previous scene. As usual, Hotspur belittles his rivals. He attempts to deflate Glendower's bragging about the importance of his nativity by saying that the heavens and earth would have shaken had Glendower never been born and, instead, his mother's cat had given birth. Using an explanation found in Aristotle's *Meteorlogica* (II.7–8), Pliny's *Natural History* (II.81), and Plutarch's *Opinions of Philosophers* (III.15), Hotspur adds that it might be "the imprisoning of unruly wind" in the earth's womb, an ailment and not Glendower's birth, that caused the "old beldam earth, . . . Our grandam earth," to shake (III.i.11–32). Glendower tries with rhetoric to overpower Hotspur and attempts to mythologize his birth further by making himself more than of woman born. Glendower wants to be his own mother. Although he is in his own mind like a god, his competitiveness with the mortal Hotspur is explicit:

> And bring him out that is but woman's son
> Can trace me in the tedious ways of art,
> And hold me pace in deep experiments.
> (III.i.44–46)

Hotspur is insulting about the Welsh language and about poetry just as he was about a woman's lies. Once the map of England and Wales has been divided to everyone's satisfaction, in contrast with Hotspur's earlier secrecy with Kate, Glendower asks the others to inform their wives of their departure and says how much his daughter will run mad on hearing that Mortimer must leave (III.i.136–40).

Like the scenes between Katharine and Henry V, the exchange between Lady Mortimer and Mortimer (with Glendower as translator) represents a marriage alliance of two people who cannot understand the other's language. Henry and Katharine can at least speak a few words of the other's language, but not Mortimer and his wife, even though they have known each other longer. Mortimer sounds like Romeo and the narrator of the sonnets addressing the young man. He is almost Petrarchan. She would go to the wars and be a soldier, for she will not part with Mortimer (III.i.189–90). Glendower translates his daughter's language of love for his son-in-law, a dialect that is unwarlike and full of pleasure and given to forgetfulness of the trials and rigors of life. When Lady Mortimer sings, Hotspur satirizes her to Kate as he had burlesqued Glendower to his face. Hotspur is intolerant of other languages—especially of those people the English have "tolerated," the Welsh and Irish—because he says he would rather hear his dog (a bitch, naturally) howl in Irish than hear Mortimer's wife sing in Welsh. Like Hamlet, he would "lay" in his lady's lap. Women in the Renaissance are often criticized for being garrulous, but Hotspur, after Kate threatens to break his head and orders him to be "still," reinforces the distinct roles of man and woman by declaring that it is "a woman's fault" to be still (III.i.231–35). Here, "still" probably means silent and motionless, a kind of passiveness that may be designed for male sexual activity. Hotspur jests that he help himself to Lady Mortimer but will not repeat it when Kate does not hear it. He then belittles his wife for speaking like a woman below her station (III.i.236f.). After Hotspur's "class act," he shows, as Glendower observes, how eager he is to leave his wife for battle, whereas Mortimer would stay by his wife's side. Hotspur may be an anti-Petrarchan satirist of love, but he also slips into the uncomfortable realms of misogyny and jingoism.

Henry compares Hal first to Richard and then to Hotspur. The dead king destroyed his authority because he allowed himself "To laugh at gibing boys, and stand the push / Of every beardless vain comparative" (III.ii.66–67). In other words, a man should not laugh at the wit of boys and beardless youths. Henry likens Hal unfavorably to Hotspur, "Mars in swaddling clothes" (III.ii.112). Mars is for men, Venus for effeminate men. Hal responds with a speech of blood and trumpets in which he redeem his honor on Hotspur's head (III.ii.129f.). This is a warrior culture where men judge other men by their ability to fight and conquer.

Falstaff is not a man of action but an apparent ne'r-do-well and coward, whose inaction and stillness threatens the warlike state. He tells Bardolph, "Why, my skin hangs about me like an old lady's loose gown" (III.iii.2–3). But Falstaff thinks of himself as a gentleman, someone who visits bawdy houses, swills and steals, and treats women accordingly—badly. He calls the Hostess "dame Partlet the hen," implying that she clucks and is fussy, and commands, "go to, you are a woman, go" (III.iii.50, 58–59). To be a man is to command women. As in earlier scenes, the comedy depends in part on males asserting their superiority over females. The Hostess will not let Sir John say that he "knows" her but, instead, speaks her own knowledge of him: he owes her money and, in order to erase his debt, is trying to tell her that a thief stole from him in her tavern. Falstaff tries to belittle the shirts that she gave him by implying that they did not live up to his station, so that he gave them away to baker's wives, who used them to sift meal. The prince's arrival reshapes the quarrel: he sides with the Hostess, but this support does not prevent Falstaff from insulting her and from avoiding repayment. Although Falstaff asks the prince to leave the Hostess and listen to him, she interrupts his fabrication about being robbed by swearing by her faith, truth, and womanhood that Falstaff slandered and threatened to cudgel Hal. This report prompts Falstaff to liken her to a "stewed prune," or bawd, and to a hunted fox drawn from cover. He says that she is worse than Maid Marian, a disreputable figure in Robin Hood ballads and a character in a May-game and morris dance whom the Puritans attacked for impropriety, impudence, and grotesque costume. A man often played this last character. Falstaff also calls the Hostess a "thing" (III.iii.110–14). She is an object—a sex object—to him. Falstaff likens her to an otter because "She's neither fish nor flesh, a man knows not where to have her" (III.iii.126–27). The Hostess plays right into his equivoque. To "have her" has three meanings: first, to take her; second, to get the better of her; third, to possess her sexually. She declares to Falstaff, "thou or any man knows where to have me" (III.iii.128–29). Shakespeare's prince and errant knight, perhaps because of their class, education, and gender, are getting the better of the Hostess. Even though the prince defends the Hostess, he participates in the jokes against her "honesty" (III.iii.154). In a comic reversal, Falstaff forgives the Hostess, who is the one who should forgive him, and, amidst his orders, Falstaff tells her, "thou shalt find me tractable to any honest reason" (III.iii.172–73). Hearing about the war, where Hal has got him the modest "charge of foot," Falstaff satirizes the departed prince's warlike words: "Rare words! Brave world! Hostess, my break-fast, come! / O, I could wish this tavern were my drum" (III.iii.204–5). This couplet encapsulates Falstaff's ambivalent gender roles, at least as they are traditionally constructed in the play and in the Renaissance. For half a line, the audience thinks that Falstaff is praising militarism; for another half, he commands the Hostess, as if their quarrel never happened, to serve him breakfast; in the second line he qualifies his praise of the prince's battle readiness. The tavern is the world of the Hostess and Falstaff. Only Hal departs the tavern for the battlefield with any resolve and relish.

The Hostess' appearance is the last by a female character in the play, even though two more acts remain. The comic company of the tavern cedes to the dark competition of the battleground. The scene shifts from the prince's jokes about having maidenheads as a result of the war to Hotspur talking about the rebels' situation after Northumberland's "sickness" as "the maidenhead of our affairs" (IV.i.59). The talk turns to Mercury and Mars, the encounter between Hal and Hotspur, even amidst the foreboding of the rebels' defeat. And Shakespeare prepares the way for the redemption of the wayward Hal into warlike manliness and honor.[53] Vernon says, "England did never owe so sweet a hope / So much misconstru'd in his wantonness" (V.ii.67–68). Hotspur is glad the king's advance "cuts me from my tale" because he avows that he is more interested in deeds than words, although he goes on talking, persuading his soldiers to fight in a way he denied he could (V.ii.90f., see 75–78). Hal speaks of his brother's "maiden sword" (V.iv.130). In war the world of women is displaced into an epithet for a weapon. Otherwise, the women are forgotten as the men contend for the kingdom.

2 HENRY IV

This play, like the first part of *Henry IV*, minimizes the role of women and represents male characters who worry about their manliness. Rumour, who begins *2 Henry IV*, resembles Virgil's Fama, a female figure who possesses many eyes, ears, and tongues and speaks about truth and falsehood. During the English Renaissance, the gender of Rumour, and the related figures of Report, Supposition, and Fame is not so clear. Whereas Stephen Hawes represents Fame as "A goodly lady, envyroned about / With tongues of fire," Holinshed writes about one of Henry VIII's pageants in 1519, "Then entered a person called Report, apparelled in crimsin sattin full of tongs."[54] Rumour is self-consciously monstrous but, using occupatio, will and will not blazon its anatomy. After characterizing itself as "a passive pipe on which the blunt monster" can play, Rumour asks,

> But what need I thus
> My well-known body to anatomize
> Among my household?
> (*2HIV*, IN.20–22)[55]

The Elizabethan audience—the theatre being one of Rumour's households—already
knew what to expect from that figure. From one interpretative vantage, that is assuming that Rumour is a female character played by a boy actor, the falsity of rumors
in this male world has been displaced onto the feminine through the "effeminate"
medium of a boy.[56] This point, although not certain, is in keeping with Virgil's use
of Fama in book 4 of *The Aeneid* and with the general attempt in the Renaissance
to separate the manly realm of deeds from the effeminate and feminine realm of
words. Even though Shakespeare shows his power through visual images on stage, like
Rumour itself, he often represents deeds through words, and much of his art arises
from verbal power. The anxiety over the status of words, even their relation to gender,
may help comprise a larger concern with values in Elizabethan England. Shakespeare
should not be equated with his characters, but they are refractions of their author's
psyche and participation in his culture. The characters are a site for the debate over
gender, which refracts a debate over the value of the theatre and of poetry, which
can be seen in the many attacks on the theatrical and poetic and the defenses against
them throughout Shakespeare's life. Are poetry and the theatre unmanly and sinful? These are central questions in the debate. They must be moral and teach men
to act morally even if they must do so with the much-questioned temptations of
pleasure. If Rumour is not a female figure, it still uses "false" images of a personified
war making the year pregnant and speaks about itself as a passive pipe. These traits
in conventional terms of the Renaissance would be identified with the female and
effeminate. This emphasis on gender, though potentially important, does not seem
to be here Shakespeare's main rhetorical concern.

Falstaff continues to speak about himself in terms of male and female. To his page
he declares, "I do here walk before thee like a sow that hath overwhelmed all her litter
but one" (I.ii.9–11). Falstaff is pregnant with an aggressive wit that would overwhelm
his page. He also satirizes the prince, the page's ultimate master, for not having a
beard, implying that he is not a man like Sir John. Falstaff belittles the manhood of his
rivals and those who thwart him. When the page tells him that Master Dommelton
will not give Falstaff satin, the knight rails, "Well, he may sleep in security, for he
hath the horn of abundance, and the lightness of his wife shines through it; and
yet cannot he see, though he have his own lanthorn to light him" (I.ii.45–48). This
is one of the many cuckold jokes in Shakespeare. Falstaff implies that Dommelton
is blind to his wife's infidelity and that although he has a cornucopia and a horn-
shaped light, he is blind to her adultery and his own cuckold horns. This invective
arises, as did his insults of the Hostess in *1 Henry IV*, from his need for money and
goods and his inability to be always successful into lying himself into further credit.
For some reason, this financial constraint leads to slander that involves the denigration of women.

Falstaff's wit derives in part from to proverbial wisdom that is not kind to women.
His suggestion that he bought Bardolph as a servant in Paul's, that Bardolph will
purchase him a horse in Smithfield, and that if he could only find a wife in the stews
echoes but alters the proverb: "A man must not make choice of 3. things in 3. places.
Of a wife in Westminster. Of a seruant in Paules. Of a horse in Smithfield. Least he
chuse a queane, a knaue or a iade."[57] Falstaff changes the order from wife, servant, and
horse to servant, horse, and wife and transforms Westminster into a brothel, so that he

can make the warning in the proverb. In jest at least, Falstaff would take a prostitute for his wife. Falstaff also regards his own "pregnancy" or wit as being undervalued in these times (I.ii.169). He must leave those who "kiss Lady Peace" for war (I.ii.207). Before he goes to the wars, Falstaff asks the page to deliver a letter to Mistress Ursula, whose identity is uncertain, as it is not clear whether she is the same person as Mistress Quickly (called Nell in *Henry V*), because he swears marriage many times to both figures, or another woman Falstaff strings along (I.ii.241–44, see II.i.86–87).

Whether or not Rumour was played a female figure there is no definitive evidence. In the body of the play, at least, the first woman does not appear until the second act. This delay in introducing female characters also occurs in the preceding two plays of the tetralogy. In a continuation of a disagreement in *Part 1*, the Hostess wants to arrest Falstaff. When the constables are afraid that Falstaff will stab them, the Hostess fleshes out the double entendre: "he stabbed me in mine own house, most beastly in good faith. A cares not what mischief he does, if his weapon be out; he will foin like any devil, he will spare neither man, woman, nor child." (I.iii.13–17). The words "stab" and "foin" can mean thrusts in sex as well as in fencing. Although equivocal, this allegation about not caring whether his object of violence or sex be man, woman, or child, implies a darker side to Falstaff, who after all profits from the deaths of his recruits, than most critics have wanted to explore. The Hostess' remark must be considered in the context of her slight command of the language and her more specific penchant for malapropisms, but her words should not be ignored and may imply a more complicated sexual world in the play. Shakespeare does not choose to emphasize this complex sexuality and blurring of gender, and how much the Hostess' remark is an interpretative issue depends on theoretical and critical practice. A deconstructive reading would, more than its predecessors, follow up on the exception just as a psychoanalytical interpretation might explore the Hostess' assertion as a Freudian slip or an unconscious displacement. Deconstructive and psychoanalytical readings are multifold and not monolithic. Judith Gardiner discusses the complexity of the various types of feminist psychoanalytical readings: "Often the feminist psychoanalytic critic relies on orthodox Freudian conceptions about the unconscious, sexuality, fantasies and defences to solve specifically feminist literary problems. Chief of these problems are the roles that gender plays in authors' projections, in characters' motivations, in readers' responses and in the latent structures of literary texts."[58] These problems take the interpreter down many forked paths. Despite the many difficulties in interpretation, readings persist. The scene continues the bawdy play, for instance Fang's "vice" and the Hostess' allusion to Falstaff's "infinitive thing upon my score," her asking pardon of the officers "(saving your manhoods)" and her having "borne" Falstaff's wrong (II.i.20–37). When the officers try to make the arrest, Falstaff orders Bardolph, "Throw the quean in the channel!" and Mistress Quickly accuses him of being a man killer and woman killer (II.i.46–52). Falstaff's page calls her a "fustilarian," which the *Riverside* glosses as a "frowsy slut," and Falstaff plays with an equivoque in which he would ride her (II.i.58–59, 74–77). In front of the Chief Justice the Hostess accuses Falstaff of breaking his promise to marry her, and the Justice tells the fat knight to pay her back and repent (II.i.84f.). But Falstaff takes the Hostess aside, apparently makes new promises, and asks her to pawn her plate. She gives in: her challenge is over. The exploitation of this woman, which underpins the comedy, will continue.

The tavern community treats women as sexual conveniences. The prince talks about Poins' bastards begot in the stews (II.ii.20–27). Poins taunts Bardolph for blushing like a maid: "What a maidenly man-at-arms you are become! Is't such a matter to get a pottle-pot's maidenhead?" (II.ii.73–75). This bawdy allusion yokes sex and drink just as the page's joke about Bardolph's red face does: "Methought he had made two holes in the ale-wife's new petticoat, and so peeped through" (II.ii.78–80). The coat is probably red and associated with prostitution. In the verbal exchange with Bardolph, when comparing his opponent's face to a firebrand, the page confuses Althaea's dream with Hecuba's, when she, pregnant with Paris, dreamt that she would bear a firebrand that would ruin Troy. But this instance shows that the power of women, even if only in a dream, is displaced by a boy onto a man's face, and he gets it wrong. Falstaff's letter, which he meant the prince to read in private but which he reads aloud, accuses Poins of trying to have the prince marry his sister Nell, in some parodic ale-house version of the dynastic marriage (II.ii.120–33). Hal himself assumes that Doll Tearsheet is a prostitute even though he has not met her. When the page declares that she is "A proper gentlewoman, sir, and a kinswoman of my master's," the prince cannot resist his punning ways that impugn Doll and yoke him to the fat, bullish Falstaff: "Even such kin as the parish heifers are to the town bull" (II.ii.146–50). By echoing the proverb "To be a great whore-master, to be the town-bull," Hal implies that Falstaff is Doll's pimp.[59] Hal and Poins agree that Doll is a "road," or a well-ridden prostitute. As in *1 Henry IV*, these two characters will disguise themselves to trick Falstaff.

Like the women at the Boar's Head, the women in the noble houses have little power over their fates. Shakespeare juxtaposes the two scenes as if each were to modify the other. Are all women kept from politics and left to the whims of men in the private sphere? Lady Northumberland seems to have given up pleading with her husband not to go to the wars, but Lady Percy, Hotspur's widow, will not desist. She reminds Northumberland how he deserted his son, so that his honor, being lost, cannot be redeemed through war but must await God's forgiveness. Lady Percy's speech becomes a eulogy for Hotspur: he was honor itself, so in speech, gait, diet, accent, inclinations to pleasure, military rules, and caprices of temperament "he was the mark and glass, copy and book, / That fashion'd others" (II.iii.31–32). In a hyperbole reminiscent of the king's in the opening scene of *Part 1*, Lady Percy calls Hotspur "O wondrous him! / O miracle of men!" (II.iii.32–33). For all of her earlier disagreements with Hotspur, she can only see him on his own terms, as a valiant, honorable soldier, even though she calls the god of war "hideous" (II.iii.35). This is no subversion of male martial values, but Lady Northumberland and Lady Percy do convince Northumberland to flee to Scotland rather than fight, a recommendation that might move toward the female subversion against male authority in Shakespeare that Woodbridge and Rackin claim.[60] The reasons that Lady Percy and Lady Northumberland give are not revolutionary but fit within the framework of male warrior culture. Lady Percy does not say that it is wrong for Northumberland to fight but that he should have fought with honor beside Hotspur and not to redeem his honor now for the mere sake of others. Lady Northumberland is concerned that the rebels are not strong enough and that her husband should wait to see how strong they are before fighting. Her daughter-in-law concurs and can only think that if Hotspur had to fight alone so should the marshal and archbishop (II.iii.41f.). Although Lady Percy is the type of mourning widows like the Duchess of Gloucester in the first act of *Richard II* and Lady Anne in the second scene of *Richard III* and it is understandable how pervasive her grief is, she does not question the wars and code of honor that helped to kill Percy. Only Falstaff satirizes honor, even if his motives are not always honorable (*IHIV*, V.i.127f.).

This scene occurs between two tavern scenes, which modify its sense of honor. Act 2, scene 4 parallels the same scene in *Part 1* but gives the women a larger role. Whereas the Hostess supports Doll Tearsheet in her drunkenness, Falstaff abuses her by generalizing about sickness in her sex: "So is all her sect; and they be once in a calm they are sick" (II.iv.37–38). Falstaff does not stop there with stereotypes, because he blames Doll for tempting him into loose-living and bloatedness (41). She denies it and blames gluttony and venereal disease for making Falstaff corpulent. Falstaff reasserts his blame, but Doll implies that women catch the diseases from men. Falstaff combines war and sex by using military terms to evoke sexual puns, of serving, occupying, deploying weapons, and firing bullets (48–52). But as much as the Hostess supports Doll elsewhere, she notes that Falstaff and Doll never get along and that Doll should bear troubles, children, and men because she is the weaker vessel (53–60). This is the same attitude Petruchio shows to Katherine in *Taming of the Shrew*: "Women are made to bear, and so are you" (II.i.201, *Riverside*; see the Arden ed.). Doll asks the Hostess whether an empty vessel like her can bear Falstaff, which seems to indicate that she will give in to the sexual jokes. She also yields because Falstaff is off to the wars but will not put up with another empty vessel, Pistol. The Hostess will also not welcome Pistol. Falstaff disparages women in his assurances that Pistol is only a cheater and not a swaggerer: "He'll not swagger with a Barbary hen, if her feathers turn back in any show of resistance" (97–98). "Barbary hen" can mean prostitute, so that the Hostess, like Doll, is reminded that she is no better than a whore. Falstaff ignores the requests of Doll and the Hostess because he lets Pistol enter and trades sexual innuendoes with him at the two women's expense. Doll will not accept Pistol's "charge," but demonstrates that, unwittingly or not, she plays by the rules of Falstaff's sexual pleasure: "Charge me? I scorn you, scurvy companion. . . . I am meat for your master" (120, 122–23). Doll heaps insults on Pistol as Hal and Falstaff had on each other in the main tavern scene in *Part 1*. Shakespeare gives comic scope to her aggression. Pistol will tear Doll's ruff, which, as Humphreys notes, happens in a number of English plays during the Renaissance, most notably when in *Bartholomew's Fair* (1614) Jordon Knockem, an expert in the sharp practice of the game of prostitution, threatens Punk Alice, a mistress of that game (to use Jonson's terminology): "Shall I tear ruff, slit waistcoat, mag rags of petticoat, ha?" (*BF*, IV.vi.78–79).[61] By calling Pistol captain, as Dover Wilson notes in the *New Cambridge Shakespeare*, the Hostess "hopes to pacify him by giving him a commission."[62] But Doll will have no part in it. She mocks Pistol in a quasi-catechismal rhetoric worthy of Falstaff: "You a captain? You slave! For what? For tearing a poor whore's ruff in a bawdyhouse? He a captain?" (140–42). Doll and the Hostess combat Pistol's threats with equivoques on "occupy" and "Peesel" for Pistol. He fights back with tags from old plays and from Elyot's *Ortho-epia Gallica* (1593), outbombasting heroes like Marlowe's Tamburlaine, and sexual quibbles on "etceteras nothings" (144–80). This is verbal warfare. It soon becomes a brawl. For some reason, Falstaff has decided to evict Pistol and not to go along with his insinuation that Doll is a "Galloway nag" or common whore, the kind of joke with which the fat knight began the scene (186). Falstaff wounds Pistol, if Bardolph can be believed. This bravery wins Doll's affection and praise as she mothers him: "Come on, you whoreson chops! Ah, rogue, i' faith, I love thee. Thou art as valorous as Hector of Troy, worth five of Agamemnon, and ten times better than the Nine Worthies" (215–18). It is as if Doll has imbibed Pistol's mock-heroic spirit. Falstaff's courage and honor has moved her so much she offers to sleep with him (220–21). The scene qualifies Hotspur's honor with Falstaff's, Lady Percy's adulation for her hero with Doll's. Paradoxically, while undermining the heroic code, this scene reinforces it—with all its gender stereotypes, such as the valiant warrior and the supportive if not sexually pliant woman. This is the ironic complexity I argue for in my interpretation of the tetralogy.

But Doll, like Hal, serves another thematic purpose in relation to Falstaff. She reminds him of his need for repentance: "when wilt thou leave fighting a-days, and foining a-nights, and begin to patch up thine old body for heaven?" (228–30). She also helps make the most of the dramatic irony by asking Falstaff questions about Hal and Poins that enable him to slander them as they work in disguise behind him. If Falstaff satirizes Poins for being a harmless follower of the prince who accompanies him in acts of bravado and flatters him, Poins and the Prince mock Falstaff for being too old to perform sexually. In counterpoint to this satire is the touching, if not slightly maudlin, exchange between Falstaff and Doll. When Falstaff says, "Thou't forget me when I am gone," Doll replies, "By my troth, thou't set me a-weeping and thou sayst so. Prove that ever I dress myself handsome till thy return" (274–77). But Shakespeare has too sure a dramatic sense to let such a tender moment linger. Poins and Hal come forward, and Falstaff tries to divert attention from his slanders to Doll's corruption because he swears by her, "by this light flesh and corrupt blood, thou art welcome" (291–93). This oath brings Doll's scorn. The Prince, who had called Doll a whore when he spoke for Poins' ears alone, now moralizes and gentrifies her with some irony, which the Hostess misses (297–301). To save himself but not his companions, as he had in the tavern scene in *Part 1*, Falstaff wants to save the prince from his wicked companions, who now include Mistress Quickly and Doll Tearsheet, with some equivocation. When the prince asks whether the women are wicked, Falstaff says that Doll is already in hell, but he does not know whether the Hostess is damned for lending him money. The Hostess does not think that she should be damned for her generosity, an act that is much in keeping with Falstaff's bold and incongruous comedy, and Falstaff agrees until he can indict her on account of serving meat during Lent. Nor will Falstaff relent in calling attention to the difference between a lady and a prostitute when, without bidding, he interprets with puns Hal's polite address to Doll—the prince's politeness calls her a gentlewoman when his flesh tells him she is a whore (334–48). As in the tavern scene in *1 Henry IV*, a knock interrupts the antics with the business of war. Hal bids Falstaff a crisp "good night" in contrast to the Hostess' extravagant compliments that arise from twenty-nine years of friendship and Doll's loving tears. Since Shrewsbury, Falstaff is much sought after in matters of war. In his words he is a man of merit rather than one of the "undeserved." He sends for Doll before he goes, far more reluctant than Hotspur ever was to leave the world of affection and sexual intimacy that women represent for the male world of destructive war (349–87).

I do not want to forget that this is a comic scene but only wish to note that it evokes laughter partly at the expense of women. It is a complex scene, so that the women seem to embody a fuller friendship with Falstaff than the prince does. Once again, this interpretation depends on point of view. If military honor and political order are the highest values, then the tavern is the place where the prince "So idly to profane the precious time," wastes. If, on the other hand, sex and affection between men and women, no matter how tainted by money and unequal social roles, are considered imperfect but better than war and political unity, then the tavern appears more savory than the battlefield. The rejection of Falstaff, even though many critics no longer view it as a problem because Hal must necessarily perform this act to rule the country, represents more than the casting off of a old fat man. The unruly affection of the tavern women is something that war will not tolerate. Today, on the verge of a possible war in Kuwait and in the Middle East, many of us may think that it is impossible after the trench warfare of the Great War and the Holocaust and nuclear bombing of the Second World War to appeal to military honor and glory.[63] But this is not what our newspapers and newscasts reflect and report. Such appeals are made over and over even in these historical circumstances. The idea that a twentieth-century view—jaded and "ironic" in the crudest sense—of war has preserved us from the horrors and insanities of battle becomes naive and self-congratulatory. The ironic view of war represents in the events of the second tetralogy and those that may come about before this work appears a multiplicity of scenes and values. Paradoxically, the tears of a prostitute wishing her John farewell may say more about survival than a hero going out to destroy the enemy. In an imperfect world, which is the greater disease: war or prostitution? The king and Warwick talk about England's diseased body (III.i.38–44). Both war and prostitution leave some women dependent. In modern war many women are killed without having weapons to fight back, though old wars were idealized. The fall of Troy meant the death of women and children, and Henry V threatens the virgins before Harfleur.

Other passing allusions to women show that while men exclude them from war, they cannot suppress them from their vocabularies. Henry IV's apostrophe to Sleep, a personified woman, is more an excuse to express a king's self-pity for having so much more responsibility than his poorer subjects than a way of filling up his bed as a result of the absence of a wife (III.i.1f.). Silence will not speak about his wife and daughter when Shallow asks him, but Shallow still asks Bardolph about Falstaff's wife. Bardolph replies, "Sir, pardon: a soldier is better accommodated with than a wife," which begins an increasingly heated discussion of the phrase "better accommodated" (III.ii.5–7, 63–66). For Bardolph, love and war do not mix. Mouldy, one of the recruits, says, "My old dame will be undone now for one to do her husbandry and her drudgery" (III.ii.112–13). The double entendres on "undone," "husbandry" and "drudgery," along with the play on "pricked," imply, one would hope, that Mouldy's old dame is not his mother but another woman he is cultivating. Falstaff quibbles on the name "Shadow," making the point that a woman often bears a son who hardly resembles his father (III.ii.128–31). This is another lame joke, but one that hints once more at the anxiety that sons do not measure up to fathers and that men are anxious about female fidelity and their own legitimate origins. Legitimate birth is like legitimate kingship. Falstaff is also punning on shadows, or death heads and faggots, who, in Elizabethan parlance, represent fictitious men on the muster rolls who enable a captain to collect their pay for his own profit. Nor is Falstaff finished spinning equivoques. Feeble says that he is a "woman's tailor," a trade that was, as Humphreys notes, often ridiculed, perhaps for effeminacy, as in Jonson's *New Inn* and Middleton's *Blurt, Master Constable*. "Tailor" could also refer to male or female genitalia, so that Falstaff continues his aggressive puns on "prick" (Humphreys 104). Amidst talk of disease, Shallow recalls the brothel Sir John and he used to frequent in their youth and, in particular, how Jane Nightwork once doted on him (III.ii.171–214). Bullcalf and Mouldy, who is concerned about his "old dame," pay off Bardolph so they do not have to serve in Falstaff's company. While parodying handbooks on war, Falstaff praises "Feeble the woman's tailor" for being able to run during a retreat. Shallow was Sir Dagonet, King Arthur's fool, in an annual exhibition in which a company of London archers took the names of the knights of the roundtable, which makes Shallow a fool while playing at war (III.ii.262–64, 274–81). Falstaff says that Shallow lies about many of his feats among the prostitutes but says that Shallow was "lecherous as a monkey, and the whores called him mandrake," which alludes to this root, whose resemblance to man included a penis, that was used in love potions. Some of the mandrakes were supposed to resemble women. Falstaff also says that Shallow used to sing old-fashioned songs to "overscutched housewives," battered or well-whipped hussies or whores. Although Falstaff is elsewhere likened to a Vice with a dagger of lath, he refers to Shallow as Vice's dagger (III.ii.295–327). Violence, especially violence to women, lies behind the comedy in this scene and others in the play. These male characters generally think about women in sexual terms, as subordinates to be whipped into submission and as possible threats to their masculinity and male identity.

No women appear from act 2, scene 4, until act 5, scene 5. These central scenes take place primarily near or on the battlefield. But the feminine appears amidst men. When Colevile surrenders to Falstaff because of the fat knight's reputation for valor, Falstaff speaks of his body in feminine terms:

> I have a whole school of tongues in this belly of mine,
> and not a tongue of them all speaks any other word
> but my name. And I had but a belly of any indifferency,
> I were simply the most active fellow in Europe: my womb,
> my womb, my womb undoes me.
> (IV.iii.18–23)

Falstaff's belly is like Rumour's. Although like the Scots "wame" "womb" can mean belly, it also represents a pun that calls attention to Falstaff's girth, which, like his wit, makes him seem pregnant. At the height of battle, when his reputation is at its apogee, Falstaff is likened to a woman. This valiant soldier, who is the very parody of military honor, is also a literary fat lady. Falstaff's boast comes right after John of Lancaster's betrayal of the rebels.

Sir John does not like Prince John's attitude toward him, so that, when Lancaster leaves, Falstaff mocks him as he had done Shallow. Falstaff's theme is that John of Lancaster is thin-blooded, sober, cowardly, and effeminate:

> There's never none of these demure boys come
> to any proof; for thin drink doth so over-cool their
> blood, and making many fish meals, that they fall
> into a kind of male green-sickness; and then when
> they marry they get wenches. They are generally fools
> and cowards—which some of us should be too, but
> for inflammation.
> (IV.iii.88–94)

Hal's brother should drink sack and eat meat to avoid being like an anemic unmarried girl who gives birth to girls. Falstaff, whose puns often liken him to a woman, wants to be valiant and manly and imputes to his enemies effeminate traits. This ambivalence to gender surrounds Falstaff. Using military metaphors, he then describes the effects of sack on the body.

Other references to the feminine and unmanly occur occasionally. The king uses the common personification of Fortune as a fickle woman: "Will Fortune never come with both hands full, / But write her fair words still in foulest letters?" (IV.iv.103–4). Gloucestershire, one of Henry's sons, speaks about the people reporting "Unfather'd heirs," which probably refers to a sprite begetting a child with a virgin, as in *The Faerie Queene* Spenser reports of Merlin's birth (*FQ*, III.iii.13). The obsession with legitimate heirs occurs in the imagery as well as the plot of the play. In the next scene Hal thinks that he is "unfathered" when he sees the crown beside his sleeping father, whom he presumes dead. Warwick tells Henry that Hal weeps at his father's "death," so that the Elizabethan division of behavior between the sexes appears not as rigid as it has since grown (IV.v.20–46, 81–87). When Henry IV dies, Henry V says to his brothers, "I'll be your father and your brother too" (V.ii.57). The new king presents himself as a replacement for his father and a benevolent patriarch, unlike the tyrannous Amurath, who killed all his brothers when he became sultan in 1574, as did his successor in 1596. No one speaks about mothers. Henry V says to the Lord Chief Justice—"You shall be a father to my youth"—and then calls him "father" (V.ii.118, 140). The scene focuses on the death of the father and the new king's assumption of the role of father as well as the adoption of a new father, which will lead to the rejection of his surrogate and theatrical father Falstaff. Shallow shows how manly and witty sack can make a man. Silence, too, shows his drunken wit by singing a song of "lusty lads" in a time "When flesh is cheap and females dear," another—

> Be merry, be merry, my wife has all,
> For women are shrews, both short and tall.
> 'Tis merry in hall, when beards wags all

—and yet others about sweethearts (V.iii.17–46). After these drinking songs, which treat women like commodities or sweethearts and wives like shrews, Pistol arrives as the man from court and, in his soldier's rant made from literary and lyrical tags, announces the death of Henry IV while insulting Shallow (V.iii.81f.). Pistol, who tells Sir John "I am thy Pistol," has been likened to a pizzle, now discharges his duty and raises Falstaff's expectations from Hal, who is, in Pistol's words, the knight's "tender lambkin." The audience knows, as Falstaff does not, that the woe he predicts for the Chief Justice is misplaced (V.iii.134).

When the audience does see women again, it is part of the crackdown against the tavern world.[64] The Hostess accuses the First Beadle: "Thou hast drawn my shoulder out of joint." He responds by threatening her with violence—"and she shall have whipping-cheer enough"—because a man or two has been murdered near her (V.iv.2–7). Doll threatens him: "and the child I go with do miscarry, thou wert better thou hadst struck thy mother, thou paper-faced villain" (9–11). Only from female characters does the audience hear of mothers. The Hostess, who seems to have problems with English, hopes that Falstaff will arrive to save them and that the child will miscarry, perhaps to scare the beadle that he will be charged with murder, but perhaps as part of the charade. Doll, if the First Beadle is to be believed, is not pregnant but uses pillows to feign pregnancy. He charges them, with Pistol, of beating a man to death (12–18). Doll threatens the First Beadle with violence: "I will have you soundly swinged for this—you blue-bottle rogue, you filthy famished correctioner, if you be not swinged I'll forswear half-kirtles" (19–22). She is as violent in her speech as are the men, but she must rely on someone else to do her thrashing even if she stakes her femininity on her ability to have him whipped by giving up wearing skirts. The First Beadle responds by calling her a "she knight-errant," which involves a quibble on a quixotic female knight and a woman who errs at night through carnal sins. The Hostess thinks of him as might and of them as right. Like Falstaff, both Doll and she attack thin people for being hard and unforgiving (23–31). Like men, women in the play use verbal violence and threats but, unlike men, they cannot do their bidding alone. If the Beadle is right, Doll and the Hostess needed Pistol's help to beat a man to death. Although in *2 Henry IV* women are subjected to the physical and verbal violence of men, they are not idealized but can also participate in that violence. This is slapstick comedy with a serious turn.

The women and the wild men of Hal's youth will be pushed aside.[65] When Pistol tells Falstaff of the arrest of Doll, "Helen of thy noble thoughts," and evokes Falstaff's revenge with an image of a Fury's snake, the fat knight swears to "deliver her" (V.v.31–39). The play ends with the rejection and arrest of Falstaff and John's talk of civil peace and war in France (41f., 97–109). This is a man's world of domestic order and the promise of foreign wars. Even if the Epilogue could curtsy, which men and women both did in Shakespeare's time, the drive toward the division of the sexes should not be underestimated (EP, 1–2). Despite the marginalization of women in war in the play, the Epilogue kneels down before the audience to pray for the queen (16–17). The queen, as several critics have noted, portrayed herself as a man and a woman, a prince unlike other women and a virgin, a Marian and revered female exempt from the trials of other women.[66] The Epilogue also tries to represent a consensus between the sexes in the playhouse, if not to imply the fiction that men would not disagree with women if they knew what was best for them: "All the gentlewomen here have forgiven me: if the gentlemen will not, then the gentlemen do not agree with the gentlewomen, which was never seen before in such an assembly" (22–25). This king of begging Epilogue is meant to bind the audience together in a community that marks the order and unity of an apparently comic ending. In the Epilogue to *As You Like It*, Rosalind, who makes something of the fact that a boy actor plays her part, attempts the same kind of ideal relation between men and women. She, too, makes much of addressing the women first, of how much men like women and of working harder to get the applause of the men. In *2 Henry IV* that men like women as women like men, on an equal footing, is not clear. The Epilogue to this play promises that the author will produce another play "with Sir John in it" and "Make you merry with fair Katharine of France" (26–34). But in *Henry V* Falstaff appears ever so briefly, and only in report, and Katharine is as powerless as she is charming. Her lack of power may ensure her charm in a male construction of ideal romance and womanhood.

HENRY V

In beginning obliquely with the suggestion that Elizabeth I was an important implied or potentially actual audience for Shakespeare when he wrote *Henry V*, I mean not to ignore my interpretation of the play in the next chapter but to provide other grounds for it.[67] I am not advocating a simplistic moral allegory in which Henry is really Elizabeth, but I am suggesting that ideas of gender and of governance in the play would be considered in terms of those in Elizabeth's England. Censorship is a commonplace of the Elizabethan playhouses. Shakespeare, Ben Jonson, and others experienced censorship. Shakespeare was probably a script-doctor for the censored and troubled *Sir Thomas More*. Shakespeare's plays were often performed at Elizabeth's court. The connection between the queen's gender and her ability to rule recurs in the debates of Elizabethan politics. Should a woman rule? Should a woman ruler marry? Should a female monarch rule her country and be ruled by her husband? Was Elizabeth primarily a "prince" or a woman? Henry V defeated the French against great odds; so too did Elizabeth rout the great Spanish Armada.

Henry V opens with clergy afraid for clerical interests and consequently advocating a foreign war based on Henry's right to the crown as a result of their interpretation of the Salic law, which came to be the rubric under which those who argued for the exclusion of females from the French throne rallied. The issue of gender in this play, and in the tetralogy of which it is the culmination, becomes more vital than it first appears. This is an issue that almost all male critics have failed to address seriously (many are charmed with Katharine) and that no female critic of whom I am aware has examined in detail.[68] The relation of Elizabeth later dawned on Elizabeth herself in 1601 when she is said to have called herself Richard II in the wake of the performance of Shakespeare's *Richard II* at the same time as the Essex rebellion of 1601. In *If You Know Not Me*, when portraying Elizabeth, Thomas Heywood takes lines from Shakespeare's Richard II and Henry V and gives them to Elizabeth, thereby making her masculine through ventriloquy and textual interplay.[69]

Some background about women's views of the feminine in the Middle Ages and the Renaissance, even if brief and barely adequate for the task, is necessary. This may seem like an indirection or digression, but I shall assume that these ideas of the feminine will have implications for male ideas of the feminine, masculine, and effeminate when we return to examining *Henry V* later in this section. These contexts will begin in the Middle Ages and move through Shakespeare's time to discussions of gender in Shakespeare to about 1990 (the 1980s being the historical moment of interest in relation to the 1590s).

Christine de Pisan (1364–1430?) is regarded in the French tradition as an early feminist. And she was not alone. Christine and those who shared her modern views of women lived at least two centuries before Shakespeare. As Joan Kelly notes, "Feminist theorizing arose in the fifteenth century in intimate association with, and in reaction to, the new secular culture of the modern European state."[70] This culture maligned and oppressed literate women, who in turn used their educations to defend themselves. For four centuries, Christine and others participated in what came to be known as the *querelle des femmes*. The defenders or advocates of women, as Kelly calls them, made polemical arguments against the defamation and subjection of women, held the idea of gender, that the sexes are culturally, and not simply biologically, constituted, and opposed the mistreatment of women. In early modern Europe, Kelly argues,

> aristocratic women lost considerable economic, political, and cultural power as compared, not only to their feudal forebears, but to men of their own class. At the same time, a class of women emerged, shaped by a new gender construction of the domestic lady. The contents of early feminist theory reflect the declining power of women of rank and the enforced domestication of middle-class women. Yet it owes its very being to the new powers of education some of these women had at their command.[71]

The attitudes of men surrounding these women were often not encouraging to the enterprise of the defenders or advocates. In *De claris mulieribus* (1355–59) Boccaccio spoke of viragos, of women whose virile souls were caught in female bodies. Allison Heisch and Kelly conclude that only viragos, exceptions to the female sex, could aspire to the Renaissance ideal of "man."[72] But to return to the Middle Ages: besides rewriting Boccaccio to illustrate a positive view of the nature of women, in *Livre de la Cité des dames* (1404), translated as *The Boke of the Cyte of Ladys* by Brian Anslay in 1521, Christine de Pisan made a case for female origins of culture and civilization and took offense against the Salic law of 1328.73 This law brings us to the hidden ground of *Henry V*. Olivier's version made the debate of the Salic law in act 1, scene 2, a slapstick comedy to interest the wartime filmgoer in a scene the director must have thought was full of irrelevant verbiage. It might be that in a production sympathetic to the position of women in the play, and certainly in a feminist production or film, the interest in this scene would be precisely in how Henry seeks glory and the French king bases his power on the exclusion of women from the throne of France. In directing a play, one has to make the abstract idea concrete in the speeches and gestures of the actors and in the set, which is always possible but difficult. A reading of the play does not always need such concretion. The reader only has to pay attention to the exclusion of women from the opening of the play. Certainly, *Richard II*, as well as *1* and *2 Henry IV*, make that exclusion unsurprising. It is the indignation of Christine in 1404 over the Salic law of 1328, a law that prevented women from inheriting the French crown, that serves as a reminder that rediscovering women in earlier periods, like the Renaissance, and reading Shakespearean histories with empathy for women and an understanding of their disinheritance represents a historical return and not an ahistorical interpretative wrenching by remaking *Henry V*, a work of the 1590s, into one of the 1990s. In *Il libro del cortegiano* (1528), translated as *The Courtyer* by Thomas Hoby in 1561, Baldassare Castiglione incorporates into his dialogues the decreasing role of women as governors and in public life generally. Although the duchess presides over the group, nineteen men and four women discuss the traits of the ideal courtier, and women are removed from bearing arms and horsemanship even if they share all other education with men.[74] The role of women in public life had declined in the early modern period, but Elizabeth I was on the throne when *Henry V* was first staged in 1599. How would she react to a scene that involved the exclusion of women from the throne of France? Queen Victoria seemed to ignore the Salic law even though she included the customary and fictitious claim to the French crown as one of her titles.[75]

To say that *Henry V* is partly about the role of Elizabeth I in her time is not to say that that is the rhetorical emphasis of the play. It may be, as I have suggested, one of its hidden grounds. But there were and are many portraits of Queen Elizabeth. Roy Strong concludes that a gap existed between the idealization and the actuality in the portraits of the queen.[76] Life could also make an art of the cult of the queen. J. E. Neale reports that on one of Elizabeth's progresses two hundred gentlemen in white velvet, three hundred in black velvet, and fifteen hundred servingmen, all mounted, met her in Suffolk, and, not to be outdone, twenty-five hundred horsemen met her in Norfolk.[77] At the end of George Peele's *The Arraignment of Paris* (1581–84) the golden apple is presented to Elizabeth as the climax of the play.[78] In John Lyly's *Endimion* (pub. 1591), which the children of Paul's performed before Elizabeth at Greenwich the night of New Year's Day in 1588, represents Cynthia as an allegorical figure for Elizabeth. The Epilogue shifts the allegory from moon to sun and explicitly states, "if your Highness vouchsafe with your favourable beams to glance upon us, we shall not only stoop, but with all humility, lay both our hand and hearts at you majesty's feet."[79] The publication of this play occurs in the same years as the inhibiting of the Paul's Boys, which was to last until 1599, probably for taking part in the Marprelate controversy.

Perhaps the best known idealization in Elizabethan literature is Spenser's *The Faerie Queene*, which includes the following tribute:

> Sunne of the world, great glory of the sky,
> That all the earth doest lighten with thy rayes,
> Great Gloriana, greatest Majesty,
> Pardon thy shepheard, mongst so many layes,
> As he hath sung of thee in all his dayes,
> To make one minime of thy poore handmayd,
> And underneath thy feete to place her prayse,
> That when thy glory shall be farre displayd
> To future age of her this mention may be made.
> (VI.x.28)

A shifting between identifying Elizabeth with the sun and moon, male and female, seems to occur in the symbology of the cult. John King aptly calls attention to Spenser's "Letter to Raleigh" (January 23, 1589–90), which prefaced *The Faerie Queene*, where the poet models his Belphoebe on Raleigh's Cynthia, presumably a missing part of the fragmentary part of Raleigh's *Ocean to Cynthia*, and observes that the "androgynous conceit that fuses solar and lunar qualities in the 'April' eclogue is akin to some queenly images in the *Faerie Queene*."[80]

That Walter Raleigh did much to disseminate the moon-cult may be seen in his nocturnal portrait (1588), in which Luna, the crescent moon in the upper left-hand corner, controls the tides. The queen manages the sailor, whose nickname, Water, as Neale reminds us, Elizabeth gave him.[81] Later, Raleigh's relations with the queen soured. Raleigh, as V. T. Harlow says, undertook a voyage to Guiana to present Elizabeth with that country of the Amazons, famous from the El Dorado legends, as a way of regaining the queen's favor, which she had denied him since his secret marriage to Elizabeth Throgmorton [Throckmorton] in 1592.[82] In the Epistle Dedicatory to *The Discoverie of the large and bewtiful Empire of Guiana* (1596) Raleigh says that he did not bring back treasure because he wanted to maintain the queen's "future honor and riches" and would not sack the kingdoms "vntill I knew whether it pleased God to put a disposition in her princely and royall heart either to follow of foreslow" that course.[83] In a book apparently written because the queen and others were skeptical about Raleigh's voyages—some actually doubted whether he traveled to South America—Raleigh addresses his "prince," who is also a woman and includes a passage in his description of Guiana that shows his ambivalent relation to his Virgin Queen:

> To conclude, Guiana is a Countrey that hath yet her Maydenhead, neuer sackt, turned, nor wrought, the face of the earth hath not beene torne, nor the vertue and salt of the soyle spent by manurance, the graues haue not beene opened for gold, the mines not broken with sledges, nor their Images puld down out of their temples. It hath neuer been entred by any armie of strength, and neuer conquered or possesed by any Christian Prince.[84]

This passage, which Montrose interprets in relation to Raleigh's desire for Elizabeth to undertake an "Amazonomachy," implies that Elizabeth, a virgin, should rape this virginal land and then, in the sentences that follow this passage, how to fortify the conquered land and conquer more. Elizabeth is a female prince, an oxymoron that, as this passage reveals, created sexual and gender doublethink. Besides grave robbing, Raleigh invokes the sexual image of penetration of the land, which in *Henry V* the king will do before Harfleur when he threatens to rape the virgins. Male violence against virgins, in the name of the prince but for the queen's eye, implies Elizabeth's double view of herself as a virgin and a prince. As her reign progresses, she denies anything ordinary about her womanhood. If Raleigh is ambivalent when he almost wrecked his life to regain the queen's favor, his idealization of Elizabeth is problematic. That is not to advocate a debunking of the queen but only to find, in Elizabethan times and now, a more balanced portrait of her.

Elizabeth did receive laudatory verses and literary tributes even after her death.[85] Shakespeare was not beyond such a paean. He waited until the queen was dead before representing the most overt praise in Cranmer's paean to the future greatness of the infant Elizabeth at the end of *Henry VIII*. King identifies the portrait of Elizabeth attaining apotheosis on the title page of William Camden's *Annales* (1625) as the height of hyperbolic representation of the queen.[86] Even longer after the death of the queen, Michael Drayton describes the earthly paradise, a favorite theme of Elizabethan literature, in a poem, *The Muses' Elizium* (1630), whose title conflates Elizabeth's name with the Elysian fields:

The Poets Paradice this is,
To which but few can come;
The Mu∫es onely bower of bli∫∫e
Their Deare *Elizium*
(the description of Elizivm)[87]

But the idealization of Elizabeth I has continued well into the twentieth century. Male historians and critics, until recently, idealized her the most and sometimes sounded like the male critics addressing Cleopatra that Woodbridge describes.
I should like to take as a representative J. E. Neale, the fine historian and chronicler
of Elizabeth and her parliaments. Of Elizabeth, he says, "She intoxicated Court and
country, keyed her realm to the intensity of her own spirit. No one but a woman
could have done it, and no woman without her superlative gifts could have attempted
it without disaster. In part instinctive, it was also conscious and deliberate."[88] Neale
implies that women are more and less than men and that, unless they are exceptional,
women should not try to excel in public life. This calls to mind Boccaccio's notion
of the virago. Neale concludes his magisterial study, *Elizabeth I and Her Parliaments*
(2 vols., 1953, 1957), "Some of her parliamentary actions, wrenched from their time
and setting, may seem harsh and despotic. Yet to understand is not merely to pardon;
it is to respect. Even when most truculent or admonitory, her messages and speeches
were suffused with queenly and motherly affection."[89] Neale appeals to Elizabeth's
female affection then adds that unless the queen's "princely" artificial style or our
own cynicism "makes disbelievers of us," Elizabeth's speeches will provide "the truest
display of the Gloriana her subjects adored: moving in their introspective moments,
inspired in their courage and confidence, transcendent in their utter dedication of self
to country and people."[90] Here is the language of religiosity and hero-worship that
we may find in the Bardolatry of Shakespeare that Shaw criticized and that Marjorie
Garber has described in apt psychoanalytical terms as "Shakespeare as Fetish."[91] Neale
invokes adoration and belief as a response to this "prince."

Predictably, a reaction against the cult of the Faerie Queene has set in just as
it did in the 1950s against Tillyard's *Elizabethan World Picture*. In discussing Dr.
Simon Foreman's dream of January 23, 1597, in which the queen becomes Foreman's
"virginal sex-object," Louis Montrose observes, "The virginal, erotic, and maternal
aspects of the Elizabethan feminine that the royal cult appropriates from the domestic domain are themselves appropriated by one of the queen's subjects and made the
material for his dreamwork."[92] This "unmastered" woman, whom Montrose says is
the only one in the kingdom, generated tensions about dependency and domination in a "patriarchal" society (68). By casting Foreman as Bottom, who falls in love
with the fairy queen, and by connecting the interest in Amazons in sixteenth-century
travel narratives and in the play, Montrose ingeniously connects *A Midsummer Night's
Dream* to this Elizabethan male anxiety over the queen as the only woman having
power over all of the men and their desire to control her.[93] Perhaps Foreman is like
Oberon because he wants to control female sexuality and her offspring, although
Foreman is not of the ruling class. During the Renaissance, the Amazonian mythology, as Montrose reminds us, "seems to embody and to control a collective anxiety
about the power of the female not only to dominate or reject the male but to create
and destroy him."[94] This may also relate to the obsession with cuckoldry in the *Henry*

IV plays and in other Shakespearean, Renaissance, and restoration plays. Montrose also evokes the New World, where Raleigh named Virginia for Elizabeth and where he discovered Guiana, which, like the Amazons, must be wooed with a sword. Montrose also links to Raleigh's description of the rape of virginal Guiana Spenser's evocation of Virginia and the Amazons in *The Faerie Queene* (*FQ*, 2 Proem 2, II.iii.31).[95] The virago distinguishes herself from other mortal women.

There are too many other male critics and historians who are fascinated with Elizabeth I to mention here, so that I shall refer only to John King as well as Peter McClure and Robin Headlam Wells, whose work builds on their predecessors. King summarizes a standard scholarly position on Elizabeth, her symbolic marriage to England, which allowed for a Petrarchan religion of love in ballads, pageants, entertainments, and plays, and her conversion of "her unprecedented weakness as a celibate queen" into a myth of public sacrifice. According to King, "her maidenly chastity was therefore interpreted not as a sign of political or social deficiency, but rather as a paradoxical symbol of the power of a woman who survived to govern despite illegitimization, subordination of female to male in the order of primogeniture, patriarchy, and masculine supremacy, and who remained unwed at a time when official sermons favored marriage and attacked the monastic vow of celibacy and veneration of the virgin Mary."[96] King attempts to historicize the changes to the myths surrounding the queen over the course of her reign. He notes that during the 1560s and 1570s the queen and her subjects assumed that she would marry.[97] During the four-year attempt to arrange a marriage between Elizabeth and the Duke of Alençon (1579–83), a symbolism and iconography of virtue and perpetual virginity develops.[98] McClure and Wells view Elizabeth as a second Virgin Mary, even though, as King points out, official Elizabethan sermons attacked the veneration of Mary.[99]

Building on E. C. Wilson's *England's Eliza* (1939) and Frances Yates' article, "Queen Elizabeth as Astrea," (1947), McClure and Wells say that they emphasize the relation of the cult of Elizabeth to the cult of Mary more than their predecessors. More generally, Roger Boase has set out the case that critics have made for interpreting courtly love in the light of Mariology. McClure and Wells argue that "a mystical kinship between the Virgin Elizabeth and the Virgin Mary was central, not peripheral, to the cult of the English monarch," as evidenced in literature, drama, and the visual arts.[100] This is a recent version of an argument with which Philippa Berry disagrees on the grounds that the cult of Mary did not use desire, worldly power, and natural imagery to define her worship.[101] Yates' concentration on Astrea, the virgin of the golden age whose return was prophesied in Virgil's *Fourth Eclogue*, as the key to Elizabethan state symbolism, according to Wells and McClure, appeals only to the mind. These critics also fault Wilson for treating Marian symbols no differently from those of classical figures like Diana. Both Yates and Wilson, they argue, do not take into account the political and religious climate of the times when they commit these errors.[102] Although in the view of McClure and Wells the moderate Elizabethan Protestant wanted to throw off the pope as part of his nation's progress, he also experienced "seductive memories and reminders of pre-Reformation beliefs and practices." At the conclusion of their own apotheosis of Elizabeth, which uses religious and sexual imagery, these critics aver that "Only in the queen's mystical fellowship with the Virgin Mary were such emotional, intellectual and spiritual conflicts resolved, and only in that typological relationship between the two women—expressed in 'the miraculous maiden circle' of Elizabeth's life and in an iconography that portrayed the embodiment of the state and the symbol of the church as a post-figuration of the Blessed Virgin—was the historical, political and theological meaning of Virgil's prophecy fully articulated."[103] Possibly, as Julia Kristeva says, the loss of the virgin has affected women's representation.[104]

Even in the revision of earlier views of Elizabeth, it is difficult, especially among male critics, not to sense a king of religiosity or obsession, whether they argue for skepticism, historical context, or a new religious analogy. This precarious relation of authority and subjection, which Montrose discusses, may be one of the traps that male projection onto women sets for itself even as it tries to locate the trap and, in some cases, eradicate it. Elizabeth is a test case just as Shakespeare's Henry V is for male ideas of honor and heroism. The two celebrations are too closely related in the person of the prince to ignore.

Female critics are increasingly wary of the myth of Elizabeth that many men helped to create. Although many women have written about the cult of Elizabeth, for the sake of brevity, I must limit my discussion to a few. In *Ester hath hang'd Haman* (London 1617) Ester Sowernam called Elizabeth "not onely the glory of our Sexe, but a patterne for the beſte men to imitate."[105] But Joan Kelly and Allison Heisch both call Elizabeth an "honorary male." According to Kelly, Elizabeth's rule was that of a virago who did little to advance the lot of women, who saw herself, at least in official propaganda, as an exception to the law of nature, and who, in her famous Tilbury speech, where she is reported to have said that she had the body of a weak and feeble woman but the heart and stomach of a king of England.[106] Mary Thomas Crane observes that Elizabeth is often constructed through male eyes in her time and ours. For Crane, the first group of critics (Marotti, Montrose, and Greenblatt) have discussed how Elizabeth manipulated and was manipulated by pastoral and Petrarchan models and how her courtiers and she used them as mediations through which they asserted and mystified their power. The second group of critics (Javitch and Whigham) have examined how the rhetorical strategies and tropes of courtesy books like Castiglione's *The Courtier* allowed for political struggles at court. Crane aptly notes that these two critical views do not fully account for Elizabeth's strategies of power because the Petrarchan, pastoral, and courtly idioms arise mainly from the writings of male courtiers and writers and not from those of the queen, so that these symbols may tell us more about what the men wished to see in Elizabeth than how she envisioned and presented herself. These two critical views of the queen emphasize her as playing at the role of the marginal and apparently powerless woman in order to mask her power and a persona that her male subjects encouraged to manage her.

As an alternative to this patriarchal queen, Crane explores political counsel to demonstrate how she asserted and protected her authority in forging public policy. Elizabeth, as Crane says, depicted herself as "educated advisor," a role that her male subjects neglected to apply to her, to subvert the patriarchy. She took up the male authority, which humanists associated with men, to play an active role in government rather than the static role of figurehead and object of male worship. Elizabeth, according to Crane, asserted and abnegated authority through the male role of political counselor, which allowed her power and put limits on those of her male advisors.[107]

Crane also opposes some female critics, who, she says, have emphasized Elizabeth's denigration of her "female" weakness while asserting her divine "body politic" as masculine or androgynous authority.[108]

Philippa Berry argues that the absolute monarchies of France and England in the sixteenth century appropriated to themselves idealized attitudes to love, notably Petrarchism and Neoplatonism. In England literary representations of an unmarried queen as an ideal of female chastity revealed the inner contradictions of this model. The female beloved in both Petrarchism and Florentine Neoplatonism, Berry says, at least when she was not a queen, usually represented "little more than an instrument in an elaborate game of masculine 'speculation' and self-determination" or male narcissism.[109] Berry argues that Frances Yates, and many other commentators on the cult of Elizabeth do not adequately emphasize gender.[110] As an alternative, Berry proposes that in order to consider Elizabeth as a woman, one has to look at the potentially subversive representation of her as a Petrarchan or Neoplatonic beloved with spiritual and political power and to remember Elizabeth's ties to her beheaded mother and to female courtiers.[111] Berry also notes that male critics too often define women in relation to men and have neglected to mention that for the first twenty years of Elizabeth's reign she was represented as an "unattainable object of male desire."[112] In the 1590s, Berry says, Chapman, Shakespeare, Raleigh, and Spenser rewrite chastity through their representations of the unmarried queen. According to Berry, during that decade, the professional poet and playwright transformed an aristocratic cult into a widely disseminated commodity. For instance, the poets and dramatists appropriated the courtly allusions to Elizabeth as Diana or Cynthia.[113] In literary works the association of Elizabeth with the moon, rather than with the more conventional symbol of kingship, the sun, in Berry's view, made the queen more problematic because of her association with a changeable and wandering planet.

Other changes in the writings of the 1590s modify the doctrine of chastity, which affected the cult of Elizabeth: the renewed emphasis on marriage; the anti-Petrarchan and antiplatonic attitudes, or the beloved as spouse, or the male beloved or patron, rather than the female beloved, as idealized object, in some of the sonnets; similar recasting of classical conventions and the comic but sometimes misogynist views of love; the absence of a representation of the female body; and the attempted manipulation and negation of female sexual desire in the epyllion or erotic narrative poem.[114]

This is a long digression from what many critics have considered important in *Henry V* but it is, I hope, warranted. The queen is the ruler and primary authority and audience for courtiers, authors, and subjects. In *Henry V* the Prologue speaks of Mars, war, and kings, not of women. In the opening scene the clergy wants a war in France to divert attention from a bill they consider detrimental to their interests. The second scene involves the debate of the Salic law, which was a collection of folk laws and customs that had nothing to do with succession but late became associated with the barring of women from the French throne, which began when the French nobles elected Philip of Valois to the throne to prevent a woman from ascending it and rejected Edward III's claim through his mother, Isabella. The principle, which is here associated with the Salic law, assumes that only the male monarch can enter into a symbolic marriage with his kingdom.[115] But when Henry V asks the advice of the Archbishop of Canterbury on the question of his right to the French crown, Canterbury argues against the Salic law, but not on the grounds that it has nothing to do with the barring of women from ascending the French throne, but because the Salic realm is in Germany and not in France. The reason Canterbury gives for the law in this German realm is that the French who lived in the Salic realm disdained "the German women / For some dishonest manners of their life" and so established the Salic law (I.ii.48–50, see 35f.). Here again is the male obsession with female chastity and the provable true heir. The French, Canterbury says, did not possess the Salic land until four hundred and twenty-one years after Pharamond, the supposed framer of the law. Appealing to more traditional scholarship, Canterbury tells Henry that the French writers enumerate a list of French kings who claim the crown as a result of their mothers or female ancestors and that the present French king, who relies on female ancestors for his claim to the throne, uses the Salic law to hide the fact that Henry has a better claim to the French throne, which descended from Isabella, daughter of Philip IV of France and mother of Edward III. Canterbury also cites the book of Numbers: "'When the man dies, let the inheritance / Descend unto the daughter'" (I.ii.99–100). Canterbury and Ely as well as the secular lords, Exeter, his uncle, and Westmoreland then switch attention from the female ancestors that enable Henry's claim to the glory of Edward the Black Prince and of the English in their bloody defeats of the French on the battlefield (100–142). The women become pawns that ensure male battle-glory. These advisors debate with the king the history and strategy of domestic defense and foreign wars (143–221). After hearing this advice, Henry concludes, "France being ours, we'll bend it to our awe / Or break it all to pieces" (224–25). Henry's warlike reply to the "sporting" insult of the Dauphin's gift of tennis balls includes a threat of war that has dire consequences for women:

> for many a thousand widows
> Shall this his mock mock out of their dear husbands;
> Mock mothers from their sons, mock castles down.
> (284–86)

These women are caught between the Dauphin's insults and Henry's threats, victims who have no say in war and peace.

The former tavern world of the *Henry IV* plays is shaken. Nell Quickly, Bardolph says, was betrothed to Nym but married Pistol. The opening scene in act 2 represents the tension between Nym and Pistol over Mistress Quickly, the first woman on stage in *Henry V*. Once again, as in *2 Henry IV* (II.iv), the Hostess is surrounded by violence, and, as if she expects respectability, she says that if she lodges a dozen or fourteen gentlewomen, then people will think her place a bawdy-house (II.i.32–37). Using a double entendre, the Hostess asks Nym to "show thy valour and put up your sword" (43–44). Pistol blusters and declares in a comic version of the third-person that Caesar uses in *The Gallic Wars*: "Pistol's cock is up" (51). This comic plot, like the main plot, has men fighting over women and marriage as their source of manliness. Bardolph achieves peace by threatening each with violence (63–65). But the verbal threats persist. Even though a betrothal was a serious legal and moral bond, so that if Bardolph is correct, Nym and the Hostess are so bound, Pistol's ethos is to treat Nym with contempt, to use violence to keep Mistress Quickly from him, and to insult him by implying that Nym is only good for whores: O hound of Crete, think'st thou my spouse to get?

> No; to the spital go,
> And from the powdering-tub of infamy
> Fetch forth the lazar kite of Cressid's kind,
> Doll Tearsheet she by name, and her espouse:
> I have, and I will hold, the quondam Quickly
> For the only she; and—pauca, there's enough.
> (II.i.73–79)

Pistol says that Nym deserves to go to a steam bath used to treat venereal disease in order to find a Cressida, portrayed as a diseased whore in Robert Henryson's *Testament of Cresseid* (pub. 1561) and later the phrase, "kite of Cressid's kind" often appears in Elizabethan literature (see George Gascoigne, *Dan Bartholomew of Bath* [1577], a verse account of the author's adventures between 1572 and 1574 in the Netherlands [line 69], where he was taken prisoner, and Greene, *Carde of Fancie* [1587], IV.132).[116] Despite the violence, the Hostess shows some affection and care about the men about her, Falstaff and Pistol. Of the first, she says, "The king has killed his heart," and to the second, she says generously, "Good husband, come home presently" (88–89). Even though Falstaff has been corrupt, Pistol is belligerent, and both are comic characters subordinated to the audience through dramatic irony, these words are tender. Nevertheless, the context of those words is two near fights between Nym and Pistol as Bardolph intervenes. Another such fight begins after the Hostess leaves with the Boy who has reported on Falstaff's sickness (90–100). This time, however, at Bardolph's request, Pistol pays his debt to Nym, and they are friends. For Nym, the loss of money was more important than the loss of his betrothed. The Hostess reports with her usual malapropisms the terrible fever Falstaff is suffering and, with the others, gently blames the king for breaking the fat knight's heart (117f.).

The death of Falstaff occurs offstage. When the Hostess asks to go with her "honey-sweet husband" on the road to Southampton, Pistol says no because his "manly heart" mourns for Falstaff, as if the presence of a woman would lessen the mourning of Pistol and his male companions (II.iii.1–6). The hostess' report of the moments before and after Falstaff's death, even as she malaprops Arthur for Abraham, provides a dramatic and physical description. As she describes reaching up the sheets to his knees and beyond it is as if she were a lover feeling his body for the last time, knowing that the various parts are colder than life ever made them (9–27). She confirms the rumor that Nym heard that on his deathbed Falstaff cried out for sack but denies the one that Bardolph heard that Sir John called out for women. The Boy contradicts the Hostess: "Yes, that a' did; and said they were the devils incarnate" (32–33). The Hostess may have wanted to forgive and forget Falstaff's misogyny to protect her sex or his memory. She thinks of "incarnate" as red rather than of its other meaning—in the flesh, and says Falstaff never liked the color. But the Hostess' irrelevancies cannot divert the tenacious Boy, who reports of Falstaff that "A' said once, the devil would have him about women" (36–37). In the Boy's view, Sir John thought of women as his temptation, a traditional view associated with Eve's temptation of Adam.[117] Falstaff's fear of women and misogyny is given a theological cast. When the Hostess responds to the Boy, "A' did in some sort, indeed, handle women; but then he was rheumatic, and talked of the whore of Babylon" (38–40), she may be implying that in health Falstaff spoke with and fondled women but in sickness or romance (the Elizabethan pronunciation allows for pun on "rheumatic"), he spoke, as a Puritan might, thus following Wyclif and the Lollards, of the Catholic Church as the "scarlet woman" of Revelation 17:4–5 or the Whore of Babylon. The Hostess' lines, which play on the redness of "incarnate" and "carnation," show traces of the first conception of Falstaff's character, Sir John Oldcastle, but they also indicate that the slander against one's male enemies, by likening them to a so-called fallen woman, also represents a general slander against women. This slander becomes common in sixteenth-century England. Pistol's instructions to his wife about how to handle their finances and his command that she occupy herself as a housewife constitute an example of male control (48–65). Pistol wants to place her as much in the domestic domain as possible. When he asks the others to kiss her, Nym cannot, perhaps an indication that his loss of Mistress Quickly touches him still and that the rift with Pistol is not entirely mended. This is the last we see of the Hostess. Except for the French princess and Alice, the rest of the play is devoid of female characters.

As in the next chapter I discuss much of the male characters' disturbing treatment of women in conjunction with other concerns, I shall look briefly at a few other instances of the male use of females to further their power. When Exeter acts as Henry's ambassador, he tells the French king that if he does not give up the crown because of Henry's rightful claim, France will suffer:

> and on your head
> Turning the widows' tears and orphans' cries,
> The dead man's blood, the prived maidens' groans,
> For husbands, fathers, and betrothed lovers,
> That shall be swallow'd in this controversy.
> (II.iv.105–9)[118]

This threat that women and children will mourn those men taken from them in war becomes one of the violence tropes that Henry and his government use, apparently to avoid violence. The victims never have a say in war and peace. Exeter also reports to the Dauphin that Henry disdains his disdain:

> He'll call you to so hot an answer of it,
> That caves and womby vaultages of France
> Shall chide your trespass and return your mock
> In second accent of his ordinance.
> (123–26)

As in the earlier plays, England and France are females on which the male acts (see *HV*, II.iii.175–77). The threats are part of a male ritual not unlike the challenges between Bolingbroke and Mowbray at the opening of *Richard II*. While the French king is remarkably restrained, the Dauphin has drawn Henry into a male competition of who is the most powerful. In response to the Dauphin's scorn, Exeter threatens him on behalf of Henry: "he'll make your Paris Louvre shake for it, / Were it the mistress-court of mighty Europe" (132–33). Here, Exeter is thinking of "mistress" as a principal, a term from tennis, which is a response to the Dauphin's gift of tennis balls, and may be punning on "Louvre" as lover. He conflates war, women, and sport. A return to the feminine occurs in the definition of the manly war. The Chorus amplifies this view and asks the audience to participate in it:

> Follow, follow!
> Grapple your minds to sternage of this navy,
> And leave your England, as dead midnight still,
> Guarded with grandsires, babies, and old women,
> Either past or not arriv'd to pith and puissance:
> For who is he, whose chin is but enrich'd
> With one appearing hair, that will not follow
> These cull's and choice-drawn caveliers to France?
> (CH. III.17–24)

England is guarded by the weak because any boy who is "enriched" with even a hair of manhood would fight in France. The Chorus also wants the audience to suppose that the French king, through his ambassador, offers his daughter and a few "petty and unprofitable dukedoms" to Henry, who rejects the offer (28–32). As Lawrence Stone notes, for at least a thousand years before the sixteenth century, the characteristic family was the open lineage family, in which, at least at the middle and upper levels of society, political and economic advantages were considered foremost and in which the parents and kin, and not the bride and groom, selected the mates. In this kind of family, primogeniture, entails, and the dowry system governed the structure of propertied families This type of family describes that which Shakespeare is representing in this and the other histories in this tetralogy, but, according to Stone, the restricted patriarchal nuclear family best describes the English family between 1580 and 1640. Shakespeare and much of his audience in the 1590s would have experienced the gradual transition from the open lineage family to a more nuclear family, from loyalties to lineage, kin, patron, and local community of the one to loyalties to country, sovereign, and a particular sect of the church of the other. A certain recognition of, as well as a certain estrangement from, the open lineage family would probably exist in the audience. Apparently, in this transition, church and state strengthened the power of the patriarch within the home over wife and children.[119] In the Chorus' report two dynasties treat a daughter like property and territory, as a potential exchange in a peace treaty.

Unlike women, men try to define themselves in terms of themselves. Before Harfleur, Henry defines masculinity:

> In peace there's nothing so becomes a man
> As modest stillness and humility:
> But when the blast of war blows in our ears,
> Then imitate the action of the tiger.
> (III.i.3–6)

Men split their personalities between peace and war. Henry also appeals to the glory of their fathers in a kind of patriarchal representation and, in a commonplace, likens war to the hunt (19f.). Less "manly" than Henry, the Boy and Pistol agree that they would rather be in an alehouse in London than at war in France (II.ii.11–20). Pistol asks Fluellen to "abate thy manly rage," which may be comic because Fluellen is a comic figure who becomes engaged in a squabble with the bombastic Pistol (23). The Boy says that although he is a boy, Bardolph, Pistol, and Nym are not men to him because they are cowards and thieves (28–57). Amid the violence, Captains Fluellen, Jamy, Gower, and Macmorris speak about their violent deeds and debate military action. These Welsh, Scottish, English, and Irish men are drawn together in an imperial war against the French, but Fluellen and Macmorris nearly fight each other (78f.). In the next scene Henry threatens the men of Harfleur in words like those he sent with Exeter to the French court. If they will not surrender, he mow down their children and virgins and rape the maidens, a theme that he amplifies repeatedly in this long speech (III.iii.1–43). If Henry plays Herod to virgins, what would Shakespeare's Henry V have been like to Elizabeth I, a virgin and a commander at Tilbury, a maiden prince? I do not wish to ventriloquize her thoughts but to suggest that a certain ambivalence may have characterized her reaction to this and other instances of male authors representing the prince in action and his relation to women. This is one reason I have cited the often contradictory critical views of both male and female critics in regard to Elizabeth's relation to the gender politics of her day.

The differences in class and language among the men in the "English" camp join those between the French and English women in decentering a common notion of men and women. The actual appearance of French in act 3, scene 4, where Alice gives Katharine an English lesson, distances the audience from these women because of the strangeness of their language. The French have been speaking English all along and now these women do not know any better and have decided to speak their "mother tongue." Fortunately, in the middle of this play about English nationalism or jingoism, they are doing so in a language lesson, where Katharine will learn English, the language of the invader. With help from Alice, Katharine anatomizes her body and does an inventory of the parts, a kind of self-imposed blazon, as if she must learn to see herself through Henry's English eyes, as she may become his property. A blazon was, as Nancy Vickers notes, a conventional heraldic description of a shield and a poet's conventional description of an object he is praising or blaming, and she says that the most celebrated examples of French blazons, in which each poem praised a separate part of the female body, was *Blasons anatomiques du corps feminin* (1543). In the English tradition the blazon consisted of a catalogue of each beautiful part in a kind of remembered dismemberment of the female body.[120]

This disturbing combination of a male article of war and his dismembered object of lust or idealized love is in keeping with the yoking of male battle lust to their subordination of women in this and the earlier plays. But Shakespeare has a female Katharine list the parts of her body in a way that is common during a language lesson. Without making too much of a common pedagogical technique, I am saying that inadvertently it has a similar effect to a blazon, a kind of trap for women that Vickers discusses and out of which women should write themselves.[121] Katharine thinks that "foot" and "count" sound like obscene French words. Her response to them is equivocal. On the one hand, she implies that she does not like obscenities against women, but more directly, she does not think that a woman of honor should utter such words, especially before French gentlemen. Nonetheless, she repeats them for Alice, as if delighting at some level in the forbidden utterance and as if women can take these words even if men cannot from the mouths of women. Then Katharine culminates her lesson by climaxing her list of the parts of her body by uttering these two words. Her prowess in English brings high praise from her older companion, Alice, who does not seem that concerned about how these two English words sound like obscenities in French (51–62). Katharine is internalizing male constructions of female honor while rebelling against the male silencing of women and management of female speech. Shakespeare assumes that his audience will understand a brief scene predominantly in French but relating an English lesson. Katharine must be taught English to become Henry's wife, but her attitudes represent contradictions over the construction of female honor.

The French lords also attribute to French women doubts about the manhood of their men, thereby revealing the uncertainties of the male speakers who report these doubts and showing that the women may have internalized the gender system that the men imposed on them.

> DAUPHIN. By faith and honour,
> Our madams mock at us, and plainly say
> Our mettle is bred out; and they will give
> Their bodies to the lust of English youth
> To new-store France with bastard warriors.
>
> BRETAGNE. They bid us to the English dancing-schools,
> And teach lavoltas high and swift corantos;
> Saying our grace is only in our heels,
> And that we are most lofty runaways.
> (III.v.27–35)

These comments are surrounded by the men's talk of fathers, lineage, honor, and overconfidence and their disdain for the English as Norman bastards. The French disdain for the nation they conquered centuries before and the feudal titles relate closely to the values the women are reported to hold—disdain of their men for being effeminate cowards worthy only to teach dance to the English. The French king's defiance and disdain for Henry V is supposed to prepare for Henry's bloody course and victory (36–54).

Another way men try to explain the world is by attributing the fickleness of the world to the goddess Fortune. Before Pistol can complete his complaint to Fluellen that Bardolph is to suffer the death penalty as a result of the fickle, blind, and restless goddess Fortune, Fluellen interrupts him with an explication of Pistol's stock symbolic representation of the goddess. He explains that her muffler represents her blindness, her wheel shows "that she is turning, and inconstant, and mutability, and variation," and her foot on the stone depicts the rolling and rolling of events (III.vi.25–59). The vices that men in classical, medieval, and early modern periods attributed to women also become those of goddesses who are blamed for the flaws and vices of men and for their faulty actions. After Fluellen and Pistol have a verbal run-in, Gower discredits Pistol as a roguish soldier who decorates himself with honors through his stories of the war rather than in the war (61–88). When Fluellen tells Henry that Bardolph is to be executed, the king does not acknowledge his former friendship with him but speaks in general terms about how important it is to execute such thieves because one should not abuse the French verbally or actively but conquer them with gentleness (99–117). This military discipline leads to a death of a friend and to a rejection of a former life, less intense but of the same kind as the rejection of Falstaff. Montjoy, who represents the French king, and Henry exchange threats and boasts, although Henry admits weakness in such an astute way that he uses it to brag about the strength and valor of the English army (118–72). Here, between kings, is a rhetorical battle: the words of men cannot escape competition.

In the next scene even the French warriors compete among themselves over the greatness of their horses (III.vii). In that competition the Dauphin reveals that he is riding a palfrey, which Walters says is a lady's horse and infers that the Dauphin is effeminate (28–30). The Dauphin boasts that he has written a sonnet to his horse, which sparks an exchange that is, through references to horses, full of male pride of the mastery of women:

> ORLEANS. I have heard a sonnet begin so to one's mistress.
>
> DAUPHIN. Then did they imitate that which I composed to
>   my courser; for my horse is my mistress.
>
> ORLEANS. Your mistress bears well.
>
> DAUPHIN. Me well; which is the prescript praise and perfection
>   of a good and particular mistress.
>
> CONSTABLE. Nay, for methought yesterday your mistress shrewdly
>   shook your back.
>
> DAUPHIN. So perhaps did yours.
>
> CONSTABLE. Mine was not bridled.
>
> DAUPHIN. O, then, belike she was old and gentle, and you rode,
>   like a kern of Ireland, your French hose off, and in your
>   straight strossers.
>
> CONSTABLE. You have good judgment in horsemanship.
>
> DAUPHIN. Be warned by me, then: they that ride so, and ride not
>   warily, fall into foul bogs. I had rather have my horse to
>   my mistress.
>
> CONSTABLE. I had as lief have my mistress a jade.
>
> DAUPHIN. I tell thee, constable, my mistress wears his own hair.

CONSTABLE. I could make as true a boast as that if I had a sow to my
mistress.

DAUPHIN. Le chien est retourné à son propre vomissement,
et la truie lavée au bourbier: thou makest use
of anything.

CONSTABLE. Yet do I not use my horse for my mistress; or
any such proverb so little kin to the purpose.
(III.vii.43–69)

In response to the Dauphin's unlikely and absurd sonnet to his horse, Orleans
begins the mockery of the Dauphin by taking an ironical position, saying that the
opening of that sonnet, "Wonder of nature," more suits a mistress. The Dauphin's wild
praise of his horse makes him take what is, perhaps, an inadvertent anti-Petrarchan
stance. A mistress is more like a horse than like the sun, but, for the Dauphin, the
absurdity does not stop there, because this is an extreme compliment because, in his
view, how could a mere woman measure up to a mare? But despite the Constable's
protest to the contrary, at the end of the exchange when Rambures changes the subject, saying that the analogy between horse and mistress shows little wit, Orleans and
he still string the Dauphin along and encourage such sexist comparisons. Orleans
says that the Dauphin's mistress, his horse, "bears well," while the Constable speaks
of it "shrewdly" shaking the Dauphin's back. The first comment plays on an obvious
equivoque while the second refers to the distasteful "practice" of a man compelling
his shrewish woman to wear a bridle. An Italian jest, which appears in Humphrey
Gifford's *A Posie of Gilloflowers* (1580), involves two brothers who marry two sisters.
Whereas the first brother treats his wife well and she becomes contrary and shrewish,
the second takes his wife to a stable and shows her how he beats his unmanageable
horse. When the horse does not learn the lesson, the second brother kills it with his
sword. The wife learns her lesson.[122] The Constable also plays on "jade," which means
a loose woman as well as a nag, so that he is also disrupting the Dauphin's analogy
but is doing so in the Dauphin's misogynist framework. Even if the Constable prefers
loose women to horses and does not believe in bridles, he does not escape sexism
and plays the Dauphin's game, perhaps because of rank. When the Dauphin has left,
Orleans and the Constable discuss him and banter about how valiant or cowardly
he is. When Orleans says, "By the white hand of my lady, he's a gallant prince," the
Constable replies, "Swear by her foot, that she may tread out the oath" (96–98). They
continue to use feminine metaphors to debate the manly valor of the Dauphin. The
Constable would have the lady in Orleans trample the oath that the Dauphin is gallant. Orleans and the Constable both think the English soldiers resemble mastiffs
who rush to have their heads crushed by Russian bears, and the Constable adds that
the English leave "their wits with their wives" (143–51). Among the French warriors,
women are either like horses, are good for sexual plunder, or are undervalued adjuncts
who collect the wits of their dim-witted soldier-husbands.

The displacement of male anxiety over war and bravado in anticipation of it as
well as the ideal of honor pervade the play. In describing how the English chide the
slow night before battle, the Chorus likens "the cripple tardy-gaited night" to the

image of a "a foul and ugly witch" limping tediously away (CH. IV:19–22). But in the debate with the disguised king, Williams uses the image of some men, dead because of the king's decision to go to battle in France, at the Last Judgment, crying "upon their wives left poor behind them, some upon the debts they owe, some upon their children rawly left" (IV.i.140–43). Except for the concern of these dead soldiers from Agincourt because of the abruptness with which they left their children, their sorrow is that they have made their wives indigent because they can no longer provide for them. The king says that some soldiers will have on their consciences their "beguiling virgins with the broken seals of perjury" (168–69). In a speech like Henry IV's on sleep, Henry V catalogues the burdens of a king, including the lives, souls, debts, anxious wives, children, and souls of his soldiers (236–39). The king speaks about how the few English soldiers will by virtue of their small number share a greater honor and valor. He concludes his speech on masculine chivalry:

> And gentlemen in England now a-bed
> Shall think themselves accurs'd they were not here,
> And hold their manhoods cheap whiles any speaks
> That fought with us upon Saint Crispin's day.
> (IV.iii.64–67)

Pistol's comic capture of the French soldier, when the ancient wants money or he will cut his captive's throat, qualifies the male honor that the king praises (IV.iv.37–80). Bourbon says that he who will not follow him against the English, who are winning the battle, should, like a "base pandar," go hence and

> hold the chamber-door
> Whilst by a slave, no gentler than my dog,
> His fairest daughter is contaminated.
> (IV.v.14–16)

This fear of violation of daughters and the bestial analogy reveal the anxiety that lies behind the earlier talk of chivalry. Enemies show their disdain and hatred for each other by threatening to victimize or by victimizing their women. Exeter recounts to Henry an honorable marriage between soldiers when he says that in death York kissed his dead cousin Suffolk:

> So did he turn, and over Suffolk's neck
> He threw his wounded arm, and kiss'd his lips;
> And so espous'd to death, with blood he seal'd
> A testament of noble-ending love.
> (IV.vi.24–27)

This idealized male love contrasts with many of the male attitudes toward women in the play and is even more ideal than Henry's courtship of Katharine, which, as the Chorus reminds the audience, is part of a dynastic negotiation. Exeter also reports that, looking on, the man in him could not stop his tears, the mother in him, which the king understands and has "mistful eyes" (28–34). But then the king orders that his men kill their French prisoners. The next scene tells of the French killing of the English boys, and Gower explains that that slaughter is the reason for the king's order against the French prisoners (IV.vii.1–11). Gower's words only modify the first impression of the king's cruel order after the fact. There is some honor, on both sides. The king reiterates his order to cut throats (65–67). When the English are triumphant in battle, the king dwells on the names of the dead French nobles, whose class make them the trophies of triumph (82–114). This epic list shows that men on both sides occupy the center of war. Only after the victory does the play mention wives (CH. V: 10). After alluding to Essex, the Chorus refers to the empress, who is Elizabeth (25–35). Here, Shakespeare places Elizabeth above Henry and Essex.

In the last act, women are appealed to for their powers but have little actual power that men do not displace on to them. Fluellen humiliates Pistol as a coward even as Pistol calls forth the Fates and Fortune, both female figures, to give him the power to fight and avenge himself (V.i.21, 84). Pistol refers to "my" Doll's death of venereal disease in the hospital (85–86). The expected reference would be to Nell. Here, textual problems may explain the slip, perhaps suggesting that the text of this play in the First Folio shows signs of revision that change the role of Falstaff from active participant in the wars to a minor or remembered character who dies in narrative report (see II.i, iii). As G. Blakemore Evans suggests, "It is even possible that much of Pistol's 'business' once belonged to Falstaff, a view that would help to explain the curious reference to Doll Tearsheet (V.i.81), which properly should be to Mistress Quickly."[123] This death leaves the way for a concentration on Queen Isabella, Alice, and Katharine, all of whom are French and will serve Henry's dynastic ambitions. Isabella's hope that Henry's eyes, once "The fatal balls of murdering basilisks," will now look on France with peace, Burgundy's personification of Peace as a female figure chased from France, Henry's wooing of Katharine, and the sexist and military jokes among Burgundy, France, and Henry at Katharine's expense all characterize the final scene of the play. As in the next chapter I discuss these matters in this scene in detail, I shall only touch on a few points here. Isabella says to Henry that she will leave him with Katherine, whom Henry calls his "capital demand" in the negotiations, because "Haply a woman's voice may do some good / When articles too nicely urg'd be stood on" (V.ii.93–98). Henry becomes more like Hotspur, the plain soldier, and amid equivoques tries to tell Katharine that he is not a flatterer but only relies on his good heart to win her (134–73). He also appeals to her that they will make a child that will conquer the Turks (215–20). After all his talk of "love," a word he uses repeatedly and is predicated on his desire to possess France, Katharine does not speak of love but agrees to marry him according to her father's wishes, which Henry assures her, as if she were a pawn, that it will be the king of France's wish (231–64). This kind of arranged marriage is in keeping with Stone's description of marriages among the upper classes before the seventeenth century. He kisses her against her wishes and, like a Petrarchan lover, claims that her lips are more eloquent than all the French council (291–97). The power he gives her is his own but only as an idealization that he can repossess. Burgundy and Henry play with double entendres, especially on "blind": love is blind, but blind also means lust; Katharine is thus the victim of their gaze and their verbal forays about sexual penetration (298–347). The French king does agree to give Henry Katharine as part of the treaty. Henry now graces Katharine with an official kiss. Isabella blesses her daughter's marriage while asking the couple to overcome the ill acts and jealousies that trouble marriage beds. Henry asks that the marriage be prepared. This promise of marriage resembles that of Shakespeare's romantic comedies, except in those plays the marriages of love overcome the arranged marriages proposed by father figures at the beginning of the plays. Katharine plays a passive role. The Chorus also modifies the diplomatic joy with news of Henry's death and how under Henry VI England lost France and itself bled in civil war. In this play love dwells in the shadow of war.

TRANSITIONS

The construction of gender in the second tetralogy is complex. The characters view gender in contradictory ways that make it difficult to discern anything but a jostle of voices. Whether Shakespeare was a vessel of Elizabethan ideology on gender or whether he was ahead of his time on this question remains a matter of debate among feminists. The representation of gender in these four plays' representation raises disturbing questions about the construct of the feminine and masculine, as does the "cross-dressing" of each gender in displacement and confusion, when women are said to be like men and men like women, in relation to a warrior culture that is turning to politics but that still denies women an active role in the new order. Shakespeare's second tetralogy is a site of contestation among characters over the question of gender. This analysis is a modest contribution to a theoretical and critical debate that still has a long way to go.

In the next chapter, I would like to concentrate on *Henry V* and do so from a more general point of view, so that questions of gender will relate to other key concerns in the history play. The mutability and malleability of this genre is something that I discuss. It is appropriate that a discussion of this protean kind of drama—which includes elements of tragedy, comedy, and satire—should end this book on Shakespeare's virtuoso experimentation in language and form, poetry and drama, as he developed as an artist. Shakespeare's sense of history and culture manifest themselves in the richness of his work. Part of this rich texture of Shakespeare's poetic and dramatic productions derives from his language and his ability to keep changing in his art. The chapter after the one on *Henry V* will examine the intricate contradictions that make *Henry VIII* such an interesting play. This is history as romance or, if one prefers, tragicomedy.

Heminge and Condell would not admit this play as anything other than a history of England and therefore one of the histories. They, of course, classed Shakespeare's plays as tragedies, comedies, and histories—nothing more or less.

Subsequent editors and critics of Shakespeare have tried something more complex. From gender to genre, there is sometimes a wide gap of time between Shakespeare and his contemporaries and Jan Kott, Angela Pitt, Marilyn French, and their contemporaries. Interpretation and reinterpretation are the lot of Western readers and audiences—it is part of the tradition and countertradition of the West. Being critical and having distance, as feminists were and did, reinvigorates the reading, viewing, criticism, and performance of Shakespeare and of his histories. The evidence of Shakespeare's women, or any of his other characters, while being related to context, comes primarily from the plays themselves. They have staying power because of the power of their language and design. The power of character and action in Shakespeare sing through the range and play of his language that has an enduring ability to astonish.

CHAPTER 8

HENRY V

THE DISCUSSION OF GENDER IN THE SECOND TETRALOGY ENDED WITH ITS last play, *Henry V*, but in that work, as important as considerations of women are, there are other significant aspects on which this chapter will focus. Shakespeare's sense of innovation marks his work in the history play and other genres. In representing history and culture, Shakespeare's poetry, dramatic and nondramatic, shows lively experimentation. The very tensions within these works create some of the dramatic power of Shakespeare's art.

Sometimes, in *Henry V*, the play bristles so much with contrary words and action that form and content seem to vie. This creates almost a problematic because the play is full of persuasion and debate, perhaps suggesting *avant la lettre* the great plays about particular social problems by Ibsen and Shaw, such as *Enemy of the People* (1882) and *Mrs. Warren's Profession* (1893, staged 1902). Perhaps the controversy that Ibsen's and Shaw's plays caused indicates why the so-called problem plays of Shakespeare became a problem for contemporary critics. I have always been more positive about the problem plays and see *Henry V* partly in this light as a play that debates the problem of war, authority, and political legitimacy, so there is no problem with problems. In fact, they provide conflict and drama and the bristling of word and action. The heroism and antiheroism coexist in and between characters. And so I turn to a critic of the 1890s—Boas—writing about a playwright of the 1590s—Shakespeare.[1]

When in the 1890s Frederick Boas first called attention to problems in some of Shakespeare's plays and laid the critical groundwork for the debate on the problem plays or problem comedies, was he uncovering a division in Shakespeare's mind or representation or in the audience of the modern period?[2] C. S. Lewis and E. M. W. Tillyard in England and W. K. Wimsatt and Monroe C. Beardsley in the United States debated the authority of the author's intention decades before the advent of reception theory, which argued for the importance of the role of the reader.[3] Possibly, the rise of irony as a critical and theoretical concept in the past two centuries has contributed to the destabilization of the text and its meaning.[4] Drama complicates the complex relation between author and audience because it is a literary and theatrical text, is written and oral. The audience is singular and plural. Psychoanalytical criticism has made us more aware that literary and dramatic texts are complex interactions of the conscious and unconscious.[5] It is difficult to understand the reader's interpretation of the text, even if it is translated into a full written response, as well as the relation of reader and auditor. To state the division between author and reader in terms familiar to the Renaissance, rhetoric is the relation between speaker and audience, writer and reader. This rhetorical relation can involve communication and persuasion, a sharing of common assumptions, or a manipulation of one party by another. Rhetoric was at the center of the education of writers like Spenser, Shakespeare, and Milton and existed well before Aristotle helped codify its rules, so that its importance to poetry and criticism is as great as it is to politics and the law.[6] Although no text can be hermetically sealed from history and is as much a product of social and historical forces as those of personality, for the purposes of exploring *Henry V* as leading to the problem play, this chapter will assume that a dramatic text involves a representation in language and a reception that is complex and not easily reducible.

Broadly speaking, all texts represent the problems that exist between the author and audience, but problem plays draw attention to that debate as well as to the difficulties of genre, of representation itself. Whether Shakespeare was divided in his representation of the reign of Henry V as the culmination of that of the previous divided reigns in the second tetralogy, or whether readers, especially in the last century or so, are divided in their reception of the way Shakespeare represents history, patriotism, love, and war, becomes a dilemma that is, perhaps, unanswerable. If we cannot reconstruct Shakespeare's intention with any certainty, we cannot dismiss Boas and his followers by saying that others before them had not seen the critical problem and thus it does not exist, because to do so would be to advocate the abandonment of all fields that have been thoroughly considered, such as classical and Shakespearian scholarship. Contrary to the wish of theorists like E. D. Hirsch and Terry Eagleton, that we should give up criticism for the former's authorial authority or the latter's idea of rhetoric, each generation reinterprets the past in terms of itself and the converse.[7] Whether Shakespeare used the Chorus in *Henry V* as a proto-Brechtian alienation effect, so that his audience would experience its distance from the civil wars of an earlier era as well as from the stage and the history play, the Chorus does sometimes distance the present from the past, the world from the theatre. The present can only use its own language, no matter how much derived from the past, to speak about past events, as the previous sentence implies. This chapter will, then, assume that the text represents signs that can be interpreted and will discuss the problems *Henry V* represents rather than deciding what may be undecidable: what is the cause of the problem.

Problems also occur in the earlier plays of the second tetralogy. If *Richard II* tends toward tragedy but extends that tragic fall from the individual to the state and includes the comic episode of the Aumerle conspiracy; if *1 Henry IV* develops the comic communal element but also contains the germs of satiric isolation and self-criticism in the tavern parodies of Hotspur and Glendower as well as in the division between Hal and Falstaff; if *2 Henry IV* represents the negative discipline, blind fallenness, and increasing incommunication of satire because Hal and Falstaff meet seldom but also includes a mixture of the tragic and the comic as well as a crisis in the relation of fiction and history in the rejection of Falstaff; then *Henry V* continues this generic friction that is characteristic of the problem play, its crisis being especially apparent in the disjunction between the comic marriage of Henry and Katherine and the tragic fall that the Epilogue describes.

In part, *Henry V* attempts to sum up the earlier plays of the second group of histories. It represents the problems of unity and division, offering a problematic ending to the second tetralogy, attempting to give its histories of many genres a unified shape.[8] The history play is an unstable genre, partly because history is a continuum of time and therefore hard to capture within the limits of a work of art and partly because the history play is always tending toward something else or, at least, is always incorporating other genres—such as tragedy in *Richard II*, comedy in *1 Henry IV*, and satire in *2 Henry IV*.

Although each of these plays contains less-prominent aspects of other genres in them, it is *Henry V* that balances or, rather, makes the different genres collide more equally. By doing this, it pushes out the boundary of its genre in a way that many critics would agree to be a primary feature of the "problem play."[9] Critics mix the terms *problem comedies* and *problem plays*, admitting the difficulty of defining them, and do not always concur on which plays come under these headings. Even though some critics include *Hamlet* (1600–1601), *Antony and Cleopatra* (1606–7), and *Timon of Athens* (1607–9), the usual "problem" triad is *Troilus and Cressida* (1601–2), *All's Well That Ends Well* (1602–3), and *Measure for Measure* (1603–4). Shakespearean scholars recognize several other aspects—which I take to be subsidiary to pressing at the bounds of the genre—that characterize problem plays.[10] These elements are numerous: incongruities of generic conventions and structure, especially endings that are theatrically achieved or do not answer the "problems" the play poses; the relation of appearance and actuality or reality, often illustrated through acting and disguise; an involved and intellectual language and discussion in which the debate and probing of ideas (often about the relation between sex and war or politics) are conducted apparently for their own sake; and the raising of complex problems that do not have easy answers—all contribute to the vexed enigma of the problem plays. As William Witherle Lawrence says, these plays demonstrate that "human life is too complex to be so neatly simplified" and show an antiheroic, dark, and critical side to life and to human nature in ways that perplex the audience.[11] Irony has already been used to cause the audience perplexity in the earlier plays of this tetralogy by showing the black humor of tragedy and the dark sides to comedy and satire in a complex view of history. *Henry V* goes beyond its predecessors in this respect and is the play in the second tetralogy that most resembles a problem play.

Although no critic seems to have developed an interpretation of the strong elements of the problem play in *Henry V*, a few scholars have pointed to *1* and *2 Henry IV* as containing the origins of the problem play, or at least some of its effects.[12] Closer inspection shows, however, that *Henry V* pushes much more radically at the bounds of the history play, for in this work tragedy, comedy, and satire collide with one another; the language of debate appears to exist for itself or, perhaps, to emphasize the problems of the play, as in the clerical debate on Henry's claim to France in I.ii. or the debate between Henry and his soldiers at IV.i.; the antiheroic and heroic constantly qualify each other; the relation of sex to war is uneasy; the public and private personalities of the king seem to lack integration; and the "tragic" death of Falstaff, Henry's violent sexual imagery, and the satire on war (especially the objections of Bates and Williams and Burgundy's description of devastated France), all serve to modify the heroic king and his comic marriage to Katharine. Other subsidiary resemblances to the problem plays also occur in *Henry V*.

Like *Troilus and Cressida*, this play shows the seamy side of war and questions the kind of heroism that had been exalted since classical times—Fluellen comically likens

Pistol to Mark Antony (III.iv.15). Some problem elements in *Henry V* also anticipate those in *All's Well That Ends Well*, most notably the relation of sex to war and a theatrically achieved ending to what begins and proceeds well into the play as a tragic action. *Troilus* also explores sex and war, whereas *Measure for Measure* looks at the relation between sex and government. *Measure*, too, has a theatrically achieved ending and although not comic, the ending of *Troilus* also appears unable to resolve the proceeding action with satisfaction. Like the Duke in *Measure*, Henry is a disguised ruler who manipulates other characters, but by doing so is brought to a more profound idea of his own responsibility.[13] The audience and critics of *Henry V* are as divided and perplexed over its forms and ideas as they are over similar matters in the problem plays.

The complicating irony of *Henry V* is compatible with its "problem" elements.[14] *Richard II* and *1* and *2 Henry IV* all reveal aspects of the generic friction that characterizes the problem play, but it is in the last play of the tetralogy that that friction reaches its highest pitch. The fall of Richard creates problems, and the fall of Falstaff creates more. Other falls over the course of these plays also represent the difficulty of a human redemption of history. Multiplicity in *Henry V* complicates the lines between appearance and actuality, heroism and antiheroism, conscious and unconscious motive, and intention and profession, so that this play "ends" the second tetralogy ironically by pushing the history play in the direction of the problem play, extending or bursting (depending on one's view) the bounds of the genre itself.

By inverting, reversing, contrasting, and blending tragic, comic and satiric conventions and tones, Shakespeare also raises questions about the multiple, ambiguous, and, therefore, ironic nature of history itself. Henry V would be the hero Richard was not, but he cannot achieve unmitigated heroism. Henry's own violent thoughts and Shakespeare's ironic use of imagery and theatricality and the juxtaposition of comic marriage and tragic Epilogue modify the king's heroic part. The end is the beginning. As in *Finnegans Wake*, the cycle of history begins again, "falls to" again, for the informed audience knows the fate of the Henry V before *Richard II* begins, and if the playgoers do not, the Epilogue tells them, thereby shaping the meaning of the action of the second tetralogy (including Richard's fall) and looking ahead to the reign of Henry VI (who falls, and after whom Richard III also falls), which Shakespeare had already shown on the stage in the first tetralogy. The irony in *Henry V* represents the history play as problem play because it depicts the problem of writing history not only in this play but also in the second tetralogy (with hints back to the first tetralogy). This irony has implications for writing and for writing history generally, for the complex relation and interpretation of history and fiction. As in the earlier plays of the tetralogy, multiplicity in *Henry V* extends beyond the established limits of the genre to which each history play is most closely related—in this case the problem play—and explores the study of history and historiography as well as the nature of the history play itself. Although the problem element cannot include all the implications of *Henry V*, it is important for an understanding of the play. More specifically, we should turn to the ways irony of theatre, structure, and words, as well as Henry's debate with Bates and Williams (IV.i.) help create the generic friction that makes this history play a problem play.

SELF-CONSCIOUS THEATRICALITY

The Chorus in *Henry V* elaborates the self-conscious theatricality in the earlier plays of the tetralogy. He examines the relation of theatre and world, history play and history, so much that he raises the audience's awareness of the problems of representing history on stage. That the main action and the Chorus qualify each other also raises questions about the relation of narrative and represented action in the history play. In the introduction to act 3 the Chorus asks the audience to "Suppose," "Hear," and "behold" the men and scenes in his description as actually existing on stage. He challenges the playgoers to do the literally impossible so that they exercise their imaginations as fully as possible. They become part of the meaning of the play and of history. The Chorus realizes the complexity of historical shaping.[15] Repetition becomes a reaching or amplification for the Chorus, who, armed with the modest accomplishment of the theatre, at the opening of act 4, commands the audience to behold, "as may unworthiness define," Henry among the troops at night, the "disgrace of four or five most vile and ragged foils" representing the armies at Agincourt. In addition to this distancing synecdoche, the Chorus also attempts to draw the audience into illusion through the mimetic and onomatopoetic descriptions of the busy hammers of the armor makers and the French playing for the English at dice. The Chorus to act 5 repeats the view that the play is unable to express actual historical events.[16] The repetition draws attention to itself and stresses the problems of the history play, limiting the genre as being inferior to the world but, at the same time, raising it above the chaos of the world with strong and precise description, ordered couplets, and the assumption (from the author's point of view at least) that poetry is more lasting than the memorials of princes. The Chorus also dispels the notion of a monolithic Elizabethan audience, promising to prompt "those that have not read the story" and asking pardon of those who have because this play is a poor copy of life. Shakespeare displaces a conceit and humility onto his Chorus regarding this history: this play is more or less than its sources and than the world.

Other aspects of the irony of theatre complicate *Henry V*. Through a character's use of theatrical terms, Shakespeare conveys that character's awareness of "acting" to an audience watching an actor playing the part. A subsidiary element in this problem play is this self-referential role playing, so that once again the irony of theatre shows the close relation of *Henry V* to that kind of drama. The other histories, however, also show this characteristic, but this self-conscious sense of theatre supplements in *Henry V* a choric presence that is stronger than anything in the previous plays. For instance, according to Canterbury, the Black Prince "play'd a tragedy" for the French in battle and the Boy says that Nym and Bardolph were much more valorous than Pistol, "this roaring devil i' the old play" (I.ii.105–6; IV.iv.69–74). Most importantly, through the Boy, Shakespeare reminds the audience of morality plays in which the devil is beaten and makes Pistol (not just any old actor) a devil whose vice Fluellen beats out of him with a leek rather than a wooden dagger. Even if the characters refer to role playing and to early English drama, they cannot understand the application of these references as much as the actors, audience, and playwright. This dramatic irony reminds us that this history is dramatic.

Shakespeare's theatrical irony shows that deceit is another disguise, revealing with it the problems of private and public and of government. The history plays especially share this concern with *Measure* and to a lesser extent with *All's Well*. In *Henry V* deceit and disguise test Henry as a ruler (or potential ruler for that matter) more directly and more critically than in *1* and *2 Henry IV*. Shakespeare ensures that the playgoers will appreciate the dramatic irony of the condemnation by Scroop, Cambridge, and Grey of a man who insulted the king when, unknown to them, Henry knows that they want to murder him (II.ii.). The king is self-consciously theatrical. In order to punish the rebels most and to achieve the greatest effect so that he may appear just when sentencing these men, Henry pretends to reward them with commissions when he hands them a list of their crimes. By way of this dramatic irony, Shakespeare links Henry with the audience and thus appears to seek its approval of the king.

Deceit and disguise, such as Pistol's deceit and Henry's disguise, relate closely to each other. The ancient's great voice and seemingly "gallant service" fool Fluellen until Pistol curses the Welsh captain for not intervening to prevent Bardolph's death and until Gower remembers Pistol as an "arrant counterfeit rascal." Henry IV had dressed counterfeits in battle to protect his life, so that kings and knaves are not always so different in their theft and deceit. According to the English captain, the ancient will pretend to be a war hero, learning his part, playing the "roles" of other soldiers and describing the "scenes" of the battles to be convincing (III.vi.12–82). To compare and contrast this deceit ironically with Henry V's disguise, the playwright has Henry assume a part among his soldiers before Agincourt and interweaves the incidents of the gloves and the leek. After encountering Bates and Williams, private soldiers, the king complains about the burden of the public man and the irresponsibility of the private man (IV.i.). This problem of the relation of public and private lies at the heart of kingship from *Richard II* to *Henry V*. With the help of the Boy, Pistol, who did not recognize the disguised king, deceives the French soldier (as Falstaff did to Colevile in *2 Henry IV*) into thinking him a great warrior. In a soliloquy the Boy exposes Pistol's empty acting to an already suspicious audience (IV.iv.). If Pistol is a hollow man, is Henry? Later, Shakespeare shows Henry "playing" with Williams as Fluellen does with Pistol, so that the playwright once more compares king and Welsh captain and complicates the ironic connections between characters. Henry shares the dramatic irony with the audience at the expense of Williams as well as Fluellen, who is equally ignorant (like Pistol) of the king's earlier disguise and the exchange of gloves and whom Henry asks to be a proxy in a fabricated quarrel with "a friend of Alençon," which is an actual disagreement with Williams (IV.vii, viii). Shakespeare uses disguise and deceit so extensively that *Henry V* seems to foreshadow *Measure*.

Even though Henry complains about the trials of kingship, he uses his "directorial" powers, like Duke Vincentio and Prospero, to arrange events and manipulate others. After Henry's good-natured fun is over and Williams and Fluellen have stopped fighting (each having the other's glove), the king rewards Williams, who claims that Henry is at fault for having disguised himself and for not having expected abuse in that guise but who then asks pardon of the king (IV.viii.1–74). It is Henry's power as king that keeps the conflict over the glove from getting out of hand. Whereas the king pretends to be less than he is, Pistol feigns that he is more. The glove gives way to the leek. The hyperbolic and out-of-fashion Fluellen punishes the boasting and antique-tongued ancient. Although Pistol likens himself to a horse-leech and is called vicious, on stage he does little to warrant the punishment he receives, except that, if the Boy is to be believed, he is a devil from the old morality plays and must be beaten.[17] In any event, the Welsh captain is less merciful than the king, who, nonetheless, may not have learned as much from Williams as he might have. The taverners continue to raise questions about the nature of kingship and about Henry's dilemmas as king, but they also reveal their own limitations. Henry's tricks as an "actor" and "director" show that he is still enraptured by the robes of office even if he sometimes sees the shortcomings of pomp and protocol.

If, most importantly, the irony of theatre in *Henry V* reveals Shakespeare's problematic use of the Chorus, consciously making the audience aware of the limitations and potentialities of the theatre and history play, it also represents other subsidiary elements from the problem plays—theatrical ending, debate, and disguise. *Henry V* often uses these aspects in ways that recall their occurrence in *Richard II* and *1* and *2 Henry IV* as well as looking ahead to their use in the problem plays. Although the irony of theatre affirms the close relation of history and the problem play in *Henry V*, it also shows that comparisons that are too close are odious. For instance, the disguised Henry is much like the disguised Duke, but Vincentio is more allegorical and shadowy, more of a god out of the machine than Henry is. On the other hand, Henry must deal with a wider range of public and historical experience, and his directorial side (although central to his character) is only one part of a complex character who seems to taste blood, feel desire, and laugh more readily than the illusive Duke. Theatrical irony raises our awareness of the problems of the history play, and so this is a problem play with a difference.

STRUCTURAL PROBLEMS

The structure of *Henry V* is ironic and displays affinities with the problem play.[18] A choric envelope modifies the heroic feats of Henry V in the main action, for the Epilogue shows that he cannot control the future, as his son, born of the marriage to Katharine, lost France and then England. Shakespeare makes structural use of debates, such as the clergy's consideration of Salic law (among themselves and with Henry); the discussion between the king, Bates, and Williams about the nature of warfare and of kingship; and the conversation between Henry and Katharine about love, marriage, and politics. The main action ironically qualifies the patriotism, optimism, and hero worship of the Chorus, and the ways in which the "lowlife" scenes modify the words and deeds of Henry and his party. In other words, a friction occurs between Chorus and main action. The worlds of the captains and of the French also provide other ironic perspectives in a complex play. An investigation of the ironic relation of some scenes in *Henry V* to the first three plays of the tetralogy casts the eye of the audience backwards, making it an historian, enabling it to observe a modified Henry and to find that in one regard history appears as fallen as humanity, a circle more like the wheel of fortune than the circle of perfection. Henry V is more like Richard than he would like to think. People change but also stay the same and—relying too much on similarity between past, present, and future—find themselves caught by and in time. Shakespeare uses references to the past structurally to create an irony that shows the many limited views of people, the collision of worlds, and the forgetfulness and ignorance of characters regarding the past as they move in the unstable present into the uncertain future.

The general structure of Henry V represents an ironic reversal. The play begins with the Prologue telling a tale of warlike Harry and the glory of Agincourt and ends with an Epilogue that speaks of the loss of France and the return of England to civil war. This choric envelope qualifies the rising fortunes Henry experiences in France during the main action. Although Shakespeare did not divide the play into acts and scenes, the choruses punctuate the play in such a way as to suggest that a brief examination act by act of the friction in the structure might be helpful. Each act begins with the Chorus, whose simple patriotism becomes modified by complex scenes.[19] For instance, in act 1 the mixed motives of the clergy about the war in France, in act 2 the dishonorable nature of the English taverners and traitors as well as Henry's possible and partial responsibility for Falstaff's death, in act 3 Henry's apparent relish in destruction and the gentleness of Katharine (and she is French!), in act 4 Bates' and Williams' criticism of the king as well as Henry's admission of the dubious Lancastrian claim to the "English" crown and of his family's mistreatment of Richard, and in act 5 the King of France's treatment of his daughter and (not in the main action but in the Epilogue) time's defeat of Henry's glory all complicate but do not negate the patriotic view of the Chorus.

The structure of *Henry V* reveals aspects of the problem play but also the characters' special concern with the nature of time and history. The design of the play emphasizes an ironic treatment of problem elements: extensive debate about love, marriage, and politics; an especially self-conscious tension between appearance and actuality and between the heroic and the antiheroic; and the theatrically achieved ending that does not seem to answer the play. After the Prologue's examination of the relation of history and drama, the first two scenes display a prolonged interest in debate itself. Canterbury complicates the question of how just the war is when he gives a detailed interpretation of the history of the Salic law, which shows that Henry is the rightful king of France. Through irony, Shakespeare qualifies Canterbury's position: Henry IV recommended this foreign war to his son, Lancaster had predicted it, the Prologue in *Henry V* confirms it with patriotism, and Exeter and Westmoreland call for war, so that the clergymen are not the only war hawks and should not be held solely responsible for the designs on France (I.ii; see *2HIV*, IV.v.212f.; V.v.105–10). Debate is very important to Canterbury and Henry as a means of justifying the invasion, but the war becomes a tangle. If Henry's advisors are corrupt, the unjust war qualifies the heroic stance; if the invasion is just, Henry's inability to acknowledge that he makes, and is answerable for, the ultimate decisions of government modifies his heroism in France. Shakespeare calls Henry's judgment into question, raising the problem of measure for measure that occurs in *Richard II* and *1* and *2 Henry IV*, as well as in *Troilus*, *All's Well*, and *Measure*. Although nearly identical to its representation in the problem plays, this problem has a history in the second tetralogy and, consequently, also becomes a problem of time and succession. On the whole, *Henry V* examines judgment from a more public point of view than do the problem plays. If reports of earlier actions or the earlier plays in the tetralogy, especially at the end of *2 Henry IV*, provide one part of the context for act 1, the subsequent acts in *Henry V* and even the pretext but postscript of the first tetralogy furnish the other part.

Acts 2 through 5 show a similar pattern. The problem elements in act 2 occur mostly in Nym's and Pistol's qualification of the Chorus—who praises Henry as the mirror of all Christian kings, extols England, and denounces the traitors—when they are involved in verbal combat because the treacherous ancient has stolen Nym's betrothed, Mistress Quickly, who says the king has killed Falstaff's heart (II.i., iii.). The king is a modified mirror. Henry's judgment of the conspirators in II.ii. may be just, but it is also reminiscent of his rejection of Falstaff. By bracketing Henry's judgment of the conspirators with the taverners' discussion of Falstaff's death and the king's responsibility for it, Shakespeare emphasizes the wider implications of Henry's "trials." The ironic structure of act 3 particularly emphasizes the relation of sex to war but brings out the tension between private and public more fully than the problem plays. *Troilus* reduces the public to the private. *All's Well* and *Measure* look at the public domain in personal terms. Achilles sulks in his tent and would make war a personal act of revenge. Bertram escapes to the wars to leave Helena, his unwanted wife. Angelo turns government to lust and Duke Vincentio would make marriage the culmination of his experiment in justice and government. The Chorus begins act 3 by saying that Henry rejects as insufficient the French king's offer of his daughter and a few petty dukedoms. Shakespeare qualifies Henry's heroic call to his men into the breach at the opening of III.i with the savagery before Harfleur in the opening lines of III.iii, where Henry once again threatens the French in violent images, likening the siege of the town to the rape of its women. What makes this verbal assault even more uneasy is the introduction of Katharine, who is innocently learning a new language (III.iv.). In III.v. Shakespeare further complicates the relation of men and women, private and public, when he represents haughty Frenchmen, including their king, as insulting the English partly as a result of the French women thinking the French men effeminate. Act 4 continues to qualify heroism, showing the complexity of war and human nature. The playwright makes the problem element a part of his representation of an historical event and, therefore, asks the audience to avoid oversimplifying history. He also uses the motif of the disguised ruler that occurs in *Measure*. The Chorus extols Henry for bravery, warmth and generosity, but the disguised king soon encounters the criticism of Bates and Williams, who try to make Henry responsible for the justice or injustice of the war, a responsibility that he has attempted to shirk from the opening of the play. Other problems arise. When Fluellen responds that the enemy has killed the defenseless boys, the French lose the sympathy of the audience. On the other hand, Henry has already ordered the killing of the French prisoners because they are reinforcing their scattered men—a cruel action, although Gower praises him for ordering these killings as a reprisal for the slaughter of the boys (IV. vi.35–38, vii.1–11). The reason for the order is ambivalent. Even if the audience perceived the Boy's portentous words that the other boys and he will guard the luggage and that "the French might have a good prey of us if he knew of it," the playgoers only know that this event occurred and not its relation to the king's order (see IV.iv.76–80). Even though the audience probably cannot untangle this problem, it witnesses a king who may think that he has to be ruthless in defending his outnumbered army or prefers revenge to turning the other cheek. Henry's action tempers the sympathy of the audience, keeping it off balance and focusing its attention on the king and his problems.

The problem elements that irony stresses in act 5 are appearance and actuality and a theatrically achieved ending. In a charming part of V.ii., Henry woos Katharine, so that if he seemed like a basilisk in war, he appears to be a shy lover in peace (7, 99f.). Nonetheless, the marriage is a theatrical solution, a public and political union under the guise of an entirely personal love, that cannot mend the animus between England and France.[20] Henry is the actor still, for, having spoken so eloquently throughout the play, he now plays the "plain king," unless he is fluent in war and halting in love: this difference or discontinuity of roles makes it difficult to read his personality (V.ii.121–73). Amid this awkward tenderness, other ironies arise. Even a heroic king can be sadly wrong in his predictions or grimly foiled in his hopes. Henry says to Katharine, "Shall not thou and I . . . Compound a boy, half French, half English, that shall go to Constantinople and take the Turk by the beard? shall we not?" (V.ii.216–19). This wish for a crusade is as ironic as the similar desire of Henry IV. The last question—"shall we not?"—which is a negative acting as an intensive affirmative, provides an answer to the king's hopes: Henry and Katharine will not produce such a conqueror. Even though Henry claims modesty, he breaks custom and kisses Kate. The Epilogue reminds the audience of the fall again into ruin in the reign of Henry VI, which Elizabethan playgoers have already seen on stage in the first tetralogy.

As *Henry V* is like a problem play, it shows incongruities of generic conventions and structure, especially in an end that is theatrically achieved and does not respond to the problems that the play poses. The sheer amount of discussion about the legitimacy and responsibility of kingship, much of it for its own sake, threatens to frustrate the historical action of the play and the very survival of the genre itself, pushing it into new regions (the first tetralogy and beyond) and into new problems—such as when a representation can properly end, and, if history is in part circular (for *Henry V* also turns back to *Richard II*), how it can end at all. One of the major problems of *Henry V* is that its ending threatens to explode the play and therefore the second tetralogy as a whole and also the Shakespearean history play as a genre because of this tension between centrifugal and centripetal forces. Like theatre and words, structure is a measure of time, of the diachronic and synchronic. Each author represents the problems of time in a different way.[21] Here, Shakespeare chooses to look at origins and ends differently, using irony of structure to represent a relation of past, present, and future that strains between order and chaos.

Some of the scenes in *Henry V* show a close affinity to others in *Richard II* and *1* and *2 Henry IV*, so for the audience that sees these plays in succession, the irony of the scenes in *Henry V* becomes more complex in light of the earlier scenes. The idea of judgment arises out of an intricate ironic pattern between different scenes in these plays, an intertextuality, and is both important to the histories in their assessment of kings, kingship, succession, order, and rebellion and to the problem plays, especially in *All's Well* and *Measure*, in which human judges are shown to be so fallible, particularly in personal relations, that they compromise their public duty or office. The audience, but especially readers, directors, and critics, will find another vantage point from which to judge, to understand, Henry's treatment of the conspirators in II.ii if it compares his judgment with Richard's sentencing of Bolingbroke and Mowbray; with Bolingbroke's handling of Bushy, Greene, Richard, Aumerle, and the conspirators; with Henry IV's condemnation of Vernon and Worcester; and with Lancaster's "trial" of Scroop and the rebels (*RII*, I.i., iii.; III.i.; IV.i.; V.iii., v.; *1HIV*, V.v.; *2HIV*, IV.ii.). The primary irony of these scenes is that a human judge may be judged as he judges others. Henry V self-righteously condemns rebels though his father was an insurgent and his brother used treachery to condemn Scroop, a relative of the man Henry vilifies most. The execution of Nym and Bardolph, petty thieves, can be viewed in relation to Bolingbroke's theft of the crown and summary execution of Bushy and Greene as well as Henry's use, then rejection, of Falstaff. Even if Fluellen's argument for military discipline were entirely convincing (and it does show merit), Henry forgets that his father's illegal actions did not meet with capital punishment. The rules of the game are ad hoc, discontinuous, and serve those who have power to enforce them. For a moment, if we assume that time is a continuum, we might judge judgment in *Henry V* a little differently, although it resembles the judging in earlier plays in the tetralogy as well as in the problem plays, which come after it. On these grounds of interpretation, Henry is breaking the same rules that his father did and for which he feels insecurity if not shame. He punishes others for the faults he shares with them. But discontinuity persists with continuity: the judgment in this play also differs from the problem plays because it occurs in the context of history in which it participates with *Richard II* and *1* and *2 Henry IV*.

An ironic use of structural references to the past invites us to look at the nature of history in these plays, individually and as a group, not in the temporal isolation of a "pure" problem play. In the opening scene Ely and Canterbury praise Henry's reform from a wild youth, and Canterbury also refers to the titles in France that Henry derives from Edward III—the king's private and public histories. It becomes apparent from Canterbury's historical account of the Salic law that wars, depositions, and usurpations characterize the history of France as much as of England. By telling Henry to go to the tombs of Edward III and the Black Prince to gain inspiration from classical times to the present, Canterbury provides moral *exempla*. Ironically. the Black Prince was the father of Richard, whom Henry's father had deposed, so that this reference can also remind us that Henry's claim to the English crown, let alone to the French crown, is tenuous. Characters use history selectively. Gaunt had invoked the spirit of Edward III to shame Richard into better government (*RII*, II.i.104–8). Even if Canterbury invokes the glorious past of England, his motives are not clear—how much does he want to protect the church from taxation? Interpretations of history affect present actions, and they can be as mythical as factual. Henry. Canterbury, Ely, and Exeter debate past strategies of fighting the French and the Scots that seem to affect both Henry's decision to invade (or at least give him a rationale for it) and the manner in which he will do it (I.ii). There is a part of Henry's personal past that comes to a close: Falstaff is dead (II.iii.5). The king has forgotten the clown, and the audience never knows whether he is aware of the death, as he never refers to it onstage. This is a past, if the taverners can be believed, that qualifies Henry's heroic nature. Henry, like his father and the rebels, interprets Richard's rule in history as a way of coming to terms with his own part. The memory of Richard is a locus for Henry's doubt and assertion over his own authority and the idea of kingship.

The irony of structure shows the history as problem play, for the fall of England once more at the end of *Henry V* and the failure of the English to reach a lasting heroic age (even in fallible human terms) create a crisis in history because such an instability in human events threatens to defy or render false any principle of artistic order or any genre applied to (or perhaps imposed on) the chaos of human time. The playwright is caught between a view of his task as supplement to nature, something that fills the gap between humanity and nature after the Fall, and as a reflection or representation of the fallen world. Whatever the solution, it is symbolic because the word can never be the world. It seems, however, that history demands a representational muse, because there is a tradition that the language and structure of history conform more closely to conventions of what was long called realism and because there is a supposition that historical representation relates directly to past events and an outside world. Shakespeare explores the relation between invented speeches, characters, and events, like the actions of Pistol, Bardolph, Williams, and Fluellen on the one hand, and those taken from the chronicles, from "real life," like Ely, Henry V, and Katharine on the other. Through irony of structure, Shakespeare represents temporal instability and temporal patterns, shapes and unshapes history, and asserts and questions the existence of history. It is the unresolved tensions between unity and dissolution, between history and fiction, and between heroism and skepticism that make *Henry V* difficult to interpret but that ultimately give the play its interest and vigor.

THE PROBLEM OF WORDS

Henry's violent images and Burgundy's description of France as a ruined garden most clearly show *Henry V* pressing at the bounds of the genre of the history play, for they reveal a qualification of the comic marriage at the end and modify Henry's heroism. Besides developing aspects of the problem play in *Henry V*, the irony of words complicates such historical patterns as the question of time, much as verbal irony has done in *Richard II* and the *Henry IV* plays. The problem and historical elements overlap.

Ironic images of war and peace best illustrate the problematic attributes of the play. The major speech that modifies Henry's gentleness in war is the threat against Harfleur (III.iii). Both in love and in war Henry uses violent images. Katharine becomes a sex object and joke about siege and rape (V.ii.309–47). Even the imagery of peace involves strife and ruin, as can be observed in Burgundy's image of France as a ruined garden (V.ii.23f.). If this personal violent language spills over into Henry's public conduct of the war and makes his kingship more problematic, references to time also call attention to a crucial question for the history play: how can we best represent and recreate time?

In exploring the problem of representing history in historical drama, we shall glance at Henry's Crispin Crispian speech, though we shall concentrate on the views of time expressed by the Chorus and other characters in *Henry V*, who share many ideas with characters in the first three plays of the tetralogy. These shared problems help unite the tetralogy even if the difference in ironic emphasis and in treating problem elements also distinguishes each play. Once again, irony creates a tension between centrifugal and centripetal forces in a history play. In addition to the Chorus' conscious references to history, the views that the characters hold of the past spur them to ironically limited actions. When the Prologue asks the audience to make leaps of imagination, to turn

> the accomplishment of many years
> Into an hour-glass: for the which supply,
> Admit me Chorus to this history,

he offers to act as an intermediary in presenting the history play, especially in making the audience aware of the difference between "historical" and "dramatic" time (PR. 30–2). For the Prologue, then, the telescoping of time is important enough to mention at the beginning, suggesting that the representation of this historical period or, more specifically, a play about this reign demands a radical selection of events and swift representation through narrative foreshortening.

The views of time reflect or refract a divided and fallen world. Shakespeare qualifies the triumph of time that the Chorus proclaims and raises questions about the nature of history. When the Chorus invites the audience to help recreate a specific time, each production creates a novel relation between the eve of Agincourt, the performances of 1599 and their references to Essex, and each new audience (IV, V: CH.). The words of the Chorus take on different meanings as time passes. If the playgoers take up the invitation to use their historical imaginations, to participate, they will involve themselves in the interpretation of history (which, with past events and the author's representation, is history) and in the change of history, not as it happened but as people perceive it to have happened. The Chorus talks about other written representations of history and asks the audience, with some irony, to accept the limitations of the theatre in representing historical time (V.CH. 1–9). The audience can admire the representation of Agincourt while realizing that it is not the battle as it happened but an interpretation of it. Playgoers can extrapolate for this limitation the shortcomings of their own interpretations. Paradoxically, Shakespeare's interpretation of the reign of Henry V is for many the only or primary representation of that period, even if it calls attention to its limitations. *Henry V* resembles the sonnets that are aware of the desolation and constraints of time while defying time with a representation that will survive its human subjects.

Shakespeare modifies the Epilogue's praise of the glory of Henry's "Small time." The playwright helps achieve multiplicity by creating a tension between the form, rhythm, and musical time of the sonnet that the Epilogue speaks and the ruin he must announce for time ahead. The sonnet is also a coda in a score that not only sings the praises of Henry but also criticizes him. Shakespeare's ironic use of time shows the problems of the genre of the history play, especially in the relation between Chorus and main action, but, perhaps above all, reveals a common ground between the four plays by representing their shared concerns about human limitations in time.

Nor is history one sided. For the French, unlike for Henry and Fluellen, Cressy represents the "memorable shame" that Edward inflicted on them at the height of his power and reminds them of Henry, Edward's descendant, who now threatens France (II.iv.53–64). Although the French king states a particular lesson of history—that the Dauphin should learn to respect the English—he later does not follow it himself and rejects Henry's "memorable" pedigree that would give him the French crown (Il. iv.88). Memory also fails the characters. It takes Gower a while to remember that Pistol is a "bawd, a cut-purse" (III.vi.6l–62). Here, Shakespeare causes an "unhistorical" character to judge another like him, as if to complicate history through the supposition of how things might have been. To inspire his own soldiers in the Crispin Crispian speech, Henry reminds them that although as old men they will forget other events, they will remember this great day, each man recalling his own feats with exaggeration, passing on the story of English honor to his son, who will teach his son, so that Crispin Crispian will never be forgotten until the "ending of the world" (IV. iii.40–66). Henry shows a subtle understanding of subjectivity, embellishment, and myth-making, of the difficulty of keeping history from becoming an epic or romantic narrative, and of the advantages to his situation and to heroism that the difficulty allows. Oral history is important to Henry for reasons of self-interest, patriotism, and heroism, even as he understands its departure from fact and truth. For Henry, as for many of us, the myth is never plain and rarely simple. The truth of fiction and the fiction of truth interact to the very end of the tetralogy. Irony of words helps reveal the problem play in *Henry V*, which presses at the bounds of its genre, including more problematic "images" such as those of war and peace as well as more commonly historic ones like "time."[22]

THE PROBLEMATIC CHALLENGE TO THE KING IN IV.I.

Act 4, scene 1, represents appearance and actuality, acting and disguise, and a friction between heroism and antiheroism, all of which are problematic and complicate the idea of history in *Henry V*. It is a scene that looks at the relation of religion to politics, which helps bind together the plays of the second tetralogy. For the sake of time and space, our analysis will focus on the debate that Henry has with his soldiers and with himself. The debate between Henry and Bates and Williams raises problems about the responsibility and legitimacy of the king. Henry also admits his doubts about his relation to Richard and regal succession and authority.

It is ironic that in a godlike disguise Henry finds even his humanity questioned. Disguised as a captain serving under Erpingham, Henry, who is playing yet another role, answers Bates that Erpingham should not tell "the king" his despairing thought, for the monarch—and here Shakespeare wrings the dramatic irony for all its worth—is "but a man, as I am: the violet smells to him as it doth me; the element shows to him as it doth to me." This speech of Henry's echoes Richard's musings on the "death of kings" after he learns that Bolingbroke has not only invaded the country but has also executed Bushy, Green, and Wiltshire: "I live with bread like you, feel want, / Taste grief, need friends." Like Richard, Henry wants others to see the man beneath the regal ceremony (99–106, cf. *RII*, III.ii.171–77). It is ironic that Henry still faces the problem of the king's two bodies that Richard experienced and that he is drawn to talk about it in the same terms. In light of Bolingbroke's deposition of Richard, irony also arises when Henry expresses this tension in an image of rise and fall. The memory of Richard throughout the tetralogy affects the action and the characters' notions of kingship. Although the king's "affections are higher mounted than ours, yet when they stoop, they stoop with the like wing" (106–8). This description can be applied to both Henrys as well as to Richard, for Bolingbroke was "base" in deposing his predecessor and Henry descends from and not only maintains a stolen crown but seeks to mount a new throne in France. From a self-interested English vantage point, Henry V is most successful because he helps stop civil war and exports strife to France.

The debate with Williams and Bates brings kingship and the Shakespearean history play to another crisis, for Henry V, the hero at the culmination of the second tetralogy, finds his judgment and policy questioned and wins a limited and not entirely convincing battle over his soldiers. In the meantime. Henry admits that a king must be an actor, hiding his fears from his men so that they will not be disheartened. His acting is political and recalls his father's dissembling more than Richard's histrionics of self-expression.

Bates takes to task one of the king's favorite topics throughout the play—the difference between the inward and the outward man—saying that no matter what courage Henry "shows" the world, the king wishes himself home in England (e.g., cf. V.ii.). Inside and outside often interpenetrate. In another reminder of dramatic irony, Shakespeare has the disguised king speak the conscience of the king and to say that Henry would wish himself only in France. "Conscience" is also an important word in the king's view of responsibility and of the inward and the outward (cf. 8, I.ii). Having shaken Henry, Bates shakes him some more. He says that the king should be fighting alone so that he might be ransomed for sure and might save the lives of innocent men, a statement that Henry answers with another intense moment of dramatic irony: "Methinks I could not die any where so contented as in the king's company, his cause being just and his quarrel honourable." Williams grumbles, "That's more than we know." As in a dark night of the soul, Henry must reexamine his assumptions, for here are men who view war with France in an opposite way to his position or to the one he professes.

Like Richard, who plays many roles and none contented, the judge is being judged. Henry's example has not resurrected the spirits of the soldiers but has, instead, caused Williams to use the image of the Resurrection against him (135f., cf. 18–23). Whereas Henry had tried Falstaff and the conspirators, he is now on trial himself (*2HIV*, V.v; *HV*, II.ii). Whereas Bates says that, owing to the obedience of the soldiers, the king will assume the responsibility for the crime if the war is unjust, Williams describes the dismembered bodies of the soldiers in battle crying at the Day of Judgment when Henry will answer if the war was wrong, for the soldiers fought as obedient subjects doing their duty whether their monarch was right or wrong. The literally dismembered body politic takes on theological as well as teleological meanings. The play and the group of history plays are also in danger of flying apart, as its own unity is the multiple questioning of kingship. Interpretations clash. Human judgment and design are fallible. Playing at God is a game no human can win, but without trying to achieve a god's eye view, people, including playwrights and audiences, can slip into solipsism and lapse into incommunication. Where Henry has found a righteous crusade in Christianity, Williams finds pacifism: "I am afeared there are few die well that die in battle, for how can they charitably dispose of any thing when blood is their argument?" (143–46). Nor will the king accept this accountability, although he used a similar argument to remind Canterbury that his conscience is answerable to God (cf. I.ii.14–32). It appears that Henry's response shows false logic for Williams, because he does not share the same premise as Henry that the war in France is just. A son sent to sea on business who dies in a sinful state is not the same as a man fighting an unjust war who dies in his sins, for only when the business is criminal and unjust is the case the same. But in Henry's public thoughts the war is just, although in his private meditations he is not so sure. Even as the father is not responsible for the state of sin in which the subject dies, he is answerable for the death, if one places the problem in the context of the play and the tetralogy, which is at least in part Christian. Eschatology is at the center of a central debate in the Shakespearean history play. The question of what is criminal and what is just is not such a simple one, and to live by the logician's rule is not easy. The king does not give the voyage or the boy a bad cause, or at least a cause that doubts its own justice, even when it might be just; Shakespeare thus creates a narrative that is more reflective of the complexity of the king's bodies, motives, politics, and psychology. The king has an enduring divine body (his public office) and a perishing mortal body (his private person), which can be seen in the phrase, "The king is dead. Long live the king." In death, the office of king passes to the heir even if two different persons have held the office of kingship in the moments before and afterward. A general knows that the probability of death for his soldiers is greater in battle than in peace even if he does not "purpose" their deaths. The king is evading the point. Bates had said that the monarch assumes the crime of the wrong cause and not the personal sins of the men (see 131–33). But then the king is playing a role and, like a playwright, with the part. For the sake of the unwanted discussion (the king had wanted to walk alone unengaged in the night), Henry has played one of Erpingham's captains, and is and is not the king.[23]

In this self-consciously theatrical situation, the king continues his line of argument. He says that even a king with a spotless cause in war will be fighting with some vicious soldiers, whose violent crimes Henry enumerates, including the seduction of virgins, an image (like that of rape) he appears to repeat if not relish in his unconscious if not conscious mind. Henry may be no better than the spotted soldiers in his example (cf. III.iii.20–21, 35; V.ii.318–19, 330–32, 343–47). The king continues to talk about men who have committed violent crimes, saying that if they outstrip human justice "they have no wings to fly from God," for whom war is a vengeance against such sinful men. The confident appeal to God characterizes the public king, even in disguise. Henry also neglects to consider the good men who perish in an unjust war or to think about the justice of his cause: he wants to have it both ways—"Every subject's duty is the king's; but every subject's soul is his own." Returning to the idea of individual "conscience," Henry argues that the soldier should prepare his soul for God because if he dies so, he gains a life in Christ, and if he lives, he has benefitted from such a spiritual exercise (135–92). Even here, in our interpretations of this and the other plays of the tetralogy, we cannot entirely escape Tillyard and cannot neglect Shakespeare's Christian and medieval heritage as well as his increasing use of debate and discontent with genre and form that leads to the problem plays.

Williams and Bates concede the argument, but Williams continues to take exception to Henry's words. This time he does not believe that the king will be ransomed. Shakespeare plays the dramatic irony for all it is worth, as Henry replies that if the king is ransomed, "I will never trust his word after." He is a king and no king. Nor can Williams tolerate the pomposity of the caped soldier, who scorns his words as "perilous shot" from a popgun, that impotent private displeasure against a monarch, that vain peacock's feather trying to turn the sun of the king to ice with fanning. Williams seems to be getting to Henry. Although there may be some truth in what Williams says soldier to soldier, Henry appears to be taking offense as a king. When Henry expresses "potential" anger, Williams says that there will be a quarrel between them, and then they exchange gages. As Henry's answers are problematic, the comic resolution of this challenge in IV.vii and viii should perplex the audience. The glove incident is resolved comically, but rather than cowering before the king, Williams appeals to decorum. The king, Williams says, came disguised as a common soldier and was answered as one. Williams did not offend the king but asks pardon still, his reward a glove full of gold crowns as well as a royal pardon. Even though the resolution shows Henry's sense of humor, power, generosity, and "mercy" and catches the aggressive Williams, who boasts like the French, in a dramatic irony, it does not remove the difficult problem of responsibility in war and makes the comic ending of the plot an uneasy one. Like the theological, political, and military debates in the first two scenes and like the debates on military history in which Fluellen finds himself, this debate resolves itself in the English victory but with the irresolution of dissent and fallen nature.

Shakespeare now represents Henry's private considerations of the nature of kingship. After Bates and Williams exit, Henry is finally "alone with his thoughts," but they are now more disturbed than before (193–235). In a soliloquy the king speaks about the burden of kingship as Richard and Henry IV had before him (*RII*, III. ii.155f.; *2HIV*, III.i.4f.). Even though Henry had described the king as a just man when he spoke with Bates and Williams, he now differentiates between the king and private men, particularly fools who feel nothing hut their own "wringing" or pain, especially intestinal.[24] Like Richard, whom Bolingbroke soon deposes, Henry V curses "ceremony" for its emptiness. Both Richard and Henry wrestle with the tension between the private and public aspects of kingship. Whereas Richard said, "throw away respect, / Tradition, form, and ceremonious duty," Henry apostrophizes ceremony, recalling the naught, the 0, the nothing in something that the Chorus conjures. Henry would personify his troubles and doubts and blame them, calling the inside out and censuring it for not being inside, for its alienation. He also apostrophizes the king's two bodies, "Twin-born with greatness," and personifies "thrice-gorgeous ceremony" in a moral allegory of king and man and vilifies it for being pompous and for being a royal burden a common man does not have to endure. Henry asks ceremony, "Art thou ought else but place, degree and form, / Creating awe and fear in other men?" He questions the very order he has asserted. Although he also discovers the same kind of flattery Richard did, he has more might than Richard, is able to suppress rebellion, and can be more concerned with the fear that power causes and how the powerful thus grow unhappy (cf. *RII*, IV.i.305–10). Like his father before him, Henry also apprehends the idea that Gaunt tried to teach Richard: a king has limited power because he cannot improve the health of another man (262–63, cf. *RII*, I.iii.226; IV.i.302f.; V.iii.78). Just as his father spoke about the cares and troubled sleep of kingship, so too does Henry (cf. *2HIV* III.i.4f.). Neither the regal clothes nor the titles nor the "tide of pomp / That beats upon the high shore of this world make the king sleep as soundly as the wretched slave." The tidal imagery may reveal Henry's recognition that time waits for no man. Henry also implies that the king is like Phoebus, who rises to light the world, whereas the private man, like a lackey, bears no responsibility for the rise and fall of the fortunes of governments and nations. The king, a little Christ here, illuminates the world and keeps the peace for men. If, as Henry told Bates and Williams, each man must show the king duty but answer for his own soul, then no king should be overburdened. To rise or fall, a king needs private men, so that they are more important than Henry says and suffer more than he admits in his idyll of the common man. Subjects can suffer exile, death in battle, and poverty. Although Henry inveighs against royal power, he does not mind using it to advantage with Williams, Fluellen, Katharine, and the French king (see IV.vii; V.ii, iii).

In private Henry now doubts his relation to God, whereas in public he proclaims his special status. After Erpingham enters, tells Henry that his nobles want to see him, and leaves, the king speaks a second soliloquy in which he prays to the God of battles to keep the hearts of his men from fear and from counting the superior numbers. Henry would take from them their sense of "reckoning," which can also mean judgment, as if the soldiers would judge Henry harshly. After all Henry's echoes of Richard's thoughts, Shakespeare seems to be showing that the heroic king is losing his confidence in his special relation with God, asking God's pardon for his father's fault in acquiring the crown, and telling what penance he has done for Richard. Lastly, Henry promises to do more penance than he has done for Richard's death but realizes this repenting—imploring pardon—"comes after all" (or "ill" as Taylor reads the text). Depending on the reading of the word "all" or "ill," the meaning is either that the sins of the fathers are visited on the sons or that having himself done ill, Henry V's penitence is worth little. The asking of forgiveness, if deeply felt, is the first step to absolution. How sincere Henry is we can only wonder. We may be willing to grant him his new understanding of his own limitation or ask why he waits such a long time to pray that God not punish him—"Not to-day, O Lord! / O not to-day"—why he is so concerned about the day of battle, why he implies that punishment is something that he can only stave off, and whether he is, like Everyman and Mankind, trying to bargain with God (231–311). This scene follows the patriotic and adulatory Chorus and precedes the French denunciations of the English, so that the context displays the ironic qualification I have been speaking about throughout. Here are different views of history modifying one another. The problem elements of disguise and debate and the historical aspects of time and interpretation are in constant and creative friction. Perhaps most of all, the collision of official and unofficial history, of private and public selves (and other roles that challenge this opposition) make us aware of how much strain persists in the genre of the history play. The idea of kingship helps relate this scene to the rest of the play and the tetralogy. Irony, here especially, creates a situation for the history play and the second tetralogy that mediates between unity and disunity without resolution.

It would be foolish to forget the heroic aspects of Henry's character. Irony qualifies and complicates but does not undercut his personality. *Henry V* possesses the chief attribute of the problem play: it pushes at the boundaries of its genre, in this case of the history play. The Aumerle conspiracy especially represented comedy ab ovo in the tragic history of *Richard II*. The promises of Hal to redeem time at the expense of others like Falstaff—as well as Sir John's and his parodies in *1 Henry IV*, mainly a comic history—begin the satire, with the attendant isolation that predominates in *2 Henry IV*. In *Part 2* the rejection of Falstaff stresses the problems of kingship that Richard's fall began and looks forward to the problem play in *Henry V*. In the last play of the second tetralogy, however, different types of irony reveal many of the same problems: irony of structure stresses the tension between the Chorus that praises heroism and the main action that is partly antiheroic; irony of theatre particularly calls attention to Henry's uses of disguise and acting and to the Chorus' emphasis on the problems of writing and viewing a history play; and irony of words uniquely uncovers the images of war and peace that modify Henry's heroic character, a heroism that has been amply documented by Tillyard and others. The examination of IV.i looks at the combination of these ironies and especially the problematic debate among Henry, Bates, and Williams. These kinds of irony, as well as the analysis of the representative scene, reveal common subjects among the four plays, such as kingship (right, responsibility, and succession) that help mold these plays into a tetralogy. Paradoxically, the problems of the history play serve not only to perplex the audience and induce a crisis in understanding history but also to unite the plays in a coherent pattern. Apparently, the tetralogy and the history play represent diversity in unity and unity in diversity. *Henry V* is the most self-critical and self-reflexive of Shakespeare's histories.

But other histories have their own contradictions and ambivalences. *Henry VIII*, written many years after *Henry V*, is a product of a Jacobean age in which Shakespeare, now that Elizabeth was dead, could write about the Tudors and could even include a paean to the dead queen under whose reign he lived roughly the first thirty-nine years of his life. The conflict in Ireland had changed and the wars with Spain were over. Shakespeare was exploring the themes of regeneration and the miraculous in a form of comedy that had enough unlikely and tragic turns that these plays came to be known as romances and tragicomedies. The ghosts of Heminge and Condell might wonder why I have taken an English history play—*Henry VIII*—and discussed it in terms of romance, but that is just one way of seeing the play from another angle and, perhaps, in bringing something different to light. And that is what I hope to do in the next chapter.

CHAPTER 9

HENRY VIII

IN *HENRY VIII*, AS IN *HENRY V*, SHAKESPEARE EXPLORES THE DRAMATIC limits of representing history. It seems there are contradictions inherent in Shakespeare's representation of the reign of Henry VIII. Although not quite like Thucydides in recording contemporary events in Athens, Shakespeare had now become closer to representing the life of his one-time queen and her family than ever before. Perhaps with her death, he could broach the topic with less chance of censorship or political risk.

Henry VIII represents a difference in time that would be similar to us writing today about the stock market crash of 1929. We know people who were alive at that time, and it is likely that Shakespeare would know of people, although they could not have been many, who were there for the birth of Elizabeth and the turbulent events of the reign of her father. People did not, on the whole, live as long then as now, but some did. It is difficult, given the changing and relative nature of time, to make a symmetrical analogy, but the notion that Shakespeare was not too far from the events he was depicting, at least emotionally, would be the same for us whose parents lived through the crash of 1929, the Depression, and the Second World War. History was something immediate, a matter of the lives of the great, an example, moral and otherwise, to those who would write or read it. Shakespeare's histories were, however, dramatic and were matters of fiction as well as works that were based on what happened rather than, to hearken back to Aristotle, what might have happened. Being a dramatic poet, in Aristotle's terms, Shakespeare put drama before history—what made the play about the past better was seemingly more important than being true to the past. In Shakespeare's age, history was not something simple that everyone agreed on or approached in the same way. Shakespeare's forging of the history play is a case in point.[1]

HISTORY AND HISTORIES

History in Renaissance England was not generally considered to be the contemptible poring over mouse-eaten records that Sidney described.[2] The many histories, historical poems, history plays, and prefatory defenses and justifications of history attest to the Renaissance fascination with and respect for history. For example, in Richard Grafton's *Chronicle at Large* of 1569, Thomas Norton praises the truth of history, as does William Camden in his history of the reign of Elizabeth.[3] History, which means so many things to different people, then and now, even if we often speak of one abstract history rather than histories, could also be dangerous. Invention and representation were not free activities under the English monarchs. Elizabeth was stringent in her censorship. We only have to think of the censoring of the *Sir Thomas More*, John Hayward's ordeal and eventual imprisonment over *The First Part of the Life and Reign of King Henry IV* (which, unfortunately, he had dedicated to Essex), and the production of *Richard II* that Shakespeare's company staged at the request of Essex's party during the Essex rebellion.

Although Elizabeth was lenient with the players, this last incident demonstrates the power and vulnerability of the theatre.[4] Only under James I, apparently, did Shakespeare think it wise or safe to represent the reign of Henry VIII, who, being Elizabeth's father, had not been a safe subject while she ruled.[5] Any complexity might be considered criticism.

It is difficult to say why Shakespeare wrote *Henry VIII* about ten years after the death of Elizabeth, and I only want to discuss the kind of history that I think he is writing in this play. Historical fiction is an oxymoron to some. Shakespeare's history plays need no apology and are a major achievement of Renaissance historiography. Certainly, he is not making the same kind of contributions to history as science and inquiry as Camden, John Stow, and John Selden are, but be is unsurpassed in his innovations in history as rhetoric. History is a story, the communication of the past to the present in present terms, as well as inquiry and the weighing of evidence. Without rhetoric, history becomes lists and half-hatched notes that few, if any, want to read. History without inquiry and the weighing of evidence becomes another story, a myth. Both evidence and myth are important for history.

If history exists, so do histories, and it is this subject that appeals to me most in discussing *Henry VIII*.[6] Shakespeare had written the *Henry VI* plays, which resembled chronicles, *Richard III*, most akin to melodrama, and *King John*, most like a polemic or propaganda play. In *Richard II* he creates a mimetic tragic history, but by the time he reaches the Chorus of *Henry V*, he is asking the audience to be a conscious part of history, to use its imagination. Shakespeare reveals a variety of history in the English histories, not to mention those plays that deal, more or less, with Roman and British history. Reason, our ability to use logic, tells us that in order to have history, we must find the past similar enough to our own time to find it interesting or useful but different enough to distinguish it from the present.[7] There would be no reason to write about historical periods or reigns without difference, but there would be no communication without similarity.

HISTORY AND *HENRY VIII*

In *Henry VIII* Shakespeare continues the type of exploration of imagination and English history that he begins in the choral part of *Henry V*. Reworking the discreet tableaux or episodic nature of the chronicle plays of the 1580s and the early 1590s in *Henry VIII*, Shakespeare uses with great effect the pageantry of the old street pageants but also of the masque, an increasingly popular genre at court.[8] I cannot discuss all these matters here but will look briefly at how Shakespeare shows a series of independent events, which many of our historians think is history, while attempting to give the reign of Henry VIII a pattern. Despite Shakespeare's use of a *de casibus* pattern—the falls of Buckingham, Katherine, and Wolsey and the near fall of Cranmer—the episodic nature of the structure and the apparent lack of political morality keep *Henry VIII* from providing an intellectually satisfying order, although the rhetorical appeal to the emotions and the attempt at a comic or happy ending qualify, or ask us to confront, our intellectual notions of history. More than any other Shakespearean history, *Henry VIII* embodies the collision of dramatic and historical expectations. Of any of the genres available to the Renaissance playwright, romance, or tragicomedy represents myth most closely and moves farthest from report and evidence, which were, after Camden, Stow, and others, becoming increasingly associated with history. The desire—passion or need—for unity, the mythic redemption through Elizabeth of Henry's rule, as if the end justifies the means, as if imagination can mend the evidence that reason finds and examines, characterizes the conclusion of *Henry VIII*.

An irony arises in the possible alternate title of this Shakespearean, perhaps Fletcherian history play, for it proclaims: *All is True*.[9] The Prologue emphasizes the title of the play while Cranmer's prophecy uses cognates of the word "truth" and is a retrospective prophecy (as much history is, though less obviously) and so relies on the perspective that the present has on the past (18, 21: V.iv.14f., esp. 16, 28, 36, 47).[10] If, literally, all were true in history, then the reader or audience would have little work to do. The truth would be represented, plain and simple. The word *history* would resolve its disjunctive etymology: inquiry, past events, and a story about the past. Drama presents and represents, so that it involves direction and literal presence as well as indirection and figuration. The play as literature is figurative, and although it has its own presence, it lacks stage presence. On a literary and linguistic level, it would be difficult to think that the author or authors were setting out the plain truth. By looking briefly at the Prologue, the fall of Buckingham, the trial of Katherine, the downfall and farewell of Wolsey, the annunciation of Elizabeth, and the Epilogue, I hope to show the friction between the tragicomic Prologue and the comic ending on the one hand and the tragic main action (at least in the *de casibus* sense) on the other.

The Prologue creates problems for those who would find unembarrassed truth embraced in *Henry VIII*. That is not a very auspicious beginning. The comic marriage of Henry and Anne Bullen is not without its own qualification. I'm afraid that we do laugh and weep in an oxymoronic reaction to the marriage, so that the Prologue is not a sure guide to the play, something that would not have surprised Shakespeare or Fletcher (Prol. 31–32: III.ii.64–71). The Chorus to *Henry V* is not a simple guide to the truth of the play, although he helps to complicate it. Besides destabilizing truth in the disjunction between its claims and the unstable words, events and structure of the main action, the Prologue reveals the friction in *Henry VIII* between tragic sadness and celebratory laughter:

> I come no more to make you laugh; things now
> That bear a weighty and a serious brow,
> Sad, high, and working, full of state and woe;
> Such noble scenes as draw the eye to flow
> We now present.
> (1–5)

Later, he adds,

> Therefore, for goodness' sake, and as you are known
> The first and happiest hearers of the town,
> Be sad, as we would make ye.
> (23–25)

The Prologue assures the audience that those who come to shed a tear of pity will find
the play a proper subject for it, who believe will find truth and who come for entertainment will get their money's worth. Only the members of the audience, perhaps
but not conclusively the groundlings, who want to hear "a merry bawdy play" and
the clash of shields will be disappointed and will not understand the intentions of the
authors.[11] At the same time the Prologue speaks of intentionality, he asks the audience
to imagine historical persons on the stage just as the Chorus in *Henry V* had done:

>   Think ye see
> The very persons of our noble story
> As they were living: think you see them great,
> And follow'd with the general throng, and sweat
> Of thousand friends: then, in a moment, see
> How soon this mightiness meets misery:
> And if you can be merry then, I'll say
> A man may weep upon his wedding day.
> (25–32)

Authorial intention and audience response are equal parts of history (see 21). Even
though the Prologue protests against comedy, inadvertently or not, he sneaks it into
his speech several times and by amplifying his denial of the comic, he calls attention
to it (13–32). In fact, the Prologue begs the question, for the play does just what he
warns against: it gives a sad story a happy end. As the Prologue is being witless while
speaking with wit, it is quite possible that the author, or authors, is indulging in a little
dramatic irony. In addition, the Prologue points out the *exempla*, lessons that might
have been learned decades before in *A Mirror for Magistrates*.

FALLS AND FALLEN HISTORY

The falls of illustrious characters also suggest that no consensus on truth exists in
Henry VIII: Buckingham's truth is not Henry's or Henry's Buckingham's, not to
mention Katherine's.[12] Another friction occurs between the pattern of comedy and
the return to exempla that are almost *de casibus*, the falls of Buckingham, Katherine,
and Wolsey. Katherine's trial is not exactly an example of justice and truth (II.iv.).
Nor can Wolsey see himself in the cold light of "fact" but interprets his life into
mythology (III.ii.350f.). The tragic falls rub against the comic ending. In this play
the desire for a pattern in history questions itself the more it wants truth.[13] This
romantic history, this comic celebration of marriage and birth, by its very insistence
on pattern and ritual and mythic intelligibility may modify those desires for order
with chaos and nothingness, may cause doubt about the power of free will and reason

in history. Shakespeare represents the close relation of each fall, as Wolsey is behind Buckingham's and Katherine's and Henry VIII must act to make the falls, including Wolsey's, happen. Wolsey simply outmaneuvers Buckingham and, if anything, is less ethical than his rival in his politics. But Wolsey does survive; Buckingham does not. If Henry blindly condemns a good man because he takes ill counsel, Buckingham heeds Norfolk's good advice and steps closer to death. The opening scene represents a power struggle between Wolsey and Buckingham. Norfolk advises Buckingham to restrain his anger against Wolsey and to use his reason (I.i.146–49). While Buckingham wavers between restraint and exposing Wolsey's secret bargain with Charles the Emperor, he is arrested as Wolsey has beaten him to the king's ear. After considering reason and passionate action, as if free will has a part in history, Buckingham resigns himself: "The will of heav'n / Be done in this and all things: I obey" (I.i.209–11). The second scene opens with the king congratulating Wolsey for discovering Buckingham's treason and with the king's desire to hear Buckingham's defense in person. Katherine interrupts this congratulatory atmosphere with complaints about Wolsey's illegal taxing of the subjects, which he, following Henry's will, denies and overturns while taking the credit for the change in "policy," showing the wiliness the playwrights established for him in the first scene. The conflict between Wolsey and his adversaries becomes a structural principle that holds together the loose episodes of the play (I.ii.1–109). Nor can the queen's pleas for Buckingham change the king's mind, because Wolsey has members of Buckingham's household perjure themselves. The king will listen to their "truth" rather than to hers (I.ii.177). After the next two scenes, which describe and represent the largesse and hospitality of Wolsey—in whose celebratory palace the king meets Anne Bullen, we hear about Buckingham's sorry predicament, that his "sharp reasons" could not save him from the perjured witnesses from his own house (II.i.14). The gentlemen, who report these matters, blame Wolsey and contrast him unfavorably with Buckingham, who appears.

Although the play makes Buckingham seem just and a victim of Wolsey's machinations, it implies, through dramatic irony, Henry's gullibility, blindness, and lack of conscience for allowing the fall and then not seeking to rehabilitate Buckingham's reputation. Buckingham is the first of the mighty to fall. Even if he appears stoic, he also seems a little naive before Wolsey's strategies, so that his piety, although admirable, is ill equipped for this world, not an entirely desirable quality for a politician. Like Henry, Buckingham sometimes sees what he wants to see as his notion of betrayal in his family confirms. Buckingham is searching for a pattern to make sense of human action. He pleads his innocence, forgives his enemies, asks for prayers to lift his soul to heaven, sends his love to the king, and gives a lesson in history. This last subject is especially appropriate for our purposes. He compares his situation to his father's and finds similarities and differences. Buckingham's father was the first to revolt against Richard III but, betrayed, was executed; in gratitude, Henry VII restored Buckingham's titles, but Henry VIII ordered his death. The wheel of fortune comes full circle, or nearly. In Buckingham's moral lesson he realizes that history does not exactly repeat itself:

> I had my trial,
> And must needs say a noble one; which makes me
> A little happier than my wretched father:

> Yet thus far we are one in fortunes; both
> Fell by our servants, by those men we lov'd most:
> A most unnatural and faithless service.
> (II.i.118–23)

Even still, Buckingham is ready to see a common pattern for people in history and how heaven purposes human events. As if this identification of faithless servants in two generations in one family could be generalized for all, Buckingham warns those gathered about him to beware such betrayal. Like Hamlet, he wants them to tell his sad tale when the audience has already heard and seen it. His last words evoke faith and pity: "God forgive me" (136). Although no one listened to his reason at the trial, he hopes they will now, as well as to his desire for the government of the world with reason—God's. But Henry never analyzes his own mistakes, and so the deaths of Buckingham and Katherine become part of a structure that is only the play's desired and overt pattern of truth and justice. That *Henry VIII* appears so forgiving of the king in order to prepare for a messianic ending obscures—or throws into relief, depending on the emotional and intellectual position of the audience—Henry's blindness to justice in the falls.

Katherine's fall calls into question the integrity of her opponents and their appeals to "truth," "honour," "conscience," and "honesty." These powerful men from court and church try to manipulate her for their own political ends. Katherine is subject to the king's wishes, although her defiance unsettles the men's authority and unmasks the motives behind their idealizing speeches. Her fall is foreshadowed by her objections to Wolsey, the introduction of Anne Bullen and Henry at Wolsey's, and the rumors of a separation between king and queen, caused by Wolsey, right after Buckingham's last speech (II.ii.40–69). The next scene furthers the rumors of Wolsey's greed for power and his design against Katherine and her brother, Charles the Emperor, who would not procure for him the archbishopric of Toledo, as well as Henry's designs on Anne. According to the Chamberlain, these rumors are "true" (II.ii.37, 39). Norfolk, Suffolk, and he hope that heaven will uncover Wolsey's plots. The cardinal still gives this history its unity. He soon slights Suffolk and Norfolk while working on the king's divorce, like Buckingham's "divorce of steel" (cf. I.ii.76, ii.73f.). Even Cardinal Campeius questions Wolsey's honesty and general character, and Henry does not escape implicit censure, for his comments on Katherine echo Suffolk's mockery. Henry says to Wolsey,

> O my lord,
> Would it not grieve an able man to leave
> So sweet a bedfellow? But conscience, conscience;
> O, 'tis a tender place, and I must leave her

whereas the Chamberlain had said, "It seems the marriage with his brother's wife / Has crept too near his conscience," to which Suffolk had answered in an aside, "No, his conscience / Has crept too near another lady" (II.ii.140–43, 16–18). The third scene shows Anne's respect for Katherine and her reluctance and naiveté as well as Henry's gifts to her. The Old Lady satirizes Anne's scruples about becoming queen, bringing up "conscience" again:

and which gifts
(Saving your mincing) the capacity
Of your soft cheveril conscience would receive,
If you might please to stretch it.
(II.iii.30–33)

While the Old Lady accuses Anne of hypocrisy, Anne swears by her "troth" that her intentions are honorable: troth may be a pun on betrothal as well as meaning truth and faith (35–36, 39). By contrasting the selfish or mixed motives of Wolsey, Campeius, Henry, and Anne with Katherine's desire for justice, the play makes it difficult to scapegoat Wolsey while forgetting Henry's part in the annulment. If the audience blames both, it should not forget that culpability during the "happy" ending.

After talk about the queen and her apparent displacement by Anne, Shakespeare represents Katherine's trial. The playwright shifts from indirect to direct means of representing Katherine's situation. She appears directly before the audience rather than through the report of others. Katherine represents herself. This representation, however, is not unmediated, as the male voices dominate the trial. The men want her to play by their rules. They will make history both event and narrative. Despite Henry's scruples, his desires dominate the court. The queen appeals to heaven and says that she was a "true and humble wife" (II.iv.20–21). Wolsey answers Katherine's plea to Henry. She then accuses him of being her enemy, but Wolsey claims his "truth" (96). As Wolsey has Henry absolve him of Katherine's accusations, the king speaks repeatedly about his "conscience" and claims that heaven punished him for marrying his brother's widow by not giving him a male heir, but after Henry's great, pious, and conscientious speech, in an aside, he reveals his disdain for the court, the law, and Rome (168, 180, 198, 201, 184–206, 233–39). Saying she has "fall'n from favour," Katherine meets Wolsey and Campeius and tells them that she has a clear "conscience" and proclaims, "truth loves open dealing" (II.i.20, 30, see 47). Evidently forgetting his own earlier accusation against Wolsey, Campeius openly speaks of Wolsey's "truth" (65). "Truth," "honour," "honesty," and the will of heaven are primary concerns in this scene and throughout the play. The characters, like historians or historical dramatists, may use these words, but to prove that they have found their meaning is another matter (e.g., 50–97). Katherine contrasts the justice of God as a judge with the injustice of human judges, will not accept the cardinals' professions of goodwill, and, like Buckingham, sees the image of divorce and death to prepare herself for her end (97f., 139–42). For the moment, however, the queen recants and will abide by the counsel of the cardinals (175f.). By recanting, Katherine allows herself (she may have no choice) to be enclosed by male narrative and legal argument. Justice slips away.

Wolsey's fall should prove that there is some poetic justice in the play, but it is not so simple. In fact, his fall also makes us wonder why Henry, who uses many of the same techniques in his personal and political machinations, does not meet the same fate. It may be a question of power. Henry has more than Wolsey does and so survives. This political ethic is hardly the one behind the birth of innocence and the pastoral vision at the end of the play. The end may be comic but the content of the play is mainly not. Actually Wolsey falls because of his scheming against Anne Bullen (III. ii.). Like the Lord Chamberlain, Suffolk prophesies a blessing will come from Anne, and the end of the play represents the obvious benefit—the infant Elizabeth (50–52, cf. II.iii.77–79). History is often the future in its presence reading the past. Norfolk and Suffolk rehabilitate Cranmer's reputation and prepare for Henry's divorce from Katherine and his marriage to Anne, a strange shift from the suffering of the old queen to the hope of the new. Interpreters of history can have short memories. When Wolsey appears, he is a victim of dramatic irony: he doesn't realize that Henry has found him out (74f.). At the end of the trial scene, Henry had already wanted Cranmer to return. Norfolk claims that the switch of packets of letters incriminated Wolsey, and Henry, whose thoughts are not exactly heavenly, disdains the cardinal's sublunar considerations (128–35). Consciously mocking Wolsey's "heavenly" calling, the king toys with him (135f.). Wolsey realizes his great fall has come and, for all his machinations, like Buckingham, he accepts his fortune:

> I shall fall
> Like a bright exhalation in the evening,
> And no man see me more.
> (III.ii.225–27)

Death shows that life is nothing. Nonetheless, he will not admit guilt in Buckingham's execution and in other crimes of which Surrey accuses him, which Wolsey says is out of spite (228f.). Besides amplifying the accusations against Wolsey, Surrey's invective prompts the Lord Chamberlain's forgiveness of this "falling man" (333)—the farewell speech. True to a Shakespearean notion of complex character, Wolsey's fall demonstrates a mixture of unrepentant defiance and a sober philosophical consideration of death.

Wolsey's farewell speech is moralized history, a "magistrate" reflecting on his fall (350f.). Shakespeare's penchant for complicating aesthetic and ethical questions often occurs through intricacy of character. As if to encourage the audience into suspicion or dislike of Wolsey, Shakespeare makes the cardinal's greatest speech his last and leaves the audience to consider its hasty judgments. Even though Wolsey and Henry are not one-dimensional and even though the play complicates their characters by sometimes using their consciences to evoke the sympathy of the audience, this does not mean that such rhetorical and dramaturgical strategies efface their shortcomings and leave the ending as wholly comic and celebratory. All too often the consciences of Wolsey and Henry are false and their concern is for pleasure, power, and reputation, so that it is difficult to gauge the audience's sympathy for them. In the farewell speech, Wolsey chastens himself for pride, like Lucifer, and for relying on the favors of princes, for being blind when one thinks the way to power is clearest, As in an epiphany, Wolsey is cured by the king of the burden of honor, his fall fortunate, less and less like Lucifer's as he proceeds (373f.). The news of Thomas More being made Lord Chancellor in his stead makes Wolsey talk about More's "conscience" and doing "justice / For truth's sake," about More staying in the king's favor a long time (393f.). Besides seeing how difficult "conscience" and "truth" have been, the audience, then and now, would know about the fall of More (13).[14] Cromwell also tells Wolsey that Henry has long been secretly married to Anne Bullen and is having her crowned this day, making the king look as worldly and Machiavellian as the cardinal whom he had just denounced. Hypocrisy and desire and not ideals and right reason propel Henry's decisions and actions. Wolsey says Anne is the true reason for his fall, reiterates that he is a fallen man, and, contrary to the cardinal's farewell to kingship, recommends that Cromwell desert him and seek the king's favor. Wolsey says he wants Cromwell to achieve glory to resurrect the forgotten Cardinal and say he taught him, that he "Found thee a way (out of his wrack) to rise in" (437). Oddly enough, Wolsey then tells Cromwell to "fling away ambition" and repeats the image of the fallen angels (438f.). The cardinal regrets he did not follow service to others and virtue, for to fall after a virtuous life would be martyrdom. At the end of such a worldly life, Wolsey's thoughts, which are contradictory, focus now on heaven, and the audience must judge his sincerity and their own, for they can be too proud if they reject him for human sins and exempt themselves from fallen humanity.

The falls of Wolsey and Katherine are nearly simultaneous. The coronation follows the cardinal's fall and precedes the queen's last appearance (IV.i). We hear about Katherine not appearing before court and being divorced *in absentia* and then hear about the crowning of the new queen with some attendant pageantry. The consciences of the two gentlemen evaporate as they compare Anne to an angel, and of the king the second gentleman says, "I cannot blame his conscience" (47). The third gentleman gives an opulent description of the coronation, which occurs offstage, as well as praising Anne. The focus of the play is shifting from Wolsey to Cranmer, Katherine to Anne. The singing of *Te Deum* and the gathering of bishops about the queen, as well as the shift of venue for the feast from the historical Westminster to the unhistorical palace where Wolsey once lived, evoke grim ironies and prefigure sadness. The mention of Cranmer and Cromwell signal a new order. The next scene represents Katherine for the last time. Festivity and sadness qualify each other: they are never allowed to last long alone. At length, Griffith tells Katherine about Wolsey's repentant death. After she forgives him while listing his sins, including "untruths," Griffith balances her account with the cardinal's virtues—scholarship and generosity—so much so that she wishes him to chronicle her life (IV.ii.). Katherine's vision of the spirits of peace, in the form of a masque, prepares her for death and brings religion, dream and myth into this history. She sees her brother's envoy, wants her daughter and serving women well looked after, forgives Henry and wants to die like a queen. Like Wolsey, she says farewell and speaks of remembrance, but cast aside, she, too, will have to face oblivion. The masque is her comet, her death her absence. The comic and mythical dramatic machinery cannot, without calling attention to an ironic gap between the desire for comedy and the reason for tragedy, make up for the injustice in her fall.

AN ALMOST FALL, THE ALREADY
PAST AS PROLOGUE, TRANSITIONS

A romantic history, *Henry VIII* rises from its own ashes. Cranmer, true and honest (as it is said repeatedly), is accused and nearly falls, but Henry toys with his accusers the way he did with Wolsey, and Cromwell, Wolsey's protégé, stands by Cranmer. Henry favors Cranmer and makes him a godfather of Elizabeth, whose birth and baptism relate closely to the accusation and acquittal of the Archbishop of Canterbury (V.ii.). There is much to say in this regard, but I will only mention that Cranmer's prophecy of Elizabeth's reign repeats the claim of truth (V.iv.16. 28. 47), predicts peace and plenty, and says, as the playwrights are doing, that "our children's children / Shall see this, and bless heaven" (54–55). Cranmer's paean to the Virgin Queen is the future reading itself back on the past. It provides a comic ending that is like the phoenix, Cranmer's description of Elizabeth, for out of sorrow it gives joy, good rising from the tragic falls of the illustrious. Henry, who has sought a male heir and power and claimed conscience, should, perhaps, be forgiven as the Lord Chamberlain and Katherine forgave Wolsey. If Elizabeth, in Cranmer's words, shall be "A pattern to all princes living with her" (22), the play urges itself as a pattern of virtue and happiness. The trouble is that the Prologue did not want the play to be comic, that more strife was to follow in the reign of Henry VIII, and that "truth" and "honour" have been difficult and changeable words in the course of the action.[15]

The structure of the play, so long relying on Wolsey, who asked and received the greatest forgiveness, asks for charity. Once forgiven, Cranmer does not seem to bear grudges but celebrates Elizabeth's birth with Henry. It is as if mythology and the desire for reason, for a pattern of virtue, has taken over. Either Shakespeare, and perhaps Fletcher, decided to allow the imagination of the audience freer play than in any of the English history plays, or they decided that there was no pattern to events in human time without the moral and aesthetic senses of the audience or that religion and mythology have as much to do with history as do fact and evidence. There are, of course, other alternatives. The pastoral tribute to Elizabeth is as touching in its nostalgia as it is in its frankness when it makes the past future and the future past. The Epilogue is about "naught" and is being naughty, using wit to ask for happy applause and, like the epilogues to *As You Like It* and *2 Henry IV*, encouraging but manipulating interpretation.

From one point of view, that of Machiavellian counsel, Shakespeare sets up Wolsey's fall by allowing him a part in the falls of two decent characters—Buckingham and Katherine—in order to prepare the way, along with the false accusation of Cranmer, for the annunciation of Elizabeth and the beginning of a great and good epoch in English history. Nonetheless, Henry VIII is partly responsible for the falls of Buckingham and Katherine and, in the latter case, wants to replace his wife with Anne Bullen. Although Shakespeare cuts off Henry's reign before his repeated replacement of wives, his persecution of Protestants as heretics, his execution of More, and other controversial acts, he cannot stir the tide of history with his history play. If the Jacobean audience focused on the praise of Elizabeth, it could not entirely forget the whole of her father's reign. Even in the play, Henry cannot escape some blame: why, for example, did he not insist on a divorce from Katherine before he met Anne Bullen? Anne becomes a strange trigger to his "conscience," a word Shakespeare makes problematic in the play. *Henry VIII* may find its power in the tension or disjunction between the religious pattern of fall and redemption or the tragicomic pattern of death and birth on the one hand and the ethical dilemmas in the action on the other. The very interest in the play may be the paradox that the more it imposes on events a movement toward a coming ending, the more we notice its injustices. These contrasts demonstrate that the problems that arise from the relation between history and tragicomedy or romance require close scrutiny and not the dismissal that has sometimes attended reactions to *Henry VIII*.

For whatever reason, Shakespeare returns to the old episodic chronicle play and supplements it with pageantry and masque. Perhaps with Fletcher's help, he cuts his play loose from the close mimesis of some of his earlier English histories, leaving his audience to follow the Chorus of *Henry V* in filling out the historical action. Long before reader response theory, Shakespeare knew that writing, and in this case historical representation, demanded more than intentionality. The tragic and comic aspects of *Henry VIII* rub together in a creative way that proclaims the variety of history and the problems of the task. *Henry VIII* is both historical and antihistorical. Its brilliant surface calls into question patterns in history while asserting them. The play is a simple historical pageant full of complexity and contradiction. What the Boy says about Pistol in *Henry V* might apply to *Henry VIII*: "I did never know so full a voice issue from so empty a heart: but the saying is true, 'The empty vessel makes the greatest sound'" (*Henry V* IV.iv.69–71).[16] If the desire for reason in history remains strong, reason itself recognizes that desire is infinite but performance not. As an experienced playwright, Shakespeare, with or without Fletcher, understood the limits of performance even as he celebrated its beauty and power. If on earth and in time, Henry can wish "That when I am in heaven I shall desire / To see what this child does, and praise my maker," the audience shares Henry's predicament but also has the benefit of the backward look and overview of history.

And so with Shakespeare's representation of history in his own and other cultures though the great range of his language, both in poetry and prose, there is something splendid and changing and surprising. He does not rest. He is a restless experimenter who will not rest on his laurels, which is not a bad thing for a poet. Shakespeare's great skill at poetry and drama enables him to reinterpret and rework through showing and telling stories ancient and modern in all the registers that different kinds of literature allow. And we who are interpreters and reinterpreters, too, give our own backward glance at Shakespeare, who looks about him and behind him. Desire has a surface and a performance, and history as event and interpretation are a pageant of contradiction and intricacy. In the play of culture there is give and take, for Shakespeare and for us. The asymptotic may be the divergent and linearity circular, but in close attention to Shakespeare's language and design we can find some signposts that suggest something beyond a worn and incurious world.

CONCLUSION

THIS BOOK BEGAN WITH BEN JONSON'S WORDS FOR SHAKESPEARE IN THE front matter of the First Folio in 1623. Marlowe, Shakespeare, and Jonson were great innovators. Jonson was ambivalent about Shakespeare and helped lead the way in the reception of Shakespeare. Still, Jonson could offer a great eulogy for this poet and playwright: "Soule of the age! / The applauſe! delight! The wonder of our Stage!"[1] As we also saw, about seven years before, Francis Beaumont had written a poem to Jonson in which he pictures heirs hearing "how farr sometimes a mortall man may goe / by the dimme light of Nature."[2] This is where the formal view of Shakespeare, poet of nature, began. In a sense, Heminge and Condell, who edited the First Folio, and Jonson and Beaumont, knew Shakespeare and brought out the idea of nature and art, their time and posterity, issues that would occur to later generations. This is the context of my book and all such books on Shakespeare.

This poet and playwright is a protean figure who assumes and assimilates classical and Romantic elements. Shakespeare inspired writers in English, German, and other languages using classical, Romantic, and other models. The beauty and power of Shakespeare's language and the dramatic and nondramatic worlds helped to create this influence in posterity. This interest could be as much about philosophy and rhetoric as it was about poetry. In rhetoric Shakespeare could persuade and show the various relations between speaker and audience, writer and reader. Part of this meeting is about cultivating interpretation, something that joins the writer and his audience. Shakespeare's play of language enriches that relation between actors and audience, words and reader.

In this book, I have explored a whole range of Shakespeare's fictional worlds. The rape and death of Lucrece, the plot against and death of Julius Caesar, the overthrow of Richard II, the invasion of France by Henry V, Cranmer's prophecy about Elizabeth in *Henry VIII*, as I argued, are all contested moments. Shakespeare the man is not much known to us, so we have before us Shakespeare the maker of his texts for stage, manuscript, and print. Shakespeare was of England as it had been attempting to expand its trade and territory. Although the book focused mostly on texts, it also presented contexts that should have shed some light on these works. In this context, I examined some of his key texts, beginning with the narrative poems and the sonnets. Afterwards, I discussed barbarism and its contexts and Shakespeare's representation of history as well as the double image or typology of England and Italy. The English history plays became the matter of the last part of the book. A large part of the discussion centered on gender in the second tetralogy (*Richard II*, *1* and *2 Henry IV* and *Henry V*) followed by an analysis of *Henry V* and *Henry VIII*. This tetralogy appears to leave women out from the dynamics of rule and power more than the first tetralogy did, and it was a challenge for the examination of gender dynamics that the texts produced. Shakespeare's *Venus and Adonis* and *The Rape of Lucrece* seem to be the only works that Shakespeare authorized for print. In them, Shakespeare explored mythology and the classical pasts of Greece and Rome. These poems are in epic cast and gesture to Homer, Virgil, and Ovid. The seduction of language and the language of seduction emerge as important aspects of these poems. I also discussed how Shakespeare's dramatic and nondramatic sonnets take up on the theme of time, which is central to Shakespeare and to my book on him. Temporality is a key to the poems and plays of Shakespeare.

The nondramatic poems are suggestive in their treatment of language, theme, and character. In *Venus and Adonis*, Shakespeare explores mimesis through reflective imagery, description (or narration) and direct speech, and self-conscious allusions to the laws of nature and their limits. This poem explores the nature of representation while expressing wit and eroticism. Art imitates life imitating art. Shakespeare describes the "war" between Venus and Adonis in terms of the stage (359–60) while using stories and personifications of nature and death: these challenge mimesis with symbol and allegory (esp. 716–44, 806, 953–1012).[3] Shakespeare mends the limited possibility of the world with the supplement of art. He gives us a poem where nature is vigorous because it strives with itself and with what is beyond it, just as Shakespeare's poem does.

The Rape of Lucrece represents a key moment surrounding the siege of Ardea, such as Tarquin's account of seduction and Lucrece's tale of rape. The poet's narrative explores love, lust, and violence. Rhetoric as persuasion and communication lies at the heart of the poem. Characters as narrators, the principal narrator, and the ways the reader is implicated in the narration were all elements examined to show how Shakespeare affects the reader.

Point of view is a key to Shakespeare's poetry and drama. In *Lucrece*, he provides an intricate representation of exempla and description of the characters', narrator's, and author's points of view that demands a great deal of the reader. The inset of Troy represents a difficult challenge. Representation can misrepresent the subject, and every reading, including my own, is on the verge of being a misreading. Further, I argued that the complicity of the narrator in Tarquin's failed seduction and then the rape of Lucrece and the violence in the sack of Troy might well embody the author's seduction of himself and of the reader. By examining narrative closely from the point of view of the relation of the characters, narrator, and poet to the reader, I hoped to show a clearer understanding of *Lucrece*. I asked how the ethic of reading and experience in the world relate.

In the sonnets, I argued that a conflict occurs between the ruins of time and the monuments of Shakespeare's poetry. I maintained that this tension lay in the desire between rhetoric and poetics, lust and love. The sonnet shows the pressure of time to produce a fiction of timelessness. The verbal world of the sonnets shows overreaching conceit while recognizing its impossibility. Shakespeare explores the limits and possibilities of poetry generally and the sonnet specifically. The compression of the sonnet in a collection of sonnets challenges the expansiveness of time. In some ways, form becomes a theme itself to be explored.

Shakespeare's dramatic and nondramatic sonnets stretch the bounds of the verse form itself. They also explore the bounds of the desire for peace and the discovery of conflict working within the confines of fourteen lines and a tight formal rhyme and rhythm. Shakespeare's sonnet sequence represents a private love made public in fame, an oscillation between permanence and oblivion, true and false love. This locus, I argued, is not always that different from the more seemingly public space of the the-atre, where the sonnets in *Romeo and Juliet* and *Henry V* were performed. In *Romeo and Juliet*, Shakespeare's humble and bold language speaks about love, time and death. It is unsure and sure and rests as much in readers' eyes as in mistress' eyes.[4] Where the eye or ear is becomes an inescapable part of Shakespeare's art.

Another aspect of Shakespeare's time was not simply the sonnets, but the shock of discovery with the expansion of Europe that occurred before and during his life. This exploration was one of the many great changes that Europeans and other cultures lived through from the fifteenth century. Like Columbus, Michel de Montaigne, and others, Shakespeare considered the question of the human. He represented worlds that included ideas of slavery and freedom and of monstrosity and barbarity.[5] In the opening of *The Histories*, Herodotus wanted to rescue great deeds from oblivion and wished "that great and marvelous deeds, some displayed by the Hellenes, some by the barbarians, not lose their glory."[6] This way the glory of Hellenes and barbarians will persist. I argued that whereas Herodotus was given to barbarians and barely men-tions monsters, Shakespeare did the opposite. Civilization and barbarism have long persisted together in texts. Walter Benjamin reminds us that point of view becomes vital in history and culture as much as I argued it did in poetics. Benjamin says that the vantage lies with the victor.[7] That might lead to the question—Is Shakespeare in *Henry V* writing from the point of view of the victor? In my discussion, I found that the few examples of monstrosity in *The Tempest* and *Othello*, plays about otherness and the exotic, yield their own surprises. To equate one group with the monstrous based on its gender, race, or class would, then, oversimplify the matter. The uses of "barbarian," "barbarous," and "barbarism" in Shakespeare's plays is intricate and con-tradictory. In history, tragedy, and comedy (including romance), Shakespeare employs these terms in many different ways. Shakespeare represents the classical past across genres. In this context, he uses barbarism in a manner that the Greeks and Romans would recognize. Columbus came to divide the world into good friendly Natives and evil and treacherous Natives, but did Shakespeare in *Titus*, *Othello*, *Coriolanus*, and *The Tempest* do anything different?[8] What interests me is that the language of contradiction in representation suggests that whatever Columbus and Shakespeare intended, their words embodied the drama of liminal states that could not seal civili-zation from barbarism.

Even though close attention to reading Shakespeare's works as poetry and drama has been at the heart of this book, some contextual matters help to reconfigure and cast some light from a different angle on how Shakespeare made his art in the time and place he did. Shakespeare's predecessors, contemporaries, and successors enter into the drama of meaning. That is part of the web of interpretation.

Temporality, as I observed, becomes a continuum in which people in the present reach into the past to project something into a present moving into the future. This poet and playwright employed many kinds of poetry and drama to explore the rep-resentation of history and was part of the Renaissance discovery of time.[9] A central question in the book became what Shakespeare makes in time and of time and how he does so through language. Throughout the study, I attempted to show that from the reversal of conventions of love through the reinterpretation of a classical myth and the rhetoric of seduction to temporality in the sonnets or the insertion of the monstrous between the civil and the barbaric, Shakespeare forged his themes through language. In poetry and drama, in sonnets, *epyllia* or brief epics, tragedy, romance, and comedy, as well as in the history plays themselves, he shaped time and history. Shakespeare's history is protean and involves the meditation on the past, personal, and public; the classical past; the biblical past; the European past; and the English past. The connections among ideology and mythology, story and argument underpin Shakespeare's representation of history. That recreation of history takes on many forms. Although there are ideological and political dimensions of Shakespeare's history, the mythological and aesthetic aspects are keys to understanding his representation of history. As Aristotle observed, the putative and possible aspect of poetry connects it to history because rhetoric shares with poetics the "what if" and "what might happen." Dramatic historical poetry can escape neither ideology nor mythology. Shakespeare is of his time but is of interest over time.[10]

A typology that is a key instance of history is Shakespeare's representation of England and Italy. In his nondramatic and dramatic poetry, Shakespeare represented an Italy of the ancients and of his own time, and in this work Rome and Italy held out an example of ancient wisdom and of bold change. As the book outlines, *The Rape of Lucrece* represented a critical moment in the history of Rome while the sonnets owed something to Petrarch and Shakespeare's comedies were indebted to Terence and Plautus and could have had Italian settings. Shakespeare's history plays, which were about England, defined the nation partly against Rome and Italy. Some of Shakespearean tragedies, such as *Titus Andronicus, Julius Caesar, Othello, Coriolanus*, and *Antony and Cleopatra*, were Roman and Italian. The tragicomedies or romances also have such concerns. *Cymbeline* represents ancient Britain and imperial Rome, and *The Tempest* has as its world an island between Italy and Africa. The focus of my discussion in this part of the book was on ancient Rome and medieval and Renaissance Italy in relation to ancient Britain and England.

In this typology between past and present, there and here, so much depends on point of view, as Benjamin observed of the writing of history. Italy and England came to inhabit the possible worlds of Shakespeare's history and fiction. Italy had been built by the ancient Roman republic and empire, and Britain had been a part of the Roman sphere, first as a colony or province. The Christian church and its connections to Rome also complicated this double image.[11] The Renaissance included the rebirth of classical languages and learning and helped to make Italy a cultural source for western Europe.

In discussing the second tetralogy (*Richard II, 1* and *2 Henry IV*, and *Henry V*), I decided to examine gender in these plays that might appear to marginalize women even though Shakespeare wrote and staged them in the 1590s when a queen was on the throne. I also returned to a time—the 1980s—when I had studied gender in these plays and when feminism had made some exciting changes to the field of Shakespearean studies, including those of the histories. In this analysis, I chose to concentrate most on the text itself rather than to make Shakespeare conform to the works of contemporaries inside and outside drama and literature. While I placed Shakespeare in the context of women critics working in a key time in feminism within Shakespearean studies, I also examined what women say and do in his texts and how others react and interact with those words and actions.[12]

Part of what I wanted to examine was whether Shakespeare's second tetralogy, the very height of the English history play, left women to the margins and silences away from the center of power.[13] I also discussed the feminine in conjunction with the masculine and the effeminate because these demarcations are interdependent.[14] Some of the female characters in the comedies and Joan of Arc in *1 Henry VI* dress as men and challenge gender codes. From the 1960s to the 1980s, feminist criticism questioned the marginalization, abuse, and neglect of women in the Roman and English histories and among male critics. But feminist critics then considered Shakespeare's first tetralogy (*Richard III, 1, 2, 3 Henry VI*) much more than his second tetralogy.[15] I found that the construction of gender in the second tetralogy is intricate and that the characters view gender in contradictory ways that are what I called a jostle of voices. Shakespeare's second tetralogy is a site of contestation among characters over the question of gender.

Following that discussion of gender in this important series of history plays, I chose to concentrate on two plays, *Henry V* and *Henry VIII*, that pushed the boundary of historical drama about England. As a supplement, I concentrated on *Henry V* in terms of language, structure, and character. How problematic and how innovative and how heroic this play is depends again on the point of view of Shakespeare in the text and the reception since. The rise of irony as a critical and theoretical concept in the past two centuries may well have contributed to the destabilization of the text and its meaning.[16] This play, like the first three of the second tetralogy, represent kingship (right, responsibility, and succession). Paradoxically, the problems of the history play perplex the audience and induce a crisis in understanding history while also creating a coherent pattern. This protean kind of drama—the history play—includes aspects of tragedy, comedy, and satire. My discussion of it provided an end to this book on Shakespeare's innovation in language and form, poetry, and drama.

When discussing *Henry VIII*, I stressed that this play is a history as romance or, if one prefers, tragicomedy. Shakespeare does not seem to have shared the view history was the antiquarian venture that Sidney described.[17] Elizabethan and Jacobean England saw many histories, historical poems, history plays, and prefatory defenses and justifications of history.

In *Henry VIII*, as I maintained, Shakespeare continues the kind of exploration of imagination and English history that he represents in the choruses to *Henry V*. Shakespeare reworks the episodic nature of the chronicle plays of the 1580s and the early 1590s in *Henry VIII*. He uses with great effect the pageantry of the old street pageants and the masque.[18] Further, Shakespeare uses a *de casibus* pattern—the falls of Buckingham, Katherine, and Wolsey and the near fall of Cranmer. More than any other Shakespearean history, it seems to me, *Henry VIII* embodies the collision of dramatic and historical expectations. The desire for unity and the mythic redemption through Elizabeth of Henry's rule are key parts of the conclusion of *Henry VIII*.

In this book, I have concentrated on Shakespeare's representations of place and time, of private and public, and the personal and the political, as well as how questions of gender, lust, and love have implications beyond the plays themselves. Shakespeare, the private man and public playwright, lived in the reign of Elizabeth I and

James I and wrote poems about Greek and Roman myths, the encounter between Venus and Adonis, Tarquin and Lucrece, as part of a recovery of the classical past, often with present purposes. The rhetoric of seduction in both narrative poems places the reader in a dilemma between aesthetic and erotic pressure and ethical decision. In the sonnets, Shakespeare explores the boundaries of gender and the friction between love and lust. In all this the language is the very power Shakespeare has over his readers. The private poems of the sonnets and the public sonnets of the plays show once more how Shakespeare can make the private and public meet through the same forms. Time is a central concern of these sonnets, and this is also a principal theme of the history plays. Shakespeare's times, how he represents history in the poems and plays, and the configuration of civility, monstrosity, and barbarity also occur in the context of the halting expansion of England and western Europe and in the context of classical notions of civilization and barbarism.

When examining these texts and contexts, I focused mainly on the language of Shakespeare and his contemporaries. In the history plays, especially *Richard II*, *1* and *2 Henry IV*, *Henry V*, and *Henry VIII*, I have paid close attention to gender and the ways in which the last two of these plays test the very boundaries of the history play, as Heminge and Condell classified them in the First Folio. As one of the great variety of readers Heminge and Condell mention in their address and a member of the posterity Shakespeare imagines in the sonnets, each of us attempts to interpret Shakespeare in performance or in print. In writing this book over decades, I am one reader being overheard by another. Rather than attempt readings of Shakespeare's complete work, I have interpreted a sample of work along the way in regard to poetry, culture, and history. This is an offering to readers somewhere in the tension between the profession of Shakespeare and our collective general readership, in the slower movement of the reception of Shakespeare and the pressing moment of research. Perhaps somewhere between is scholarship and interpretation, both of which have a long history before natural philosophy became science. Time itself is a way to scholarship in the humanities and in letters, to use an old term, and the republic of letters has many members. The pressure of the moment is scientific discovery and the progress of the most recent experiments have many benefits, but being too much in that moment in the study of Shakespeare may well mean that we have forgotten what went before and how to take up shards of old vessels.

There is no one way into Shakespeare, and this is another by someone balancing the point of view of poet, literary scholar, and historian. More important than any of this is that Shakespeare is always there—for Beaumont, for Jonson, for us, and for those after we are gone—his poetry and dramatic power enduring despite the odds when the First Folio came out, in English and so many other cultures and languages. It might be, as Oscar Wilde's Vivian, in *The Decay of Lying*, said: "Paradox though it may seem—and paradoxes are always dangerous things—it is none the less true that Life imitates art far more than Art imitates life."[19] However someone construes that balance between life and art, it is hard to know the division between how Shakespeare helped to produce our culture and why our culture still needs Shakespeare. He was of a time and of many times past and to come. He has given the fiction of timelessness a good run, which is not surprising for the author of Sonnet 55 and a few other works with a passing interest in time.

NOTES

INTRODUCTION

1. *Mr. William Shakespeare's Comedies, Histories, & Tragedies. Published According to the True Originall Copies* (London: Isaac Iaggard and Ed. Blount, 1623), A5r.
2. Ibid.
3. Ibid.
4. Ibid.
5. Ibid.
6. Ibid., A5r–A5v.
7. E. K. Chambers emends "deere" to "cleere," and, as G. Blakemore Evans notes, the Holgate MS, fol. 110 (Pierpont Morgan Library), and Additional MS. 30982 at the British Library read "deere." See Chambers, *William Shakespeare* (Oxford: Clarendon, 1930), 2:224; Evans, "Early Critical Comment on the Plays and Poems," in *The Riverside Shakespeare*, 2nd ed., ed. G. Blakemore Evans, with J. J. M. Tobin (Boston: Houghton Mifflin, 1997), 1971.
8. Evans, "Early Critical Comment," 1971–72.
9. Ibid., 1973.
10. Ibid.
11. *Mr. William Shakespeares*, A5v.
12. Ibid.
13. Ibid.
14. Ibid.
15. Ibid.
16. A good example of an accomplished scholar writing a general book for what he calls "a non-professional audience" is Frank Kermode, *Shakespeare's Language* (2000; repr., London: Penguin, 2001), vii.
17. Gilbert Murray, *The Classical Tradition in Modern Poetry* (1927; repr., New York: Vintage Books, 1957), vii. On Ben Jonson, see Anne Barton, *Ben Jonson, Dramatist* (Cambridge: Cambridge University Press, 1984).
18. Rather than go into this topic, I refer to my other discussions of Shakespeare's relation to irony and Romanticism in a number of works, including *Theater and World: The Problematics of Shakespeare's History* (Boston: Northeastern University Press, 1992), esp. 9–11, 228–31.
19. William Lambard, in John Nichols, *Progresses and Processions of Queen Elizabeth* (1823), quoted in *The Shakespeare Allusion-Book*, ed. and rev. J. Munro (1909; repr., Freeport, NY: Books for Library Press, 1970), 100.
20. Walter Kaufman, *From Shakespeare to Existentialism* (Princeton: Princeton University Press, 1980), 3.

21. The Platonic Socrates, particularly in the tenth book of *Republic*, shows skepticism over the role of Homer in Greek education and would prefer that poetry serve philosophical and political ends. This is an attempt to displace poetry with philosophy. Still, Plato is also uncomfortable with the rhetoricians, comparing these professionals with someone devoted to education without financial interests—Socrates, poetry, philosophy, and rhetoric are not—as his student, Aristotle, recognized—easy to separate. To persuade is, for Aristotle, the end of the rhetoric: "Persuasion is clearly a sort of demonstration, since we are most fully persuaded when we consider a thing to have been demonstrated." Aristotle, *Rhetoric*, trans. W. Rhys Roberts (1924; repr., New York: Dover, 2004), 1355a. Aristotle does not portray the study and practice of rhetoric, which originated in the Greek colony in Sicily and was exported back to Athens, as something insincere and manipulative. No cheap lawyer jokes for him. Instead, Aristotle says that rhetoric is of use "because things that are true and things that are just have a natural tendency to prevail over their opposites, so that if the decisions of judges are not what they ought to be, the defeat must be due to the speakers themselves, and they must be blamed accordingly." Aristotle, *Rhetoric*, 1355a. See Plato, *The Republic of Plato*, trans. Francis MacDonald Cornford (1941; repr., Oxford: Clarendon, 1945), Book X, 595 A-608 B. Poetry, according to Aristotle, sprang from imitation and harmony and rhythm. He considers these aspects to be two elements deep in human nature. Poetry, for Aristotle, comes down to a relation between the character of the author and the choice of genre. On Aristotle, see Jonathan Hart, "The Author Writes Back (and Speaks Up)," *Primerjalna književnost* 31, no. 2 (2008): 15–37.

22. Clifford Geertz, *Available Light: Anthropological Reflections on Philosophical Topics* (2000; repr., Princeton, NJ: Princeton University Press, 2001), 3. For my own recent discussions of culture, poetics, interpretation, recognition and other topics, see *Interpreting Cultures: Literature, Religion, and the Human Sciences* (New York: Palgrave Macmillan, 2006).

23. See Aristotle, *Poetics*, chapter 9.

24. In a well-known passage, Philip Sidney gives us a view of the historian as lost in a slowly vanishing archive: "The Historian, scarcely giueth leysure to the Moralist, to say so much, but that he loden with old Mouse-eaten records, authorising himselfe (for the most part) vpon other histories, whose greatest authorities, are built vpon the notable foundation of Heare-say, hauing much a-doe to accord differing VVriters, and to pick trueth out of partiality, better acquainted with a thousande yeeres a goe, then with the present age." See *An apologie for poetrie. VVritten by the right noble, vertuous, and learned, Sir Phillip Sidney, Knight, At London: Printed [by James Roberts] for Henry Olney, and are to be sold at his shop in Paules Church-yard, at the signe of the George, neere to Cheap-gate, Anno. 1595*. In the opening paragraphs of "Preface to Shakespeare," Samuel Johnson also says famously, "*Shakespeare* is above all writers, at least above all modern writers, the poet of nature; the poet that holds up to his readers a faithful mirrour of manners and of life. . . . His persons act and speak by the influence of those general passions and principles by which all minds are agitated, and whole system of life is continued in motion. In the writings of other poets a character is too often an individual; in those of *Shakespeare* it is commonly a species." See *Mr. Johnson's Preface to His Edition of Shakespear's Plays* (London: J. and R. Tonson, H. Woodfall, J. Rivington, R. Baldwin, L. Hawes, Clark and Collins, T. Longman, W. Johnston, T. Caslon, C. Corbet, T. Lownds, and the Executors on B. Dodd, 1765), A4v–A5r. In *Jerusalem*, William Blake takes a contrary view to Johnson's: "He who would do good to another must do it in Minute Particulars. / General Good is the plea of the scoundrel, hypocrite & flatterer: / For Art & Science cannot exist but in minutely organized Particulars, / And not in generalizing Demonstrations of the Rational Power." See William Blake, "Jerusalem," in *The Complete Poetry and Prose of William Blake*, rev. ed., ed. David V. Erdman and Harold Bloom (Berkeley: University of California Press, 1982), 205.

25. For a discussion of the London of Shakespeare and its material culture at the turn of the seventeenth century, see *Material London, ca. 1600*, ed. Lena Cowen Orwin (Philadelphia: University of Pennsylvania Press, 2000). In this volume, on the theatres in London, see Andrew Gurr, "The Authority of the Globe and the Fortune," 251–67.

26. Ben Jonson, *The Workes of Beniamin Ionson* (London: Will Stansby, 1616).

27. See Rosalind Miles, *Ben Jonson: His Life and Work* (London: Routledge & Kegan Paul, 1986), 166–69. See also David Riggs, *Ben Jonson: A Life* (Cambridge MA: Harvard University Press, 1989); Sarah Van Den Berg, "True Relation: the Life and Career of Ben Jonson," in *The Cambridge Companion to Ben Jonson*, ed. Richard Harp and Stanley Stewart (Cambridge: Cambridge University Press, 2000), 1–13; and, in the same volume, Leah Marcus, "Jonson and the Court," 30–42. My thanks to Jane Wong for discussing Jonson as laureate.

28. For records on Shakespeare's life, see, for example, E. K. Chambers, *William Shakespeare*, 2:1–18. See also Samuel Schoenbaum, *William Shakespeare: A Documentary Life* (Oxford: Clarendon Press, 1975); *William Shakespeare: Records and Images* (New York: Oxford University Press, 1981).

29. Mark Harrison, *Disease and the Modern World: 1500 to the Modern World* (Cambridge: Polity Press, 2004), 27–29. See also F. P. Wilson, *The Plague in Shakespeare's London* (Oxford: Oxford University Press, 1927); William H. McNeill, *Plagues and Peoples* (Oxford: Blackwell, 1977); Clare Gittings, *Death, Burial and the Individual in Early Modern England* (London: Croom Helm, 1984); Paul Slack, *The Impact of Plague in Tudor and Stuart England* (Oxford: Clarendon Press, 1985); J. Leeds Barroll, *Politics, Plague, and Shakespeare's Theatre: The Stuart Years* (Ithaca, NY: Cornell University Press, 1991); F. David Hoeniger, *Medicine and Shakespeare in the English Renaissance* (Newark: University of Delaware Press, 1992); Nat Wayne Hardy, "Anatomy of Pestilence: The Satiric Disgust of Plague in Early Modern London (1563–1625)" (PhD thesis, University of Alberta, 2000); Colin Heywood, *A History of Childhood* (Cambridge: Polity Press, 2001).

30. See John Seeley, *The Expansion of England* (London: Macmillan, 1883).

31. In 1734, Voltaire showed ambivalence toward Shakespeare (he wrote about Shakespeare from about 1733 to 1776): "The *English* as well as the *Spaniards* were posses'd of Theatres, at a Time when the French had no more than moving, itinerant Stages. . . . *Shakespear* boasted a strong, fruitful Genius: He was natural and sublime, but had not so much as a single Spark of good Taste, or knew one Rule of the Drama." See "Shakespeare's Montrous Farces . . . Lettres Philosophiques, *1734*," in *Four Centuries of Shakesperian Criticism*, ed. J. Frank Kermode (New York: Discus/Avon, 1965), 73. In 1765, Samuel Johnson observed, "When *Shakespeare's* plan is understood, most of the criticisms of *Rymer* and *Voltaire* vanish away." See "Samuel Johnson, Edition of Shakespeare 1765," in *William Shakespeare: The Critical Heritage*, ed. Brian Vickers (London: Routledge, 1974), 45. Elizabeth Montagu also came to the defense of Shakespeare against Voltaire's charges of barbarism in "Essay on the Writings and Genius of Shakespeare," in Vickers, *William Shakespeare*, 169; see also 328–29. On Voltaire's view of Shakespeare, see also Alphonse de Lamartine, *Shakespeare et son oeuvre* (Paris: A. Lacroix, Verboeckhoven et Cie., 1865) and a translated excerpt from this book from March 5, 1916, in the *New York Times*. Lamartine says, "if one judges from the errors of taste, improprieties, vulgarities, and obscenities, from the shortcomings of style even, which mar the plays of the English Æschylus and Molière, one must confess that Voltaire was not too severe." On the other hand, "if one bases judgment on the conception, eloquence, fecundity, truth, and sublimity of genius of this incomparable man, Voltaire is wrong." Lamartine sees the beginning of national literature in England, France, and Italy as being contra barbarism: "This does not imply that the literary century of Elizabeth, the sixteenth century, when Shakespeare wrote, was a

barbarous century: it was rather an overrefined century, and age of affectation and corruptions of style. For it must be borne in mind that in Italy and France, as well as in England, national literature does not commence with barbarism, but with affectation." Voltaire also saw Shakespeare's power and helped to spread his reputation in France and the continent, given the importance of French as a language at that time. See Thomas R. Lounsbury, *Shakespeare and Voltaire* (New York: Charles Scribner's Sons, 1902), esp. 41–42.

32. Aristotle's theory of natural slavery found an advocate in Juan Ginés de Sepúlveda and an opponent in Bartolomé de Las Casas in the debate over the nature of the American Indian (*los Indios*).

33. On natural slavery, see Aristotle, *Politics*, trans. Benjamin Jowett (New York: Dover, 1992), bk. 1, chs. 4–5; Lewis Hanke, *Aristotle and the American Indians: A Study in Race Prejudice in the Modern World* (Chicago: Henry Regnery, 1959); and Anthony Pagden, *The Fall of Natural Man: The American Indian and the Origins of Comparative Ethnology* (1982; rev., Cambridge: Cambridge University Press, 1986). See Herodotus, *The Persian Wars*, trans. G. Rawlinson (New York: Modern Library, 1942); on Herodotus, see François Hertog, "Herodotus and the Historiographical Operation," *Diacritics* 22 (1992): 83–93; Donald R. Kelley, *Faces of History: Historical Inquiry from Herodotus to Herder* (New Haven, CT: Yale University Press, 1998); Rosalind Thomas, *Herodotus in Context: Ethnography, Science and the Art of Persuasion* (Cambridge: Cambridge University Press, 2000); Jonathan Hart, *Interpreting Cultures*, esp. 54–55.

34. An early response by a woman, Margaret Cavendish, Duchess of Newcastle (1624–74), raises the question of Shakespeare's feigning and the world and does so in relation to Shakespeare's representation of gender, which will occupy a later part of my book. Of Shakespeare, she says, "one would think that he had been Metamorphosed from a Man to a Woman, for who could Describe *Cleopatra* Better than he hath done, and many other Females of his own Creating." See Cavendish, "*A Letter on Shakespeare* (from CCXI Sociable Letters, *1664*," in Kermode, *Four Centuries*, 42.

35. For an important earlier discussion, see Anne Righter [Barton], *Shakespeare and the Idea of the Play* (London, Chatto & Windus, 1962).

36. See Thomas M. Greene, *The Vulnerable Text: Essays on Renaissance Literature* (New York: Columbia University Press, 1986).

37. *Mr. William Shakespeares*, A4r.

38. Ibid., A3v.

CHAPTER 1

1. Ovid, *The. xv. Bookes of P. Ovidus Naso, entytuled Metamorphosis*, translated oute of Latin into Englysh meeter, *by Arthur Golding Gentleman, A worke very pleasaunt and delectable* (London: Willyam Seres, 1567). For work on *Venus and Adonis* that is subsequent to mine (the original of my essay having been written in 1986–87—see note 13) but contributions that discuss concerns related to rhetoric and eroticism, what I have called the rhetoric of seduction, see, for example, Jonathan Bate, "Sexual Perversity in *Venus and Adonis*," *Yearbook in English Studies* 23 (1993): 80–92; Catherine Belsey, "Love as Trompe-l'oeil: Taxonomies of Desire in *Venus and Adonis*," *Shakespeare Quarterly* 46 (1995): 251–76; Gary Kuchar, "Narratives and the Form of Desire in Shakespeare's *Venus and Adonis*," *Early Modern Literary Studies* 5 (1999): 1–24. For a more general discussion, see Peter Hyland, *An Introduction to Shakespeare's Poems* (New York: Palgrave Macmillan, 2003).

2. Dolce, Letter to Contarini, in G. G. Botari, *Racolta di Lettere sulla Pittura, Scultura e Architettura* (Rome, 1759), 3:257–60, quoted in Paola Tingali, *Women in Renaissance Art: Gender, Representation, Identity* (Manchester: Manchester University Press, 1997),

141. See also Ludovico Dolce, *Dialogo della Pittura*, in P Barocchi, ed., *Trattati d'Arte del Cinquecento fra Manierismo e Controriforma* (Laterza, Bari, 1960–62), 1:143–206.

3. Tingali, *Women in Renaissance Art*, 140, discusses the erotic aspect of Titian's painting in *Venus and Adonis* and his other works. See Tingali, *Women in Renaissance Art*, 141–2. See also Mary Pardo, "Artifice as Seduction in Titian," in James Grantham Turner, ed., *Sexuality and Gender in Early Modern Europe* (Cambridge: Cambridge University Press, 1993), 55–90, esp. 55. Pardo wants to shift the traditional emphasis from theme to means of representation or artifice in discussing Titian's *Urbino Venus*. Tingali also notes the critical discussion of Titian, seeing his paintings as *poesie*. For an earlier specific comparison, see John Doebler, "The Reluctant Adonis: Titian and Shakespeare," *Shakespeare Quarterly* 33 (1982): 480–90.

4. For a discussion of Ronsard, Sonnet XC, lines 9–14, in this context, see Lawrence D. Kritzman, *The Rhetoric of Sexuality and the Literature of the French Renaissance* (Cambridge: Cambridge University Press, 1991), 127.

5. For a discussion of Venus' female independence in this garden, see Pamela Joseph Benson, *The Invention of the Renaissance Woman: The Challenge of Female Independence in the Literature and Thought of Italy and England* (University Park: Penn State Press, 1992), 253–57.

6. Christopher Hibbert, *The Virgin Queen: Elizabeth I, Genius Of The Golden Age* (London: Da Capo Press, 1992), 130–31.

7. Susan Doran, *Queen Elizabeth I* (New York: New York University Press, 2003), 116–17.

8. On the dedication, see, for example, Jonathan Bate, *The Genius of Shakespeare* (New York: Oxford University Press, 1998), 20. Stephen Greenblatt provides a good context for Southampton's life and the relation to Lord Burghley as background to Shakespeare dedicating the poem to Southampton: see his *Will in the World: How Shakespeare Became Shakespeare* (New York: W. W. Norton & Company, 2004), esp. 228–30.

9. For an interesting discussion of this in the context of republicanism, in which he implies that *Venus and Adonis* is not overtly political but reads the poem as a critique of Elizabeth's failure to procreate and to have the monarchy survive in contrast to the virtue of Lucrece set out in his later narrative poem, see Andrew Hadfield, *Shakespeare and Republicanism* (Cambridge: Cambridge University Press, 2005), 80, 100, 130–36.

10. John Clapham, *Narcissus. Siue amoris iuuenilis et praecipue philautiae breuis at que moralis descripto* (Londini: Excudebat Thomas Scarlet, 1591). The translation here and below is mine, but has benefitted from the advice of David Porter, whose ability in poetry and poetics and in translation is admirable. I give particular thanks for his advice and for sharing his Latin translation when I asked him about these two parts of Clapham. It was interesting to see his subtle and clear analysis of the prose sentence and line of verse, which kept me honest and accurate when I got too loose or metaphorical. Another aspect of the last line of poem that we discussed is the richness of "infoelicis" from "infelix." As the saying goes, the faults are my own.

11. Clapham, *Narcissus*.

12. Citations and quotations are from William Shakespeare, *The Poems*, ed. F. T. Prince (London: Methuen, 1960).

13. Since the writing of this piece in 1986–87 for the meetings of the Shakespeare Association of America, there has been some interesting work done on this poem. The first published version appeared as "'Till forging Nature be condemned of treason': Representational Strife in *Venus and Adonis*," *Cahiers Élisabéthains* 36 (1989): 37–47. My thanks to the editors for permission to include this material here. The following notes survey the scene at the time of writing in 1986–87, whereas notes 1–11 and 19–22 represent more recent supplements.

14. For a fine and detailed discussion of the relation between rhetoric and character in the poem, see Heather Dubrow, *Captive Victors: Shakespeare's Narrative Poems and Sonnets*

(Ithaca: Cornell University Press, 1987), 15–80. For other recent studies of *Venus and Adonis* and especially of its rhetoric, see Gordon R. Smith, "Mannerist Frivolity and Shakespeare's *Venus and Adonis*," *Hartford Studies in Literature* 3 (1971): 1–11; Michael Goldman, *Shakespeare and the Energies of Drama* (Princeton: Princeton University Press, 1972), 12–19; Heather Asals, "*Venus and Adonis*: The Education of a Goddess," *Studies in English Literature* 13 (1973): 31–51; Lucy Gent, "*Venus and Adonis*: The Triumphs of Rhetoric," *Modern Language Review* 69 (1974): 721–9; Richard A. Lanham, *The Motives of Eloquence: Literary Rhetoric in the Renaissance* (New Haven: Yale University Press, 1976): 82–94; Hallet Smith, "The Non-Dramatic Poems," in *Shakespeare: Aspects of Influence*, ed. G. B. Evans (Cambridge, MA: Harvard University Press, 1976), 43–53; William Keach, *Elizabethan Erotic Narratives: Irony and Pathos in the Ovidian Poetry of Shakespeare, Marlowe, and Their Contemporaries* (New Brunswick, NJ: Rutgers University Press, 1977), 52–85; Clark Hulse, *Metamorphoric Verse: The Elizabethan Minor Epic* (Princeton: Princeton University Press, 1981), 143–75.

15. For some other views of imagery in the poem, see Hereward T. Price, "Function of Imagery in *Venus and Adonis*," *Papers of the Michigan Academy of Science, Arts, and Letters* 31 (1945): 105–15; Robert S. Jackson, "Narrative and Imagery in Shakespeare's *Venus and Adonis*," *Papers of the Michigan Academy of Science, Arts, and Letters* 43 (1958): 315–20; Eugene B. Cantelupe, "An Iconographical Interpretation of *Venus and Adonis*: Shakespeare's Ovidian Comedy," *Shakespeare Quarterly* 14 (1963): 141–51; Alan B. Rothenberg, "The Oral Rape Fantasy and Rejection of Mother in the Imagery of Shakespeare's *Venus and Adonis*," *Psychoanalytic Quarterly* 40 (1971): 447–68; Lanham, 87; Dubrow, 22, 78. Like Dubrow afterwards, Griffin and Allen note the importance of hunting imagery in the poem: see Robert J. Griffin, "'These Contraries Such Unity Do Hold': Patterned Imagery in Shakespeare's Narrative Poems," *Studies in English Literature* 4 (1964): 43–55; and Michael J. B. Allen, "The Chase: The Development of a Renaissance Theme," *Comparative Literature* 20 (1968): 301–12.

16. Besides the contrasting positions of Lanham and Dubrow on the rhetorical relation of Venus and Adonis, see Robert P. Miller, "Venus, Adonis, and the Horses," *English Literary History* 19 (1952): 249–64; Clifford Leech, "Venus and her Nun: Portraits of Women in Love by Shakespeare and Marlowe," *Studies in English Literature* 5 (1963): 247–68; J. D. Jahn, "The Lamb of Lust: The Role of Adonis in Shakespeare's *Venus and Adonis*," *Shakespeare Studies* 6 (1970): 11–25; William E. Sheidley, "'Unless It Be a Boar': Love and Wisdom in Shakespeare's *Venus and Adonis*," *Modern Language Quarterly* 3, no. 5 (1974): 3–15; David N. Beauregard, "*Venus and Adonis*: Shakespeare's Representation of the Passions," *Shakespeare Studies* 8 (1975): 83–98; Kahn, 360–4; Wayne A. Rebhorn, "Mother Venus: Temptation in Shakespeare's *Venus and Adonis*," *Shakespeare Studies* 11 (1978): 1–11; Donald G. Watson, "The Contrarieties of *Venus and Adonis*," *Studies in Philology* 75 (1978): 32–63; Lennet J. Daigle, "*Venus and Adonis*: Some Traditional Contexts," *Shakespeare Studies* 13 (1980): 31–46; James J. Yoch, "The Eye of Venus: Shakespeare's Erotic Landscape," *Studies in English Literature* 20 (1980): 59–71. Some of these studies mention narcissism, but I agree with Heather Dubrow (44) that this subject requires more attention.

17. Not enough has been said about rhetoric in this poem, although, as I have said, Lanham and Dubrow make contributions. Surprisingly, critics have said too little on the relation between art and nature, the role of mimesis, and the use of narrative in the poem. In part, my analysis attempts to contribute in these areas. For brief discussions of narrative, see, for example, Huntington Brown, "*Venus and Adonis*: The Action, the Narrator, and the Critics," *Michigan Academician* 2 (1969): 73–87; Keach, 60, 72, 84; Jackson, 315–20; Hulse, chap. 1.

18. I have not come across an argument for art as a supplement of nature in *Venus and Adonis*. For works that relate to mimesis and genre in the poem, and so are related to art as supplement, see R. H. Bowers, "Anagnorisis or the Shock of Recognition in Shakespeare's *Venus and Adonis*," *Renaissance Papers* (1962): 3–8; Kenneth Muir, "*Venus and Adonis*: Comedy or Tragedy?" in *Shakespearean Essays*, ed. Alwin Thaler and N. Sanders (Knoxville: University of Tennessee Press, 1964); James H. Lake, "Shakespeare's Venus: An Experiment in Tragedy," *Shakespeare Quarterly* 25 (1974): 351–5; Beauregard 83–98; Dubrow 16.

19. For a detailed view of allegory in the poem and its relation to Spenser's representation, see Sayre N. Greenfield, "Allegory to the Rescue: Saving Venus and Adonis from Themselves," in *The Ends of Allegory* (Newark: University of Delaware Press, 1998), 86–110. On allegory more generally but also including the role of Venus, see Gordon Teskey, *Allegory and Violence* (Ithaca, NY: Cornell University Press, 1996), esp. 38, 58, 75–76, 85–86, 160, 193.

20. See Hadfield, 130–33. For republicanism in Stuart England, see David Norbrook, *Writing the English Republic: Poetry, Rhetoric and Politics, 1627–1660* (Cambridge: Cambridge University Press, 1999). For a recent general collection on the narrative poems and sonnets, see *The Cambridge Companion to Shakespeare's Poetry*, ed. Patrick Cheney (Cambridge: Cambridge University Press, 2007). In this volume, see Coppélia Kahn, "*Venus and Adonis*," 72–89.

21. "Sylvan historian" occurs in John Keats, "Ode on a Grecian Urn," *Lamia, Isabella, the Eve of St. Agnes, and Other Poems* (London: Taylor and Hessey, 1820), line 3.

22. There are differing views on Keats and this poem, especially the last lines, even as a tale of the two Cambridges in a relatively short period of time, as can be seen in I. A. Richards, *Practical Criticism* (London: Kegan Paul, Trench, Trubner, 1929), esp. 186; T. S. Eliot, "Dante," in *Selected Essays* (London: Faber and Faber, 1932), esp. 230; Douglas Bush, "Introduction," in *John Keats: Selected Poems and Letters*, ed. Douglas Bush (Cambridge MA: Harvard University Press, 1959); Walter Jackson Bate, *John Keats* (Cambridge, MA: Belknap Press, 1963), esp. 510. See also Helen Vendler, *The Odes of John Keats* (Cambridge, MA: Harvard University Press 1984).

CHAPTER 2

1. See, for example, Eliane Fantham, "The *Fasti* as a Source for Women's Participation in a Roman Cult," *Ovid's "Fasti": Historical Readings at Its Bimillennium*, ed. Geraldine Herbert-Brown (Oxford: Oxford University Press, 2002), 23–46, esp. 28; Peter Mark Keegan, "Seen, Not Heard: *Feminea Lingua* in Ovid's *Fasti* and the Critical Gaze," in ibid., 129–54, esp. 130. For a modern view, see Ian Donaldson, *The Rapes of Lucretia: A Myth and Its Transformations* (Oxford: Clarendon, 1982).

2. See Carole Newlands, *Playing with Time: Ovid and the "Fasti"* (Ithaca NY: Cornell University Press, 1995), 1–2, 21–22.

3. See Anthony James Boyle and Roger D. Woodard, introduction to Ovid, *Fasti* (Harmondsworth: Penguin Books, 2000), xxxv, l.

4. Livy (Titus Livius), *The History of Rome*, ed. Ernest Rhys, trans. Rev. Canon Roberts, Everyman's Library (New York: E. P. Dutton, 1912), 1:1.59.

5. Ibid.

6. Ovid, *Fasti*, trans. A. J. Boyle and R. D. Woodard (London: Penguin, 2000). These lines are from *Fasti* 2.

7. This theme of private and public has been a part of the debate on Shakespeare for many years. Long after the writing of my analysis of *Lucrece*, it persists. On another view of republicanism, and one that is detailed and suggestive, see Andrew Hadfield, *Shakespeare*

and Republicanism (Cambridge: Cambridge University Press, 2005), esp. 1, 13, 55, 131–63, and Lynn Enterline, *The Rhetoric of the Body from Ovid to Shakespeare* (Cambridge University Press, 2000), 169–95.

8. Since this analysis of *Lucrece* was written in 1988 (and presented at the Shakespeare Association of America), more work has appeared on the poem that relates to the analysis I presented (see also note 1 above). See, for example, Catherine Belsey, "Tarquin Dispossessed: Expropriation and Consent in *The Rape of Lucrece*," *Shakespeare Quarterly* 52 (2001): 315–35; Colin Burrow, "Introduction," *The Complete Poems and Sonnets*, The Oxford Shakespeare (Oxford: Oxford University Press, 2002); Patrick Cheney, *Shakespeare, National Poet-Playwright* (Cambridge: Cambridge University Press, 2004); Catherine Belsey, "The Rape of Lucrece," *The Cambridge Companion to Shakespeare's Poetry*, ed. Patrick Cheney (Cambridge: Cambridge University Press, 2007), 90–107. For an earlier version of this chapter, see "Narratorial Strategies in *The Rape of Lucrece*," *Studies in English Literature, 1500–1900* 32, no. 1 (Winter, 1992): 59–77. My thanks to the editors for permission to use this earlier material in this version. In notes 9 to 18, I have preserved the bibliographical context of the original.

9. For a discussion of narrative theory, see Jonathan Culler, *The Pursuit of Signs: Semiotics, Literature, Deconstruction* (Ithaca: Cornell University Press, 1981), 169–86. It is obvious from my rhetorical method that I agree with Heather Dubrow's call to reassess *Venus and Adonis* and *The Rape of Lucrece*. The poems are Shakespeare "displaying the tropes and other formal devices that he, like his contemporaries, had so thoroughly learned in grammar school," but I take the critics' censure of Lucrece (as Dubrow describes it) to be on the right track for the wrong reason: the display is far more complex and interesting than a schoolboy's rhetorical play (although this tutelary play may be more worthy than critics too often think). See her *Captive Victors: Shakespeare's Narrative Poems and the Sonnets* (Ithaca: Cornell University Press, 1987), 15. Dubrow's interpretation of *Lucrece* is ample and subtle. She discusses rhetoric well: see, for example, her discussion of *syneciosis*, the image of the besieged city, speech patterns, character, literary conventions, identity, self-centeredness, ambiguity, praise and flattery, the dangers of story-telling, language and power, speechlessness and powerlessness, the complaint, *epyllia*, the problems of reading and writing history, and synecdoche (80–168). Unlike Dubrow, I focus on the narrator and narration and do not privilege one rhetorical trope (*syneciosis*—or contrapositum, which is like oxymoron: see her title for an example) as the trope behind the tropes. See also my analysis of *Venus and Adonis*.

10. Aristotle and A. C. Bradley differ but show the close relation between plot and character. The former says, "Again, tragedy is the imitation of an action; and an action implies personal agents, who necessarily possess certain distinctive qualities both of character and thought, for it is by these that we qualify actions themselves, and these—thought and character—are the two natural causes from which actions spring, and on actions again all success or failure depends" (Aristotle, *Poetics* 6:5, in *Critical Theory Since Plato*, ed. Hazard Adams [New York: Harcourt Brace Jovanovich, 1971], 51). The latter says, "The centre of tragedy, therefore, may be said with equal truth to lie in action issuing from character, or in character issuing in action . . . . What we do feel strongly, as a tragedy advances to its close, is that the calamities and catastrophe follow inevitably from the deeds of men, and that the main source of these deeds is character" (A. C. Bradley, *Shakespearean Tragedy*, 2nd ed. 1905 [1957; repr., London: Macmillan, 1966], 7).

11. All quotations and citations from *Lucrece* and *Venus and Adonis* are from the Arden edition of *The Poems*, ed. F. T. Prince (London: Methuen, 1960). Parenthetical references are to line numbers unless otherwise indicated. Other Shakespearean quotations and citations are from *The Riverside Shakespeare*, ed. G. Blakemore Evans (Boston: Houghton Mifflin, 1974).

12. See Prince, *Poems*, 73.

13. Thomas Whitfield Baldwin, *On the Literary Genetics of Shakespeare's Poems and Sonnets* (Urbana: University of Illinois Press, 1950), 117, cited in Prince, *Poems*, 74; see also *Ad Herennium*, 4:23.

14. In addition to reexamining Ovid's influence on Shakespeare in the narrative poems, Richard Lanham has helped rekindle interest in the rhetoric of *Lucrece* and has examined its use of dramatic motive. See *The Motives of Eloquence: Literary Rhetoric in the Renaissance* (New Haven and London: Yale University Press, 1976), 82–83, 94–110. In *The Rapes of Lucretia* (1982), Ian Donaldson provides a context for Shakespeare's version. See Prince, *Poems*, 125. For a discussion of eroticism, see William Keach, *Elizabethan Erotic Narratives: Irony and Pathos in the Ovidian Poetry of Shakespeare, Marlowe and Their Contemporaries* (New Brunswick, NJ: Rutgers University Press, 1977). On narcissism and self-reflexive narrative, see Hart; Lanham, 99, 103; Dubrow, 118; and R. Rawdon Wilson, "Shakespearean Narrative: *The Rape of Lucrece* Reconsidered," *Studies in English Literature* 28, no. 1 (Winter 1988): 39–59, 49. For a postmodern study, see Linda Hutcheon, *Narcissistic Narrative: The Metafictional Paradox* (London: Methuen, 1984).

15. For a more general view of the relation of the poem to the tragedies, see Harold R. Walley, "*The Rape of Lucrece* and Shakespearean Tragedy," *PMLA* 76, no. 5 (December 1961): 480–87.

16. For a pertinent discussion of King John, see Jane Donawerth, *Shakespeare and the Sixteenth-Century Study of Language* (Urbana: University of Illinois Press, 1984), 169–70.

17. R. Rawdon Wilson has looked carefully at narrative in *Lucrece*. His able and interesting analysis concentrates on ekphrasis, which is especially relevant for the discursive picture of Troy (1366–1568). He extends his argument to embedded narratives and their conventions and rhetorical strategies such as copia, listing, characterization, interior monologue, recursiveness, reflexivity, alternate tales, and fictional worlds. See Wilson, "Shakespearean Narrative," 39–59. For a discussion of the verbal and pictorial (iconographical), see Clark Hulse, *Metamorphic Verse: The Elizabethan Minor Epic* (Princeton: Princeton University Press, 1981), 175–94; David Ronsand, "'Troyes Painted Woes': Shakespeare and the Pictorial Imagination," *Hebrew University Studies in Literature* 8, no. 1 (Spring 1980): 77–97, esp. 81; G. B. Evans, ed., 1738; see *The Winter's Tale*, V.ii.97. For other fine works that examine narrative and rhetoric in Lucrece, see Katharine Eisaman Maus, "Taking Tropes Seriously: Language and Violence in Shakespeare's *Rape of Lucrece*," *Shakespeare Quarterly* 37, no. 1 (Spring 1986): 66–82; Joel Fineman, "Shakespeare's Will: The Temporality of Rape," *Representations* 20 (1987): 25–76.

18. Quintilian, *Institutio Oratoria*, trans. H. E. Butler, Loeb ed. (London, 1921–22), 3:VIII. vi.67 ff.

19. For a perceptive book on Shakespeare's rhetoric and poetics, but one that really concentrates on the plays, see Frank Kermode, *Shakespeare's Language* (London: Penguin, 2000). A good general introduction to the topic in the poems and plays is Cheney, *The Cambridge Companion to Shakespeare's Poetry*.

CHAPTER 3

1. Edmund Spenser, "*Ruines of Rome: By Bellay*," in *Spenser's Minor Poems*, ed. Ernest de Sélincourt (Oxford: Oxford University Press, 1910).

2. See also Joachim Du Bellay, *L'olive augmentee depuis la premiere edition. La Musagnoeomachie & aultres oeuvres poëtiques . . .* (Paris: Gilles Corrozet & Arneul L'angelier, 1550). My thanks once more to Philip Ford for his expert advice and guidance on this translation.

3. A. Kent Hieatt, "The Genesis of Shakespeare's *Sonnets*: Spenser's *Ruines of Rome: By Bellay*," *PMLA* 98 (1983): 800; see 801–14.

4. George Puttenham, *The Arte of English Poesie* (London: Richard Field, 1589).

5. Earlier views that support this appreciation of Wyatt can be found in George Putten-ham, *The Arte of English Poesie*, and D. G. Rees, "Sir Thomas Wyatt's Translations from Petrarch," *Comparative Literature* 7 (1955): 15; see 16–24.

6. On the variety of sonnets (fourteen different rhyme patterns in the fifty-four sonnets in the collection—twenty-seven by Wyatt and fifteen by Surrey), see William R. Parker, "The Sonnets in Tottel's *Miscellany*," *PMLA* 54 (1939): 669–77.

7. Alan Stewart, *Philip Sidney: A Double Life* (London: Pimlico, 2001), 7; see 1–8.

8. Petrarch, *Petrarch's Lyric Poems: The Rime Sparse and Other Lyrics*, trans. and ed. Robert M. Durling (Cambridge MA: Harvard University Press, 1976), 46–47. I quote from this edition in Italian and English here and below.

9. Ibid., 90–91.

10. Hallet Smith, "Sonnets," in *The Riverside Shakespeare*, 2nd ed., ed. G. Blakemore Evans (Boston: Houghton Mifflin, 1997), 1842.

11. H. E. Rollins and T. W. Baldwin give extensive genealogies of critical commentary in this and other instances of reading the sonnets. See William Shakespeare, *Sonnets*, ed. Hyder Edwards Rollins, 2 vols., New Variorum (Philadelphia: Lippincott, 1944); and T. W. Baldwin, *On the Literary Genetics of Shakespeare's Poems and Sonnets* (Urbana: University of Illinois Press, 1950), 31.

12. Discussing Shakespeare's sonnets, Joel Fineman provides a useful reminder about praise: "the poetry of praise is regularly taken to be, from Plato and Aristotle through the Renaissance, the master model of poetry per se: furthermore, . . . this is a central fact for the renaissance sonnet, which, from Dante onward, characteristically presents itself as something panegyric" (1). Fineman argues that the poetry of praise relates to poetic subjectivity in the techniques, conceits and literary personality of the poet (1). Heather Dubrow also discusses the character of the speaker of Shakespeare's sonnets in terms of rhetorical paradox and suggests that closure and flattery are problems that occur in sonnet cycles (213–14, 226, 252, 257). Whereas, for Fineman, Shakespeare rewrites praise through paradox to invent a new persisting subjectivity (2), for Dubrow, the speaker of Shakespeare's sonnets at once desires "to express and deny his aggressions, to be victor and captive" (253). See Joel Fineman, *Shakespeare's Perjured Eye: The Invention of Poetic Subjectivity in the Sonnets* (Berkeley: University of California Press, 1986) and Heather Dubrow, *Captive Victors: Shakespeare's Narrative Poems and Sonnets* (Ithaca: Cornell University Press, 1987).

13. On the structure of comedy, see Francis Cornford, *The Origin of Attic Comedy* (1914; repr., Cambridge: Cambridge University Press, 1934); Northrop Frye, "The Argument of Comedy" (1948): *Shakespeare: Modern Essays in Criticism*, rev. ed., ed. Leonard F. Dean (1957; repr., London: Oxford University Press, 1967), 79–89; Z. J. Jagendorf, *The Happy End of Comedy: Shakespeare, Jonson, Molière* (Newark: University of Delaware Press, 1984); Harry Levin, *Playboys and Killjoys: An Essay on the Theory and Practice of Comedy* (Oxford: Oxford University Press, 1987); Jonathan Hart, "The Ends of Renaissance Comedy," in *Reading the Renaissance: Culture, Poetics, and Drama*, ed. Jonathan Hart (New York: Garland, 1996), 91–127, 232–33. For a suggestive and apt discussion of comedy more generally, see Michael Corder, Peter Holland, and John Kerrigan, "Introduction," in *English Comedy* (Cambridge: Cambridge University Press, 1994), 1–11.

14. See Jonathan Hart, *Theater and World: The Problematics of Shakespeare's History* (Boston: Northeastern University Press, 1992), esp. 21–28, 166–99.

15. For a good summary of whether the order of the quarto of *The Sonnets* (1609) is chronological or Shakespeare's arrangement, including a brief outline of the key views of John Benson (1640), Charles Knight (1841), H. E. Rollins (1944), and Katherine Duncan-Jones (1983), see G. Blakemore Evans, "The Commentary," in *The Sonnets*, ed. G. Blakemore Evans, The New Cambridge Shakespeare (Cambridge: Cambridge University Press,

1996), 113–14. W. H. Auden makes some of the most sensible observations on the writing, order, and publication of Shakespeare's sonnets, which he calls a "jumble." See W. H. Auden, "Introduction," in *William Shakespeare, The Sonnets*, ed. William Burto, the Signet Classic Shakespeare (New York: New American Library, 1964, rev, 1988), xxiii; see xxi–xxii, xxiv, xxxv–xxxvi. John Kerrigan refers to John Benson's reprint of the *The Sonnets* in 1640 (London: By Tho. Cotes) as inflicting on the poems "a series of unforgivable injuries"—Benson made longer poems and "began the long-running tiresome game of re-ordering"; see John Kerrigan, "Introduction," in William Shakespeare, *"The Sonnets" and "A Lover's Complaint,"* New Penguin ed., ed. John Kerrigan (Harmondsworth: Penguin, 1986), 46.

16. All references to the plays are to *The Riverside Shakespeare*, ed. G. Blakemore Evans, 2nd ed. (Boston: Houghton Mifflin, 1997); and to *The Sonnets*, ed. G. Blakemore Evans, the New Cambridge Shakespeare (Cambridge: Cambridge University Press, 1996). This chapter is based on an earlier version that appeared as "Conflicting Monuments: Time, Beyond Time and the Poetics of Shakespeare's Dramatic and Non-dramatic Sonnets," in *The Company of Shakespeare: Essays on English Renaissance Literature in Honor of G. Blakemore Evans*, ed. Thomas Moisan and Douglas Bruster (Madison, NJ: Associated University Presses, 2002), 177–205, and is incorporated here with the kind permission of the publisher. Since my writing this essay in the late 1990s, some interesting related work has been done. See, for example, Michael Schoenfeldt, "The Sonnets," in Cheney, *Cambridge Companion to Shakespeare's Poetry*, 125f.; see also note 39.

17. For a reading of this Epilogue in the context of the other choruses in *Henry V*, see Hart, *Theater and World*, 149–57; see *Henry VIII* for the fourteen-line chorus that ends the play.

18. For a suggestive study that places Shakespeare between Petrarch and Baudelaire and that attends to the nuances of language and style, see Sandra Bermann, *The Sonnet over Time: A Study in the Sonnets of Petrarch, Shakespeare, and Baudelaire* (Chapel Hill: University of North Carolina Press, 1988), esp. 51–92.

19. To follow up on the discussion of the order that occurs in note 15, it is debatable whether Shakespeare authorized Thorpe's quarto of Shakespeare's *Sonnets* in 1609, so critics have questioned the ordering of the poems. Whereas Katherine Duncan-Jones (1983) thinks that Thorpe was so authorized, G. Blakemore Evans (1996) does not; see Katherine Duncan-Jones, "Was the 1609 Shake-speare's *Sonnets* Really Unauthorized?" *Review of English Studies* 34 (1983): 151–71. Brents Stirling explores the ordering and reordering of *The Sonnets*; see Brent Stirlings, *Shakespeare's Sonnet Order: Poems and Groups* (Berkeley: University of California Press, 1968). Heather Dubrow (1987) questions the narrative of the *Sonnets* and later expresses the view, which must have crossed the mind of many readers, that sonnets that do not specify the gender of the addressee cannot neatly fit into the conventional split of sonnets 1–126 (young man) and sonnets 127–52 (dark lady) and be identified with certainty with either the young man or the dark lady; see Heather Dubrow, *Echoes of Desire: English Petrarchanism and Its Counterdiscourses* (Ithaca: Cornell University Press, 1995), 121–23, and her "'Uncertainties now crown themselves assur'd': The Politics of Plotting Shakespeare's Sonnets," *Shakespeare Quarterly* 47 (1996): 291–305. As W. H. Auden reminds us, Michelangelo's nephew altered the sex of the addressee of his uncle's sonnets to Tomasso de Cavaleri, just as Benson was to do with Shakespeare's *Sonnets* in 1640 ("Introduction," in William Shakespeare *The Sonnets*, ed. William Burto, revised Signet edition [1964; New York: New American Library, 1988], xxxvi). Shakespeare may be shifting the gender of the addressee, but the motif of age and death is a *carpe diem* convention of the sonnet. See, for example, Ronsard's *Sonnets pour Hélène*, II, 42. Whereas Auden does not think that Shakespeare wanted the sonnets published, let alone created in the order in which they appear, Stephen Booth discusses the principle of structure in the individual sonnet

and the collection of sonnets, analyzing the dilemma over order that faces the critics of these poems; see Stephen Booth, *An Essay on Shakespeare's Sonnets* (New Haven: Yale University Press, 1969), esp. 1–28.

20. For a discussion of homosexuality in these poems and in the Elizabethan context, see, for example, Auden, "Introduction," xxviii–xxix, xxxi; Alan Bray, *Homosexuality in Renaissance England* (London: Gay Men's Press, 1982); Joseph Pequigney, *Such Is My Love: A Study of Shakespeare's Sonnets* (Chicago: University of Chicago Press, 1985); Bruce R. Smith, *Homosexual Desire in Shakespeare's England: A Cultural Poetics* (Chicago: University of Chicago Press, 1991), ch. 7.

21. The role of the eyes ('I's) has not gone without notice. On the Petrarchan distinction between eye and heart, see Auden, "Introduction," xxxii–xxxiii; on the lying figure of eyes/'I's, see Joel Fineman's *Shakespeare's Perjured Eye*.

22. See Evans, "Commentary," 125, Sonnet 12:13n34.

23. Evans, "Commentary," 127, Sonnet 28:15 headnote; see Horace, *Odes* III, 30; Ovid, *Metamorphoses*, xv, 871–9, xv, 234–6.

24. See Edmund Spenser, *Amoretti*, 58:7.

25. See Evans, "Commentary," 142, Sonnet 30:1–2n.

26. Helen Vendler discusses the use of metonymy in Sonnet 128, including associations and displacements of "eye/I," whereas, as we have seen, Joel Fineman gives a more deconstructive turn to the general use of "eye/I"; see Helen Vendler, "Shakespeare's Sonnets: The Uses of Synecdoche," in Shakespeare, *The Sonnets*, ed. Burto (Signet, 1988), 233–40.

27. See Evans, "Commentary," 162, Sonnet 54:11–12n33.

28. Evans, "Commentary," 163, Sonnet 14n.

29. Stephen Booth reminds us of Falstaff's allusion to Bardolph's face as "a death's head or a memento mori" in *1 Henry IV* (III.iii.29–31 in the *Riverside Shakespeare*); see Booth's "Commentary," in William Shakespeare, *Shakespeare's Sonnets*, ed. Stephen Booth (New Haven: Yale University Press, 1976), 266.

30. John Kerrigan aptly argues that Shakespeare begins the *Sonnets* with a "breeding group" and why poems concerned with metaphor, such as 21, 78–96, follow a group of sonnets on marriage: "In reproduction, Shakespeare found the most moral means to similitude." Kerrigan suggests that the Elizabethans had an ideal of copiousness with which we have lost touch. See John Kerrigan, "Introduction," in Shakespeare, *"The Sonnets" and "A Lover's Complaint,"* 27.

31. See Shakespeare, *The Sonnets*, 84n14.

32. Evans, "Commentary," 192, Sonnet 83n6.

33. Perhaps this prize, as G. B. Evans suggests, is like booty from the New World such as Francis Drake seized, except that Drake was a national hero as well as a mercenary whom the court sanctioned; see Evans, "Commentary," 193, Sonnet 86n2. The Spanish gold in this analogy would be the young man, an ambivalent praise at best, as Raleigh, Hakluyt the Younger, Bacon, and others wanted England to seek such riches but also warned that this American or Spanish gold was a source of Spain's power and the corruption of European courts. I have written extensively on God and gold in the colonization of the New World and on what I call the example of Spain, a full treatment of which occurs in my book, *Representing the New World: English and French Uses of the Example of Spain* (New York: Palgrave Macmillan, 2001), which was in manuscript when I wrote the original essay on the sonnets.

34. In his edition of the sonnets, John Kerrigan notes how this envoy, 126, sums up the themes from the preceding 125 sonnets to the young man such as love, beauty, time, destruction, and death.

35. Petrarch, "*Rime sparse*," 11: 8–10; *Petrarch's Lyric Poems*, trans. and ed. Robert M. Durling, bilingual edition (Cambridge, MA: Harvard University Press, 1976), 46–47. As Robert Durling notes, Petrarch, who did not have the apostrophe as an aspect of his punctuation, identifies Laura with laurel (*lauro*), breeze (*l'aura*) and gold (*l'auro*); see During, Introduction, *Petrarch's Lyric Poems*, 27. For our purposes of contrast between black and blonde, the association with gold is important.

36. See also Evans, "Commentary," 243–44, Sonnet 127 headnote and n10. In Sonnet 15, Sidney's speaker proclaims, "You that poore *Petrarch's* long deceased woes,/ With new-borne sighes and denisend wit do sing" (15:7–8); Philip Sidney, *The Poems of Sir Philip Sidney*, ed. William A. Ringler, Jr. (Oxford: Clarendon Press, 1962), 466. Mary Wroth's importance in this discussion of Petrarchanism and anti-Petrarchanism should not be underestimated. Heather Dubrow speaks of "Mary Wroth's juxtaposition of the most conventional Petrarchanism with its most rebellious counterdiscourses"; see Dubrow, *Echoes of Desire*, 135. On Wroth and the context of women writers in the Renaissance, see Elaine V. Beilin, *Redeeming Eve: Women Writers of the English Renaissance* (Princeton: Princeton University Press, 1987), ch. 8; Ann Rosalind Jones, *The Currency of Eros: Women's Love Lyric in Europe, 1540–1620* (Bloomington: Indiana University Press, 1990), ch. 4; Mary Ellen Lamb, *Gender and Authorship in the Sidney Circle* (Madison: University of Wisconsin Press, 1990); Barbara Kiefer Lewalski, *Writing Women in Jacobean England* (Cambridge, MA: Harvard University Press); Katy Emck, "'A Wanton Woman and a Wise': Women Writing about Desire in Renaissance Europe, 1540–1620" (Ph.D. thesis, University of Alberta, Fall 1996), ch. 2.

37. Shakespeare should also be viewed in the context of European poetry. For example, the unsunlike eyes of the mistress of Shakespeare's Sonnet 130 is like the dark eyes of the mistress in Ronsard's *Amours de Cassandre*, 152.

38. For example, in a sonnet, Mary Wroth describes Cupid as the "great King of Love"; see Mary Wroth, *Pamphilia to Amphilanthus* 89:11, *The Poems of Lady Mary Wroth* (Baton Rouge: Louisiana State University Press, 1983).

39. More generally, since the original writing of the essay (on which this chapter is based), some important related work has appeared, such as William Shakespeare, *Shakespeare's Sonnets*, ed. Katherine Duncan-Jones (London: Thomas Nelson, 1997); Helen Vendler, *The Art of Shakespeare's Sonnets* (Cambridge, MA: Belknap Press, 1997); Shakespeare, *"The Sonnets" and "A Lover's Complaint,"* ed. John Kerrigan (Harmondsworth: Penguin, 2000). Beyond these detailed introductions, notes, and sustained arguments are general collections like *A Companion to Shakespeare's Sonnets*, ed. Michael Schoenfeldt (Oxford: Blackwell, 2007). A recent student guide also shows the continued interest in Shakespeare's poetry in the classroom: see John Blades, *Shakespeare: The Sonnets* (New York: Palgrave Macmillan, 2007).

40. For this term, see, for example, my *Theater and World* (1992).

CHAPTER 4

1. About the time of the first draft of my discussion of barbarism and its contexts, an interesting and provocative book appeared: see Harold Bloom, *Shakespeare: The Invention of the Human* (New York: Riverhead Books, 1998). Here I am trying to provide a wider context for the human to Shakespeare's alone.

2. See Jonathan Hart, "Portugal and the Making of the English Empire: The Case of Richard Hakluyt the Younger," *Literatura de Viagem*, ed. Ana M. Falcão, Maria T. Nacimento, and Maria L. Leal (Lisboa: Edições Cosmos, 1997), 155–68.

3. Barbarism is a widespread topic that persisted into the nineteenth and twentieth centuries and beyond. A few examples will show that this topic never seems to go away, at least thus far. There are many faces of barbarism in the various discourses. One book looks to the time of Judges in the Bible and sees a decline into barbarism, which is the danger of the age, as well as the threat of "Romanism"; see Horace Bushnell, *Barbarism the First Danger: A Discourse for Home Missions* (New York: American Home Missionary Society, 1847), esp. 1–6. Another volume begins with the search for routes to Asia, including the Northwest Passage: see Charles Roger, *The Rise of Canada: From Barbarism to Wealth and Civilization* (Quebec: Peter Sinclair, 1856), esp. 3–10. A book with an ironic title that suggests that history is an "advance" to barbarism (which the subtitle contradicts just in case) is F. J. P. Veale, *Advance to Barbarism: How the Reversion to Barbarism in Warfare and War-Trials Menaces Our Future* (Appleton, Wisconsin: C. C. Nelson, 1953), esp. 1–7, 297 (originally published under a *nom de plume* in England in 1948). A significant study is J. G. A. Pocock's *Barbarism and Religion*; see particularly vol. 4, *Barbarians, Savages and Empires* (1999; Cambridge: Cambridge University Press, 2005). Pocock discusses theories of barbarism as well as expansion in Eurasia and the New World and the question of seaborne empires. See also Bernard Wasserstein, *Barbarism and Civilization: A History of Europe in Our Time* (Oxford: Oxford University Press, 2007), esp. 1–36 on Europe before and leading up to 1914. Since the later 1990s, when my paper on barbarism was first written, I have published further work relevant to this topic such as "Representing Spain: The Ambivalence of England and France to Spanish Colonization in the Americas," *CRCL/RCLC* 25, no. 1–2 (1998): 24–50; *Representing the New World* (New York: Palgrave, 2001); *Empires and Colonies* (Cambridge: Polity, 2008); and "Las Casas in French and Other Languages," in *Approaches to Teaching the Writings of Bartolomé de Las Casas*, ed. Santa Arias and Eyda M. Merediz (New York: Modern Language Association of America, 2008), 224–34. There are a large number of publications in this area, and I have suggested only a few that are particularly relevant.
4. Herodotus, *The Histories*, Greek with an English translation by A. D. Godley (London: Heinemann, 1920), 1.1.
5. The discussion of Aristotle and mimesis is vast and informative. For this debate on approaching and being distanced from nature through art in Aristotle's theory of poetics, see Jonathan Hart, "The Author Writes Back (and Speaks Up)," *Primerjalna književnost* 31, no. 2 (2008): 15–37.
6. There are various versions of this essay under the original name "On the Concept . . ." and the alternative "Theses . . ." The version I am using is the Zohn translation: see Walter Benjamin, "Theses on the Philosophy of History," in *Illuminations*, ed. Hannah Arendt and trans. Harry Zohn (1955; New York: Harcourt, Brace & World, 1968), 258. See also Walter Benjamin, "On the Concept of History," in *Materialist Theology, 1940*, vol. 4 of *Selected Writings*, ed. Howard Eiland and Michael W. Jennings (Cambridge MA: Belknap, 2006), part 5 (orig. titled "Thesis VII"). For the French version, see *Les Temps Modernes* 2, no. 25 (October 1947).
7. All citations and quotations are from *The Riverside Shakespeare*, 2nd ed., ed. G. Blakemore Evans, with J. J. M. Tobin (Boston: Houghton Mifflin, 1997). This chapter was first written as "Barbarism and Its Contexts," presented in "Shakespeare and the Nature of Barbarism," at the Shakespeare Association of America (SAA), San Francisco, 1999. My thanks to the SAA, Mary Floyd-Wilson, and my fellow seminar participants. Since my original paper on Shakespeare and barbarism, there has been some interesting work in the area of the theme of barbarism in Shakespeare, some of which I will mention here. On language and barbarism, see Ian Smith, "Barbarian Errors: Performing Race in Early Modern England," *Shakespeare Quarterly* 49 (1998): 168–86. For a discussion of the influence of Seneca's *Hercules Furens* in the overcoming

of barbarism, see Robin Headlam Wells, "An Orpheus for a Hercules: Virtue Redefined in *The Tempest*," in *Neo-Historicism: Studies in Renaissance Literature, History, and Politics*, ed. Robin Headlam Wells, Glenn Burgess, and Rowland Wymer (Cambridge: Brewer, 2000), 240–62. On the Scythians and barbarism, see Christopher Baker, "Ovid, Othello, and the Pontic Scythians," in *A Search for Meaning: Critical Essays on Early Modern Literature*, ed. Paula Harms Payne (New York: Lang, 2004), 61–80. About gender, rhetoric, and barbarism, see Richard W. Grinnell, "Witchcraft, Race, and the Rhetoric of Barbarism in *Othello* and *1 Henry IV*," *Upstart Crow* 24 (2004): 72–80. Concerning discourse and images of purgation and barbarism, see Ben Saunders, "Iago's Clyster: Purgation, Anality, and the Civilizing Process," *Shakespeare Quarterly* 55 (2004): 148–76. On language and violence, see Jessica Lugo, "Blood, Barbarism, and Belly Laughs: Shakespeare's *Titus* and Ovid's Philomela," *English Studies* 88 (2007): 401–17.

8. On the relation between Caliban and Prospero in the context of travel or encounter narratives and of the tensions between civilization and barbarism, see Ileana Azor Hernández, "Dos instantes de una parábola teatral sobre el colonialismo: *La tempestad* de William Shakespeare y Aimé Césaire," *Conjunto* 49 (1981), 95–108.

9. Concerning civility and barbarism and its relation to moral shortcomings in this play, see John Rooks, "Mental and Moral Wilderness in *Titus Andronicus*," *Shakespeare and Renaissance Association of West Virginia: Selected Papers* 16 (1993): 33–42. On the binary of civilization and barbarism, see Annie Gagiano, "'Barbarism' and 'Civilization' in Shakespeare's *Titus Andronicus* and in Marechera's *Black Sunlight*," *The Literary Griot* 10, no. 1 (1998): 12–27. For an analysis of civility barbarism in the context of empire, colonizer, and colonized in regard to Rome, England, and the New World in relation to *Titus Andronicus*, see Virginia Mason Vaughan, "The Construction of Barbarism in *Titus Andronicus*," in *Race, Ethnicity, and Power in the Renaissance*, ed. Joyce Green MacDonald (Madison NJ: Fairleigh Dickinson University Press, 1997), 165–80. Another play that might be discussed in the context of barbarism is *Antony and Cleopatra*. Mary Nyquist discusses female rule as something represented as barbaric in early modern England and places her discussion in the context of work by Charles Sedley, John Milton, and John Dryden; see her "'Profuse, proud Cleopatra': 'Barbarism' and Female Rule in Early Modern English Republicanism," *Women's Studies* 24, no. 1–2 (1995): 85–130. On barbarism, masculinity, and femininity, see Patricia Parker, "Barbers, Infidels, and Renegades: *Antony and Cleopatra*," in *Center or Margin: Revisions of the English Renaissance in Honor of Leeds Barroll*, ed. Lena Cowen Orlin (Selinsgrove: Susquehanna University Press, 2006), 54–87.

10. On two African versions that counter the dichotomy of civilization and barbarism, see Jyotsna Singh, "Othello's Identity, Postcolonial Theory, and Contemporary African Rewritings of *Othello*," in *Women, "Race," and Writing in the Early Modern Period*, ed. Margo Hendricks and Patricia Parker (London: Routledge, 1994), 287–99. On art overcoming law and the regenerative aspect of the arts as a counter to barbarism, see Robin Headlam Wells, "Civility and Barbarism in *The Winter's Tale*," in *Intertestualità shakespeariane: Il Cinquecento italiano e il Rinascimento inglese*, ed. Michele Marrapodi (Rome: Bulzoni, 2003), 275–92.

11. See Edward W. Said, *Orientalism* (New York: Vintage, 1978) and Anthony Pagden, *The Fall of Natural Man: The American Indian and the Origins of Comparative Ethnography* (Cambridge: Cambridge University Press, 1982, rev. 1986). Monsters were key in Renaissance travel and encounter narratives, maps, and images. Even in the field of medicine and anatomy, the monstrous was important. See, for example, Ambrose Paré, *On Monsters and Marvels*, trans. Janis L. Pallister (1982; Chicago: University of Chicago Press, 1996). Monstrosity and barbarity, although related in Herodotus, are not always connected and are certainly not in Paré's work. The medieval background is also important, even though

the monstrous and the barbarous are not brought together by scholars in the following study: *The Monstrous Middle Ages*, ed. Bettina Bildhauer and Robert Mills (Toronto: University of Toronto Press, 2003). In that collection, see especially Sarah Salih, "Idols and Simulacra: Paganity, Hybridity and Representation in Mandeville's Travels," 113–33. On sexuality and monsters, see particularly the relation between the encounter and the monstrous, see Samantha J. E. Riches, "Virtue and Violence: Saints, Monsters and Sexuality in Medieval Culture," in *Medieval Sexuality: A Casebook*, ed. April Harper and Caroline Proctor (London: Routledge, 2007), 59–78. On monstrosity as it relates to gender (female power or the rule of women), see Patricia Parker, *Literary Fat Ladies: Rhetoric, Gender and Property* (London: Methuen, 1987), esp. 60, 245. See Edward W. Said, *Culture and Imperialism* (1993. London: Vintage, 1994), xxviii; *Orientalism* (New York: Pantheon Books, 1978); Anthony Pagden, *The Fall of Natural Man*, esp. 14–26; and Lisa Lowe, *Critical Terrains: French and British Orientalisms* (Ithaca: Cornell University Press, 1991). The following parts of this chapter draw on some of my earlier work such as Jonathan Hart, "Images of the Native in Renaissance Encounter Narratives," *ARIEL* 25 (1994): 55–76; "Mediation in the Exchange Between Europeans and Native Americans in the Early Modern Period," in "Ross Chambers," special issue, *CRCL/RCLC* 22 (1995): 319–43; "Redeeming *The Tempest*: Romance and Politics," *Cahiers Élisabéthains* 49 (1996): 23–38; "Strategies of Promotion: Some Prefatory Matter of Oviedo, Thevet, and Hakluyt," *Imagining Culture: Essays in Early Modern History and Literature*, ed. Jonathan Hart (New York: Garland, 1996), 73–92; "Translating and Resisting Empire: Cultural Appropriation and Post-colonial Studies," in *Borrowed Power; Essays in Cultural Appropriation*, ed. Bruce Ziff and Pratima Rao (New Brunswick, NJ: Rutgers University Press, 1997), 137–68. The work that I present here is in a new context.

12. Pagden, *The Fall of Natural Man*, 15. The following discussion draws on Pagden, 15–26.

13. Ibid., 16.

14. Aristotle, *De mirabilibus auscultationibus* 836 a 10–15, cited in Pagden, *The Fall of Natural Man*, 16.

15. Aristotle, *Politics* 1338 b 19, and *Nichomachean Ethics* 1148 b 19ff., cited in Pagden, *The Fall of Natural Man*, 18.

16. Pagden, *The Fall of Natural Man*, 15.

17. My discussion is here indebted to the thread of empire and its translation in Ernst Breisach, *Historiography: Ancient, Medieval & Modern* (Chicago: University of Chicago, 1983). Herodotus, *History*, trans. A. D. Godley (London: Heinemann, 1920–25), 4 vols. Greek, with English trans., 7.9.

18. Breisach, *Historiography*, 13.

19. Herodotus, *The Persian Wars* 7.9.

20. Breisach, *Historiography*, 23–4.

21. Ibid., 29–30.

22. Ibid., 34.

23. See, for example, Gonzalo Fernández de Oviedo, *Natural History of the West Indies*, trans. Sterling A. Stoudemire, University of North Carolina Studies in Romance Languages and Literatures 32 (Chapel Hill: University of North Carolina Press, 1959); André Thevet, *Les Singularités de la France antarctique* (Paris: Le Temps, 1982); Richard Hakluyt, *Voyages*, vol. 1 (London: Dent, 1907).

24. Christopher Columbus, *The Four Voyages of Columbus: A History in Eight Documents, Including Five By Christopher Columbus, In the Original Spanish, with English Translations*, ed. and trans. Cecil Jane (1930; repr. New York: Dover, 1983), 3.

25. Hernán Cortés, *Letters from Mexico*, ed. and trans. Anthony Pagden (1971; repr., New Haven: Yale University Press, 1986), 98–99.

26. Richard Hakluyt, *Voyages and Documents*, ed. Janet Hampden (1958; repr., London: Oxford University Press, 1963), 8–9.

27. Jacques Cartier, *The Voyages of Jacques Cartier*, ed. H. P. Biggar (Ottawa: Publications of the Public Archives, 1924), 116; see 337–38n284; Marcel Trudel, *Histoire de la Nouvelle-France* (Montreal: Fides, 1963), 1:20. See also Jacques Cartier, *Relations*, ed. Michel Bideaux (Montreal: Les Presses de l'Université de Montréal, 1986).

28. Haie, "A report of the voyage and successe thereof, attempted in the yeere of our Lord 1583 by sir Humfrey Gilbert knight . . . ," in Hampden, 239–40.

29. L. C. Green and Olive P. Dickason, *The Law of Nations and the New World* (Edmonton: University of Alberta Press, 1989), 36, 176–80, 268; Bartolomé de Las Casas, *A Short Account of the Destruction of the Indies*, ed. and trans. Nigel Griffin and introduction by Anthony Pagden (London: Penguin, 1992). See Jonathan Hart, *Representing the New World* (2001) and "Language, European," and "Papal Donations and Colonization," *Encyclopedia of Western Colonization Since 1450* (Woodbridge, CT: Macmillan/Thomson Gale, 2006).

30. Green and Dickason, 221, 235, see 87; Neal Salisbury, "Squanto: Last of the Patuxets," *Struggle and Survival in Colonial America*, ed. David G. Sweet and Gary B. Nash (Berkeley: University of California Press, 1981), 239–40. On Squanto, see also William Bradford, *Of Plymouth Plantation, 1620–47*, ed. Samuel Eliot Morison (1952; repr., New York: Alfred A. Knopf, 1991).

31. Oviedo, *Natural History of the West Indies*; Thevet, *Les Singularités de la France antarctique*; Hakluyt, *Voyages*. See my "Strategies of Promotion," which I draw on briefly here.

32. Columbus, *The Four Voyages of Columbus*, 3. This in brackets is Cecil Jane's English translation.

33. Las Casas, *Short Account*, 3.

34. See Anthony Pagden, "History and Anthropology, and the History of Anthropology: Considerations on a Methodological Practice," in Hart, *Imagining Culture*, 27–40, 199–201; Ross Chambers, "No Montagues Without Capulets: Some Thoughts on 'Cultural Identity,'" *Explorations in Difference: Law, Culture, and Politics*, ed. Jonathan Hart and Richard W. Bauman (Toronto: University of Toronto Press, 1996), 25–66. On a number of occasions, I have written on otherness, recognition, and misrecognition, most recently in "Recognitions, Otherness and Comparing Literatures and Histories," *Journal of Literary Criticism* 12.1–2 (June/December 2008), 130–59.

35. Michel de Montaigne, *The Essays of Montaigne*, trans. E. J. Treichmann (London: Oxford University Press, 1953), 119.

36. See Edward Said, *Orientalism* and *Culture and Imperialism* as well as Trinh T. Minh-ha, *Woman, Native, Other: Writing Postcoloniality and Feminism* (Bloomington: Indiana University Press, 1988), 63–65.

37. Michel de Montaigne, *The Essays of Montaigne*, 108–9. See Michel de Montaigne, *Essais* (Paris: Garnier Freres, 1962).

38. William Hawkins, "A brief relation of two sundry voyages made by the worshiful M. William Haukins of Plimmouth . . . ," in Hampden, 21. See Thomas More, *Utopia* (Berlin: Weidmann, 1895), for Latin and *Utopia*, trans. Edward Surtz (New Haven: Yale University Press, 1964) for English.

39. John Hawkins, "The first voyage of the right worshipfull and valiant knight sir John Hawkins . . . ," in Hampden, 99.

40. John Hawkins, "The third troublesome voage made with the Jesus of Lubeck . . . in the yeeres 1567 and 1568 by M. John Hawkins," in Hampden, 110–14; on Hawkins, see also Job Hortop, "The travailes travailes of Job Hortop," in Hampden, 114–36.

41. Anon., "A true report of such things as happened in the second voyage of captaine Frobisher . . . Ann. Dom. 1577," in Hampden, 169, 182.

42. Christopher Hall, "The first Voyage of M. Martine Frobisher, to the Northwest, . . . in the yeere of our Lord 1576," in Hampden, 153.

43. Anon., "A true report . . . the second voyage of captaine Frobisher," in Hampden, 171–74.

44. Haie, "A report of the voyage . . . by sir Humfrey Gilbert," in Hampden, 261, 265.

45. Arthur Barlowe, "The first voyage made ot the coasyts of America, . . . Anno 1584," in Hampden, 292.

46. Columbus, *The Four Voyages of Columbus*, 294–95; see also 30–40; and see Peter Hume, *Colonial Encounters: Europe and the Native Caribbean 1492–1797* (1986; repr., London: Routledge, 1992), 45–87.

CHAPTER 5

1. Here I echo a phrase from a work I first read in the 1970s when I began to write on Shakespeare's histories, that is, Ricardo J. Quinones, *The Renaissance Discovery of Time* (Cambridge, MA: Harvard University Press, 1972). Quinones examines Shakespeare's various genres but does so mainly seeing discovery as means of triumphing over time for those in the Renaissance. Although I, too, discuss time and genre, I do so from a related but different point of view. See Quinones, 3. For an important discussion of time and narrative, see Paul Ricœur, *Temps et récit*, 3 vols. (Paris: Le Seuil, 1983–1985); vol. 1, *L'intrigue et le récit historique* (1983); vol. 2, *La configuration dans le récit de fiction* (1984); vol. 3, *Le temps raconté* (1985). Ricœur explores the relation between the literary and the historiographical, of the account or narrative with time, of philosophy and poetics or language. For the English translation, see *Time and Narrative*, 3 vols. trans. Kathleen McLaughlin and David Pellauer (Chicago: University of Chicago Press, 1984, 1985, 1988). In Paris in 1981, Richard Keaney interviewed Ricœur (published in 1984, reprinted in 1991): in the interview, they discuss the creativity of language. Ricœur notes the interpretation and reinterpretation in Western culture, noting that neither Homer nor Aeschylus invented his stories but that each is a reinterpreter of myth, or a reinventor of new narrative meanings in the retelling of the same story. Keaney sees Chaucer and Shakespeare as also reinventing the Iliad myth. See *A Ricoeur Reader*, ed. Mario J. Valdés (Toronto: University of Toronto Press, 1991), 471. Another book that discusses philosophy and time, but in relation to Shakespeare, is Agnes Heller, *The Time Is Out of Joint: Shakespeare as Philosopher of History* (Lanham, MD: Rowman and Littlefield, 2002).

2. Although I discussed the German connection early on and in a few places, the most accessible work is Jonathan Hart, *Theater and World: The Problematics of Shakespeare's History* (Boston: Northeastern University Press, 1992).

3. This chapter is a slightly expanded and a revised version of a lecture delivered at the University of Aarhus, Denmark, in 1997. My thanks to my hosts, and for sharing with me their interest in fictional markers. There was no discussion of Ricœur there.

4. *Narrative and Dramatic Sources of Shakespeare*, ed. Geoffrey Bullough, 8 vols. (London: Routledge, 1962–75). See also Kenneth Muir, *The Sources of Shakespeare's Plays* (London: Methuen, 1977). More specifically, for recent discussions of Shakespeare's use of the sources in the history plays, see Peter Sacchio, *Shakespeare's English Kings: History, Chronicle, and Drama*, 2nd ed. (1977; repr., Oxford: Oxford University Press, 2000); Katherine Bailey, "Shakespeare's Histories," *British Heritage* 22, no. 5 (2001): 52–55; and Dominique Goy-Blanquet, "Elizabethan Historiography and Shakespeare's Sources," *The Cambridge Companion to Shakespeare's History Plays*, ed. Michael Hattaway (Cambridge: Cambridge University Press, 2002), 57–70. More generally, see Mary Ann McGrail, "From Plagiaries to Sources," *Poetica: An International Journal of Linguistic-Literary Studies* 48 (1997): 169–85; Robert S. Miola, *Shakespeare's Reading* (Oxford: Oxford University

Press, 2000); Leonard Barkan, "What Did Shakespeare Read?" in *The Cambridge Companion to Shakespeare*, eds. Margreta De Grazia and Stanley Wells (Cambridge and New York: Cambridge University Press, 2001), 31–47; Stuart Gillespie, *Shakespeare's Books: A Dictionary of Shakespeare's Sources* (London: Athlone Press, 2001); Leah Scragg, "Source Study," *Shakespeare: An Oxford Guide*, ed. Stanley Wells (Oxford: Oxford University Press, 2003), 373–90; and *Shakespeare and Elizabethan Popular Culture*, ed. Stuart Gillespie and Neil Rhodes (London: Arden Shakespeare, 2006).

5. Aristotle, "On the Art of Poetry," in *Classical Literary Criticism*, ed. T. S. Dorsch (1965; repr., Harmondsworth: Penguin, 1975), 33–75. As I have argued elsewhere, the question of recognition is central to dramatic and narrative representations of historical fiction: most recently, see "The Author Writes Back (and Speaks Up)," *Primerjalna književnost* 31, no. 2 (2008): 15–37 and "Recognitions, Otherness and Comparing Literatures and Histories," *Journal of Literary Criticism* 12.1–2 (June/December 2008), 130–59. Rhetoric and mimesis (representation) are places where Plato and Aristotle differ. See Plato, *The Republic of Plato*, trans. Francis MacDonald Cornford (1941; repr., London: Oxford University Press, 1945), bk. 10, 595 A-608 B. On rhetoric, see, for example, W. Rhys Roberts, "References to Plato in Aristotle's Rhetoric." *Classical Philology* 19 (1924): 342–46; Everett Lee Hunt, "Plato and Aristotle on Rhetoric and Rhetoricians," *Essays on the Rhetoric of the Western World*, ed. Edward P. J. Corbett, James L. Golden, and Goodwin F. Berquist (Dubuque, IA: Kendall/Hunt, 1990), 129–61; Amâelie Rorty, *Essays on Aristotle's Rhetoric* (Berkeley: University of California Press, 1996); Sara. J. Newman, "Aristotle's Definition of Rhetoric in the *Rhetoric*: The Metaphors and Their Message," *Written Communication* 18 (2001): 3–25.

6. See, for example, Paul Murray Kendall, *Richard III* (New York: Norton, 1956); and Peter Geyl, "Shakespeare as a Historian: A Fragment," in *Encounters in History* (Cleveland: World, 1961), 49–83.

7. See E. M. W. Tillyard, *Shakespeare's History Plays* (London: Chatto & Windus, 1944); A. W. Schlegel, *Lectures on Dramatic Art and Literature*, trans. John Black, 2nd ed. rev. (London: George Bell & Sons, 1900), esp. 368–72; Samuel Taylor Coleridge, *Lectures and Notes on Shakspere and Other English Poets* (1895; repr. London: Bell, 1883); Edward Hall, *The vnion of the two noble and illustre femelies of Lancastre [and] Yorke*, 2nd ed. (London: Richard Grafton, 1548); Raphael Holinshed, *The first and second volumes of Chronicles . . .* , 2nd ed. (London: [Henry Denham], 1587).

8. For another view, see Mercedes Maroto Camino, "'My Honour I'll Bequesh unto the Knife': Public Heroism, Private Sacrifice, and Early Modern Rapes of Lucrece," in *Imagining Culture: Essays in Early Modern History and Literature*, ed. Jonathan Hart (New York and London: Garland, 1996), 95–108.

9. I am using W. Jackson Bate's term, "the burden of the past" and Harold Bloom's "the anxiety of influence." In his first edition Bloom exempts Shakespeare from the anxiety of influence, although I think Shakespeare felt Marlowe's influence. See W. Jackson Bate, *The Burden of the Past and the English Poet* (Cambridge MA: Belknap Press, 1970); Harold Bloom, *The Anxiety of Influence: A Theory of Poetry* (New York: Oxford University Press, 1973). In the preface to the second edition, Bloom revisits the relation between Shakespeare and Marlowe and, while admitting the extraordinariness of Marlowe as a poet (not so much as a dramatist), he qualifies his earlier view that implied that Shakespeare not only invented the modern (as Bloom was to say more fully and explicitly in *Shakespeare and the Invention of the Human*) but, to a large extent, himself: "But to say, as I did in this book, that Shakespeare swallowed up Marlowe the way a whale scoops up a minnow was to ignore the extraordinary case of indigestion that Marlowe caused the Moby-Dick of all playwrights"; see *The Anxiety of Influence*, 2nd ed. (New York: Oxford University Press,

1997), xxi. Bloom continues on xxii to give Marlowe more credit than he had in the first edition as well as to clarify his view of the anxiety of influence by saying that he favors a Shakespearean reading of Freud rather than a Freudian reading of Shakespeare and wittily asserting that Freud had a Hamlet complex.

10. See John Gower, Book VIII, *Confessio Amantis* (London, 1554), cited in Hallett Smith, introduction to *Pericles*, in *The Riverside Shakespeare*, ed. G. Blakemore Evans (Boston: Houghton Mifflin, 1974), 1480.

11. For perceptive views Shakespeare's use of the comic genre, see Anne Barton's introductions to the comedies in *The Riverside Shakespeare*.

12. See Harold Jenkins, introduction to William Shakespeare, *Hamlet*, ed. Harold Jenkins (London: Methuen, 1982).

13. Frank Kermode, introduction to *Hamlet* in *The Riverside Shakespeare*, 1136–37, here and below.

14. All quotations from the plays in this chapter are from *The Riverside Shakespeare* (1974).

15. Frank Kermode, introduction to *Coriolanus* in *The Riverside Shakespeare*, 1392–93, here and below.

16. G. Blakemore Evans, "The Additions Ascribed to Shakespeare," in *The Riverside Shakespeare*, 1683–85. On Anthony Munday's original manuscript, on Hand D and other matters regarding this play, see Giorgio Melchiori, "The Booke of Sir Thomas Moore: A Chronology of Revision," *Shakespeare Quarterly* 37 (Autumn, 1986), 291–308.

17. Jonathan Hart, "*The Tempest*: Romance and Politics," *Cahiers Elisabéthains* 49 (1996): 28.

18. L. C. Green, and Olive P. Dickason, *The Law of Nations and the New World* (Edmonton: University of Alberta Press, 1989), 221, 235, see 87; Neal Salisbury, "Squanto: Last of the Patuxets," in *Struggle and Survival in Colonial America*, ed. David G. Sweet and Gary B. Nash (Berkeley: University of California Press, 1981), 239–40.

19. See Jonathan Hart, "Representing Spain: The Ambivalence of England and France to Spanish Colonization in the Americas," *CRCL/RCLC* 25 1/2 (1998): 24–50; and "The Black Legend: English and French Representations of Spanish Cruelty in the New World," *Comparative Literature Today: Theories and Practice/ La Littérature comparée d'aujourd'hui. Théories et réalisations* (Paris: Champion, 1999), 375–87.

20. See Aristotle, "The Art of Poetry," and G. Bernard Shaw, preface to *Plays for Puritans* (London: Contable, 1900), in which he speaks of Bardolatry: this origin is set out in the *Oxford English Dictionary*.

CHAPTER 6

1. Since the first version during the 1990s, other work has appeared in the field. I would like to call attention to a few examples here. My thanks to Holger Klein and the Edwin Mellen Press for permission to reprint the earlier "Shakespeare's Italy and England: The Translation of Culture and Empire," *Shakespeare Yearbook* 10 (1999): 460–80, as part of this chapter. On the relation between representations of Rome and the theatrical space in London, see D. J. Hopkins, *City/Stage/Globe: Performance and Space in Shakespeare's London* (New York: Routledge, 2008). On the importance of imperial Rome and its rules on the stage in early modern England, see Lisa Hopkins, *The Cultural Uses of the Caesars on the English Renaissance Stage* (Aldershot, UK: Ashgate, 2008). See also Willy Maley, "Postcolonial Shakespeare: British Identity and Identity Formation and Cymbeline," in *Shakespeare's Late Plays: New Readings*, ed. Jennifer Richards and James Knowles (Edinburgh: Edinburgh University Press, 1999), 145–57; Michele Marrapodi, ed., *Shakespeare and Intertextuality: The Transition of Cultures between Italy and England in the Early Modern Period* (Rome: Bulzoni, 2000); Brian Lockey, "Roman Conquest and English

Legal Identity in Cymbeline," *EMCS: Journal for Early Modern Cultural Studies* 3 (2003): 113–46; Barbara L. Parker, *Plato's Republic and Shakespeare's Rome: A Political Study of the Roman Works* (Newark, DE: University of Delaware Press, 2004); John Alvis, "Liberty and Responsibility in Shakespeare's Rome," in *The Inner Vision: Liberty and Literature*, ed. Edward B. McLean (Wilmington: ISI Books, 2006), 13–35; James Kuzner, "Unbuilding the City: Coriolanus and the Birth of Republican Rome," *Shakespeare Quarterly* 58 (2007): 174–99.

2. See Jonathan Hart, "Language, European," and "Papal Donations and Colonization," *Encyclopedia of Western Colonization Since 1450* (Detroit: Macmillan/Thomson Gale, 2006), 695–703, 902–6.

3. E. M. W. Tillyard, *The Elizabethan World Picture* (London: Chatto & Windus, 1943), and his *Shakespeare's History Plays* (London: Chatto & Windus, 1944). Some early examples of questioning the order of the Tudor myth that Tillyard saw in Shakespeare's plays generally and in his histories specifically, see A. P. Rossiter, "Ambivalence: The Dialectic of the Histories," in *Angel with Horns and Other Shakespeare Lectures*, ed. Graham Storey (London: Longmans, 1961), esp. 47, 51, 62; E. W. Talbert, *The Problem of Order: Elizabethan Political Commonplaces and an Example of Shakespeare's Art* (Chapel Hill: University of North Carolina Press, 1962); Leonard Dean, "From Richard II to Henry V: A Closer View," in *Shakespeare: Modern Essays in Criticism*, ed. L. Dean (1967; repr., New York: Oxford University Press, 1975), esp. 192–95. Shakespeare's dramatic history, in these accounts, is more open: for Rossiter, whose lecture was delivered in 1950, the history plays are ambivalent; for Talbert, they involve York, Lancastrian, and Tudor myths; and for Dean, they are ironic. As is well known, Tillyard faced increasing opposition during the 1980s.

4. Italy in English Renaissance drama is a vast topic, and so it is necessary to find a focus. Harry Levin begins his fine essay with a discussion of Violet Paget, who wrote about this topic under the name of Vernon Lee and dedicated her volume, *Euphorion* (2nd ed., 1884) to Walter Pater. In the volume in which Levin's "Shakespeare's Italians" appears (17–29), Michele Marrapodi, in his introduction, which is an excellent survey of the topic and the collection it introduces, discusses many approaches to this question (1–13). The various essays in the volume are enlightening, but none examines the translation of empire and the typology of Italy in the building of the mythology and history of the English nation. See *Shakespeare's Italy: Functions of Italian Locations in Renaissance Drama*, ed. Michele Marrapodi et al. (Manchester: Manchester University Press, 1993). For an earlier study, see Ernesto Grillo, *Shakespeare and Italy* (1949; New York: Haskell House, 1973); Mario Praz, "Shakespeare's Italy," *Shakespeare Survey* 7 (1954): 95–106. For some useful studies of Shakespeare and Rome, see Paul A. Cantor, *Shakespeare's Rome: Republic and Empire* (Ithaca: Cornell University Press, 1976); Robert S Miola, *Shakespeare's Rome* (Cambridge: Cambridge University Press, 1983); Charles and Michelle Martindale, *Shakespeare and the Uses of Antiquity: An Introductory Essay* (London: Routledge, 1990); Geoffrey Miles, *Shakespeare and the Constant Romans* (Oxford: Clarendon, 1996); and Coppélia Kahn, *Roman Shakespeare: Warriors, Wounds and Women* (London: Routledge, 1997).

5. On the translation of empire, see Ernst Breisach, *Historiography: Ancient, Medieval & Modern* (Chicago: University of Chicago Press, 1983), 178–79. See also Jonathan Hart, "Translating and Resisting Empire: Cultural Appropriation and Postcolonial Studies," in *Borrowed Power; Essays in Cultural Appropriation*, ed. Bruce Ziff and Pratima Rao (New Brunswick, NJ: Rutgers University Press, 1997), 137–68. G. Wilson Knight's discussion of empire in *The Imperial Theme* (London: H. Milford, Oxford University Press, 1931) is still one point of departure. With a nod to Wilson and to Jan Kott, Michele Marrapodi contributes to this debate in "Shakespeare, la storia e il tema imperiale," *Incontri meridionali: Rivista di storia e cultura*, series 3, 1–2 (1983): 21–50. On the double image

of imperial Rome and Britain in productions of the Roman plays by Herbert Beerbohm-Tree and Henry Irving during the last few years of Victoria's reign, see Ralph Berry, "The Imperial Theme," in *Shakespeare and the Victorian Stage*, ed. Richard Foulkes (Cambridge: Cambridge University Press, 1986), 153–60.

6. See Roy Strong, *The Cult of Elizabeth: Elizabethan Portraiture and Pageantry* (London: Thames and Hudson, 1977), esp. 190.

7. In this chapter I have attempted to avoid duplicating my related work that appears elsewhere, such as, "Images of the Native in Renaissance Encounter Narratives," *ARIEL* 25 (1994): 55–76; "Mediation in the Exchange Between Europeans and Native Americans in the Early Modern Period," in "Ross Chambers," special issue, *CRCL/RCLC* 22 (1995): 319–43; "Redeeming *The Tempest*: Romance and Politics," *Cahiers Élisabéthains* 49 (1996): 23–38; "Portugal and the Making of the English Empire: The Case of Richard Hakluyt the Younger," in *Literatura de Viagem*, ed. Ana M. Falcão, Maria T. Nacimento, and Maria L. Leal (Lisbon: Edições Cosmos, 1997), 155–68; "Review Article: Rediscovering Alternative Critique of Europe in the New World," *Bulletin of Hispanic Studies* 76, no. 4 (1999): 533–41; "The Black Legend: English and French Representations of Spanish Cruelty in the New World," *Comparative Literature Today: Theories and Practice/ La Littérature comparée d'aujourd'hui. Théories et réalisations* (Paris: Honoré Champion, 1999), 375–87; "French and English Translations of Spanish Representations of the New World in the Early Modern Period," in *Colonizer and Colonized*, ed. T D'haen and Patricia Krüs (Amsterdam: Rodolpi, 2000), 337–56.

8. Here I am thinking particularly of De Certeau's and Todorov's work on alterity or otherness. Whereas a theoretical view of otherness is not the focus of my chapter, which is more inductive, such work has been important in the field; see Michel de Certeau, *Heterologies: Discourse of the Other*, trans. Brian Massumi (Minneapolis: University of Minnesota Press, 1986); Tzvetan Todorov, *The Conquest of America*, trans. Richard Howard (1984; repr., New York: Harpers, 1992)

9. All citations and quotations to the poems and plays are from William Shakespeare, *The Riverside Shakespeare*, 2nd ed., ed. G. Blakemore Evans (Boston: Riverside, 1997).

10. For a discussion of such Roman and Italian sources, see William A. Armstrong, "The Influence of Seneca and Machiavelli on the Elizabethan Tyrant," *Review of English Studies* 24 (1948): 19–35. See also Felix Raab, *The English Face of Machiavelli: A Changing Interpretation, 1500–1700* (London: Routledge & Kegan Paul, 1964).

11. David B. Quinn, ed., *New American World* (New York: Arno, 1979), 96.

12. For more of the Italian role in the New World, see *The Italians and the Creation of America*, ed. Samuel J. Hough (Providence, RI: John Carter Brown Library, 1980).

13. Stephen Orgel, "Introduction," in William Shakespeare, *The Tempest*, ed. S. Orgel (1987; repr., Oxford: Oxford University Press, 1994), 39. On the influence of Virgil, see, for example, J. M. Nosworthy, "The Narrative Sources of *The Tempest*," *Review of English Studies* 24 (1948); and Robert Wiltenburg, "The *Aeneid* in *The Tempest*," *Shakespeare Survey* 39 (1987): 159–68.

14. For example, Ferdinand's words at the first sight of Miranda echoes Aeneas' words on seeing Venus (I.ii.422; see *Aeneid* I.38); Ceres' welcome of Iris in the masque draws on Virgil's description of the goddess (IV.i.76–8, *Aeneid* IV.700f.); Ariel and his spirits acting as harpies echo an episode from Virgil, where Aeneas and his companions find refuge on islands, the Strophades, where the harpies dwell; these creatures, part woman, part bird, devour the banquet the Trojans prepare, and the leader of the harpies, Celaeno, sends Aeneas off with a dreadful prophecy (III.iii.52f., *Aeneid* III.225f.); see Orgel 39–40, 52n2, 166, for a more detailed discussion of these Virgilian contexts.

15. See Orgel, 41.

16. Orgel, 34–35.

17. Thomas Hariot, *A briefe and true report of the new found land of Virginia . . .* (Frankfurt ad Moenum: Ioannis Wecheli, 1590), E recto.

18. This is an aspect I barely touch on in *Theater and World: The Problematics of Shakespeare's History* (Boston: Northeastern University Press, 1992).

19. In the comedies Shakespeare can make Italian settings and politics a matter of humor. For example, Machiavelli becomes part of a tavern joke when the Host in *The Merry Wives of Windsor* says, "Peace, I say. Hear mine host of the Garter. Am I politic? am I subtle? am I a Machiavel?" (III.i.100–101).

20. As elsewhere I have discussed *The Rape of Lucrece* in detail, I examine it here only in terms of the establishment of an arc of history and mythology concerning ancient Rome. See Jonathan Hart, "Narratorial Strategies in *The Rape of Lucrece*," *Studies in English Literature* 32 (1992): 59–77. Reprinted in *Shakespearean Criticism* (Detroit: Gale, 1993).

21. *Narrative and Dramatic Sources of Shakespeare*, ed. Geoffrey Bullough (London: Routledge & Kegan Paul, 1957–75), 4:46–53; *Riverside Shakespeare*, 836n23, 29–30.

22. In this chapter, I have, for reasons of focus and space, not to concentrate on the comedies, such as *Taming of the Shrew*, *Love's Labour's Lost*, *Merchant of Venice*, *Much Ado About Nothing*, *Two Gentlemen of Verona*, *Measure for Measure*, *All's Well That Ends Well*, or tragedies like *Romeo and Juliet* and *Hamlet* (which has its Roman allusions).

23. For a brief discussion of the allusion, including the possibility that it is to Lord Mountjoy, see Herschel Baker, "Henry V," in *The Riverside Shakespeare*, 974.

24. For the colonial model in Ireland and Virginia, see Nicholas Canny, *Kingdom and Colony: Ireland in the Atlantic World 1560–1800* (Baltimore: Johns Hopkins University Press, 1988). For discussions more specific to the Shakespearean Ireland, see Mark Burnett and Ramona Wray, eds., *Shakespeare and Ireland: History, Politics, Culture* (London: Macmillan, 1997).

25. For a discussion of these monarchs and their symbolic connections between ancient Rome and Renaissance England, see H. A. MacDougall, *Racial Myth in English History: Trojans, Teutons, and Anglo-Saxons* (Hanover, NH: University Press of New England, 1982), 17f.; Jonathan Goldberg, *James I and the Politics of Literature: Jonson, Donne and Their Contemporaries* (Baltimore: Johns Hopkins University Press, 1983), 33f.; and Philip Brockbank, "Myth and History in Shakespeare's Rome," in *Mythe et histoire*, ed. Marie-Thérèse Jones-Davies (Paris: Touzot, 1984), 95–111.

26. See Jonathan Hart, "Strategies of Promotion of Promotion: Some Prefatory Matter of Oviedo, Thevet and Hakluyt," in *Imagining Culture: Essays in Early Modern History and Literature*, ed. J. Hart (New York: Garland, 1996), 73–94.

27. On editing and feminism, see Suzanne Gossett on Pericles, Lois Potter on Desdemona, and Barbara Hodgdon on *Taming of the Shrew*, in *Arden: Editing Shakespeare: Essays in Honour of Richard Proudfoot*, ed. Ann Thompson and Gordon McMullan (London: Thomson, 2003), 65–108.

28. On editing Shakespeare generally, see Thompson and McMullan. In this volume, see especially Ann Thompson and Gordon McMullan, "Introduction," xi–xxiv, and John J. M. Tobin, "Sources and Cruces," 221–38. On recognition and misrecognition, see Terence Cave, *Recognitions: A Study in Poetics* (Oxford: Clarendon, 1990), esp. 190–91; and Jonathan Hart, *Interpreting Cultures: Literature, Religion, and the Human Sciences* (New York: Palgrave Macmillan, 2006), esp. 7–8, 21–72.

CHAPTER 7

1. Here I shall outline some of the work on women and gender in, or relating to, the second tetralogy since 1990, that is, after the drafting of my original analysis on that topic. For a discussion that includes female reproduction in the last three plays of the tetralogy, see Valerie Traub, *Desire and Anxiety: Circulations of Sexuality in Shakespearean Drama* (London: Routledge, 1992). On misogyny and homoeroticism in these plays and the desiring of Hal, see Jonathan Goldberg, *Sodometries: Renaissance Texts, Modern Sexualities* (Stanford: Stanford University Press, 1992), 145–75. On the marginalization of heteroerotic desire in the histories, especially *1 Henry IV*, see Phyllis Rackin, "Historical Difference/ Sexual Difference," in *Privileging Gender in Early Modern England*, ed. Jean R. Brink (Kirksville, MO: Sixteenth Century Journal Publishers, 1993), 37–63. On gender in the histories and other genres, see Jean E. Howard, *The Stage and Social Struggle in Early Modern England* (London: Routledge, 1994). Concerning perspectives, especially in relation to marginalized groups like women, see Paola Pugliatti, *Shakespeare the Historian* (New York: St. Martin's Press, 1996). For a view that the Shakespearean history play is not contra women, see Martha A. Kurtz, "Rethinking Gender and Genre in the History Play," *Studies in English Literature 1500–1900* 36 (1996): 267–87. On the role of gender and nation, see Jean E. Howard and Phyllis Rackin, *Engendering a Nation: A Feminist Account of Shakespeare's English Histories* (London: Routledge, 1997). For a variety of views in the poems and plays, see *Shakespeare and History*, ed. Stephen Orgel and Sean Keilen (New York: Garland, 1999). On Henry IV and Henry V, see Margaret W. Ferguson, *Dido's Daughters: Literacy, Gender and Empire* (Chicago: University of Chicago Press, 2003), esp. 110, 152–62. On marriage, see Linda Gregerson, "French Marriages and the Protestant Nation in Shakespeare's History Plays," in *A Companion to Shakespeare's Works*, ed. Richard Dutton and Jean E. Howard (Oxford: Blackwell, 2003), 2:246–62. On masculinity in *1* and *2 Henry IV*, see Michael Mangan, *Staging Masculinities: History, Gender, Performance* (New York: Palgrave Macmillan, 2003). On foreign marriage, see Cheang Wai Fong, "Women and Boundary Crossing: Foreign Brides in Shakespeare's History Plays," *Tamkang Review* 37 (2007): 177–204. In addition to Alan Bray's work on homosexuality, which was available to me at the time, see a later work: Bruce R. Smith, *Homosexual Desire in Shakespeare's England* (Chicago: University of Chicago Press, 1991).

2. See Ann Jennalie Cook, *The Privileged Playgoers of Shakespeare's London: 1576–1642* (Princeton, NJ: Princeton University Press, 1981), 64. This discussion of gender in the second tetralogy considered critical views from the 1970s and 1980s and was largely written in the 1980s and 1990. One of my regrets in the delay in publication is that friends, like Gwynne Evans and Harry Levin, are no longer here to see the work, which was supposed to be part of a larger project, "Translating Shakespeare," that was to appear in the early 1990s. A small and related part of the discussion in this chapter also occurs in my *Theater and World: The Problematics of Shakespeare's History* (Boston: Northeastern University Press, 1992), 263–70, and was originally to be included in it in its entirety. Although I have updated the bibliography and the critical apparatus, I have kept the original in terms of what I considered then because this was and is part of my contribution to the debate in my work on the histories from the 1970s in classes, talks, seminars at the Shakespeare Association of America, and articles and books. The original impetus for this work was that, at the time, there had not been much discussion of gender in the second tetralogy and I thought it crucial, even though I had not been able to discuss the question at length in my articles and books of the period. This analysis now becomes part of my thinking about poetry, history, and culture in Shakespeare, that is, a new context. In the humanities, the scientific model of recent "scholarly literature" has some important

applications, but taking time to shape an argument and to consider something (perhaps an older humanistic view) is also valuable. While paying attention to the first in the bibliographical apparatus, I have concentrated more on the second, realizing the risks of countervailing the prevailing model in the field. A good portion of this book was written in the 1980s, some in the 1990s, and some recently to draw these vantages on Shakespeare into view. Time can help sift whether something might hold up and be worth being part of a larger whole in a new context.

3. Natalie Zemon Davis, "'Women's History' in Transition: The European Case," *Feminist Review* 3–4 (1975–76), 90.

4. For an interesting discussion of this issue in its social context, see Jean E. Howard, "Crossdressing, the Theatre and Gender Struggle in Early Modern England," *Shakespeare Quarterly* 39 (1988): 419–20; see also 418–40.

5. See Angela Pitt, "Women in the Histories," *Shakespeare's Women* (London: David & Charles, 1981), 136–63; and Marilyn French, "Power: The First Tetralogy," *Shakespeare's Division of Experience* (New York: Ballantine Books, 1981) 35–69. See also Carol Rutter and others, *Clamorous Voices: Shakespeare's Women Today*, ed. Faith Evans (London: Women's Press Limited, 1988), which discusses actresses' interpretations of Kate in *The Taming of the Shrew*, Isabella in *Measure for Measure*, Lady Macbeth, Helena in *All's Well That Ends Well*, Imogen, and Rosalind but does not discuss the roles of women in the histories.

6. L. T. Fitz (Linda Woodbridge) says, "I do not think that it would be going too far to suggest that many male critics feel personally threatened by Cleopatra and what she represents to them. In Cleopatra's case, critical attitudes go beyond the usual condescension toward female characters or the usual willingness to give critical approval only to female characters who are chaste, fair, loyal, and modest: critical attitudes toward Cleopatra seem to reveal deep personal fears of aggressive and manipulative women." See L. T. Fitz, "Egyptian Queens and Male Reviewers: Sexist Attitudes in *Antony and Cleopatra* Criticism," *Shakespeare Quarterly* 18 (1977): 298; see 297–316.

7. Rose Grindon (Mrs. Leo Grindon), *A Woman's Study of "Antony and Cleopatra"* (Manchester, England: Sherratt and Hughes, 1909), 68; and Lucie Simpson, "Shakespeare's 'Cleopatra,'" *Fortnightly Review*, new series, 123 (March 1928): 332.

8. Phyllis Rackin, "Anti-Historians: Women's Roles in Shakespeare's Histories," *Theatre Journal* 37 (October 1985): 329–44; Patricia Parker, *Literary Fat Ladies* (London: Methuen, 1987), 17–23, 237n18, n22; see Lisa Jardine, *Still Harping on Daughters* (Brighton, England: Harvester, 1983), esp. 131; and Gayle Whittier, "Falstaff as a Welshwoman: Uncomic Androgyny," *Ball State University Forum* 20 (1979): 25–35.

9. Lawrence Stone supports this view that the new learning of the Renaissance and the Reformation reduced the learning, prestige, and power of women, though Stone does attribute some power to Elizabethan women, but most of the powers he lists are passive. See Lawrence Stone, *The Family, Sex, and Marriage in England, 1500–1800* (London: Weidenfeld & Nicolson, 1977), 154–55, 199. Bonnie S. Anderson and Judith P. Zinsser contend that the early phase of the Reformation accepted women as spiritual equals to men, but as the Reformed churches became more institutionalized, men in those churches, like those in the Counter-Reformation, asserted their authority over women and viewed women as inferiors. See *A History of Their Own: Women in Europe from Prehistory to the Present*, 2 vols. (New York: Harper & Row, 1988), esp. 1:254, 259, and 2:28–30.

10. Ruth Kelso, *Doctrine for the Lady of the Renaissance* (Urbana: University of Illinois Press, 1956); Joan Kelly, *Women, History, and Theory: The Essays of Joan Kelly* (Chicago: University of Chicago Press, 1984), 22; see Parker, 6.

11. Kelly, 33.

12. Kelly, 34–36.

13. Kelly, 39–42; for more on Aristotle's views on women, see Ian Maclean, *The Renaissance Notion of Woman: A Study in the Fortunes of Scholasticism and Medical Science in European Intellectual Life* (Cambridge: Cambridge University Press, 1980), 7–8.

14. Kelly, 43–47; for more on Neoplatonic views of women, see Maclean 24–26. Maclean asserts that "in spite of the influence of Neo-platonism, then, the scholastic infrastructure of the Renaissance notion of woman remains intact" (25).

15. Coppélia Kahn, "The Absent Mother in *King Lear*," *Rewriting the Renaissance: The Discourses of Sexual Difference in Early Modern Europe*, ed. Margaret W. Ferguson, Maureen Quilligan, and Nancy J. Vickers (Chicago: University of Chicago Press, 1986), 35. See Kahn's *Man's Estate: Masculine Identity in Shakespeare* (Berkeley: University of California Press, 1981).

16. Nancy Chodorow, *The Reproduction of Mothering: Psychoanalysis and the Sociology of Gender* (Berkeley: University of California Press, 1979), 36. See Kahn's *Man's Estate*.

17. Parker, 23.

18. See Cook, 67, for her praise of the Duchess for having a definite personality.

19. All quotations for the plays from the second tetralogy are from the Arden Shakespeare unless otherwise noted (usually the first edition of the *Riverside Shakespeare*). The Ardens are as follows: William Shakespeare, *King Richard II*, ed. Peter Ure (London: Methuen, 1961); *The First Part of King Henry IV*, ed. A. R. Humphreys (1960; repr., London: Methuen, 1965); *The Second Part of King Henry IV*, ed. A. R. Humphreys (1966; repr., London: Methuen, 1966); *King Henry V*, ed J. H. Walter (1954; repr., London: Methuen, 1977). G. B. Evans, in William Shakespeare, *The Riverside Shakespeare*, ed. G. Blakemore Evans (Boston: Houghton Mifflin, 1974), 820. See Peter Ure in William Shakespeare, *King Richard II*, 91.

20. Alan Bray, *Homosexuality in Renaissance England* (London: Gay Men's Press, 1982); and Eve Kosofsky Sedgwick, *Between Men: English Literature and Male Homosocial Desire* (New York: Columbia University Press, 1985).

21. Kristian Smidt, *Unconformities in Shakespeare's History Plays* (London: Macmillan, 1982).

22. Peter Stallybrass, "Patriarchal Territories: The Body Enclosed," in *Rewriting the Renaissance*, ed. Margaret Ferguson and others (Chicago: University of Chicago Press, 1986), 129; see Roy Strong, *Portraits of Queen Elizabeth I* (Oxford: Clarendon, 1963), 75–76, plate xv.

23. *The Letters and Epigrams of Sir John Harington*, ed. N. E. McClure (Philadelphia: University of Pennsylvania Press, 1930), 122, quoted in Louis A. Montrose, "*A Midsummer Night's Dream* and the Shaping Fantasies of Elizabethan Culture: Gender, Power, Form," in *Rewriting the Renaissance*, ed. Margaret Ferguson et al. (Chicago: University of Chicago Press, 1986), 68.

24. J. E. Neale, *Elizabeth I and Her Parliaments 1559–1581* (New York: St. Martin's Press, 1958), 127, in Montrose, 81.

25. *In Felicem Memoriam Elizabethae* (ca. 1608), in *The Works of Francis Bacon*, ed. James Spedding et. al., 15 vols. (Boston: Brown and Taggard, 1860), 2:450, cited in Montrose, 80.

26. Cited in Kelly 88; see Allison Heisch, "Queen Elizabeth I and the Persistence of Patriarchy," *Feminist Review* 4 (February 1980), 45–56; and Margaret King, "Thwarted Ambitions: Six Learned Women of the Italian Renaissance," *Soundings* 3 (1976): 280–304.

27. For a discussion of transvestism, sexual ambiguity, and effeminacy, see Linda Woodbridge, *Women and the English Renaissance: Literature and the Nature of Womankind, 1540–1620* (Urbana: University of Illinois Press, 1984), 156–71. For male views of female obedience in private, such as John Aylmer's, see Carroll Camden, *The Elizabethan Woman* (Houston: Elsevier, 1952), esp. 254; and Edmund Spenser, *The Faerie Queene* V.5.25. See *The Works*

of Edmund Spenser, ed. Edwin Greenlaw and others, Variorum ed. 10 vols. (Baltimore: Johns Hopkins University Press, 1932–49).

28. Kelly, 88.

29. A. P. Rossiter, "Ambivalence: The Dialectic of the Histories," in *Angel with Horns*, esp. 47, 51, 62. The lecture was delivered in 1950.

30. Stephen Greenblatt, *Shakespearean Negotiations: The Circulation of Social Energy in Renaissance England* (Berkeley: University of California Press, 1988), 73–86.

31. Woodbridge, 27. See also Phyllis Rackin, "Women's Roles in Shakespeare's Histories," *Theatre Journal* 37 (1985), who says that cuckold jokes, like Lady Faulconbridge's infidelity in *King John*, shows the anxiety behind strident patriarchal claims, "the repressed knowledge of women's subversive power" (341). Although there is much to Rackin's insight, it is too simple to create the opposition of men as power and women as subversion because other factors like class, race, and religion complicate it. Jack Cade, Falstaff, Othello, and Shylock all qualify patriarchal power. Whether male or female characters can subvert patriarchy is a larger question. At best, perhaps, such power can only be modified, but how optimistic one is about any social and political change depends on one's assumptions and beliefs.

32. Bray, 13–14.

33. *The Compact Edition of The Oxford English Dictionary* (Oxford: Oxford University Press, 1971).

34. *Compact Oxford English Dictionary, Volume II, Supplement and Bibliography* (Oxford: Oxford University Press, 1971).

35. *Narrative and Dramatic Sources of Shakespeare*, ed. Geoffrey Bullough (London: Routledge & Kegan Paul, 1957–75), 4:182.

36. Parker, 20–23; see Whittier, 25–35.

37. This leads to what appears to be a bawdy pun on "reckoning," although I can find no commentary on this point.

38. Woodbridge, 169, see 170.

39. G. B. Evans in *Riverside Shakespeare*, 1183; see Harold Jenkins, introduction to William Shakespeare, *Hamlet*, ed. Harold Jenkins, Arden ed. (London: Methuen, 1982), 405.

40. See Parker, 22. For a discussion of language in the second tetralogy, see Steven Mullaney, "Strange Things, Gross Terms, Curious Customs: The Rehearsal of Cultures in the Late Renaissance," *Representations* 3 (1983): 53–62.

41. Constance Jordan, "Feminism and the Humanists: The Case for Sir Thomas Elyot's *Defense of Good Women*," in Ferguson and others, 253.

42. A. R. Humphreys, in William Shakespeare, *The First Part of King Henry IV*, ed. A. R. Humphreys, Arden ed. (London: Methuen, 1962), 51; see *Caes*, II.i.233f. Cook 67–68 stresses the affection between them.

43. Harry Levin, *Playboys and Killjoys: An Essay on the Theory and Practice of Comedy* (New York: Oxford University Press, 1987), 14.

44. Stone, 93.

45. Ibid., 96.

46. Woodbridge, 275–83.

47. Ibid., 275, 278–83.

48. Ibid., 297.

49. See, for instance, Greenblatt; Mullaney; Hélène Cixous, "Le Sexe ou la tête," *Cahiers du GRIF* 13 (1976): 5–15; and Julia Kristeva, *Étrangers à nous-mêmes* (Paris, Fayard, 1988).

50. Jordan, 249.

51. See Jonathan Hart, "Playboys, Killjoys and a Career as Critic: the Accomplishment of Harry Levin," *CRCL/RCLC* 16 (1989): 118–35.

52. See Jonathan Hart, "The Body Divided: Kingship in Shakespeare's Lancastrian Tetralogy," *CIEFL Bulletin*, new series, 2 (1990): 24–52.

53. See Juliet Dusinberre, *Shakespeare and the Nature of Women* (London: Macmillan, 1975), 33–34, for a discussion of honor in the context of chastity.

54. Stephen Hawes, *The Pastime of Pleasure*, The Early English Text Society (London: H. Milford, Oxford University Press, 1928), vol. 173, lines 156–57; and Raphael Holinshed, *Chronicles of England, Scotland, and Ireland* (1587; repr., London: J. Johnson, 1807–8), iii.634, in William Shakespeare, *The Second Part of King Henry IV*, ed. A. R. Humphreys (1966; repr., London: Methuen, 1977), 4.

55. Nancy Vickers, "'The blazon of sweet beauty's best': Shakespeare's *Lucrece*," *Shakespeare and the Question of Theory*, ed. Patricia Parker and Geoffrey Hartman (London: Methuen, 1985), esp. 95–97; Parker, *Fat Ladies*, esp. 126–40.

56. See W. Robertson Davies, *Shakespeare's Boy Actors* (New York: Macmillan, 1939); Harold Hillebrand, *The Child Actors* (New York: Russell & Russell 1964); and Dusinberre, 10.

57. S(imon) R(obson), *Choise of Change* (1585), sig. L.iiiv, quoted in *The Second Part of King Henry IV*, 22; see M. P. Tilley, *A Dictionary of the Proverbs in England in the Sixteenth and Seventeenth Centuries* (Ann Arbor: University of Michigan Press, 1950), W276.

58. Judith Kegan Gardiner, "Mind Mother: Psychoanalysis and Feminism," in *Making a Difference: Feminist Literary Criticism*, ed. Gayle Greene and Coppélia Kahn (London: Methuen, 1985), 117.

59. See Tilley, *Proverbs*, B716.

60. Woodbridge, 208; Rackin, "Women's Roles," 329.

61. Ben Jonson, *Bartholomew Fair*, ed. G. R. Hibbard (London: Ernest Benn, 1977).

62. William Shakespeare, *The Second Part of the History of Henry IV*, ed. J. Dover Wilson (Cambridge: Cambridge University Press, 1946).

63. The final version of this chapter was completed on the verge of the First Gulf War.

64. See Simon Shepherd, *Amazons and Warrior Women: Varieties of Feminism in Seventeenth Century Drama* (Brighton, England: Harvester, 1981) for background on "tavern wenches," 93–106, and a sympathetic view of the arrest of Doll and Mistress Quickly, 96, 101–3.

65. For a view of this marginalization as something that enables the reestablishment of a "strong regime," see Pitt, 138–39).

66. Kelly and Montrose share a similar view, but Philippa Berry is against these readings. See *Philippa Berry, Of Chastity and Power: Elizabethan Literature and the Unmarried Queen* (London: Routledge, 1989).

67. In the next chapter this is the play in which I examine the role of women most closely, so that if this section appears shorter than the play warrants it is because I am avoiding repetition.

68. This was true at the time of writing the final draft (before August 1990).

69. Shepherd, 29. See, for instance, Thomas Heywood, *If you knovv not me, you know no bodie: or, The troubles of Queene Elizabeth* (London: Nathaniel Butter, 1605) and *The second part of, If you know not me, you know no bodie VVith the building of the Royall Exchange: and the famous victorie of Queene Elizabeth, in the yeare 1588* (London: Nathaniell Butter, 1606).

70. Kelly, 66.

71. Ibid., 67.

72. Ibid., 71; Allison Heisch, "Persistence," 45–56. For a similar view, see Catherine Belsey, *The Subject of Tragedy: Identity and Difference in Renaissance Drama* (London: Methuen, 1985), 180. In discussing moral philosophy in *The Cambridge History of Renaissance Philosophy* (1988), Jill Kraye entitles a section, "Renaissance Concepts of Man," where she concludes that although there was nothing original about Renaissance views of man because they borrowed from classical, biblical, patristic, and medieval sources, these views

reflected a greater and more intense exploration of man's nature. At this point, not mentioning anything about women, Kraye notes a book that does, Ian Maclean's *The Renaissance Notion of Woman* (1980). Possibly, Kraye, whose essay is learned, does not want to duplicate Maclean's work, but a few sentences, paragraphs, or pages on women might help to increase an understanding of "man" (*The Cambridge History of Renaissance Philosophy*, ed. Charles B. Schmitt and others [Cambridge University Press, 1988], 306).

73. Christine de Pisan, *Here begynneth the boke of the cyte of ladyes the whiche boke is deuyded into. iij. partes . . .* (London: Henry Pepwell, 1521); Pisan (Anslay) 1:13; Kelly, 84–85.

74. See Kelly 86.

75. In 1837, Queen Victoria, at the death of her uncle, William IV of Britain, was unable to take up the throne of Hanover, which had been united with Britain since 1714 because Hanover was subject to the old Teutonic laws, issued late in the reign of Clovis (ca. 507 to 511), also called the Salic law or *Lex Salica* or *leges barbarorum*, which barred a woman from being the ruler. On Salic law, Victoria, and Hanover, see Helen Rappaport, *Queen Victoria: A Biographical Companion* (Santa Barbara, CA: ABC-CLIO, 2003), 137, 186.

76. Roy Strong discusses the gap between the ideal and actual in Elizabeth I.

77. Neale, 192.

78. George Peele, *The araygnement of Paris a pastorall. Presented before the Queenes Maiestie, by the Children of her chappell* (London: Henrie Marsh, 1584).

79. Lyly, John. *Endimion, the man in the moone Playd before the Queenes Maiestie at Greenewich on Candlemas day at night, by the Chyldren of Paules* (London: I. Charlewood, for the widdowe Broome, 1591). See John Lyly, "Endimion," in *Pre-Shakespearean Comedies*, vol. 2, of *Minor Elizabethan Drama, In Two Volumes*, intro. Ashley Thorndike (1910; repr., London: J. M. Dent, 1960), 128.

80. John N. King, *Tudor Royal Iconography: Literature and Art in the Age of Religious Crisis* (Princeton: Princeton University Press, 1989), 63. See Philippa Berry, *Of Chastity* (1989), 134–36, for a detailed discussion of the images of sun and moon in the cult of Elizabeth. Lauren Silberman asserts that Spenser transforms the encomium of unsung heroines in Ariosto's *Orlando Furioso* (XX.1–3, XXX.1.24) into a compliment for Elizabeth, which allows for iconoclasm beneath the convention because Spenser shifts the emphasis from Ariosto's fictitious heroines to "the false men who have suppressed the exploits of heroic women" (*FQ*, III.ii.1–2); see Silberman, "Singing Unsung Heroines: Androgynous Discourse in Book 3 of *The Faerie Queene*," in Ferguson and others, 259. For another view of Spenser's place in the cult of Elizabeth, see Philippa Berry, 153–65. Berry says that in *The Faerie Queene* Spenser creates a complex view of the feminine, even at the conclusion of the two *Cantos of Mutability*, where Nature passes judgment on Mutibility's plea. Paradoxically, Berry implies, "*The Faerie Queene* accorded Elizabeth as a female beloved greater imaginative or spiritual powers than ever before. Simultaneously, it restricted the exercise of these powers in the world of human affairs, by distinguishing between two different spheres of existence, the mythic and the historical, which paralleled the Platonic division between an ideal and a real world" (153).

81. Neale, 200; see Strong 127, fig. 135.

82. V. T. Harlow, introduction to Walter Raleigh, *The discoverie of the large and bewtiful empire of Guiana*, ed. V. T. Harlow (London: Argonaut, 1928), xcviii. See Philippa Berry for a sensible account on the queen's actual power and the subsequent limits of Raleigh's imaginative role as Petrarchan or Neoplatonic lover. Berry also thinks that in *The 11th: and laste booke of the Ocean to Scinthia*, Raleigh no longer distinguishes between Elizabeth and other women, as well as the other Elizabeth, Raleigh's wife, so that he can blame her (them) for being descended from Eve and being the cause of his own sexual "transgression" (146–53); see also Stephen Greenblatt, *Sir Walter Ralegh: The Renaissance Man and His*

Roles (New Haven: Yale University Press, 1973); and Leonard Tennenhouse, "Sir Walter Ralegh and the Literature of Clientage," *Patronage in the Renaissance*, ed. Guy Fitch-Lytle and Stephen Orgel (Princeton: Princeton University Press, 1981), 235–60.

83. Walter Raleigh, 6.

84. Ibid., 73.

85. See John N. King, *Tudor Royal Iconography* (Princeton, NJ: Princeton University Press, 1989), 65–72, for another view of these Jacobean praises of Elizabeth.

86. Ibid., 71–72.

87. Michel Drayton, *The Muses Elizium: Lately discouered, by a new way ouer Parnassus* (London: Thomas Harper, 1630), 4.

88. Neale, 200.

89. Ibid., 439.

90. Ibid.

91. Marjorie Garber, "Shakespeare as Fetish," *Shakespeare Quarterly* 41 (1990): 242–50.

92. Montrose, 67. The queen's power over male and female subjects was intricate and pervasive, as Frank Whigham notes: "Both her own indulgence in elaborate dress and her restriction of her subject's sumptuary rights were parts of the same project of controlling the forces of control, adjusting them to the uses of the established order, and making exceptions only when they might enhance its power." See *Ambition and Privilege: The Social Tropes of Elizabethan Courtesy Theory* (Berkeley: University of California Press, 1984) 160.

93. Montrose, 68–73, 77.

94. Ibid., 71. For a view that contrasts George Chapman's narrative poem, *The Shadow of Night* (pub. 1594) with Shakespeare's *A Midsummer Night's Dream* (1595) because the former stresses Cynthia's spiritual autonomy and supremacy whereas the latter restores her to the patriarchy's control, see Berry, 143–46.

95. Pamela Joseph Benson observes, "Elizabeth I's sex posed a problem for Edmund Spenser in his attempt to praise her in *The Faerie Queene*. Her unmarried state and chastity offered opportunities for enthusiastic praise of her personal virtue, but her sex itself was an obstacle to his celebration of her public character as a ruler because the natural right of women to rule was not universally accepted in Elizabethan England. Spenser's two major treatments of this controversial issue seem to contradict each other. Book III is dedicated to epic praise of the Queen's ancestry and a pair of encomia of her celebrate great women of the past (ii.1–3, iv.1–3). In Book V Britomart deposes the Amazon queen Radigand and installs a male ruler. . . . The handling of the issue of the rule of women in Books III and V can only be understood accurately when set in the context of the contemporary debate about the legitimacy of rule by women, the debate from which Spenser drew his rhetoric. Two views of the subject of rule by women predominated in Spenser's day, each one allied with a major political-religious faction. The Anglicans asserted the near equality of the sexes and the propriety of rule by women; the Calvinists argued that women as a group were unsuited to rule and that only women specially raised by God to office ought to rule." See "Rule, Virginia: Protestant Theories of Female Regiment in *The Farie Queene*," *ELR* 15 (1985): 277; see 277–92. Like Albert Baugh, Maureen Quilligan thinks that Elizabeth liked the comedy of the braggadocchio in Antony Munday's reworking of an Italian play acted before the queen in 1585, as she later showed her affection for Falstaff—which the tradition of her command performance of *The Merry Wives of Windsor* may bear out, that Spenser, aware of her sense of humor, had Braggadocchio and Trompart accompany Belphoebe on her first appearance in *The Faerie Queene* (II.ii). Quilligan asserts that Spenser had to be very careful about his representation of Elizabeth's beauty and chastity because her regime was very careful about pictorial and verbal representations

of the queen. For instance, she disliked what John Stubbs said about her "marriage pro-
gram" and had his hand cut off. *A Literary History of English*, ed. Albert C. Baugh (New
York, 1948), 450, in Quilligan, "The Comedy of Female Authority in *The Faerie Queene*,"
ELR 17, no. 2 (spring 1987), 156–57; see 158–71. Dore Levy compares female rule in
Spenser's epic and *The Journey to the West*, a Chinese *hsiao-shuo*, or prose fiction dating
from the late sixteenth century. She finds parallels between the two works that may be
less incidental than she thinks: "The countries of the women themselves, dream visions,
men stopped in mid-journey by aggressive females unaccustomed to acknowledging male
authority, men's embarassment in female roles (Artegall's dress and apron, Tripitaka's and
Pa-chieh's pregnancies), are highly suggestive." "Female Reigns: *The Faerie Queene* and
The Journey to the West," *Comparative Literature* 39 (1987): 219; see 218–35. Using Der-
rida's claim that every written text originates in the vocative, in its writer's desire to achieve
the union of speaking and being, and testifies in the continuance of writing in the equivocal nature of language, Elizabeth J. Bellamy writes, "Spenser's *The Faerie Queene* 'lets itself
be read' because its ultimate quest is the poet's unsuccessful effort to nominate Elizabeth.
If we argue that *The Faerie Queene* has its origin in the vocative, then it is time to consider
the crucial interrelationship between Spenser's vocational role in *The Faerie Queene*, the
fulfillment of his epic role as England's Virgil, and his vocative goal, his desire quite simply
to name his queen, to call forth her image from behind her 'couert vele' (2 proem 5.2)
as the ultimate sanctioner of the epic task." See "The Vocative and the Vocational: The
Unreadability of Elizabeth in *The Faerie Queene*," *English Literary History* 54 (1987): 1; see
1–30. Gabrielle Bernhard Jackson relates Amazons to Joan of Arc in *1 Henry VI*; see "Topi-
cal Ideology: Witches, Amazons, and Shakespeare's Joan of Arc," *English Literary Renaissance*
18 (1988): 40–65. For Raleigh's Elizabeth and Spenser's Britomart, in Montrose's view, "the
woman who has the prerogative of a goddess, who is authorized to be out of place, can best
justify her authority by putting other women in their places" (79). For a similar view, see
also Shepherd, *Amazons*, esp. 29. Shepherd makes some interesting observations about the
changes in the word *Amazon* and in the way it connects government and religion: "The term
'Amazon' was used in the sixteenth century. In general it denotes Amazons of classical antiquity, virtuous fighting women, who did useful things, such as defending Troy. In the period
in hand [the seventeenth century] it comes to indicate a woman who uses her strength for
non-virtuous, specifically lustful ends. Hence her opposition to the warrior. Both types draw
on associations in classical mythology, Pallas Athene and the goddess of justice, Astraea, and
on associations from Christianity, the true and false churches seen as maiden and whore"
(1–2); see also Peter Stallybrass' interesting analysis of the connection between the refashion-
ing of the female body and the nation state through incorporation and exclusion and for his
related discussion of the Ditchley portrait, where Elizabeth stands on a map of England and
a Dutch engraving of 1598, where Elizabeth's body encloses Europe ("Patriarchal Territories:
The Body Enclosed," in Ferguson and others, 129–33).

96. John N. King, "Queen Elizabeth I: Representations of the Virgin Queen," *Renaissance
Quarterly* 43 (1990): 30.

97. Ibid., 38–39.

98. Ibid., 30.

99. Ibid., 58.

100. Peter McClure and Robin Headlam Wells, "Elizabeth I as a Second Virgin Mary," *Renais-
sance Studies* 4 (1990): 38–40. See Boase, *The Origin and Meaning of Courtly Love: A
Critical Study of European Scholarship* (Manchester, England: University of Manchester
Press 1977).

101. Philippa Berry, 9–10. Ian Maclean discusses the prominence of the Virgin Mary in the
Middle Ages and the Counter-Reformation. Mary is the "second Eve," whose virtues are

"humility, obedience, silence (Luke 2:19; cf. the female vice of garrulity), mortification, modesty, prudence," all, except for prudence, consistent with traditional female virtue, so that Mary can "be transformed into a perfect model of womanhood." But she is "exempt from all female vice and imperfection, and thus can accede directly to heaven by assumption unlike any other human being. Far from being the glory of her sex, she is not of her sex in its malediction, tribulation and imperfection" (23, see 24). "The Cult of Mary and the Practice of Misogyny," the fourth chapter of C. R. Boxer, *Mary and Misogyny: Women in Iberian Expansion Overseas 1415–1815 Some Facts, Fancies and Personalities* (London: Duckworth, 1975), 97–114, outlines some of the relations between the cult of Mary and woman-hating in peninsular and colonial Portuguese and Spanish culture. A similar study might bear interesting results for English culture, even if in a reformed and repressed version of those relations.

102. McClure and Wells, 38–40, 70.

103. Ibid., 70.

104. Julia Kristeva, "Stabat Mater," trans. Arthur Goldhammer, *Poetics Today* 6, no. 1–2 (1985): 133–52.

105. Ester Sowernam, *Ester hath hang'd Haman, or, An ansvvere to a lewd pamphlet, entituled, The arraignment of women* (London: Nicholas Bourne, 1617), 21. In modernized spelling, Sowernam is quoted in Kelly, 85.

106. Kelly, 88; Heisch, 45–56. Woodbridge is sceptical about attributing the revival of the formalist controversy about women, after lying dormant in the 1550s, to the death of Queen Mary and the ascension of Elizabeth (71).

107. Mary Crane, "'Video et Taceo': Elizabeth I and the Rhetoric of Counsel," *Studies in English Literature* 28 (1988) 1–2, see 3–15. The works of the first group of male critics that Crane has in mind are Louis Adrian Montrose, "'Eliza, Queene of Shepheardes,' and the Pastoral of Power," *English Literary Renaissance* 10 (1980): 153–82; "Of Gentlemen and Shepherds: The Politics of Elizabethan Pastoral Form," *English Literary History* 50 (1983): 415–59; and "'Shaping Fantasies': Figurations of Gender and Power in Elizabethan Culture," *Representations* 1 (1983): 61–94; Stephen J. Greenblatt, *Sir Walter Ralegh*, 52–59, and his *Renaissance Self-Fashioning: From More to Shakespeare* (Chicago: University of Chicago Press, 1980), 165–69; Arthur F. Marotti, "'Love is not Love': Elizabethan Sonnet Sequences and the Social Order," *English Literary History* 49 (1982): 398–400. The works of the second group are: David Javitch, *Poetry and Courtliness in Renaissance England* (Princeton: Princeton University Press, 1978); and Frank Whigham, *Ambition and Privilege: The Social Tropes of Elizabethan Courtesy Theory* (Berkeley: University of California Press, 1984).

108. As examples, Crane cites Leah Marcus, "Shakespeare's Comic Heroines, Elizabeth I, and the Political Uses of Androgyny," *Women in the Middle Ages and the Renaissance: Literary and Historical Perspectives*, ed. Mary Beth Rose (Syracuse: Syracuse University Press, 1986), 137–43; Allison Heisch, "Queen Elizabeth I: Parliamentary Rhetoric and the Exercise of Power," *Signs* 1 (1975): 31–55; and "Persistence," 45–54; Catherine Belsey, 180.

109. Philippa Berry, *Of Chastity and Power* (1989), 1–2. See Luce Irigaray, *Speculum of the Other Woman*, trans. Gillian C. Gill (Ithaca: Cornell University Press, 1986).

110. See Frances Yates, *Astraea: The Imperial Theme in the Sixteenth Century* (London: Routledge & Kegan Paul, 1975). Berry includes Montrose and E. C. Wilson and Roy Strong, *The Cult of Elizabeth* (London: Thames and Hudson, 1977), as examples of those who do not emphasize gender enough or do not elaborate the role of feminism in the debate and cites the contributors to *Men in Feminism*, ed. Alice Jardine and Paul Smith (London: Methuen, 1987).

111. Philippa Berry, 5–6. For a contrary view of the effectiveness of Neoplatonism to change attitudes to gender, see Maclean 24–26.

112. Philippa Berry, 62.

113. Ibid., 134–65.

114. For an interesting view of women and history in Shakespeare's poetry and a learned treatment of the epyllion, see Heather Dubrow, *Captive Victors: Shakespeare's Narrative Poems and Sonnets* (Ithaca, NY: Cornell University Press, 1987).

115. See Ernst H. Kantorowicz, *The King's Two Bodies: A Study in Mediaeval Political Theology* (Princeton, NJ: Princeton University Press, 1957), 221. See Philippa Berry, 61.

116. See J. H. Walter, in *King Henry V*, ed. J. H. Walter (1954; repr., London: Methuen, 1977), 34.

117. Ian Maclean (8–19) discusses the theological debate over the relation of women to Eve and the Fall as well as male views of females in the Middle Ages and Renaissance. For recent discussions of the two creation stories in Genesis, the one at 1:26–28 (which leads to the legend of Lilith, in Parker's words, "the first feminist") and the other at 2: 18–24 about Eve (who is named at 3:20); see Mary Nyquist, "Gynesis, Genesis, Exegesis, and the Formation of Milton's Eve," in *Cannibals, Witches, and Divorce: Estranging the Renaissance*, ed. Marjorie Garber (Baltimore: Johns Hopkins University Press, 1987), 148f., and Patricia Parker, "Coming Second: Woman's Place," in *Literary Fat Ladies*, 178; see 179–233.

118. On the advice of G. B. Evans, I have treated the "widow's" in the Arden as an error and made the correction according to the Riverside, which Wells' and Taylor's Oxford edition corroborates.

119. Lawrence Stone, *The Family, Sex and Marriage in England 1500–1800* (New York: Harper & Row, 1979), 5–6, 7–8, 89–90, 151, 154–55.

120. Vickers in Parker and Hartman, 95; see 96–116. For a similar analysis to my own of blazon in relation to Katharine's inventory of female parts that is also indebted to Vickers, see Parker, *Literary Fat Ladies*, 131–32.

121. Vickers, 112.

122. Walter, in Shakespeare, *Henry V*, Arden ed., 85. See Woodbridge, 205; see 201–7 for a discussion of shrew taming.

123. G. B. Evans in *The Riverside Shakespeare*, 972.

CHAPTER 8

1. This chapter is a revised version of my article, "Shakespeare's *Henry V*: Towards the Problem Play," *Cahiers Elisabethains* 42 (October 1992): 17–35, which derives from a chapter of "Irony in Shakespeare's Second Tetralogy" (1983). I thank the editors of *Cahiers Elisabethains* for permission to include it in this book. Here are some selected works on Henry V in the past two decades: On irony and ambiguity as part of the craft of acting of, see John Barton, "Irony and Ambiguity," *Playing Shakespeare: An Actor's Guide* (1984; repr., New York: Anchor Books, 2001), 149–66. For a later view of irony in *Henry V* than my own, see John S. Mebane, "'Impious War': Religion and the Ideology of Warfare in *Henry V*," *Studies in Philology* 104 (2007): 250–66. On international law, see Theodor Meron, "Shakespeare's *Henry the Fifth* and the Law of War," *American Journal of International Law* 86 (1992): 1–45. Concerning the ambivalence of history and politics, see Paola Pugliatti, "The Strange Tongues of *Henry V*," *Yearbook of English Studies* 23 (1993): 235–53. On Henry V and disguise, see Anne Barton, *Essays, Mainly Shakespearean* (Cambridge: Cambridge University Press, 1994). For a discussion of rhetoric and national identity, see Thomas Healy, "Remembering with Advantages: Nation and Ideology in *Henry V*," in *Shakespeare in the New Europe*, ed. Michael Hattaway, Boika Sokolova, and Derek Roper (Sheffield: Sheffield Academic Press, 1994), 174–93. On language and plainness, see P. K. Ayers, "'Fellows of Infinite Tongue': Henry V and the King's English," *Studies in English*

Literature 1500–1900 34 (1994): 253–77. For a discussion of authority, see Peter C. Herman, "O, 'tis a gallant king': Shakespeare's *Henry V* and the Crisis of the 1590s," in *Tudor Political Culture*, ed. Dale Hoak (Cambridge: Cambridge University Press, 1995), 204–25. On nation and memory, see Jonathan Baldo, "Wars of Memory in *Henry V*," *Shakespeare Quarterly* 47 (1996): 132–59. About law, power, and justification, see Janet M. Spencer, "Princes, Pirates, and Pigs: Criminalizing Wars of Conquest in *Henry V*," *Shakespeare Quarterly* 47 (1996): 160–77. On religion and power, see Steven Marx, "Holy War in *Henry V*," *Shakespeare Survey* 48 (1996): 85–97. Concerning Ireland and England in Holinshed and in *Richard II* and *Henry V*, see Willy Maley, "Shakespeare, Holinshed, and Ireland: Resources and Con-Texts," in *Shakespeare and Ireland: History, Politics, Culture*, ed. Mark Thornton Burnett and Ramona Wray (New York: St. Martin's Press, 1997), 27–46. On irony and postmodernism in relation to performance, see Robert Shaughnessy, "The Last Post: *Henry V*, War Culture, and the Postmodern Shakespeare," *Theatre Survey* 39 (1998): 41–61. For the controversy surrounding Henry as hero and antihero, see John Sutherland and Cedric Watts, *Henry V, War Criminal? and Other Shakespeare Puzzles* (Oxford: Oxford University Press, 2000). Concerning conflict, see Ellen C. Caldwell, "The Hundred Years' War and National Identity," in *Inscribing the Hundred Years' War in French and English Cultures*, ed. Denise N. Baker (Albany: State University of New York Press, 2000), 237–65. About characterization and metadrama, see Dennis Kezar, "Shakespeare's Guilt Trip in *Henry V*," *Modern Language Quarterly* 61 (2000): 431–61. On Katharine and marriage, see Corinne S. Abate, "'Once more unto the breach': Katharine's Victory in *Henry V*," *Early Theatre* 4 (2001): 73–85. About different kings of conscience, see Camille Wells Slights, "The Conscience of the King: *Henry V* and the Reformed Conscience," *Philological Quarterly* 80 (2001): 37–55. Concerning the debate between Williams and the king, see William Leahy, "'All would be royal': The Effacement of Disunity in Shakespeare's *Henry V*," *Shakespeare Jahrbuch* 138 (2002): 89–98. On the heroic uniting of opposites by Henry V at the end of the play, see Thomas McAlindon, "Natural Closure in *Henry V*," *Shakespearean International Yearbook* 3 (2003): 156–71. For the differences between text and stage script in *Henry V*, see Andrew Gurr, "A New Theatre Historicism," in *From Script to Stage in Early Modern England*, ed. Peter Holland and Stephen Orgel (New York: Palgrave Macmillan, 2004), 71–88. On ambiguity, see Sara Munson Deats, "Henry V at War: Christian King or Model Machiavel," in *War and Words: Horror and Heroism in the Literature of Warfare*, ed. Sara Munson Deats, Lagretta Tallent Lenker, and Merry G. Perry (Lanham, MD: Lexington, 2004), 83–101. On the difficulties in staging the Folio version of *Henry V*, see Andrew Gurr, "The Transforming of *Henry V*," *Shakespearean International Yearbook* 5 (2005): 303–13. Concerning the invasion of France, see Clayton G. Mackenzie, "*Henry V* and the Invasion of France: Rethinking the Moral Justification," *Upstart Crow* 25 (2005): 65–70. For an examination of memory in the quarto and folio versions, see Dermot Cavanagh, "History, Mourning, and Memory in *Henry V*," in *Shakespeare's Histories and Counter-Histories*, eds. Dermot Cavanagh, Stuart Hampton-Reeves, and Stephen Longstaffe (Manchester: Manchester University Press, 2006), 32–48. On the connection between Jean Bodin in Shakespeare, including in *Henry V*, see B. J. Sokol, "Tolerance in Shakespeare: An Introduction," *Shakespearean International Yearbook* 7 (2007): 177–96. Concerning the importance of the structure of the royal entry and a comparison of Elizabeth I and Henry V, see Anny Crunelle-Vanrigh, "*Henry V* as a Royal Entry," *SEL: Studies in English Literature 1500–1900* 47 (2007): 355–77. For a discussion of war that includes *Henry V*, see Simon Barker, *War and Nation in the Theatre of Shakespeare and His Contemporaries* (Edinburgh: Edinburgh University Press, 2007). A discussion of self for Hal and Henry V occurs in

Terry Sherwood, *The Self in Early Modern Literature: For the Common Good* (Pittsburgh: Duquesne University Press, 2007). For the Irish dimension of *Henry V*, see Stephen O'Neill, *Staging Ireland: Representations in Shakespeare and Renaissance Drama* (Dublin: Four Courts, 2007). On performance, speech acts, and conquest, see David Schalkwyk, "Proto-nationalist Performatives and Trans-theatrical Displacement in *Henry V*," in *Transnational Exchange in Early Modern Theatre*, ed. Robert Henke and Eric Nicholson (Aldershot, UK: Ashgate, 2008), 197–213. On the difference between the chorus and staged events and how Olivier addresses that gap, see James Hirsch, "Shakespeare's Stage Chorus and Olivier's Film Chorus," in *Shakespeare on Screen: The Henriad*, ed. Sarah Hatchuel and Nathalie Vienne-Guerrin (Mont-Saint-Aignan: Publications des Universités de Rouen and du Havre, 2008), 169–92. Concerning how Roman honor occurs in the second tetralogy as a spur to the representation of Roman history in the Roman plays, see Alexander Welsh, *What Is Honor? A Question of Moral Imperatives* (New Haven: Yale University Press, 2008), 50–66. On work and class, see Tom Rutter, *Work and Play on the Shakespearean Stage* (Cambridge: Cambridge University Press, 2008). On rhetoric in *Henry V* and other plays, see Laetitia Coussement-Boillot, *Copia et cornucopia: La poétique shakespearienne de l'abondance* (Bern: Lang, 2008).

2. Frederick Boas, *Shakspere and his Predecessors* (New York: Scribners, 1899), 345.

3. C. S. Lewis and E. M. W. Tillyard, *The Personal Heresy*, cited in W. K. Wimsatt and Monroe C. Beardsley. "The Intentional Fallacy," in *Critical Theory Since Plato*, ed. Hazard Adams (San Diego: Harcourt Brace Jovanovich, 1971), 1015: see Wimsatt's and Beardsley's view, 1015–22. For reader response theory, see, for example, Roman Ingarden, *The Literary Work of Art* (Evanston, IL: Northwestern University Press, 1973) and *Reader-Response Theory*, ed. Jane Tompkins (Baltimore: Johns Hopkins University Press, 1980). For discussions of the relation of theatre audience and reader, see Keir Elam, *The Semiotics of Theatre and Drama* (London: Methuen, 1980), esp. 208–10; and Marvin Carlson, *Theories of the Theatre* (Ithaca, NY: Cornell University Press, 1984), 454–515. Carlson calls attention to many relevant works on this relation, such as the following special issues: *Études littéraires* 13, no. 3 (1980) and *Poetics Today* (1981).

4. See, for example, J. A. K. Thomson, *Irony: An Historical Introduction* (London: Allen & Unwin, 1926); D. C. Muecke, *The Compass of Irony* (London: Methuen, 1969): Lilian Furst, *Fictions of Romantic Irony* (Cambridge, MA: Harvard University Press, 1984).

5. See B. A. Farrell, *The Standing of Psychoanalysis* (Oxford: Oxford University Press, 1981) and Elizabeth Wright, *Psychoanalytic Criticism: Theory in Practice* (London: Methuen, 1984).

6. See T. W. Baldwin, *William Shakspere's Small Latin and Lesse Greeke*, 2 vols. (Urbana: University of Illinois Press, 1944); Alexander Sackton, *Rhetoric as a Dramatic Language in Ben Jonson* (New York: Columbia University Press, 1948); Donald Clark, *John Milton at St. Paul's School: A Study of Ancient Rhetoric in English Renaissance Education* (New York: Columbia University Press, 1948).

7. E. D. Hirsch, *Validity in Interpretation* (New Haven: Yale University Press, 1967); and Terry Eagleton, *Literary Theory: An Introduction* (Oxford: Basil Blackwell, 1983), esp. 194–217.

8. Although I find Norman Rabkin's view provocative, I think that *Henry V* is a both–and play rather than an either–or play. Richard Levin's views also contribute to the debate, but he thinks of irony too much as undercutting. Unlike Levin, I would say that William W. Lloyd's view of irony (1856) is ironic. See Rabkin's, "Rabbits, Ducks and *Henry V*," *Shakespeare Quarterly* 28 (1977): 279–96; and his "Either/ Or: responding to *Henry V*," in *Shakespeare and the Problem of Meaning* (Chicago: University of Chicago Press, 1981), 33–62. See Levin's *New Readings vs. Old Plays* (Chicago: University of Chicago

Press, 1977), esp. 4–5, 90–142; and his "Hazlitt on *Henry V*, and the Appropriation of Shakespeare," *Shakespeare Quarterly* 35 (1984): esp. 138. For other views, see John Jump, "Shakespeare and History," *Critical Quarterly* 17 (1953): 233–44; Zdenek Strí-brný, "Henry V and History," in *Shakespeare in a Changing World: Essays on His Times and His Plays*, ed. A. Kettle (London: Lawrence & Wishart, 1964), 84, 101; Pierre Sahel, "Henry V, Roi Ideal?" *Études Anglaises* 28 (1975): 1–4; Gordon R. Smith, "Shakespeare's *Henry V*: Another Part of the Critical Forest," *Journal of the History of Ideas* 37 (1976): 3–26: E. W. Ives, "Shakespeare and History: Divergencies and Agreements," *Shakespeare Survey* 38 (1985): 19–37; Jonathan Dollimore and Alan Sinfield, "History and Ideology: the Instance of *Henry V*," in *Alternative Shakespeares*, ed. J. Drakakis (London: Methuen, 1985), 206–27; Stephen Greenblatt, "Invisible Bullets: Renaissance Authority and Its Subversion, *Henry IV* and *Henry V*," in *Political Shakespeare*, ed. J. Dollimore and A. Sinfield (Ithaca, NY: Cornell University Press, 1985), 18–47. All citations and quotations from the primary texts will be from the New Arden Shakespeare: William Shakespeare, *King Henry V*, ed. J. H. Walter (1954, repr., London: Methuen, 1977).

9. William W. Lawrence, *Shakespeare's Problem Comedies* (1931; repr., Harmondsworth: Penguin, 1960), 24; Peter Ure, *William Shakespeare: The Problem Plays* (London: Longmans & Green, 1961), 7–8; R. A. Foakes, *Shakespeare: The Dark Comedies to the Last Plays: From Satire to Celebration* (London: Routledge & Kegan Paul, 1971), 61: Richard P. Wheeler, *Shakespeare's Development and the Problem Comedies: Turn and Counter-Turn* (Berkeley: University of California Press, 1981), 1–2; Northrop Frye, *The Myth of Deliverance: Reflections on Shakespeare's Problem Comedies* (Toronto: University of Toronto Press, 1983), 8, 61–63.

10. In addition to these problems of structure and genre, critics have often stated the difficulty of defining a problem play or problem comedy. For example, see E. M. W. Tillyard, *Shakespeare's Problem Plays* (Toronto: University of Toronto Press, 1949), 1; Ure, 7; Ernest Schanzer, *The Problem Plays of Shakespeare: A Study of "Julius Caesar," "Measure for Measure" and "Antony and Cleopatra"* (London: Routledge & Kegan Paul, 1963), ix, 5–6.

11. For the incongruities of structure, see the references listed in note 10. For the relation of appearance and actuality, see A. P. Rossiter, "The Problem Plays," in *Angel with Horns*, 117–20; Terence Hawkes, *Shakespeare and the Reason: A Study of the Tragedies and Problem Plays* (London: Routledge & Kegan Paul, 1964), 73; Northrop Frye, 63. For the difficult language of these plays, see Ure, 8; Foakes, 61–62; Northrop Frye, 63. For views of the complexity of the problem plays and their effect on the audience, see Lawrence, 21–22; see also Boas, 345; Rossiter, 128; Schanzer, 5; Wheeler, 1–2. The critics of the problem plays have mentioned the antiheroic brooding and dissatisfied nature of these plays. See Kenneth Muir and Stanley Wells, eds., *Aspects of Shakespeare's "Problem Plays"* (Cambridge: Cambridge University Press, 1982).

12. Lawrence, 28; Tillyard, 6; Rossiter, 124, 128; Northrop Frye, 70–72.

13. Tillyard (6–7) thinks that two common attributes of the problem play are that a young man gets a shock and the shock or "business that most promotes the process of growth is transacted at night." The young king, Henry V, gets such a shock at night when he debates with Williams and Bates.

14. Rossiter, who elsewhere views *Henry V* as a propaganda play, almost equates ambivalence in the history plays with the definition of the problem play; see Rossiter, 126–28. Frye thinks that *Troilus* stresses a fallen world and fails to deliver its audience from it and connects the division and the collision of different worlds in the *Henry IV* plays, *Troilus* and *Antony;* Northrop Frye, 72; see Hawkes, *Reason*, 73.

15. The complexity of Shakespeare's history plays can be seen in the diverse response to them in detailed discussions, from Thomas Courtenay's *Commentaries on the Historical Plays of*

Shakespeare (1840; repr., New York: AMS, 1972) through E. M. W. Tillyard's *Shakespeare's History Plays* (London: Chatto &Windus, 1944) to Graham Holderness' *Shakespeare's History* (New York: St. Martin's Press, 1985).

16. For an examination of temporal crisis, see, for instance, John W. Blanpied, *Time and the Artist in Shakespeare's English Histories* (Newark: University of Delaware Press, 1983).

17. Fluellen exposes Pistol as a "counterfeit": V.i.69, cf. III.vi.61.

18. For another view, see Brownwell Solomon, "Thematic Contraries and the Dramaturgy of *Henry V*," *Shakespeare Quarterly* 31 (1980): 343–56. For an analysis of satire in the play, see Allan Gilbert, "Patriotism and Satire in *Henry V*," in *Studies in Shakespeare*, eds. Arthur D. Matthews and C. M. Emery (1953; repr., New York: AMS, 1971), 40–64.

19. For act and scene division, see J. H. Walter, introduction to *King Henry V* (1954; repr., London: Methuen, 1977), xxxv. For other views of the Chorus, see Anne Barton, "The King Disguised: Shakespeare's *Henry V* and the Comical History," in *The Triple Bond*, ed. Joseph G. Price (University Park: Pennsylvania State University Press, 1975), 92; G. P. Jones, "*Henry V*: The Chorus and the Audience," *Shakespeare Survey* 31 (1978): 93–105; Lawrence Danson, "*Henry V*: King, Chorus, and Critics," *Shakespeare Quarterly* 34 (1983), esp. 27–33. For a more general article, see Jean-Marie Maguin, "Shakespeare's Structural Craft and Dramatic Technique in *Henry V*," *Cahiers Elisabéthains* 7 (1975): 51–67.

20. Laurence Olivier's film captures the theatricality of the courtship and plans for marriage by drawing the scene back from the "fields of France" to the stage. For Olivier's consciously patriotic interpretation, see his "*Henry V*," in *On Acting* (New York: Simon & Schuster, 1986), 90–105.

21. For more general views on time and ending in fiction, see Frank Kermode, *The Sense of an Ending* (New York: Oxford University Press, 1967), esp. 76–89, and Barbara Herrnstein Smith, *Poetic Closure* (Chicago: University of Chicago Press, 1968). For a different view of parts of the structure, see Marilyn Williamson, "The Episode with Williams in *Henry V*," *Studies in English Literature, 1500–1900* 9 (1969): 275–82; and her "The Courtship of Katherine and the Second Tetralogy," *Criticism* 17 (1973): 326–34.

22. For the first systematic ironic reading of the language of this play, see Gerald Gould, "A New Reading of *Henry V*," *English Review* 29 (1919): 42–55. See also C. H. Hobday, "Imagery and Irony in 'Henry V,'" *Shakespeare Survey* 21 (1968). 107–13.

23. William Shakespeare, *Henry V*, ed. Gary Taylor (Oxford: Clarendon, 1982), 208.

24. Taylor, 217; Walter, 102.

CHAPTER 9

1. Thanks to the editors for giving permission for me to include a revised version of my article, "*Henry VIII*: The Play as History and Anti-History," *Aevum* 65, no. 3 (September–December 1991): 561–70, for inclusion in this book. This essay was written in the late 1980s. Since the original publication, a number of interesting analyzes of the play have appeared. Here is a selection of them. For a discussion of the public and private sides of Protestantism, see Camille Wells Slights, "The Politics of Conscience in *All Is True* (or *Henry VIII*)," *Shakespeare Survey* 43 (1991): 59–68. On contradiction, see Peter L. Rudnytsky, "*Henry VIII* and the Deconstruction of History," *Shakespeare Survey* 43 (1991): 43–57. For essays on Henry VIII, including a couple of Shakespeare, see *Henry VIII in History, Historiography, and Literature*, ed. Uwe Baumann (Frankfurt am Main: Lang, 1992). Concerning speech acts, gender, and class, see A. L. Magnusson, "The Rhetoric of Politeness and *Henry VIII*," *Shakespeare Quarterly* 43 (1992): 391–409. On this play at the Globe Theatre, see Julia Gasper, "The Reformation Plays on the Public Stage," in *Theatre*

and Government under the Early Stuarts, ed. J. R. Mulryne and Margaret Shewring (Cambridge: Cambridge University Press, 1993), 190–216. On style and speech, see Maurice Hunt, "Shakespeare's *King Henry VIII* and the Triumph of the Word," *English Studies* 75 (1994): 225–45. About spectacle and representation, see Bill Readings, "When Did the Renaissance Begin? The Henrician Court and the Shakespearean Stage," in *Rethinking the Henrician Era: Essays on Early Tudor Texts and Contexts*, ed. Peter C. Herman (Urbana: University of Illinois Press, 1994), 283–302. Concerning queens and heirs, see Jo Eldridge Carney, "Queenship in Shakespeare's *Henry VIII*: The Issue of Issue," in *Political Rhetoric, Power, and Renaissance Women*, ed. Carole Levin and Patricia A. Sullivan (Albany, NY: SUNY Press, 1995), 188–202. On the questioning of truth, see Gordon McMullan, "Shakespeare and the End of History," *Essays and Studies* 48 (1995): 16–37. Concerning truth and Holinshed, see Annabel Patterson, "'All is true': Negotiating the Past in *Henry VIII*," in *Elizabethan Theater: Essays in Honor of S. Schoenbaum*, ed. R. B. Parker and S. P. Zitner (Newark: University of Delaware Press, 1996), 147–65. On Providence and the example of great men, see Ivo Kamps, *Historiography and Ideology in Stuart Drama* (Cambridge: Cambridge University Press, 1996), 91–139. For a discussion of confliction aspects of ideology, see Albert Cook, "The Ordering Effect of Dramatized History: Shakespeare and *Henry VIII*," *Centennial Review* 42 (1998): 5–28. Concerning truth, see Anston Bosman, "Seeing Tears: Truth and Sense in *All Is True*," *Shakespeare Quarterly* 50 (1999): 459–76. On historical interpretation, see Thomas Healy, "History and Judgement in *Henry VIII*," in *Shakespeare's Late Plays: New Readings*, ed. Jennifer Richards and James Knowles (Edinburgh: Edinburgh University Press, 1999), 158–75. About knowing the past, see Barbara Kreps, "When All Is True: Law, History, and Problems of Knowledge in *Henry VIII*," *Shakespeare Survey* 52 (1999): 166–82. On masculinities, see Gordon McMullan, "'Thou hast made me now a man': Reforming Man(ner)liness in *Henry VIII*," in *Shakespeare's Late Plays: New Readings*, ed. Jennifer Richards and James Knowles (Edinburgh: Edinburgh University Press, 1999), 40–56. For an examination of the play in the context of martyrological controversies, see Susannah Brietz Monta, "'Thou fall'st a blessed martyr': Shakespeare's *Henry VIII* and the Polemics of Conscience," *English Literary Renaissance* 30 (2000): 262–83. On mythology and history, see Ruth Vanita, "Mariological Memory in *The Winter's Tale* and *Henry VIII*," *Studies in English Literature 1500–1900* 40 (2000): 311–37. For an analysis of knowledge and conscience in the trials, see Gerard Wegemer, "Henry VIII on Trial: Confronting Malice and Conscience in Shakespeare's *All Is True*," *Renascence* 52, no. 2 (2000): 111–30. On metatheatre, metahistory, form and historiography, see Zenón Luis Martínez, "'Maimed narrations': Shakespeare's *Henry VIII* and the Task of the Historian," *Explorations in Renaissance Culture* 27 (2001): 205–43. Concerning memory, rhetoric, and structure, see Donatella Montini, "*Henry VIII* e la scena della memoria," *Memoria di Shakespeare* 2 (2001): 55–67. On subjectivity, see Anita Howard, "'The king's soul': The Reformed Subject in Shakespeare/Fletcher, *Henry VIII* and Calderón de la Barca, *La cisma de Inglaterra*," *Shakespeare Yearbook* 13 (2002): 129–46. For a discussion of the representation of the king and his reputation, see Jean-Christophe Mayer, "Revisiting the Reformation: Shakespeare and Fletcher's *King Henry VIII*," *Reformation and Renaissance Review* 5 (2003): 188–203. On the connections between the Tudor and Stuart monarchs, see Susan Frye, "Anne of Denmark and the Historical Contextualisation of Shakespeare and Fletcher's *Henry VIII*," in *Women and Politics in Early Modern England, 1450–1700*, ed. James Daybell (Aldershot, U.K.: Ashgate, 2004), 181–93. Concerning Spanish culture and treatment of Katherine of Aragon, see Hugh M. Richmond, "Elizabeth I in Shakespeare's *Henry VIII*," in *Queen Elizabeth I: Past and Present*, ed. Christa Jansohn (Münster: Lit, 2004), 45–58. For an examination of conscience and theatricality, see Tomás Jajtner, "Hulling in the Wild Sea of Protestant Conscience: The Problem of Conscience in Shakespeare's *Henry VIII*," *Litteraria Pragensia* 14 (2004): 47–61. On the figure of the crowd in *Henry VIII* and related plays, see Ian Munro, *The Figure of the Crowd in Early Modern London: The City and Its Double* (New York: Palgrave Macmillan, 2005). Concerning Shakespeare's and Calderón's plays in relation to Providence, see Ali Shehzad Zaidi, "Self-Contradiction in *Henry VIII* and *La cisma de Inglaterra*," *Studies in Philology* 103 (2006): 329–44. For a discussion of forgetting and remembering, see Jonathan Baldo, "Forgetting Elizabeth in *Henry VIII*," in *Resurrecting Elizabeth I in Seventeenth-Century England*, ed. Elizabeth H. Hageman and Katherine Conway (Madison, NJ: Fairleigh Dickinson University Press, 2007), 132–48. On rises and falls as part of the representation of history, see Chris R. Kyle, "*Henry VIII*, or *All Is True*: Shakespeare's 'Favorite' Play," in *How to Do Things with Shakespeare: New Approaches, New Essays*, ed. Laurie Maguire (Oxford: Blackwell, 2008), 82–100.

2. Philip Sidney, *The Defense of Poesy*, in *Literary Criticism: Plato to Dryden*, ed. A. Gilbert (1940; repr., Detroit: Wayne State University Press, 1962), 418.

3. Herschel Baker, *The Race of Time: Three Lectures on Renaissance Historiography* (Toronto: University of Toronto Press, 1967), 15–17.

4. Matthew H. Wikander, *The Play of Truth and State: Historical Drama from Shakespeare to Brecht* (Baltimore: Johns Hopkins University Press, 1986), esp. 13–49. I have found Wikander's views of *Henry VIII* to be especially provocative.

5. For discussions of the complex views of power and rule during the Renaissance, including the ambivalent view that the court of James I had of Elizabeth I, see *The Historical Renaissance: New Essays on Tudor and Stuart Life, Nature and Culture*, ed. Heather Dubrow and Richard Strier (Chicago: University of Chicago Press 1988).

6. For other recent related views of history in *Henry VIII*, see W. H. Baillie, "*Henry VIII*: A Jacobean History," *Shakespeare Studies* 12 (1979): 247–64; L. S. Champion, Shakespeare's *Henry VIII*: A Celebration of History," *South Atlantic Bulletin* 44 (1979): 1–18; R. W. Uphaus, "History, Romance and *Henry VIII*," *Iowa State Journal of Research* 53 (1979): 177–83; F. V. Cespedes, "'We are One in Fortunes': The Sense of History in *Henry VIII*," *English Literary Renaissance* 10 (1980): 413–38; Alexander Leggatt, "*Henry VIII* and the Ideal England," *Shakespeare Survey* 38 (1985): 131–44; Paul Dean, "Dramatic Mode and Historical Vision in *Henry VIII*," *Shakespeare Quarterly* 34 (1986): 175–89.

7. I owe much to Lionel Gossman's unpublished essay, "The Rationality of History." For more of Gossman's work on the relation of history and literature, see "History and Literature: Reproduction or Signification," in *The Writing of History: Literary Form and Historical Understanding*, ed. R. H. Canary and H. Kozicki (Madison: University of Wisconsin Press, 1978), 3–39, and "Literature and Education," *New Literary History* 13 (1982): 341–71. See also Suzanne Gearhart, *The Open Boundary of History and Fiction: A Critical Approach to the French Enlightenment* (Princeton, NJ: Princeton University Press, 1984), esp. 4–28.

8. For another more detailed view, see J. D. Cox, "*Henry VIII* and the Masque," *English Literary History* 45 (1978): 390–409; Edward I. Berry, "*Henry VIII* and the Dynamics of Spectacle," *Shakespeare Studies* 12 (1979): 229–46; Janet Clare, "Beneath Pomp and Circumstance in *Henry VIII*," *Shakespeare Studies* 21 (1982–83), 65–81.

9. See, for example, Foakes, xxviii–xxix, 179–83 and H. R. Woudhuysen, "*King Henry VIII and All is True*," *Notes and Queries* 31 (1984): 217–18.

10. All quotations and citations from the play will be from William Shakespeare, *King Henry VIII*, ed. R. A. Foakes (1957; repr., London: Methuen, 1968).

11. How popular and privileged audiences were in Renaissance England represents a controversy among theatre scholars. Unlike Ann Jennalie Cook, Andrew Gurr concentrates on a

shorter period and does not consider the playgoers an entirely privileged group. See Anne Jennalie Cook, *The Privileged Playgoers of Shakespeare's London, 1576–1642* (Princeton, NJ: Princeton University Press, 1981) and Andrew Gurr, *Playgoing in Shakespeare's London* (Cambridge: Cambridge University Press, 1987). The Prologue, like Hamlet who warns the First Player to speak the lines as written, does not seem to think that the audience is composed entirely of sophisticates unless playwright and audience are sharing a joke about less sophisticated audiences in other theatres or other times.

12. For another view of the uncertainty of points of view and truth in *Henry VIII*, see Pierre Sahel, "The Strangeness of a Dramatic Style: Rumour in *Henry VIII*," *Shakespeare Survey* 38 (1985): 145–52. The importance of rumor here is reminiscent of the Induction to *2 Henry IV*.

13. Other views of structure include: Foakes, ed., lviii–lxiv; Anne Shaver, "Structure and Ceremony: A Case for Unity in *King Henry VIII*," *Selected Papers from the West Virginia Shakespeare and Renaissance Association* 2 (1977): 1–23, and Glynne Wickham, "The Dramatic Structure of *King Henry VIII*: An Essay in Rehabilitation," *Proceedings of the British Academy* 70 (1984): 149–66.

14. For a more detailed view of conscience in the play, see Alan R. Young, "Shakespeare's *Henry VIII* and the Theme of Conscience," *English Studies in Canada* 7 (1981): 38–53.

15. William Shakespeare, *King Henry V*, ed. J. H. Walter (1954; repr., London: Methuen, 1977).

16. Northrop Frye notes the troubled ending that depicts "the triumph of Cranmer, Cromwell, and Ann Boleyn, along the audience's knowledge of what soon happened to them"; Northrop Frye, *Fools of Time* (Toronto: University of Toronto Press, 1967), 15, quoted in John Wilders, *The Lost Garden: A View of Shakespeare's English and Roman History Plays* (London: Macmillan, 1978), 21. David M. Bergeron maintains that Shakespeare's preceding romances and the Stuart royal family bear closely on this play, so that the reign of Henry VIII finds an implied comparison with the rule of Cymbeline, Pericles, Prospero, and James I. See Bergeron, *Shakespeare's Romances and the Royal Family* (Lawrence: University Press of Kansas, 1985), 203–22. For another view of *Henry VIII*, see Paul Bacquet, *Les pièces historiques de Shakespeare: La deuxième tetralogie et "Henri VIII*," vol. 2 (Paris: Presses Universitaires de France, 1979). Although Graham Holderness does not say much about *Henry VIII*, he discusses much that illuminates the play: historiography, the relation of drama and society, the reproduction of history, history plays in performance, and the relation of text and history. Only in passing does he allude to or quote others like Wilson Knight alluding to *Henry VIII*. See Holderness, *Shakespeare's History* (Dublin, Ireland: Gill and Macmillan, 1985), 14, 184.

CONCLUSION

1. *Mr. William Shakespeares Comedies, Histories, & Tragedies. Published According to the True Originall Copies* (London: Isaac Iaggard, and Ed. Blount, 1623), A5r.

2. See E. K. Chambers, *William Shakespeare*, vol. 2, 224; and G. Blakemore Evans, "Early Critical Comment on the Plays and Poems," in *The Riverside Shakespeare*, 2nd ed., ed. G. Blakemore Evans, with J. J. M. Tobin (Boston: Houghton Mifflin, 1997), 1971.

3. See Sayre N. Greenfield, "Allegory to the Rescue: Saving Venus and Adonis from Themselves," in *The Ends of Allegory* (Newark: University of Delaware Press, 1998), 86–110, and Gordon Teskey, *Allegory and Violence* (Ithaca, NY: Cornell University Press, 1996), esp. 38, 58, 75–76, 85–86, 160, 193.

4. See William Shakespeare, *Shakespeare's Sonnets*, ed. Katherine Duncan-Jones (London: Thomas Nelson, 1997); Helen Vendler, *The Art of Shakespeare's Sonnets* (Cambridge, MA: Belknap Press, 1997); William Shakespeare, *"The Sonnets" and "A Lover's Complaint,"* ed. John Kerrigan (Harmondsworth: Penguin, 2000).

5. See Harold Bloom, *Shakespeare: The Invention of the Human* (New York: Riverhead Books, 1998).

6. Herodotus, *The Histories*, Greek with an English translation by A. D. Godley (London: Heinemann, 1920), 1.1.

7. See Walter Benjamin, "Theses on the Philosophy of History," in *Illuminations*, ed. Hannah Arendt, trans. Harry Zohn (1955; repr., New York: Harcourt, Brace & World, 1968), 258. See also Walter Benjamin, "On the Concept of History," in *Materialist Theology*, 1940, vol. 4 of *Selected Writings,* ed. Howard Eiland and Michael W. Jennings (Cambridge MA: Belknap, 2006), part 5.

8. Christopher Columbus, *The Four Voyages of Columbus: A History in Eight Documents, Including Five By Christopher Columbus, In the Original Spanish, with English Translations*, ed. and trans. Cecil Jane (1930; repr. New York: Dover, 1983), 294–95; see also 30–40; and see Peter Hume, *Colonial Encounters: Europe and the Native Caribbean 1492–1797* (1986; repr., London: Routledge, 1992), 45–87.

9. See Ricardo J. Quinones, *The Renaissance Discovery of Time* (Cambridge, MA: Harvard University Press, 1972).

10. See Aristotle, "The Art of Poetry," and G. Bernard Shaw's preface to *Plays for Puritans* (London: Constable, 1900), in which he speaks of Bardolatry.

11. See D. J. Hopkins, *City/Stage/Globe: Performance and Space in Shakespeare's London* (London: Routledge, 2008); and Lisa Hopkins, *The Cultural Uses of the Caesars on the English Renaissance Stage* (Aldershot, UK: Ashgate, 2008).

12. See Michael Mangan, *Staging Masculinities: History, Gender, Performance* (New York: Palgrave Macmillan, 2003); and Cheang Wai Fong, "Women and Boundary Crossing: Foreign Brides in Shakespeare's History Plays," *Tamkang Review* 37 (2007), 177–204.

13. See Ann Jennalie Cook, *The Privileged Playgoers of Shakespeare's London: 1576–1642* (Princeton, NJ: Princeton University Press, 1981), 64.

14. Natalie Zemon Davis, "'Women's History' in Transition: The European Case," *Feminist Review* 3–4 (1975–76), 90.

15. See Angela Pitt, "Women in the Histories," in *Shakespeare's Women* (London: David & Charles, 1981), 136–63; and Marilyn French, "Power: The First Tetralogy," in *Shakespeare's Division of Experience* (New York: Ballantine, 1981) 35–69.

16. See, for example. J. A. K. Thomson, *Irony: An Historical Introduction* (London: Allen & Unwin, 1926); D. C. Muecke, *The Compass of Irony* (London: Methuen, 1969); Lilian Furst, *Fictions of Romantic Irony* (Cambridge, MA: Harvard University Press, 1984).

17. Philip Sidney, *The Defense of Poesy*, in *Literary Criticism: Plato to Dryden*, ed. A. Gilbert (1940; repr., Detroit: Wayne State University Press, 1962), 418.

18. For another view, see J. D. Cox, "*Henry VIII* and the Masque," *English Literary History* 45 (1978): 390–409; Edward I. Berry, "*Henry VIII* and the Dynamics of Spectacle," *Shakespeare Studies* 12 (1979): 229–46; Janet Clare, "Beneath Pomp and Circumstance in *Henry VIII*," *Shakespeare Studies* 21 (1982–83), 65–81.

19. Oscar Wilde, *The Complete Works of Oscar Wilde: Criticism: Historical Criticism, Intentions, the Soul of Man*, vol. 4, ed. Josephine M Guy, Russell Jackson, Ian Small, Joseph Bristow (Oxford: Oxford University Press, 2007), 90.

INDEX

DISCARDED
CONCORDIA UNIV. LIBRARY

CONCORDIA UNIVERSITY LIBRARIES
MONTREAL